AGES

from

COURT RECORDS

1636–1700

VOLUME I

Essex, Middlesex, and Suffolk Counties, Massachusetts

Melinde Lutz Sanborn

CLEARFIELD

Originally published by
Genealogical Publishing Co., Inc.
Baltimore, Maryland, 2003

Copyright © 2003 by
Melinde Lutz Sanborn
All Rights Reserved

Library of Congress Catalog Card Number 2002117816

Reprinted for Clearfield Company by
Genealogical Publishing Company
Baltimore, Maryland, 2014

ISBN 978-0-8063-1720-5

For Roberta,

who deserved better

ACKNOWLEDGMENTS

This started out as a little list, compiled for convenience's sake, and evolved into something quite necessary and surprisingly large. Efforts to make it comprehensive were futile, but after ten years of tinkering, it was time to share.

This list makes accessible over 11,000 depositions from the earliest years of Massachusetts settlement, and frequently answers the question, "Where did they get that?" when an unreferenced quote from an antique genealogy gives an age.

Sources for this list include microfilms, published public records, and sometimes original documents. Access was a critical issue, and for that there are many people to thank. The staff at the Phillips Library, Peabody-Essex Museum in Salem, Massachusetts, home of the Essex Quarter Court records, understood the importance of seeing original papers, even though transcriptions exist. Janice Hourigan at the Massachusetts Archives could *always* find it, no matter how obscure! Paul Mahoney patiently added up the copying costs. Elizabeth Bouvier, Head of Archives for the Supreme Judicial Court Archives, shared historical facts about the arrangement and survival of some court records, and granted access to seldom-handled items. Diane Greene and Sue Moran looked up a few items in Salt Lake City when my local microfilms were too scratched to read.

I am grateful to Robert H. Rodgers for his invitation to visit the Harvard Law School library one hot summer afternoon in 1996, where many now-lost Middlesex County Court records survive in photostatic form. Dr. Rodgers' flawless transcription of these early documents sets a high bar even higher. Thank-you to Robert Charles Anderson for reassuring me that that word I thought I couldn't read really was "whales." Thanks to Leslie Mahler, whose sheer endurance for reading old handwriting is matched only by his curiosity about what comes next.

I have proved or disproved many identities with these records. May they be as useful for you.

Melinde Lutz Sanborn
Derry, N.H., December 2002

INTRODUCTION

Among the richest caches of personal information surviving from New England's first century of European settlement are the depositions of the people themselves. While these depositions are located in a variety of places, the greatest number are found in court records throughout the colonies. So many people in early New England were deponents for one reason or another that no biography or genealogy can be complete without a search through court records to see if a pertinent deposition exists.

Unfortunately--because of the defective nature of most indexes to court records and the extreme obscurity in which the few published series of indexes languish--depositions are rarely used. Although we can see that depositions have been tapped to great effect in several extensive studies, most notably the work leading to the *Genealogical Dictionary of Maine and New Hampshire*,[1] the authors' notes in such cases have never been published or cannot be found, leaving the time-consuming and almost impossible task of sorting through hundreds of thousands of court papers for only the most ambitious.

Depositions can vary in quality from being virtually useless to being incontrovertible proof of something otherwise unsuspected. When people were asked to witness in front of authority, they often said little of interest. For instance, the great majority of depositions simply consist of one person saying he or she saw another person do a certain, routine thing, like make a deed, pay for goods, or sign a will.

Since the odds are greatly in favor of such an innocuous result, why do an extensive search for a deposition that may or may not exist? For this early period, the single most useful bit of evidence included in the format of many depositions **is the age of the deponent.**

Value of This Index

Indexes to early court records, where they exist, usually limit themselves to alphabetical listings of plaintiffs or defendants, or sometimes just plaintiffs, and almost never include the most informative item: the deponents brought in to prove or disprove a case. One sterling exception is the "Index to the Calendar Index of the Supreme Judicial Court"--designated the "Suffolk Files"– which covers the period up to 1700 for various courts in what was the Massachusetts Bay Colony and successors. This voluminous handwritten manuscript, bound in oversized copybooks, is the

---

[1]Sybil Noyes, Charles Thornton Libby and Walter Goodwin Davis, *Genealogical Dictionary of Maine and New Hampshire* (reprint of original published in five parts 1928-1939, Baltimore, Md.: Genealogical Publishing Co., 2002).

result of almost forty years of labor. Funded by the Massachusetts legislature, the entire work, except for the final volume Wo-Z, has been microfilmed; however, it is not often used.

This volume will hopefully fill the void by providing an index to depositions from court records from 1636 to 1700 in which the deponent's age is given. With this index--which lists the name and age of the deponent, and the year and source of the court record--researchers can quickly determine whether it is worthwhile to track down the original record.

The percentage of deponents who give their ages in the pre-1700 era defies easy determination for a variety of reasons. Certain court officers never asked a deponent for an age, merely using the phrase "of lawful age." Other officers usually asked; some simply guessed. Certain deponents--particularly those of high social standing, those who were officers of the court themselves, or those who were well known to the court--were rarely asked to give their ages. Travelers, strangers, mariners, the very old, and the very young were most often asked. Although the number of depositions with ages given probably hovers around 15 percent of the total, this varies greatly depending on the court, the year, the individual, the clerk, and the circumstances. It does not mean that if someone was deposed twenty times, three of the depositions would contain ages.

Traditionally, "invisible" people appeared as deponents as well. Scottish slaves, African slaves, Native Americans, and bound servants could be witnesses and deponents, and frequently provided their ages when they took their oaths. The challenge in these cases is not to find a deposition with an age given but to decode the clerk's invariably exotic spelling of the deponent's name.[2]

An effort was made in this index to standardize names, but often there was so much doubt that it seemed wiser to leave the spelling as is. For example, is Nathaniel "Bacor" a Bacon or a Baker? Are the Whitemores, the Whitmores, and the Whittemores all the same family? Kemble and Kimball? Knop and Knap? Pierce, Pearce, Peirce, Pearse? Read, Reade, Reed, Reede, Reid? Sometimes it is impossible to know whether a Howard is actually a Hayward. All phonetic and graphic variants should be searched to make best use of this index.

The Contribution of Ages

Sometimes the age of a deponent was very important to the case. Men over sixty were often brought into court to support the claims of the ancient boundaries of litigants' property. Part of their authority stemmed from the fact that they were alive at the time the boundaries were set, so their ages are often given. Likewise, many older women who were experienced midwives were called upon to offer opinions on the timeliness of a birth in a fornication case. Young children were sometimes the only witnesses to violent crimes such as rape or assault, but also were relied upon to identify cattle or horses. Since they were not of "lawful age," their ages were usually stated.

One of the most common errors in genealogical work is confusing two or more men (or women) of the same name. If senior or junior or tertius or grandsenior is not used, it is very difficult to assign events to the correct individual. Frequently, fathers and sons with the same given name came to court together. With stated ages, they are clearly differentiated, being twenty or more

---

[2]Scottish names were the worst to decode, followed by French mariners, then Native Americans. In most cases these names appear in this index just as they were written. Some unusual Biblical first names were also creatively written, "Jerathmiel" being one of them. Such names were standardized here.

years apart in age. But men of the same generation can be a problem, and a deposition with the deponent's age given can be very helpful in such an instance. Take the case of the common name Nathaniel Brown. By comparing the ages stated during depositions in the 1660s through 1680 in this index, it is obvious that there are two men by that name, born about eight years apart. Basic caution should be used in such cases because ages stated can be less than precise.

There are quite a number of ways in which an error can be made in stating a person's age. Aside from the obvious instances where someone lied, someone guessed, or someone exaggerated, it is also likely that extremes of handwriting, poor preservation of documents, and inexperience with reading numbers by a transcriber all contribute to error. In compiling this index, the name Henry Stich came up twice. In both instances, his age was given as 102, once read by a WPA transcriptionist for the EQC project, and once by a court clerk in Boston prior to 1920. Since the deposition had to do with heavy physical labor, a look at the original deposition seemed in order. Sure enough, the age looked a lot like 102. However, this particular 17th-century scribe liked to make his 8 "lazy" (lying on its side), and what looked like 102 was actually 18.

Some Peculiarities of the Records

More often than not, a deposition was written on its own individual piece of paper. The usual format was to give the deponent's name, with a title (if any), age, and sometimes place of residence; indicate that he or she "makes oath and says"; give the text of the evidence; and then close with "and further this deponent saith not" and "given before me [clerk's name] on [date]." It is not unusual for the date to be left off. This is a problem for a number of reasons. First, many depositions were made before the case was heard, sometimes weeks or months before the court sat. If this happened and it was clear which case the deposition belonged in, an age could be calculated plus or minus a year from the date of the term of court. However, many cases were appealed, and the same deposition could be brought to numerous subsequent courts years, even decades, later. Each instance needs to be examined with care before it is linked to the term of court. The abbreviation "nd" is used in this index when no date appears on the deposition and assignment of a date is questionable. A question mark indicates a good guess.

Although only the year is given in this index, most court depositions give the full day and month as well. When the full date falls between 1 January and 24 March under the Julian calendar, a split year is used, such as 1675/6. Often the clerk would write 1 January 1675; this is assumed to be 1675/6, but could be 1674/5.

In a few cases, the reply to the question "What is your age?" could be stated as, "I am in my sixty-fifth year," which means the individual was sixty-four by our reckoning. Give or take a year is the rule rather than the exception. It is also important to view ages that look like rough estimates with some suspicion. In the same court appearance, a deponent speaking more than once can have more than one stated age. People can age very erratically from deposition to deposition, further illustrating how often an estimate was used. For instance, when William Allen deposed in 1667, the court clerk wrote that he was "41 or 55."

The very oldest deponent in these records was William Nickalls, and no wonder, at the rate that he was aging!

The Testimony of William Nickalls aged about one hundred years Testifieth & Saith that forty two, years agoe, or above I bought the farme I doe now live on, of Mr Bartholmew, of Salem, & the said farme was granted to the said Bartholmew, by the Town, of Salem, & this Deponant went to the said farme and lived on it about forty two years agoe, & Some short time after I lived upon the said farme Topsfeild Constable demanded Rates of me. I Tould him I did not know, wheither I Lived In Topsfield or no, Some short time after there Came Some men from Topsfeild & Tould me that they were sent by the Towne of Topsfeild to pull up my fence, to make me a molestation, that I might know what Towne I Lived in, & they pulled up my fence, & Soon after I went to Salem to Speak with Mr Bartholmew, to Know of him what I must doe about my Rates, & Then Mr Bartholmew was not at home, at that day I went to Major Hathorne to Know of him what I should Doe In the Case, & he said he would Inquire at the Generall Court, & Soon after he Tould me that the Court had determined that Such, as had Lands Laid out on the Other side of the Six miles should Enjoy their Lands, but should pay Rates to Topsfeild, so then I paid my Rates to Topsfeild & have done ever since, & this was above thirty six years agoe, that I payd Rates to Topsfeild & have been Counted a Topsfeild man & priveledged with Division Land as thay ware & I never was molested by Salem for Rates from that Day to this & Topsfeild hath been In the queit posession of all the Land between the agreement line & Ipswich River for near forty Years to the best of my Knowledg

This farme that I live on & that I bought of the Said Bartholmew lyeth between the agreement Line settled by Salem & Topsfeild & Ipswich River but only a part of the farme lyeth on Salem side the Line, and most of Topsfeild Side,

...William Nickalls aged about one hundred & four (or five) Years, being to appearance of perfect memory & understanding appeared & gave oth to the Truth of the above written febr 1694(5) before me Thos Wade Justice of peace SJC #3064

In a few cases husbands and wives came forward together to depose, and while the husband's full name was given, his wife's name might not have been, as in "Robert Lord aged 70 and his wife, aged 65." Rather than presume the identity of the wife, she is indexed as "goodwife."

Depositions were not the only kind of records in these courts that stated ages for individuals. In a number of cases, when minor children were left at the death of a parent, the court clerk recorded the children's ages. For this reason there is one entry for a child as young as three months old in this index. Another notable instance of ages stated in non-depositions was the 1678 oath of allegiance signed by adult men in Newbury, Massachusetts. Like the clerks in other Essex county towns, the Newbury clerk returned a list of men who signed, but uniquely, he included the age of every man. This list has long been a buried resource for Newbury families.

Buried Treasure

Having said how mediocre most pre-1700 depositions are, it would be a mistake to suggest they are all that way. An example of how much more valuable depositions can be than other records is the case of Joseph[1] Hills (1602-1688), who came to court in 1638 and stated that he,

Joseph Hills of Charlestowne, in New England, Woollen Draper, aged about 36 yeares, sworne, saith upon his oath that he came to New England undertaker in the ship called Susan & Ellen of London...in the yeare of our Lord one thousand six hundred thirty and eight. ...[3]

A search for the same man in passenger lists is fruitless because his record didn't survive, his death record doesn't give his age, and deeds that list occupation usually call him "gentleman."

---

[3]*New England Historical and Genealogical Register*, 30[1876]: 459. This particular deposition, although sworn in court, does not survive in public records. It was transcribed from the original, which was in private hands in 1876. The date for the earliest deposition found in the records presented here was 1640.

For every classic, often-quoted deposition, there are hundreds of less famous statements that rarely see the light of day, yet are vibrant with detail and unique value. For the study of customs, events, standards, and even language, few records equal depositions, as shown by the examples given below from people in all walks of life.

Property rights, particularly those that were not of written record, were a constant cause of conflict to be settled in early courts:

Betty an indian Woman of about sixty or seventy years of age testifieth & saith that Josiah & Nannisnit was always generally Esteemed to be the acknowledged sachims of takemmy & that the line deviding between them was by a straight line drawn from a little pond by the sound caled nuppossoo to a spring caled neagasha and so to nistotunkquanuk & that she never heard any Challing the sachimship to the westward of sd line but the sd nananenat who always Challinged the prorogative of hunting on sd land & that she her self has often sene him shaire out whales to his people and that she has had shairs made out to her by him & that she never heird him denied the sachimship until of late years Josiah has made some Challeng there unto and further saith obadiah has bin always esteemed to be son and heir to sd nananenat
Sworn in Court attst Matt: Mayhew Clk SJC 25792

When the Bunkers and the Jenkinses argued about the ownership of land, witnesses such as John Greene were brought to court to present evidence:

John Greene Senr aged 63 years or thereabouts testifieth yt in the year 1649 or thereabouts, his Father Thomas Green Entered as a Tennant on mr George Bunkers Farme in Maldon and Continued on said Farme the term of four years and as long as [blot] the fall of the year and the Spring. And I the said John Green lived with my Father the above said four years. Further Saith yt on the Land in Controversy between Lemuel Jenkins and Ezekiel Jenkins and John Bunker there stood a raile fence, and that his said Father Green Improved to the fence as mr Bunkers Land. This Deponent further Saith that no man ever laid any Claime to any Land within the bounds of said Farme during the above said terme as he know of. Cambr. Septembr 10th 1695 Middlesex Court Files, folio 179.

In the very complicated settlement of the late Governor Richard Bellingham's estate, there was no written deed of land given by Bellingham to Angola, a free African who had saved his life. To prove ownership, the depositions of witnesses such as Meneno were brought into the case:

...Meneno Negro aged about 60 years deposed saith that some fowre yeare since beeing at Carrieing of the Late Governrs. Richards Bellingham Esqr. Wood into his yard when Wee that is my selfe & Angola had done the Governor giveing us a Cup of Sack Said Stroakeing Angola on the head I have given you a peice of Land of fivety foot square Now I am in a good mood goe & take itt & some while after the sd Menene was present wth the said Richard Bellingham Govr. & John Jaxson James Penniman & Henry Tyte & is declared in the Said Penimans & Cloughs oath Sawe the said Jaxson & penniman to Lay out the Said Land & heard the Governor Say to Angola now it is thine & Further Saith not Taken upon the Oaths of the 3 severall persons heerein Mentioned this 16th: of 12th: m 73 before Symon Bradstreet Edward Tyng Assist SD 8:298-299.
The saga of an early printing press is captured in Steven Day's words:

I Steven Day aged 62 years do attest that the charges wch mr Glover Expended in Engl[and] for the p[ro]cureing of the printing presse, was besides freight & other petty Expenses, at least Twenty pounds, the wch presse hath been imp[ro]ved by order of m^r Dunster, as appeareth by another testimony I have given in. also I do attest that the same materials that were brought over *hither as above said are worth in this place at least 40[lb]. Sworne in Court 1 (2) 56 Tho: Danforth Recorder* MCC folio 11

In a rare and sensational divorce case, the neighbors lined up to detail the unloving behavior of the wife:

The Testimony of John Fuller about 40 years of age is that I heard the wife of Willyam Clements say that she did never Love him nor never should, and when her Husband would have kissed her that her heart died within her and when that her Husband came to my house to sawing I told her that they should lye in a bede together she answered that she had rather see his heart blood out in the house then that hee should com so nigh too touch her for she did not like the breed so well as to have any by him; and I asked her why shee sayd that shee had rather lye with the oxe then with him for she Loved that oxe well: and that if her husband had one that could love him; hee might have children by her Taken upon oath this 16 (11) 1[656] before mee Humphrey

When Stephen Gates of Cambridge died, his sons took exception to the terms of his will and evidence was brought regarding his state of mind:

The Evidence of Hannah Wilson aged 36 yeares Saith that She being att Goodman Robberts house one time the wife of Stephen Gates being there some words was spoken to her about her husbands condition, and she was desired for to move him abkout making his will She seemed to be unwilling to it for two reasons the one was because she thought he would give the greatest part of his estate to his eldest Sonn, and the other was that she did apprehend him oft times not to be of a right understanding and I my self being oft with him in the time of his sicknes that she did both see and hear so much from him that he was oft times not in his right understanding and further saith not the marke of
Hannah W Wilson

Marriage customs also found their way to court:

Edward Johnson aged abt 65 & Susan Johnson aged about 66 testifie that Peeter Palfray of Redding, comeing to or house to mak up the match between or sonne Mathew Johnson, & his eldest daughter Hannah Palfrey, the which wee could not formerly agree unto, Hee said Hee was desirous the match should go on. & therefore although Hee could give but little at p[re]sent (his estate being mixed with his wife) yet at the day of his death Hee should have fifty pounds out of his estate which was accordingly accepted: & there upon the matter was accomplished Edward Johnson
Susan Johnson
21.4.64 Sworne in Court his O mark
by Capt Johnson and Susanna his wife as attests Thomas Danforth R MCC Harvard #2584

Bigamy was not unheard of:

John Larkin aged about eight & thirty yeares testifyeth & saith, that Hannah Goss wife of Philip Goss is marryed in Jamaica I have seen here there severall times and both she & her husband John Murray invited mee to Dinner on Christmas day last was a twelve month and I being there she owned to me, and he sd Murray also that they were man & wife, and further that she had a child by sd Murray.
The mark of John Larkin
John Larkin mad oath to the Above written
the first of November 1689 Beore me John Phillips Assist[ant] SJC #2553

Sources

EQC - Essex County Quarterly Courts

The Essex County Quarterly Courts have been abstracted and published for the period 1636-1686 in a series of nine volumes produced by the Essex Institute, in Salem, Massachusetts. *Records and Files of the Quarterly Courts of Essex County, Massachusetts*, volumes 1 through 9 (Salem, Mass.: The Essex Institute, 1911-1975) was reprinted in a limited run by Parker River Researchers of Newburyport, Mass., in 1988. Copies printed on demand may be ordered from Higginson Books. A typescript version of the original papers and minute books was produced for the period through 1692 by the WPA, but the years between 1686 and 1692 have never been published. Some of the original documents have not been microfilmed, but are available for limited use at the Peabody-Essex Museum in Salem, Massachusetts. Entries taken from the WPA transcript for 1686-88 are cited as EQC WPA, then the volume number, folio number, and item number. Frequently, more than one deponent was recorded on a single page.

MCC - Middlesex County Court

The Middlesex County Court papers, a massive collection of unpublished court documents dating from 1649, are currently in the custody of the Judicial Archives and stored at the Massachusetts Archives at Columbia Point. A partial card-file index of court cases was made by Harvard Law School students in the 1930s after a quick sort that organized the loose papers into folios. A comparison with notes made in the 1860s by historian Thomas Wyman demonstrates that a large number of the original papers have disappeared.

A photostatic copy of the first twenty years of the surviving papers was made before WWII. This photostat has been microfilmed and is available for purchase through Harvard University. Quite a few of the papers on this film are no longer in the original files. The Harvard photostat identifies the papers by number, not by folio, and is cited here as MCC Harvard #. No detailed comparison of the two collections has been made for this index. A later filming of the folios done in the 1970s may be purchased, with permission from the Judicial Archivist, through the LDS Church. Microfilms are available for use at the Massachusetts Archives at Columbia Point and on loan at LDS Family History Centers worldwide.

Some depositions pertaining to probate matters are being published in the NEHGS series edited by Robert Rogers on early *Middlesex Probate Records*.[4] Some of the more outrageous cases have been abstracted and mentioned in Roger Thompson's *Sex in Middlesex*.[5] Beyond random abstracts of these cases in dissertations and genealogies, the majority of the materials remain unpublished.

SD - Suffolk Deeds

Suffolk Deeds, Volumes 1 through 14 (Boston: The City of Boston, 1880-1906), were published by the County Commissioners and included entries dating from the beginning of the

---

[4]*Middlesex County In the Colony of the Massachusetts Bay in New England. Records of Probate and Administration October 1649- December 1660, Vol. 1*, and *March 1660/61 - December 1670, Vol. 2*, Robert H. Rodgers, ed. (Boston: The New England Historic Genealogical Society, 1999, 2001).
[5]Roger Thompson, *Sex in Middlesex: Popular Mores in a Massachusetts County, 1649-1699* (Amherst, Mass.: University of Massachusetts Press, 1986).

Massachusetts Bay Colony to 6 November 1697. Because the recorder, Isaac Addington, began a new volume, 15, following the overthrow of the government of Sir Edmund Andros in 1689, and continued through volume 17 before going back and completing volume 14, there is a considerable gap in the published years. The unpublished original volumes 15, 16, and 17 have not been included in this index, although they doubtless contain pre-1700 depositions with ages.

Depositions with ages in these deeds routinely followed the format of a witness to a deed stating his or her age, making oath and testifying that he or she was present when the grantor signed the deed. This was only necessary when the grantor died, was of questionable competency, or was removed from the colony before personally acknowledging the deed.

SJC - Suffolk Files

Manuscript court file papers, 1629-1700, Supreme Court of Judicature. This massive collection has been indexed and re-indexed alphabetically, chronologically, and by subject and geography. Both the papers and indexes are available on microfilm.

Rather than belonging to any particular court, the "Suffolk Files" encompass loose legal papers, sometimes with unknown provenance. The papers were painstakingly sorted, primarily chronologically, and affixed into oversized scrapbooks. Cases were numbered sequentially, and some encompass hundreds of papers. These papers are similar to, and often duplicate, the court files found in Essex, Middlesex, and Suffolk counties.

SCC - Suffolk County Court

The first surviving volume of the minute books from the Suffolk County Court dates from 1671, although the court had existed for decades previously. A few of its records can be found in the manuscript "Suffolk Files" and in *Records of the Governor and Company of the Massachusetts Bay In New England,* Nathaniel B. Shurtleff, ed., vols. 1-3 (Boston: The Commonwealth of Massachusetts, 1853-54). The years 1671-1680 were published as *Records of the Suffolk County Court, 1671-1680* in *Publications of The Colonial Society,* Samuel Eliot Morison, ed., vols. 29 and 30 (Boston: The Society, 1933). The minutes of years 1681-1698 were contained in a subsequent volume that has now been lost. A photostat of this volume, in two parts, survives at the Massachusetts Archives at Columbia Point, but as a minute book it contains few, if any, depositions, let alone depositions with ages. The bulk of the entries from this source come from the uniformly excellent transcriptions of "Suffolk Files" papers edited into Morison's volumes.

Name	Age	Year	Source
Native Americans			
Betty	60 or 70	nd	SJC 25792
Betty	9	1672	SJC 1173
Andrew	58	1669	MCC folio 53
Awoosamage, John	60	1681	MCC folio 94
Beck	14	1679	MCC folio 87
Cappe	35	nd	SJC 2989
Nobhow	44	1669	MCC folio 53
Panawye	31	1669	MCC folio 53
Piambahoh	67	1681	MCC folio 96
Sasoomit	70	1681	MCC folio 101
Thomas, John	30	nd	SJC 24972
Timothy	30	1669	MCC folio 53
Tray, Tom	50	1681	MCC folio 96
Tuphors, Peter	62	nd	SJC 28857
Wanapenos	90	1690	SJC 2568
Wowoshouwet	60	1690	SJC 2568
Africans			
(maid)	16	1673	EQC 5:180
Cornelius	50	1660	EQC 2:231
Frances	18	1676	MCC folio 72
Hagar	21	1682	EQC 8:341
Manturo	30	1670	SJC 982
Meneno	60	1673/4	SD 8:298
Quaqua, John	15	1672	MCC folio 60
Sambo	18	1677	MCC folio 74
Sambo	17	1673	MCC folio 62
Sambo	18	1677	MCC folio 77
Santo	30	1695	SJC 4214
Simon	24	1680	MCC folio 91
Use, Mingo	19	1677	MCC folio 74
Europeans			
Abbey, John	16	1682	EQC 8:436
Abbott, Arthur	34	1674	EQC 5:284
Abbott, Elizabeth	25	1674	EQC 5:267
Abbott, George	26	1657	EQC 2:40
Abbott, George	30	1661	EQC 2:327
Abbott, George	40	1657	EQC 2:39
Abbott, George	40	1661	EQC 2:307
Abbott, George	44	1676	EQC 6:237
Abbott, George	50	1662	EQC 2:404
Abbott, George	50	1662	EQC 2:412
Abbott, George	50	1681	EQC 8:83
Abbott, George	54	1669	EQC 4:150
Abbott, George	60	1673	MCC folio 62
Abbott, John	24	1685	MCC folio 120
Abbott, John	27	1679	EQC 7:257

Abbott, John	28	1679	EQC 7:297
Abbott, John	33	1684	SJC 2011
Abbott, Richard	41	1672	MCC folio 65
Abbott, Richard	41	1672	SJC 1288
Abbott, Thomas	20	1653	SJC 168
Abbott, Thomas	26	1664	EQC 3:132
Abdy, Mathew	28	1654	SJC 236
Abdy, Mathew	37	1691	MCC folio 146
Abdy, Mathew	37	1691	MCC folio 147
Abdy, Mathew	37	1691	MCC folio 163
Abdy, Mathew	37	1691	MCC folio 173
Abdy, Mathew	48	1669	EQC 4:157
Abey, John	38	1679	EQC 7:292
Aborne, Moses	21	1667	EQC 3:415
Aborne, Moses	35	1680	EQC 7:426
Aborne, Nathaniel	26	1689	MCC folio 133
Aborne, Samuel	40	1680	EQC 7:426
Aborne, Samuel	52	1666	EQC 3:380
Aborne, Samuel	53	nd	SJC 2770
Aborne, Samuel	58	1670	EQC 4:279
Aborne, Samuel	68	1678	EQC 7:24
Aborne, Samuel	68	1678	EQC 7:9
Abye, Samuel	31	1680	EQC 7:362
Abye, Samuel	34	1682	EQC 8:384
Abye, Thomas	24	1680	EQC 7:362
Acey, John	40	1678	EQC 7:83
Acey, William	90	1682	EQC 8:269
Acres, Henry	26	1678	EQC 7:157
Adams, Abraham	10	1651	EQC 1:212
Adams, Abraham	37	1678	EQC 7:157
Adams, Ann	64	1691	MCC folio 148
Adams, Derrick	36	1677	SCC 902
Adams, Derrick	36	1678	SJC 1734
Adams, Edward	35	1663	SJC 606
Adams, Edward	60	1699	SJC 4696
Adams, Eleazer	54	1699	SJC 4696
Adams, Elizabeth	47	1669	MCC folio 52
Adams, George	15	1662	MCC folio 32
Adams, George	15	1663	MCC folio 35
Adams, Isaac	30	1678	EQC 7:137
Adams, Isaac	33	1678	EQC 7:157
Adams, Jacob	23	1678	EQC 7:157
Adams, Jacob	28	1684	EQC 9:238
Adams, James	47	1677	MCC folio 76
Adams, Joane	17	1651	EQC 1:212
Adams, John	22	1670	MCC folio 53
Adams, John	35	1656	MCC folio 15
Adams, John	37	1662	MCC folio 28
Adams, John	40	1699	SJC 4696
Adams, John	60	1686	MCC folio 121
Adams, John	60	1686	MCC folio 128
Adams, John	64	1686	MCC folio 121
Adams, John	70	1691	MCC folio 146
Adams, John	70	1695	MCC folio 195

Adams, John	71	1692/3	MCC folio 206
Adams, John	71	1692/3	SJC 3925
Adams, Joseph	25	1686	MCC folio 121
Adams, Joseph	25	1686	MCC folio 128
Adams, Joseph	27	1682	SJC 2126
Adams, Joseph	33	1692	MCC folio 152
Adams, Mary	17	1670	MCC folio 53
Adams, Mary	28	1683	EQC 9:236
Adams, Mary	60	1694	SJC 2957
Adams, Nathan	30	1683	MCC folio 104
Adams, Nathaniel	28	1681	EQC 8:192
Adams, Nathaniel	40	1693	MCC folio 155
Adams, Nathaniel	40	nd	SJC 2848
Adams, Nathaniel	50	1680	SJC 1909
Adams, Nathaniel	50	1681	EQC 8:192
Adams, Nathaniel	60	1662/3	SJC 507
Adams, Richard	25	1677	MCC folio 76
Adams, Robert	77	1678	EQC 7:157
Adams, Samuel	15	1670/1	MCC folio 56
Adams, Samuel	29	1681	MCC folio 92
Adams, Samuel	39	1658	MCC folio 20
Adams, Samuel	40	1660	MCC folio 25
Adams, Thomas	20	1681	MCC folio 104
Adams, Thomas	20	1681	MCC folio 97
Adams, Thomas	30	1659	MCC folio 32
Adams, Thomas	65	1677	MCC folio 77
Adams, Walter	48	1682	EQC 8:338
Adams, Walter	50	1683	EQC 9:90
Adams, William	35	1681	MCC folio 92
Addis, Hillery	15	1659	MCC folio 23
Adkins, Thomas	37	1680	SJC 1953
Ager, Jonathan	43	1682	EQC 8:412
Alborne, Henry	23	1675	SJC 1425
Alborne, Margaret	24	1655	MCC folio 12
Albridge, Catherine	60	1670	MCC folio 53
Alcock, Samuel	30	1676	MCC folio 74
Alcock, Samuel	39	1676/7	SJC 1721
Alden, John	44	1672	SCC 213
Alden, John	44	1672	SJC 1471
Aldis, John	60	nd	SJC 2252
Aldis, Nathan	73	1669	SJC 966
Aldrich, Joseph	32	1668	EQC 4:2
Aldrich, Joseph	47	1682	MCC folio 98
Aldrich, Thomas	40	1685	SJC 2370
Alexander, David	24	1685	MCC folio 114
Alexander, John	45	1673	MCC folio 63
Alexander, Joseph	42	1695/6	SJC 4249
Alger, Andrew	34	1664	SJC 652
Allanson, Ralph	54	1676	SJC 1526
Allen, Andrew	66	1682	EQC 8:381
Allen, Benjamin	30	1674	SJC 1341
Allen, Bozoun	28	1681	SJC 2029
Allen, Bozoun	30	1684	SJC 2205
Allen, Charles	24	1695	SJC 4189

Allen, Daniel	26	1682	SJC 2104
Allen, David	26	1682	MCC folio 106
Allen, Edward	62	1685	SJC 2377
Allen, Elizabeth	18	1682	EQC 8:382
Allen, Faith	60	1682	EQC 8:383
Allen, Faith	74	1695	MCC folio 162
Allen, Hannah	18	1671/2	SJC 1148
Allen, Henry	47	1667	SJC 1911
Allen, Henry	54	1674/5	SJC 1432
Allen, Henry	59	1679/80	SJC 1833
Allen, James	45	1678	EQC 7:12
Allen, James	47	1680	SCC 1145
Allen, James	47	1680	SJC 1910
Allen, James	48	1681	EQC 8:120
Allen, James	48	1681	SJC 2018
Allen, Jeremiah	18	1691	SJC 98515
Allen, Jeremy	23	1682	MCC folio 103
Allen, John	28	1678	EQC 6:413
Allen, John	35	1684	EQC 9:394
Allen, John	45	1683	EQC 9:89
Allen, John	52	1668	MCC folio 47
Allen, Mercy	33	1698	SJC 3718
Allen, Nathaniel	50	1699	SJC 4696
Allen, Nehemiah	30	1677	SJC 1586
Allen, Rebecca	23	1662	SJC 468
Allen, Rebecca	28	1681	EQC 8:226
Allen, Rebecca	30	1683	EQC 9:52
Allen, Rebecca	32	1683	EQC 9:90
Allen, Richard	19	1693/4	SJC 2989
Allen, Samuel	50	1679	EQC 7:296
Allen, Samuel	50	1679	EQC 7:296
Allen, Samuel	50	1679	SJC 2011
Allen, Samuel	50	1681	EQC 8:108
Allen, Thomas	25	1679	EQC 7:326
Allen, Thomas	26	1679	MCC folio 86
Allen, Thomas	26	1679	MCC folio 88
Allen, Walter	76	1677	MCC folio 76
Allen, William	14	1683	EQC 9:2
Allen, William	33	1679	EQC 7:296
Allen, William	33	1679	SJC 2011
Allen, William	37	1684	EQC 9:310
Allen, William	41 or 55	1667	SJC 813
Allen, William	62	1664	EQC 3:207
Alley, Geoles	42	1669	EQC 4:168
Alley, Hugh	25	1680	EQC 8:103
Alley, Hugh	53	1662	EQC 2:394
Alley, Hugh	53	1662	SJC 448
Alley, John	18	1662	SJC 508
Alley, John	30	1682	EQC 8:293
Alley, Sarah	18	1689	SJC 2541
Alling, Andrew	40	1658	EQC 2:113
Allison, James	28	1679/80	SCC 1119
Allison, James	28	1679/80	SJC 1837
Allison, Richard	29	1662	SJC 470

Ambrose, Abigail	17	1672	SJC 1178
Ambrose, Henry	35	1682	EQC 8:330
Ambrose, Henry	40	1653	MCC folio 7
Ambrose, Henry	42	1655	SJC 227
Ambrose, Richard	35	1677	SJC 1686
Ambrose, Susanna	38	1687	EQC WPA 47-53-1
Amee, John	59	1684	MCC folio 107
Ames, Henry	44	nd	SJC 2755
Ames, John	53	1672	MCC folio 59
Ames, Robert	31	1671	EQC 4:422
Ames, Thomas	60	1676	SJC 1799
Amsden, Jacob	35	1692	MCC folio 146
Amsden, Jacob	38	nd	SJC 2807
Anderson, David	28	1671	EQC 4:452
Anderson, David	29	1674	EQC 5:317
Anderson, John	26	1676	EQC 6:328
Andres, Daniel	20	1671	EQC 4:434
Andrew, Samuel	50	1672	MCC folio 59
Andrew, William	23	1681	EQC 8:188
Andrew, William	23	1681	EQC 8:188
Andrews, Daniel	16	1660	MCC folio 25
Andrews, Daniel	33	1677	EQC 6:247
Andrews, James	37	1662	SJC 561
Andrews, Jenne	62	1685	EQC 9:463
Andrews, John	22	1668	EQC 4:69
Andrews, John	22	1668	EQC 4:70
Andrews, John	22	1668	SJC 897
Andrews, John	31	1659	EQC 2:145
Andrews, John	31	1659	EQC 2:185
Andrews, John	32	1661	EQC 2:284
Andrews, John	36	1684	EQC 9:259
Andrews, John	40	1659	EQC 2:187
Andrews, John	40	1695	SJC 162383
Andrews, John	45	1659	EQC 2:184
Andrews, John	48	1668	EQC 4:69
Andrews, John	48	1668	SJC 897
Andrews, John	57	1678	EQC 6:416
Andrews, John	63	1684	EQC 9:209
Andrews, John	63	1685	EQC 9:463
Andrews, John	70	1691	SJC 3138
Andrews, John	72	1693	SJC 3138
Andrews, John	72	nd	SJC 2827
Andrews, Joseph	37	1693	SJC 162299
Andrews, Joseph	37	1693	SJC 3138
Andrews, Nicholas	38	1680	EQC 7:386
Andrews, Nicholas	40	1685	EQC 9:570
Andrews, Renew	60	1653	SJC 168
Andrews, Sarah	17	1681	EQC 8:192
Andrews, Thomas	16	1670	EQC 4:243
Andrews, Thomas	17	1660	MCC folio 25
Andrews, Thomas	22	1678	EQC 8:191
Andrews, Thomas	50	1695	MCC folio 178
Andrews, Thomas	56	1695/6	SJC 4225
Andrews, Thomas	56	1696	SJC 3323

Andrews, William	45	1693	SJC 162299
Andrews, William	45	1693	SJC 3138
Andros, Grace	50	1674	EQC 5:422
Andros, Grace	60	1674	EQC 5:353
Andros, John	37	1684	EQC 9:175
Andros, Robert	25	1674	EQC 5:354
Andros, Robert	28	1674	EQC 5:422
Andruff, John	33	1661	EQC 2:286
Anger, Anna	41	1673	EQC 5:177
Anger, Anna	41	1673	EQC 5:178
Angier, Anna	47	1676	MCC folio 73
Angier, Ephraim	17	1669	MCC folio 52
Annable, John	20	1670	EQC 4:257
Annable, John	21	1671	EQC 4:341
Annable, Joseph	21	1680	EQC 7:362
Annable, Mathew	18	1672	EQC 5:12
Annable, Mathew	25	1680	EQC 7:362
Annis, Curmac	40	1678	EQC 7:156
Anthony, Joseph	31	nd	SJC 4793
Anthro, Martha	23	1667	EQC 3:395
Appleford, John	25	1658	EQC 2:139
Appleton, John	30	1683	EQC 9:224
Appleton, John	36	1659	EQC 2:179
Appleton, John	50	1672	EQC 5:38
Appleton, John	57	1678	EQC 7:120
Appleton, Samuel	19	1674	EQC 5:318
Appleton, Samuel	19	1674	EQC 5:319
Appleton, Samuel	28	nd	SJC 2828
Arbit, Arthur	35	1674	EQC 5:341
Archard, Hannah	20	1662	EQC 2:420
Archard, Samuel	50	1665	EQC 3:276
Archard, Samuel	58	1666	EQC 3:420
Archer, Benjamin	20	1686	EQC WPA 46-79-2
Archer, Henry	66	1671	EQC 4:342
Archer, John	19	1685	EQC 9:524
Archer, John	28	1666	EQC 3:324
Archer, Samuel	22	1686	EQC WPA 46-79-2
Arington, Hannah	21	1677	MCC folio 78
Armitage, Eleazer	23	1668	SJC 924
Armitage, Jonathan	15	1662	SJC 508
Armitage, Joseph	53	1652	MCC folio 5
Armitage, Joseph	55	1657	EQC 2:30
Armitage, Joseph	57	1657	EQC 7:128
Armitage, Joseph	60	1661	EQC 2:269
Armitage, Joseph	60	1662	MCC folio 32
Armitage, Joseph	60	1670	EQC 4:253
Armitage, Joseph	60	1670	EQC 4:271
Armitage, Joseph	60	1672	EQC 5:44
Armitage, Joseph	60	1673	EQC 5:194
Armitage, Joseph	60	1674	EQC 5:424
Armitage, Joseph	60	1677	SJC 1973
Armitage, Joseph	67	1674	EQC 5:386
Armitage, Joseph	69	1677	EQC 6:286
Armitage, Joseph	70	1677	EQC 6:368

Armitage, Timothy	18	1662	SJC 874
Armitage, Timothy	36	1677	EQC 6:330
Armstrong, Mathew	27	1661	EQC 2:286
Arnold, Joseph	23	1675	EQC 6:79
Arnold, Samuel	58	1680	SJC 1915
Arnold, William	41	1691	MCC folio 151
Arnold, William	43	1692	SJC 162281
Arthur, Elizabeth	61	1677	SJC 1635
Arthur, Priscilla	36	nd	SJC 2818
Arthur, Thomas	45	1696	SJC 3377
Ashby, Elizabeth	15	1683	EQC 9:28
Ashton, Henry	26	1672	MCC folio 65
Ashton, Henry	26	1672	SJC 1221
Ashton, Henry	30	1673	SCC 349
Ashton, Henry	30	1673	SJC 1341
Ashton, John	45	1684	EQC 9:210
Aspinwall, Peter	52	1664	MCC Harvard #2583
Aspinwall, Peter	67	1680	SJC 1908
Aston, Anthony	27	1663	EQC 3:30
Aston, Anthony	27	1663	SJC 162054
Aston, Anthony	27	1663	SJC 565
Athearn, Simon	56	1696	SJC 4605
Atherton, Jonathan	42	1677	MCC folio 74
Atkins, Hatton	21	1663	SJC 571
Atkinson, Abigail	20	1694	SJC 3153
Atkinson, John	14	1682	EQC 8:284
Atkinson, John	15	1682	EQC 8:263
Atkinson, John	15	1682	EQC 8:419
Atkinson, John	17	1684	EQC 9:347
Atkinson, John	28	1665	SJC 721
Atkinson, John	28	1668	EQC 4:13
Atkinson, John	40	1676	EQC 6:159
Atkinson, John	40	1676	EQC 6:164
Atkinson, John	40	1678	EQC 6:414
Atkinson, John	43	1679	EQC 7:163
Atkinson, John	44	1678	EQC 7:156
Atkinson, Samuel	18	1694	SJC 3153
Atkinson, Sarah	19	1684	EQC 9:347
Atkinson, Theodore	27	1670	SJC 1276
Atkinson, Theodore	62	1676	EQC 6:155
Atkinson, Theodore	62	1676	SJC 162146
Atkinson, Thomas	16	1686	EQC WPA 46-119-2
Atkinson, Thomas	16	1686	EQC WPA 46-121-2
Atway, John	33	1679	EQC 7:326
Atwell, Joan	60	1688	SJC 162249
Atwell, Mary	21	1692	MCC folio 154
Atwood, Ephraim	17	nd	SJC 3630
Atwood, Philip	40	1660	MCC folio 25
Atwood, Philip	40	1660	MCC folio 26
Atwood, Philip	42	1662	MCC folio 31
Atwood, Philip	42	1662	SJC 478
Atwood, Philip	45	1663	MCC folio 35
Atwood, Thomas	32	1684	EQC 9:173
Auger, Agnes	48	1669	SJC 1046

Auger, Andrew	26	1679/80	SJC 1828
Auger, John	28	1669	SJC 1046
Auger, John	30	1670	SJC 1046
Auger, Mather	27	1685	SJC 2346
Auger, Mathew	28	1685	SJC 2346
Austin, Anthony	28	1664	EQC 3:214
Austin, Anthony	28	1664	EQC 3:215
Austin, Anthony	31	1667	EQC 3:426
Austin, Anthony	35	1671	EQC 4:340
Austin, Ebenezer	29	1692	MCC folio 154
Austin, Hopestill	29	1673	SJC 1228
Austin, Leonard	45	1679	EQC 7:182
Austin, William	22	1695	MCC folio 180
Averill, James	67	1670	SJC 986
Averill, James	70	1673	SJC 1212
Averill, James	72	1674/5	SJC 1458
Averill, James	74	1676/7	SJC 1549
Averill, James	77	1680/1	SJC 1972
Averill, Thomas	36	1672	SJC 1126
Awesioame, Thomas	11	nd	SJC 2906
Ayers, Mark	20	1682	EQC 8:282
Ayers, Robert	72	1678	SJC 27131
Ayers, Samuel	40	1662	EQC 2:356
Ayers, Samuel	40	1694	SJC 3237
Ayers, Thomas	23	1678	EQC 6:403
Ayres, John	13	1673	SJC 1254
Ayres, John	31	1680	EQC 7:372
Ayres, John	35	1683/4	SJC 2183
Ayres, Mary	34	1668	EQC 4:83
Ayres, Nathaniel	22	1678	EQC 7:156
Ayres, Samuel	45	1668	EQC 4:84
Baasham, Nathaniel	45	1690	MCC folio 135
Bab, Thomas	28	1684	EQC 9:349
Babell, Hugh	31	1679	EQC 7:263
Babill, Susannah	23	1680	EQC 7:374
Babill, Susannah	23	1680	SJC 1894
Babson, Isabel	80	1657	EQC 2:38
Babson, James	30	1663	EQC 3:40
Babson, John	18	1679	EQC 7:254
Bachiler, David	38	1681	MCC folio 96
Bachiler, John	47	1658	EQC 2:107
Bachiler, John	63	1674	EQC 5:291
Bachiler, Joseph	15	1663	MCC folio 34
Bachiler, Joseph	23	1669	MCC folio 52
Bachiler, Joseph	24	1669	MCC folio 51
Bachiler, Joseph	37	1682	MCC folio 99
Bachiler, Mark	38	1673	EQC 5:175
Bachiler, William	25	1676	EQC 6:198
Bacon, Abigail	20	1685	MCC folio 120
Bacon, Daniel	30	1671	MCC folio 59
Bacon, Daniel	38	1678	EQC 7:246
Bacon, Daniel	40	1681	EQC 8:109
Bacon, Daniel	44	1684	EQC 9:345
Bacon, goodwife	36	1681	EQC 8:109

Bacon, John	44	1672	MCC folio 60
Bacon, Mary	18	1685	MCC folio 116
Bacon, Mary	18	1685	SJC 2327
Bacon, Mary	52	nd	SJC 1050
Bacon, Mary	60	1668	MCC folio 48
Bacon, Michael	22	1659	MCC folio 21
Bacon, Michael	24	1684	MCC folio 109
Bacon, Michael	40	1684	MCC folio 109
Bacon, Michael	60	1668	MCC folio 45
Bacon, Michael	67	1676	MCC folio 71
Bacon, Sarah	15	1678	SJC 2327
Bacon, Sarah	38	1678	SJC 2327
Bacon, Sarah	38	1685	MCC folio 116
Bacor, Nathaniel	66	1677	EQC 7:126
Badcock, Deborah	70	1694	SJC 4111
Badger, Edward	23	1684	EQC 9:284
Badger, Elizabeth	20	1663	MCC folio 34
Badger, John	36	1678	EQC 7:156
Badlam, Joane	24	1684	SJC 2242
Bagworth, Benjamin	21	1671	SJC 1071
Bailey, Henry	50	1661	EQC 2:299
Bailey, Henry	70	1676	EQC 6:147
Bailey, Henry	70	1679	EQC 7:182
Bailey, Henry	78	1679	EQC 7:182
Bailey, Isaac	24	1678	EQC 7:156
Bailey, James	51	1663	EQC 3:30
Bailey, James	60	1675	EQC 6:15
Bailey, James	65	1677	EQC 6:275
Bailey, John	65	1678	EQC 7:156
Bailey, Joseph	30	1678	EQC 7:156
Bailey, Joseph	33	1682	EQC 8:430
Bailey, Joshua	20	1678	EQC 7:156
Bailey, Theophilus	31	1653	EQC 2:95
Baker, Elizabeth	20	1666	SD 5:53
Baker, Joan	30	1676	EQC 6:193
Baker, John	20	1653	MCC folio 1
Baker, John	22	1669	MCC folio 51
Baker, John	28	1669	EQC 4:116
Baker, John	36	1676	EQC 6:193
Baker, Joseph	23	1685	MCC folio 114
Baker, Josiah	40	1695	MCC folio 162
Baker, Judith	30	1676	MCC folio 71
Baker, Katherine	28	1677	EQC 6:352
Baker, Mary	33	1691	MCC folio 151
Baker, Mary	35	1683	MCC folio 101
Baker, Roger	47	1680/1	SJC 2014
Baker, Ruth	42	1682	MCC folio 99
Baker, Ruth	50	1691	MCC folio 141
Baker, Thomas	23	1675	SJC 1417b
Baker, Thomas	25	1662	EQC 2:359
Baker, Thomas	25	1673	EQC 5:232
Baker, Thomas	31	1683	SJC 2224
Baker, Thomas	39	1691	MCC folio 151
Baker, Thomas	43	1695	SJC 162375

Baker, William	36	nd	SJC 2660
Baker, William	52	1652	MCC folio 4
Balch, Freeborn	22	1681	EQC 8:190
Balch, John	16	1670	EQC 4:309
Balch, John	27	1681	EQC 8:190
Balch, Samuel	29	1681	EQC 8:190
Balden, Pheby	17	1671	MCC folio 58
Balding, Peter	29	1679	EQC 7:221
Baldwin, Phebe	50	1682	MCC folio 101
Baldwin, Thomas	25	1670	MCC folio 53
Ball, Abraham	33	1653	MCC folio 8
Ball, Francis	55	1680	SCC 1094
Ball, Isaac	25	1686	EQC WPA 46-100-3
Ball, Isaac	28	1686	EQC WPA 46-137-2
Ball, Jane	21	1686	EQC WPA 46-100-1
Ball, John	30	1676	MCC folio 72
Ball, John	39	1683	MCC folio 104
Ball, John	60	1693/4	SJC 3006
Ball, Kathrine	35	1660	MCC folio 25
Ball, Richard	26	1679	EQC 7:221
Ball, William	43	1662	MCC folio 33
Ballard, Elizabeth	16	1679	SJC 2025
Ballard, Gervais	53	1685	SJC 2377
Ballard, Jarvis	40	1672	SJC 1341
Ballard, John	21	1655	EQC 1:392
Ballard, John	25	1678	EQC 7:97
Ballard, John	50	1684	EQC 9:341
Ballard, Jon.	25	1659	EQC 2:193
Ballard, Joseph	26	1671	EQC 4:371
Ballard, Nathaniel	37	1675	EQC 6:10
Ballard, Nathaniel	48	1684	EQC 9:341
Ballard, William	44	1662	EQC 2:438
Ballard, William	45	1662	EQC 2:404
Ballard, William	45	1662	EQC 2:409
Ballard, William	45	1662	EQC 2:412
Ballard, William	50	1671	EQC 4:371
Ballatt, Anna	35	1684	MCC folio 113
Ballatt, Lydia	19	1690	MCC folio 137
Ballatt, Samuel	38	1676	MCC folio 72
Bally, Joseph	34	1681	EQC 8:215
Banbrick, Justin's widow	64	1663	MCC folio 34
Bancroft, Thomas	50	1674	MCC folio 75
Bancroft, Thomas	50	1675	EQC 6:35
Bancroft, Thomas	58	1681	EQC 8:121
Banes, Richard	34	1666	MCC folio 40
Banfield, Elizabeth	28	1679	MCC folio 85
Banfield, Elizabeth	32	1681	MCC folio 104
Banfield, Elizabeth	32	1681	MCC folio 97
Banfield, Elizabeth	35	1683	MCC folio 104
Banfield, Rebecca	32	1673	EQC 5:199
Bankes, Richard	40	1679	MCC folio 84
Bant, Gilbert	36	1695	MCC folio 180
Barbar, Hannah	45	1690	MCC folio 131
Barber, John	48	1677	EQC 6:413

Barber, Priscilla	21	1694	SJC 3030
Barber, William	46	1667/8	SJC 841
Bardall, Robert	25	nd	SJC 1738
Barden, William	31	1657	MCC folio 18
Bardens, John	33	1684	SJC 2196
Bare, John	21	1668	EQC 4:70
Bare, John	22	1668	EQC 4:48
Bare, John	22	1669	EQC 4:105
Barge, Ellenor	16	1676	SJC 1526
Barker, John	16	1661	EQC 2:287
Barker, Judith	30	1676	MCC folio 71
Barnard, Benjamin	17	1662	MCC folio 32
Barnard, Benjamin	17	1662	MCC folio 35
Barnard, James	23	1663	SJC 573
Barnard, John	18	1661	EQC 2:287
Barnard, John	20	1675	SJC 1403
Barnard, John	24	1679	SJC 1965
Barnard, John	29	1683	SJC 2183
Barnard, John	30	1662	MCC folio 35
Barnard, John	42	1674	MCC folio 63
Barnard, Joseph	20	1662	MCC folio 32
Barnard, Mathew	25	1653	MCC folio 9
Barnard, Mathew	34	1662/3	SD 4:88a
Barnard, Mathew	40	1667	SJC 909
Barnard, Richard	36	1672/3	SJC 1216
Barnard, Samuel	28	1662	MCC folio 35
Barnard, Samuel	35	1669	MCC folio 52
Barnard, Sarah	21	1662	MCC folio 32
Barnard, Sarah	30	1672	MCC folio 60
Barnard, Sarah	43	1685	SJC 2348
Barnard, Steven	22	1671	EQC 4:421
Barnard, Thomas	24	1680	SJC 2045
Barnard, Thomas	27	1684	MCC folio 107
Barnard, Thomas	27	1684	SD 13:121
Barnard, Thomas	51	1663	SJC 718
Barnard, Thomas	64	1675	SJC 1414
Barnes, Elizabeth	36	1683	SJC 2145
Barnes, James	26	1675	SJC 1402
Barnes, James	45	1696	SJC 3470
Barnes, Jane	18	1682	EQC 8:364
Barnes, John	24	1666	MCC folio 40
Barnes, Mathew	50	1656	SJC 262
Barnes, Nathaniel	27	1678	MCC folio 81
Barnes, Nathaniel	28	1679	SJC 1788
Barnes, Nathaniel	34	1685	SJC 2324
Barnes, Richard	26	1663	SJC 612
Barnes, Richard	40	1672	MCC folio 59
Barnes, Richard	48	1679	MCC folio 84
Barnes, Thomas	28	1660	EQC 2:206
Barnes, Thomas	40	1677	MCC folio 76
Barnes, William	50	1665	SJC 1321
Barnes, William	63	1675	SJC 1414
Barnett, John	30	1662	MCC folio 31
Barnett, Mathew	38	1665	MCC folio 38

Barnett, Steven	20	1669	EQC 4:177
Barnett, Thomas	56	1681	MCC folio 93
Barney, Jacob	71	1672	EQC 5:57
Barnham, Mary	46	1670	EQC 4:287
Barnum, Samuel	28	1662	MCC folio 32
Barrell, James	35	1684?	SJC 2242
Barrell, John	27	1684	SJC 2242
Barrett, Hannah	46	1662	MCC folio 31
Barrett, Hannah	50	1665	MCC folio 40
Barrett, Hannah	50	1665	MCC folio 41
Barrett, Humphrey	38	1670	MCC folio 55
Barrett, James	33	1677	MCC folio 75
Barrett, James	35	1658	MCC folio 16
Barrett, James	40	1678	MCC folio 187
Barrett, James	45	1662	MCC folio 31
Barrett, James	45	1662	SJC 478
Barrett, James	50	1665	MCC folio 40
Barrett, John	40	1671	MCC folio 58
Barrett, John	40	1692	SJC 3063
Barrett, John	40	1694	MCC folio 182
Barrett, John	51	1677	MCC folio 77
Barrett, John	65	1692	SJC 26914
Barrett, John	65	1694	MCC folio 182
Barrett, Joseph	32	1682	EQC 8:382
Barrett, Margaret	15	1678	MCC folio 82
Barrett, Mary	20	1679	EQC 7:183
Barrett, Mary	26	1665	MCC folio 39
Barrett, Rebecca	17	1689	MCC folio 133
Barrett, Rebecca	17	1690	MCC folio 133
Barrett, Rebecca	17	1690	MCC folio 140
Barrett, Samuel	30	1667	MCC folio 43
Barrett, Thomas	77	1665	MCC folio 39
Barrett, William	23	1658	MCC folio 16
Barrett, William	49	1685	MCC folio 117
Barron, Elizabeth	17	1677	MCC folio 76
Barron, Hannah	63	1678	MCC folio 81
Barron, Lydia	37	1677	MCC folio 76
Barron, Moses	34	1677	MCC folio 77
Barry, John	28	1669	EQC 4:195
Barry, John	30	1673	EQC 5:226
Barry, John	37	1679	EQC 7:177
Barry, John	41	1683	EQC 9:29
Barsham, John	28	1669	EQC 4:114
Barstow, Michael	30	1685	MCC folio 115
Barstow, Michael	30	1685	MCC folio 117
Barstow, Michael	30	1685	SJC 2348
Bartell, John	43	1674	EQC 5:348
Bartholomew, Henry	22	1679	SJC 1815
Bartholomew, Henry	60	1669	EQC 4:110
Bartholomew, Henry	62	1669	EQC 4:102
Bartholomew, Henry	72	1680	EQC 7:394
Bartholomew, Joseph	24	1662	EQC 2:402
Bartlett, Bethiah	30	1680	EQC 7:335
Bartlett, Christopher	23	1678	EQC 7:156

Bartlett, Christopher	33	1657	EQC 2:29
Bartlett, John	23	1678	EQC 7:156
Bartlett, John	28	1672	EQC 5:6
Bartlett, John	36	1680	EQC 7:335
Bartlett, John	36	1680	EQC 7:386
Bartlett, John	36	1680	EQC 7:386
Bartlett, John	36	1682	EQC 8:331
Bartlett, John	39	1678	EQC 7:156
Bartlett, John	65	1678	EQC 7:156
Bartlett, Joseph	41	1680	SJC 1915
Bartlett, Joseph	51	1681	MCC folio 95
Bartlett, Richard	30	1678	EQC 7:156
Bartlett, Richard	47	1669	EQC 4:127
Bartlett, Richard	50	1679	SJC 1791
Bartlett, Richard	53	1674	EQC 5:417
Bartlett, Richard	57	1678	EQC 7:156
Bartlett, Samuel	32	1678	EQC 7:157
Bartlett, Samuel	50	1693	SJC 3301
Bartlett, Thomas	25	1678	EQC 7:156
Bartoll, John	42	1673	EQC 5:172
Bartoll, Mary	55	1684	EQC 9:206
Bartoll, William	32	1662	EQC 2:441
Barton, Edward	33	1680	SJC 1909
Bartrom, Sarah	56	1677	EQC 6:299
Bartrom, William	40	1661	EQC 2:285
Bass, John	31	1678	EQC 7:74
Bassett, Henry	26	1680	SJC 1935
Bassett, William	33	1662	SJC 508
Bassett, William	42	1689/90	SJC 2541
Bassett, William	50	1675	EQC 6:10
Bassett, William	58	1677	EQC 6:360
Bassett, William	60	1684	EQC 9:316
Bassett, William	62	1681	EQC 8:121
Bassett, William	63	1682	EQC 8:398
Bassett, William	63	1682	EQC 8:403
Bassett, William	71	1689/90	SJC 2541
Bastard, Joseph	48	1667	SJC 909
Baston, Hannah	28	1680	EQC 7:372
Baston, Hannah	28	1680	SJC 1894
Bate, Benjamin	44	1677	SJC 1633
Bate, Benjamin	46	1678	SJC 1722
Bateman, Hannah	58	1676/7	SJC 1544
Bateman, John	62	1676/7	SJC 1544
Bateman, Joseph	21	1680	SJC 1916
Bateman, Mary	18	1680	EQC 7:371
Bateman, Thomas	33	1684	MCC folio 108
Bateman, Thomas	47	nd	SJC 3615
Baten, Susannah	18	1683	EQC 9:2
Bates, Ann	36	1670	SJC 1334
Bates, John	38	1680	EQC 7:423
Bates, John	44	1686	EQC WPA 46-79-1
Bates, Martha	29	1678	EQC 7:147
Bates, Martha	29	1678	EQC 7:90
Bates, Martha	31	1680	EQC 7:423

Batman, John	34	1691	MCC folio 140
Batt, Ann	72	1673	EQC 5:178
Batt, Barnabas	21	1665	SJC 709
Batt, Thomas	35	1676	SJC 1048
Batt, Timothy	30	1676	SJC 1459
Batt, William	30	1667	EQC 3:461
Batten, Susannah	16	1680	EQC 7:362
Batter, Edmund	50	1658	EQC 2:128
Batter, Edmund	50	1658	EQC 2:134
Batter, Edmund	50	1659	EQC 2:148
Batter, Edmund	57	1665	EQC 3:276
Batter, Edmund	58	1667	EQC 3:419
Batter, Edmund	60	1669	EQC 4:103
Batter, Edmund	61	1670	EQC 4:266
Batter, Edmund	64	1673	EQC 5:211
Batter, Edmund	68	1676	EQC 6:189
Batter, Edmund	70	1678	EQC 7:132
Batter, Edmund	72	1681	EQC 8:120
Batter, Edmund	72	1681	SJC 2018
Batter, Edmund	73	1682	EQC 8:323
Batter, Hannah	46	1682	MCC folio 99
Batter, Sarah	48	1658	EQC 2:134
Baxter, Anna	18	1681	MCC folio 97
Baxter, Hannah	18	1681	MCC folio 104
Baxter, Hannah	36	1676	MCC folio 73
Baxter, John	15	1681	MCC folio 104
Baxter, John	15	1681	MCC folio 97
Baxter, John	37	1669	EQC 4:114
Bayer, John	22	1669	EQC 4:104
Bayer, John	22	1669	EQC 4:142
Bayley, Henry	77	1678	SJC 1770
Bayley, James	51	1663	SJC 565
Bayley, John	54	1668/9	SJC 924
Bayley, Robert	35	1671	SD 7:215
Bayley, Theophilus	29	1653	SJC 225
Bayley, Thomas	18	1668	SJC 911
Beacker, John	30	1672	EQC 5:92
Beadish, Joseph	42	1681	MCC folio 94
Beadle, Nathaniel	30	1673	EQC 5:171
Beadle, Nathaniel	30	1673	SJC 1226
Beadle, Robert	36	1669	EQC 4:178
Beale, James	14	1672	EQC 5:42
Beale, James	17	1675	EQC 6:77
Beale, Martha	13	1669	EQC 4:163
Beale, Martha	14	1670	EQC 4:271
Beale, Martha	22	1654	EQC 1:331
Beale, Martha	26	1686	MCC folio 124
Beale, Martha	30	1669	EQC 4:163
Beale, Martha	40	1673	EQC 5:169
Beale, Martha	40	1673	EQC 7:5
Beale, Samuel	14	1669	EQC 4:162
Beale, Samuel	14	1669	EQC 4:163
Beale, Samuel	16	1670	EQC 4:271
Beale, Samuel	17	1672	EQC 5:42

Beale, Samuel	21	1675	EQC 6:77
Beale, Samuel	21	1675	EQC 6:78
Beale, William	22	1654	EQC 1:331
Beale, William	38	1666	EQC 3:368
Beale, William	38	1667	EQC 3:419
Beale, William	38	1669	EQC 4:163
Beale, William	40	1674	EQC 5:279
Beale, William	40	1674	EQC 5:283
Beale, William	43	1673	EQC 5:168
Beale, William	49	1679	EQC 7:201
Beale, William	49	1679	EQC 7:257
Beale, William	49	1679	EQC 7:297
Beale, William	49	1679	SJC 2011
Beale, William	50	1679	SJC 2011
Beale, William	50	1680	EQC 8:5
Beale, William	57	1686	MCC folio 124
Beamon, Symon	22	1677	MCC folio 77
Beamont, Thankful	18	1681	MCC folio 104
Beamsly, Martha	62	1663	SJC 591
Beamus, Joseph	60	1678	MCC folio 81
Beare, John	21	1668	EQC 4:67
Beare, John	30	1679	EQC 7:293
Beaumont, John	40	1690	MCC folio 136
Beck, Alexander	84	1672	SJC 1092
Beckett, John	27	1685	EQC 9:449
Beckett, John	32	1659	EQC 2:186
Beckett, John	42	1670	EQC 4:265
Beckett, John	53	1679	EQC 7:253
Beckett, John	57	1682	EQC 8:236
Beckett, Mary	19	1674	EQC 5:348
Becon, Susannah	26	1675	MCC folio 69
Bedford, Nathan	37	1676	SJC 1592
Beedle, Robert	36	1678	EQC 7:157
Beere, Philip	40	1663	EQC 3:102
Beford, Richard	58	1666	EQC 3:327
Belcher, Andrew	34	1679	MCC folio 89
Belcher, Andrew	44	1690	SJC 2563
Belcher, Andrew	45	1691	SJC 2563
Belcher, Andrew	48	1695	SJC 3101
Belcher, Elizabeth	56	1677	MCC folio 78
Belcher, Elizabeth	59	1678	MCC folio 79
Belcher, Gregory	60	1665	EQC 3:256
Belcher, Jeremiah	50	1666	EQC 3:373
Belcher, Jeremiah	52	1667	EQC 3:424
Belcher, Jeremiah	54	1668	EQC 4:7
Belcher, Jeremiah	59	1671	SJC 1102
Belcher, John	22	1671	EQC 4:376
Belcher, Joseph	26	1671	SJC 1290
Belcher, Samuel	27	nd	SJC 2910
Belknap, Joseph	42	1676	SJC 1656
Bell, Mary	18	1671	MCC folio 57
Bell, Thomas	33	1679	SCC 1089
Bell, Thomas	33	1679	SJC 1919
Belle, Thomas	50	1681	EQC 8:199

Bellflower, Hannah	17	1674	MCC folio 66
Bellflower, Henry	26	1656	MCC folio 15
Bellhouse, John	44	1669	MCC folio 51
Bellows, John	44	1670	MCC folio 53
Beman, John	20	1670/1	MCC folio 56
Bemes, Sary	38	1657	MCC folio 18
Bemish, Joseph	40	1658	MCC folio 16
Bendall, Ephraim	25	1674	SJC 1330
Bengrian, Benjamin	25	1672	EQC 5:92
Benham, Johannah	19	nd	SJC 1972
Benjamin, Abigail	72	1671	MCC folio 59
Benjamin, John	80	1698	MCC folio 207
Benjamin, Samuel	29	1657	MCC folio 18
Bennet, Aphra	35	1676	SCC 761
Bennett, Anthony	17	1678	EQC 7:101
Bennett, Aphra	35	1676	SJC 1569
Bennett, Aphra	45	1691	MCC folio 141
Bennett, Aughter	40	1679	EQC 7:216
Bennett, Edmund	20	1674	EQC 5:421
Bennett, Edward	16	1670	EQC 4:255
Bennett, Edward	17	1673	EQC 5:180
Bennett, Edward	23	1678	EQC 7:118
Bennett, Elizabeth	25	1681	MCC folio 97
Bennett, Francis	30	1653	EQC 1:317
Bennett, Henry	21	1685	EQC 9:528
Bennett, Henry	21	1685	EQC 9:528
Bennett, Henry	33	1670	EQC 4:264
Bennett, Henry	55	1684	EQC 9:243
Bennett, Jacob	21	1673	EQC 5:145
Bennett, Jacob	23	1675	EQC 6:86
Bennett, Jacob	25	1676	EQC 6:221
Bennett, Jacob	25	1679	EQC 7:382
Bennett, Jacob	33	1685	EQC 9:528
Bennett, John	20	1675	EQC 6:84
Bennett, John	33	1663/4	SJC 632
Bennett, John	35	1680	EQC 8:6
Bennett, John	37	1669	MCC folio 49
Bennett, John	37	1682	EQC 8:403
Bennett, Joseph	15	1674	EQC 5:347
Bennett, Lydia	36	1669	EQC 4:136
Bennett, Margaret	61	1669	EQC 4:115
Bennett, Margaret	64	1670	EQC 4:281
Bennett, Martha	24	1678	MCC folio 82
Bennett, Mary	42	1682	EQC 8:279
Bennett, Peter	23	1670/1	SJC 1015
Bennett, Peter	34	nd	SJC 1157
Bennett, Samuel	48	1653	EQC 2:92
Bennett, Samuel	62	1670	EQC 4:298
Bennett, Sarah	22	1663/4	SJC 632
Bennett, Sarah	65	1676	SJC 1659
Bennett, Sarah	68	1676	SJC 1544
Bennett, William	19	1676	EQC 6:221
Bennett, William	21	1680	EQC 8:9
Bennett, William	21	1680	SJC 1967

Bennett, William	24	1684	EQC 9:189
Bennett, William	24	1684	EQC 9:243
Bennett, William	28	1685	EQC 9:528
Bennett, William	50	1676	EQC 6:221
Bennett, William	70	1681	EQC 8:108
Bennett, William	70	1681	SJC 2011
Bennett, William	73	1677	EQC 6:247
Benny, John	19	1672	SJC 1163
Bent, Elizabeth	19	nd	SJC 1972
Bent, John	66	1660	MCC folio 22
Bent, Joseph	20	1660	MCC folio 22
Berbene, James	23	1691	MCC folio 147
Berh, May	15	1657	MCC folio 18
Bernard, John	18	1661	EQC 2:308
Bernard, Joseph	21	1663	MCC folio 35
Bernard, Sarah	21	1663	MCC folio 35
Bernard, Sarah	45	1685	MCC folio 115
Berry, Rebecca	30	1684	EQC 9:251
Besum, John	14	1669	EQC 4:108
Besum, John	29	1684	EQC 9:250
Bett, Elizabeth	54	1653	MCC folio 7
Betts, John	33	1681	MCC folio 184
Betts, John	36	1679	MCC folio 83
Betts, John	37	1679	MCC folio 185
Bickford, Christian	17	1666	EQC 3:376
Bickford, Jeremiah	17	1694	SJC 2989
Bickford, Samuel	21	1669	EQC 4:119
Bickford, Samuel	25	1668	EQC 4:28
Bickford, Thomas	36	1676	SJC 1526
Bidell, Robert	24	1667	EQC 4:14
Bigelow, James	13	1680	MCC folio 91
Bigelow, John	60	1678	MCC folio 81
Bigelow, John	60	1678	MCC folio 81
Bigelow, John	63	1680	MCC folio 91
Bigelow, John	75	1695	MCC folio 179
Bigelow, John	75	nd	SJC 3175
Bigelow, Joshua	37	1693	MCC folio 176
Bigelow, Joshua	40	1694	MCC folio 161
Bigelow, Samuel	32	1685	MCC folio 114
Bigelow, Samuel	33	1686	MCC folio 125
Bill, Catherine	50	1676	MCC folio 72
Bill, John	24	1678	EQC 7:23
Billing, John	38	1677	MCC folio 76
Billing, Nathaniel	40	1677	MCC folio 74
Billington, John	29	1672	SJC 1341
Bing, Robert	20	1653	SD 1:28
Binmore, Elizabeth	27	1673	EQC 5:228
Bird, John	23	nd	SJC 26748
Bird, Thomas	56	1695	SJC 4180
Birkby, Thomas	58	1672	EQC 5:18
Bisco, John	55	1677	MCC folio 76
Bisco, John	56	1678	MCC folio 81
Bisco, Mary	19	1671	EQC 4:397
Bishop, Dinah	17	1675	EQC 6:7

Bishop, Dulzebella	50	1654	EQC 1:361
Bishop, Edward	35	1681	EQC 8:108
Bishop, Edward	35	1681	EQC 8:110
Bishop, Edward	61	1680	EQC 7:391
Bishop, Edward	63	1681	EQC 8:191
Bishop, Esther	26	1682	EQC 8:315
Bishop, Job	20	1677	EQC 6:366
Bishop, Mary	20	1654	EQC 1:361
Bishop, Mary	64	1675	EQC 6:106
Bishop, Nathaniel	55	1663	SJC 573
Bishop, Nathaniel	70	1677	SCC 839
Bishop, Nathaniel	70	1677	SJC 1644
Bishop, Samuel	21	1666	EQC 3:346
Bishop, Samuel	29	1675	EQC 6:12
Bishop, Thomas	22	1673	SJC 1234
Bishop, Thomas	24	1675	SJC 1400
Bishop, Thomas	48	1695/6	SJC 4225
Bishop, Thomas	48	nd	SJC 3323
Bishop, Thomas	52	1670	EQC 4:288
Bishop, Thomas	52	1684	EQC 9:343
Bishop, Thomas	54	1685	EQC 9:439
Bishop, Thomas	54	1685	SJC 2285
Bisson, John	17	1674	EQC 5:276
Bisson, John	17	1674	EQC 5:310
Bisson, John	25	1682	EQC 8:411
Bixby, Joseph	54	1674	EQC 5:354
Black, Daniel	36	1664	EQC 3:160
Black, Faith	29	1674	EQC 5:354
Black, Freeborn	40	1674	EQC 5:291
Black, John	27	1675	SJC 1425
Black, John	28	1675	SJC 1425
Black, John	31	1673	EQC 5:216
Black, John	54	1645	EQC 1:84
Black, Mary	21	1693	SJC 2819
Blagg, Abraham	24	1677	SCC 734
Blake, Bridget	57	1699	SJC 3896
Blake, Deborah	19	1671	SJC 1100
Blake, George	55	1667	EQC 3:390
Blake, John	32	1676	EQC 6:328
Blake, William	25	1683	EQC 9:113
Blake, William	25	1684	EQC 9:189
Blanchard, Hannah	17	1681	MCC folio 94
Blanchard, Joseph	15	1670	MCC folio 53
Blanchard, Joseph	15	1670	MCC folio 54
Blanchard, Joseph	19	1673	MCC folio 62
Blanchard, Joseph	20	1673	MCC folio 65
Blanchard, Joseph	20	1674	MCC folio 66
Blanchard, Joseph	25	1679	MCC folio 185
Blanchard, Nathaniel	21	1657	MCC folio 18
Blanchard, Samuel	34	1663	MCC folio 35
Blancher, Joseph	21	1674	MCC folio 66
Blancher, Joseph	26	1680	MCC folio 183
Blancher, Joseph	26	1680	MCC folio 183
Blancher, Mary	28	1664	MCC folio 38

Blancher, Samuel	16	1672	MCC folio 60
Blancher, Thomas	20	1689	MCC folio 134
Blaney, John	29	1659	EQC 2:185
Blaney, John	51	1681	EQC 8:179
Blaney, John	51	1686	EQC WPA 46-102-2
Blaney, John	54	1684	EQC 9:317
Blano, John	22	1653	EQC 2:95
Blano, John	51	1681	EQC 8:198
Blanye, John	46	1676	EQC 6:258
Bleasee, Caleb	20	1674	MCC folio 70
Blethen, John	68	nd	SJC 2770
Bligh, Dorothy	60	1677	SJC 1582
Bligh, Edmund	13	1685	EQC 9:484
Bligh, John	20	1685	EQC 9:481
Bligh, John	36	1675	EQC 6:107
Bligh, John	47	1685	EQC 9:484
Bligh, Rebecca	43	1685	EQC 9:480
Bligh, Thomas	31	1658	EQC 2:128
Bligh, Thomas	53	1679/80	SJC 1837
Blight, Thomas	37	1665	MCC folio 38
Blish, John	47	1684	EQC 9:274
Blish, John	47	1685	EQC 9:480
Blodget, Jonathan	21	1682	MCC folio 100
Bloggett, Samuel	42	1679	SJC 1836
Bloggett, Thomas	23	1690	MCC folio 137
Blood, James	64	1670	MCC folio 55
Blood, Josiah	20	1684	MCC folio 108
Blood, Josiah	21	1685	MCC folio 116
Blood, Josiah	21	1685	SJC 2306
Blood, Richard	43	1660	MCC folio 25
Blood, Robert	24	1684	MCC folio 108
Blood, Robert	25	1685	MCC folio 116
Blood, Robert	58	1684	MCC folio 107
Blood, Sarah	25	1684	MCC folio 107
Blood, Simon	23	1685	MCC folio 116
Blood, Simon	23	1685	SJC 2306
Bloyse, Edmund	72	1662	MCC folio 35
Bloyse, Edmund	90	1677	MCC folio 77
Bloyse, Richard	24	1685	MCC folio 115
Bloyse, Richard	32	1692	MCC folio 172
Bloyse, Richard	40	1664	MCC folio 36
Blunt, Ann	28	1681	MCC folio 97
Blunt, Anna	28	1681	MCC folio 104
Blunt, Samuel	22	1669	MCC folio 52
Blunt, Samuel	24	1672	MCC folio 60
Bly, Dorothy	55	1674	SD 8:406
Bly, Samuel	22	1681	EQC 8:124
Boade, Sarah	15	1683	EQC 9:148
Boan, Thomas	56	1677	EQC 6:363
Boarman, Jacob	26	1697	SJC 162425
Boarman, Offin	17	1694	SJC 3223
Boarman, Offin	18	1695	SJC 3223
Boarman, Thomas	23	1694	SJC 2660
Boarman, Thomas	47	nd	SJC 2660

Boatsen, Sarah	17	1660	MCC folio 25
Bodkin, Domini	30	1678	MCC folio 80
Bodman, Mary	20	nd	SJC 2003
Bodwell, Henry	24	1678	EQC 6:413
Bodwell, Henry	24	1678	EQC 7:157
Boin, Thomas	47	1672	EQC 5:115
Bolston, Rachel	22	1684	SJC 2228
Bolston, Sarah	27	1685	SJC 2354
Bolton, Daniel	18	1676	MCC folio 72
Bolton, Elizabeth	50	1681	SJC 2024
Bolton, William	48	1678	EQC 7:156
Boltwood, Samuel	42	1692	SJC 3301
Bond, Hester	33	1663	EQC 3:98
Bond, John	17	1678	EQC 7:51
Bond, Joseph	22	1675	EQC 6:11
Bond, William	35	1685	MCC folio 115
Bond, William	35	1685	SJC 2348
Bond, William	46	1672	MCC folio 60
Bond, William	53	1679	MCC folio 88
Bond, William	55	1681	MCC folio 97
Bonfield, George	50	1685	EQC 9:468
Bonfield, Thomas	30	1676	MCC folio 72
Bonner, John	30	1673	MCC folio 65
Bonner, John	30	1673	SCC 178
Bonner, John	30	1673	SJC 1221
Bonnick, Thomas	23	1668	SJC 873
Bonnitton, Gabragan	20	1671	SJC 1137
Bonsall, Frances	62	1679	MCC folio 87
Boobier, Joan	19	1674	EQC 6:19
Boobier, Joan	20	1676	EQC 6:150
Boobier, Joseph	29	1674	EQC 6:19
Boobier, Joseph	30	1681	EQC 8:148
Bool, Thomas	40	1690	MCC folio 139
Boone, Margaret	54	1685	SJC 2354
Boone, William	25	1665	SJC 705
Booth, Alice	35	1675	EQC 6:81
Booth, Alice	37	1678	EQC 7:148
Booth, George	35	1675	EQC 6:81
Booth, George	37	1678	EQC 7:148
Booth, Recha	39	1680	EQC 8:60
Booth, Robert	68	1670	SJC 1078
Booth, Robert	68	1679	EQC 7:286
Booth, Symon	39	1680	EQC 8:60
Bootman, Mary	16	1678	EQC 7:51
Borbeen, John	18	1682	MCC folio 100
Bordman, Aaron	27	1676	MCC folio 73
Bordman, Moses	17	1658	MCC folio 16
Bordman, William	20	1677	MCC folio 76
Boreman, Thomas	24	1674	EQC 5:321
Boreman, Thomas	34	1679	EQC 7:187
Boreman, William	56	1672	MCC folio 61
Boreman, William	57	1672	MCC folio 61
Borlay, Andrew	21	1679	EQC 7:189
Borson, Walter	26	1672	EQC 5:110

Boswell, Hanniel	66	1681	EQC 8:153
Bosworth, Abigail	27	1680	EQC 7:371
Bosworth, Benjamin	48	nd	SJC 25037
Bosworth, goodwife	60	1679	EQC 7:270
Bosworth, Samuel	28	1671	SJC 1092
Boult, John	39	1691	MCC folio 147
Boulton, Ruth	15	1682	EQC 8:282
Bouvy, Joseph	27	1653	EQC 2:94
Bovington, Thomas	23	1668	MCC folio 47
Bovington, Thomas	39	1683	EQC 9:19
Bowalls, Christopher	30	1683	EQC 9:29
Bowden, Michael	25	1677	EQC 6:360
Bowden, Michael	25	1677	EQC 6:361
Bowden, Michael	30	1681	EQC 8:179
Bowditch, William	39	1680	EQC 7:347
Bowen, Elizabeth	26	1654	EQC 1:330
Bowen, Thomas	24	1646	EQC 1:104
Bowen, Thomas	26	1654	EQC 1:333
Bowen, Thomas	45	1669	EQC 4:155
Bowen, Thomas	45	1672	EQC 5:42
Bowen, Thomas	47	1670	EQC 4:284
Bowen, Thomas	50	1675	EQC 6:78
Bowen, Thomas	55	1681	EQC 8:180
Bowers, Jerathmiel	26	1677	MCC folio 76
Bowers, Jerathmiel	32	1681/2	MCC folio 98
Bowers, Jerathmiel	36	1685	MCC folio 116
Bowers, Susannah	35	1681	SJC 2010
Bowing, Thomas	60	1684	EQC 9:240
Bowland, John	34	1680	SJC 1935
Bowles, Christopher	30	1680	EQC 7:380
Boyce, Joseph	60	1669	EQC 4:144
Boyd, Andrew	22	1691	MCC folio 147
Boyer, Thomas	22	1668/9	SJC 911
Boyes, Antipas	28	1662	SJC 561
Boyes, Antipas	32	1667	SJC 828
Boyes, Joseph	21	nd	SJC 2770
Boyes, Joseph	40	nd	SJC 2770
Boyes, Mathew	50	1665	EQC 3:235
Boyes, Mathew	50	nd	SJC 717
Boylston, Thomas	23	1673	MCC folio 63
Boylston, Thomas	28	1673	MCC folio 63
Boylstone, Mary	20	1689	SJC 2536
Boynton, Caleb	32	1682	EQC 8:404
Boynton, John	30	1681	EQC 8:92
Boynton, John	48	1662	EQC 2:362
Boynton, Joshua	22	1669	EQC 4:159
Boynton, Joshua	30	1678	EQC 7:157
Boynton, Samuel	18	1678	EQC 7:101
Boynton, Samuel	21	1682	EQC 8:279
Boynton, Sarah	9	1681	EQC 8:278
Boynton, William	56	1662	EQC 2:397
Boynton, William	68	1673	EQC 5:188
Brabiner, Alexander	50	1663	EQC 3:31
Brabiner, Alexander	50	1663	SJC 577

Brabrook, Joseph	20	1669	EQC 4:180
Brabrook, Mehitable	16	1668	EQC 4:56
Brabrook, Mehitable	16	1668	EQC 4:81
Brabrook, Richard	50	1667	EQC 3:457
Brabrook, Richard	54	1666	EQC 3:372
Brabrook, Richard	67	1679	EQC 7:262
Brackett, James	36	1682	SJC 2126
Brackett, John	40	1677	MCC folio 76
Brackett, Ruth	60	1677	MCC folio 78
Bracy, John	24	1664	SJC 746
Bradbury, William	23	1672	SJC 1563
Bradford, Nathaniel	28	1667	SJC 824
Bradford, Robert	32	1664	EQC 3:209
Bradford, Robert	47	1673	EQC 5:216
Bradford, William	70	1694/5	SJC 3185
Brading, James	16	1678	EQC 7:156
Brading, James	29	1662	EQC 2:408
Brading, James	48	1680/1	SJC 1965
Bradish, John	27	1673	MCC folio 64
Bradish, John	31	1677	SCC 1102
Bradshaw, Humphrey	14	1674	MCC folio 62
Bradshaw, Humphrey	63	1679	MCC folio 84
Bradshaw, Martha	63	1679	MCC folio 84
Bradshaw, Martha	63	1679	SJC 1799
Bradshaw, Sarah	28	1691	MCC folio 141
Bradstreet, Dudley	22	1671	EQC 4:345
Bradstreet, Dudley	27	1676	EQC 6:120
Bradstreet, Dudley	27	1676	EQC 6:121
Bradstreet, Dudley	27	1676	EQC 6:125
Bradstreet, Dudley	33	1682	EQC 8:382
Bradstreet, John	17	1669	EQC 4:117
Bradstreet, John	24	1654	EQC 1:332
Bradstreet, John	24	1654	EQC 1:333
Bradstreet, Moses	36	1679	EQC 7:291
Bradstreet, Samuel	29	1664	SJC 754
Bradstreet, Samuel	30	nd	SJC 754
Bradstreet, Samuel	31	1666	SJC 754
Bradstreet, Sarah	16	1654	EQC 1:330
Bradstreet, Sarah	16	1654	EQC 1:332
Bragg, Thomas	20	1668	EQC 4:82
Bragg, Timothy	17	1668	EQC 4:57
Brakenbury, William	52	1655	MCC folio 13
Bramble, Robert	17	1664	MCC folio 36
Brandall, John	30	1679	EQC 7:260
Brandbrook, Richard	55	1668	EQC 4:67
Brandbrook, Richard	56	1669	EQC 4:142
Brandbrooke, Richard	55	1668	EQC 4:80
Brandon, Mary	16	1657	MCC folio 18
Branson, Francis	36	1680/1	SJC 1955
Branson, Mary	28	1680	SJC 1935
Brash, John	21	1691	MCC folio 140
Brasher, Magdalen	56	1678	MCC folio 84
Brattle, Edward	21	1691	SJC 98515
Brattle, Thomas	38	1661	SJC 418

Brattle, Thomas	44	1661	SJC 983
Brattle, Thomas	47	1671/2	SJC 1069
Brattle, Thomas	49	1673/4	SJC 1341
Brattle, Thomas	55	1679	SD 11:269
Brattle, Thomas	56	1680	EQC 8:80
Brattle, Thomas	56	1680/1	SJC 2017
Brawton, Perne	43	1691	MCC folio 157
Bray, John	50	1670	SJC 979
Braybrook, Richard	67	1679	EQC 7:293
Braybrook, Thomas	36	1678	MCC folio 82
Brayton, Francis	60	1671	MCC folio 55
Brazier, Edward	80	1683	MCC folio 90
Brazier, Edward	84	1686	MCC folio 122
Brazier, Thomas	31	1692	MCC folio 157
Bread, Elizabeth	59	1666	EQC 7:198
Bred, Allen	70	1671	EQC 4:384
Breedon, James	36	1699	SJC 4705
Breedon, Thomas	48	1668	SJC 873
Brentnell, Thomas	35	1664	MCC folio 36
Brett, Elihu	44	1694/5	SJC 3185
Brewer, Judith	30	1674	EQC 5:412
Brewer, Thomas	14	1672	EQC 5:108
Brian, William	47	1691/2	SJC 2653
Brickenden, Robert	26	1665/6	SJC 728
Brickett, Nathaniel	25	1678	EQC 7:159
Brickett, Nathaniel	26	1676	EQC 6:121
Brickett, Nathaniel	29	1678	EQC 7:156
Brickett, Nathaniel	30	1679	MCC folio 85
Bridane, Brian	28	1671	MCC folio 58
Bridge, Mathew	50	1674	MCC folio 67
Bridgen, Nathaniel	26	1691	MCC folio 144
Bridgen, Nathaniel	26	1693	MCC folio 156
Bridges, Edmund	27	1664	EQC 3:160
Bridges, Edmund	27	1664	EQC 3:183
Bridges, Edmund	29	1666	EQC 3:312
Bridges, Edmund	38	1674/5	SJC 1397
Bridges, Edmund	38	1675	EQC 6:5
Bridges, Edmund	38	1675	EQC 6:80
Bridges, Edmund	39	1674	EQC 5:354
Bridges, Edmund	40	1678	MCC folio 81
Bridges, Edmund	40	1679	EQC 7:252
Bridges, Edmund	40	1679	EQC 7:297
Bridges, Edmund	42	1678	EQC 7:119
Bridges, Edmund	46	1658	EQC 2:117
Bridges, Edward	39	1677	EQC 6:369
Bridges, Edward	40	1678	EQC 6:404
Bridges, Hannah	16	1686	EQC 9:606
Bridges, John	22	1669	EQC 4:177
Bridges, John	36	1667	SJC 905
Bridges, John	52	1700	SJC 4703
Bridges, Josias	22	1676	EQC 6:239
Bridges, Mary	60	1685	EQC 9:544
Bridges, Obadiah	20	1667	EQC 3:444
Bridges, Obadiah	24	1669	EQC 4:195

Bridges, Sarah	30	1664	EQC 3:138
Bridges, Sarah	37	1679	EQC 7:250
Bridgham, Henry	52	1664	SJC 648
Bridgham, Jonathan	31	1681/2	SJC 1956
Bridgham, Jonathan	33	1681	SJC 2029
Bridgham, Joseph	32	1684	SJC 2547
Bridgham, Marcy	15	nd	SJC 2627
Briers, Richard	30	1678	EQC 7:79
Brigden, Nathaniel	26	nd	SJC 2848
Brigden, William	30	1671	MCC folio 57
Brigden, Zachary	16	1674	MCC folio 66
Briggs, Abraham	30	1681	EQC 8:225
Briggs, George	46	nd	SJC 28783
Briggs, Job	27	nd	SJC 2787
Briggs, Sarah	37	nd	SJC 2941
Briggs, Thomas	22	1658	EQC 2:112
Briggs, William	24	1697	SJC 4005
Brigham, John	40	1692	MCC folio 174
Brigham, Nathan	19	1691	MCC folio 174
Brigham, Thomas	24	1653	MCC folio 7
Brigham, Thomas	27	1669	MCC folio 51
Bright, Henry	60	1661	MCC folio 27
Bright, John	30	1677	MCC folio 77
Brimblecom, Tabitha	70	1680	EQC 8:29
Brimsden, Robert	33	1672/3	SCC 208
Brimsden, Robert	33	1672/3	SJC 1165
Brinley, William	23	1690	MCC folio 137
Brintnole, Thomas	50	1680	EQC 7:423
Brisco, Joseph	17	1675	SJC 1422
Brisco, Joseph	34	1691/2	SJC 98524
Brisco, Robert	22	1684	EQC 9:208
Britton, Edward	22	1686	EQC WPA 46-31-2
Britton, Peter	18	1677	EQC 6:347
Broadish, John	27	1673	SJC 1214
Broadish, John	31	1677	SJC 1636
Brocke, John	24	1680	EQC 7:334
Brocke, John	24	1680	EQC 7:335
Brocke, John	30	1679	MCC folio 86
Brocklebank, Samuel	33	1662	EQC 2:397
Brocklebank, Samuel	35	1663	EQC 3:29
Brocklebank, Samuel	35	1663	SJC 565
Brocks, John	43	1668	MCC folio 44
Brodbent, Joshua	35	1690	MCC folio 133
Bromehall, Ann	55	1677	SJC 1718
Bromwell, Ann	54	1677	EQC 6:294
Bronsdon, Robert	46	1685	SD 13:382
Brooking, Henry	35	1676	SJC 1526
Brooks, Caleb	44	1677	MCC folio 74
Brooks, Caleb	51	1684	EQC 9:214
Brooks, Caleb	52	1684	MCC folio 114
Brooks, Caleb	63	1695	MCC folio 162
Brooks, Henry	19	1671	MCC folio 59
Brooks, Henry	66	1658	MCC folio 16
Brooks, Henry	85	1675	MCC folio 70

Brooks, Isaac	25	1668	MCC folio 44
Brooks, Isaac	26	1668	MCC folio 45
Brooks, Isaac	26	1669	MCC folio 51
Brooks, Isaac	27	1670	MCC folio 53
Brooks, Isaac	28	1670	MCC folio 54
Brooks, Isaac	40	1683	EQC 9:124
Brooks, Isaac	43	1685	SJC 2325
Brooks, John	34	1659	MCC folio 21
Brooks, John	41	1665	MCC folio 39
Brooks, John	46	1668	MCC folio 45
Brooks, John	47	1668	MCC folio 48
Brooks, Joshua	31	1662	MCC folio 32
Brooks, Joshua	50	1679	MCC folio 88
Brooks, Noah	23	1679	MCC folio 88
Brooks, Richard	46	1684	SJC 2228
Brooks, Timothy	33	1668	MCC folio 45
Brosher, Magdlen	56	1679	MCC folio 84
Broughton, George	28	1672	MCC folio 60
Broughton, Thomas	44	1658	EQC 2:125
Broughton, Thomas	54	1667	SJC 817
Broughton, Thomas	63	1676	SJC 1469
Broughton, Thomas	64	1678	SJC 1726
Broumage, Edward	50	1673	EQC 5:155
Brown, Abigail	56	1671	SJC 1334
Brown, Abraham	55	1683	SJC 2198
Brown, Anne	15	1673	EQC 5:245
Brown, Beriah	20	1668	EQC 4:54
Brown, Charles	30	1685	SJC 2345
Brown, Ebenezer	20	1686	MCC folio 120
Brown, Edmund	29	1682/3	SJC 2120
Brown, Elizabeth	26	1662	SJC 874
Brown, Elizabeth	50	1667	EQC 3:419
Brown, Hannah	18	1665	SJC 826
Brown, Hannah	18	1667	SJC 817
Brown, Hannah	32	1680	EQC 7:426
Brown, Henry	58	1671	SJC 1334
Brown, Henry	60	1672	SJC 1563
Brown, Ichabod	19	1686	MCC folio 120
Brown, Jacob	32	1672	SJC 1137
Brown, James	18	1680	SJC 1916
Brown, James	18	1680/1	SJC 1953
Brown, James	23	1670	MCC folio 55
Brown, James	24	1677	MCC folio 77
Brown, James	24	1695	SJC 3214
Brown, James	30	1677	EQC 6:356
Brown, James	31	1678	MCC folio 81
Brown, James	31	1678	SJC 1829
Brown, James	53	1658	MCC folio 16
Brown, Jane	48	1684	SJC 2198
Brown, John	20	1686	EQC WPA 47-15-1
Brown, John	25	1692/3	SJC 2712
Brown, John	26	1687	EQC WPA 47-60-3
Brown, John	27	1675	MCC folio 69
Brown, John	28	1660	MCC folio 25

Brown, John	28	1671	EQC 4:432
Brown, John	30	1665	EQC 3:285
Brown, John	40	1671/2	SJC 1097
Brown, John	40	1675	MCC folio 70
Brown, John	40	1683	EQC 9:2
Brown, John	45	1681	MCC folio 96
Brown, John	46	1681	MCC folio 92
Brown, John	48	1682	MCC folio 101
Brown, Jonathan	36	1672	MCC folio 60
Brown, Joseph	18	1676/7	SJC 1560
Brown, Joseph	23	1682	EQC 8:258
Brown, Joseph	25	1664	EQC 3:161
Brown, Joseph	25	1685	EQC 9:525
Brown, Joseph	25	1685	SJC 2344
Brown, Joshua	53	1695	SJC 162370
Brown, Marcy	23	1678	MCC folio 78
Brown, Mary	19	1682	EQC 8:286
Brown, Mary	76	1696/7	SJC 162413
Brown, Mary	76	1696/7	SJC 3504
Brown, Nathaniel	22	1674	EQC 5:310
Brown, Nathaniel	22	1674	EQC 5:321
Brown, Nathaniel	25	1669	EQC 4:104
Brown, Nathaniel	29	1680	EQC 7:362
Brown, Nathaniel	30	1672	SJC 1563
Brown, Nathaniel	49	1692	SJC 3153
Brown, Philip	17	1664	EQC 3:124
Brown, Richard	31	1682	EQC 8:250
Brown, Richard	32	1682	EQC 8:261
Brown, Richard	35	1686	EQC WPA 46-121-3
Brown, Roger	25	1678	MCC folio 82
Brown, Roger	30	1677	SJC 1672
Brown, Roger	37	1685	SJC 2332
Brown, Samuel	17	1673	EQC 5:245
Brown, Samuel	25	1678/9	SJC 1838
Brown, Samuel	25	1679	SJC 1896
Brown, Samuel	32	1672	SJC 1120
Brown, Samuel	32	1672	SJC 1137
Brown, Thomas	19	1670	MCC folio 55
Brown, Thomas	30	1658	MCC folio 17
Brown, Thomas	40	1666	EQC 7:197
Brown, Thomas	40	1668	EQC 4:32
Brown, Thomas	60	1686	MCC folio 120
Brown, Thomas	61	1670	MCC folio 55
Brown, William	26	1679	MCC folio 85
Brown, William	26	1682	EQC 8:269
Brown, William	26	1682	EQC 8:279
Brown, William	33	1670	SJC 989
Brown, William	35	1668	SJC 924
Brown, William	35	1673	SJC 1232
Brown, William	36	1668/9	SJC 924
Brown, William	38	1671	SJC 1071
Brown, William	77	1697	SJC 3193
Browne, Abigail	56	1671	EQC 4:347
Browne, Benjamin	29	1677	EQC 6:288

Browne, Boaz	27	1692	MCC folio 173
Browne, Charles	30	1685	EQC 9:467
Browne, Charles	42	1668	EQC 4:53
Browne, Dinah	21	1699	MCC folio 207
Browne, Eliazer	46	1695	MCC folio 207
Browne, Elizabeth	56	1673	EQC 5:181
Browne, Francis	46	1678	EQC 7:156
Browne, George	60	1684	EQC 9:323
Browne, Hugh	39	1657	MCC folio 18
Browne, James	30	1678	EQC 7:111
Browne, James	31	1678	EQC 6:404
Browne, James	31	1678	EQC 7:245
Browne, James	31	1678	EQC 7:246
Browne, James	31	1678	EQC 7:52
Browne, James	31	1679	MCC folio 87
Browne, James	71	1675	EQC 6:44
Browne, John	27	1658	EQC 2:112
Browne, John	27	1658	MCC folio 17
Browne, John	29	1660	MCC folio 25
Browne, John	30	1674	EQC 5:415
Browne, John	30	1678	EQC 7:109
Browne, John	38	1672	EQC 5:85
Browne, John	42	1679	EQC 7:269
Browne, John	44	1682	EQC 8:287
Browne, John	45	1682	EQC 8:286
Browne, John	66	1695	MCC folio 181
Browne, John	67	1680	EQC 7:394
Browne, Jonathan	33	1669	MCC folio 52
Browne, Jonathan	35	1670	MCC folio 46
Browne, Jonathan	36	1672	MCC folio 59
Browne, Joseph	25	1685	EQC 9:434
Browne, Joshua	36	1678	EQC 7:157
Browne, Josiah	46	1683	EQC 9:21
Browne, Mary	19	1682	EQC 8:287
Browne, Mary	24	1661	EQC 2:286
Browne, Mary	31	1668	EQC 4:32
Browne, Nathaniel	17	1668	EQC 4:83
Browne, Nathaniel	18	1670	EQC 4:243
Browne, Nathaniel	23	1674	EQC 5:321
Browne, Nathaniel	25	1679	EQC 7:189
Browne, Nathaniel	26	1671	EQC 4:331
Browne, Nathaniel	30	1683	EQC 9:2
Browne, Nathaniel	34	1686	EQC 9:584
Browne, Nicholas	24	1661	EQC 2:308
Browne, Philip	33	1691	MCC folio 146
Browne, Priscilla	14	1683	EQC 9:28
Browne, Richard	27	1678	EQC 7:157
Browne, Robert	37	1660	MCC folio 25
Browne, Thomas	19	1699	MCC folio 207
Browne, Thomas	22	1677	EQC 6:258
Browne, Thomas	24	1669	MCC folio 51
Browne, Thomas	55	1682	EQC 8:258
Browne, Thomas	72	1678	EQC 7:156
Browne, William	35	1673	MCC folio 64

Browne, William	42	1691	MCC folio 157
Browne, William	57	1672	EQC 5:12
Browne, William	69	1678	EQC 7:132
Brownson, John	16	1664	EQC 3:246
Bruer, Daniel	40	1677	SD 10:186
Bruff, Steven	30	1662	SJC 570
Brusey, William	30	1680	EQC 8:26
Brush, George	30	1663	MCC folio 34
Brush, Richard	18	1658	EQC 2:112
Brusse, Richard	18	1658	MCC folio 17
Buck, Ephraim	24	1670	MCC folio 53
Buck, Roger	80	1686	MCC folio 121
Buck, Roger	81	1686	MCC folio 127
Buckley, John	24	1685/6	SJC 2385
Buckley, Sarah	16	1673	EQC 5:144
Buckley, William	56	1673	EQC 5:129
Bucknam, Edward	17	1675	MCC folio 70
Bucknam, John	56	1668	SJC 869
Bucknam, Samuel	24	1698	MCC folio 167
Bucknam, Samuel	24	1698	MCC folio 169
Bucknam, Sarah	34	1656	MCC folio 11
Bucknam, William	63	1665	MCC folio 40
Bucknell, George	56	1676/7	SJC 1568
Bucknell, Richard	20	1676/7	SJC 1568
Bucknell, Samuel	38	1671	SJC 1108
Bucknell, Samuel	42	1673	MCC folio 63
Bucknell, Samuel	42	1673	SJC 1222
Bucknell, Sarah	27	1663	SJC 573
Budd, Edward	33	1665	SJC 721
Buff, Abel	22	1671	MCC folio 59
Buffington, Thomas	42	1686	EQC WPA 46-22-4
Buffington, Thomas	42	1686	SJC 2770
Buffum, Joshua	43	1680	EQC 7:331
Buffum, Joshua	43	1680	EQC 7:386
Buffum, Mary	30	1678	EQC 7:137
Bulkeley, Richard	26	1685	SJC 2324
Bulkeley, William	56	1673/4	SJC 1246
Bull, Elisha	29	1691	MCC folio 146
Bull, Elisha	29	1691	MCC folio 163
Bull, Elisha	29	1691	MCC folio 173
Bull, John	40	1684	MCC folio 110
Bull, John	46	1680/1	SJC 1964
Bull, John	51	1685	SJC 2354
Bull, Joseph	50	1692	SJC 3301
Bull, Margaret	25	1665	SJC 714
Bull, Samuel	27	1686	MCC folio 121
Bull, Samuel	27	1686	MCC folio 128
Bull, Samuel	33	1692	MCC folio 152
Bull, William	30	1686	MCC folio 121
Bull, William	43	1662	MCC folio 33
Bull, William	43	1662	SJC 495
Bull, William	60	1686	MCC folio 121
Bull, William	60	1686	MCC folio 128
Bull, William's wife	60	1686	MCC folio 121

Bullard, George	50	1658	MCC folio 16
Bullard, George	81	1680	MCC folio 91
Bullard, Jacob	38	1680	MCC folio 91
Bullard, John	66	1667	SJC 830
Bullard, Joseph	33	1699	SJC 4696
Bullard, Mary	46	1685	MCC folio 114
Bullard, Mathew	16	1685	MCC folio 114
Bullard, Nathaniel	44	1678	MCC folio 84
Bullard, Nathaniel	50	1685	MCC folio 114
Bullen, Ephraim	68	nd	SJC 28866
Bullens, John	40	1664	MCC folio 36
Bullock, John	24	1679	EQC 7:252
Bullock, John	25	1680	EQC 7:330
Bully, Peter	25	1667	SJC 909
Bulstrode, Samuel	36	1666	SD 5:72
Buncker, John	28	1691	MCC folio 143
Bunger, Daniel	60	1696	MCC folio 208
Bunker, Ann	4	1658	EQC 2:99
Bunker, Elizabeth	12	1658	EQC 2:99
Bunker, Martha	1	1658	EQC 2:99
Bunker, Mary	6	1658	EQC 2:99
Bunker, William	10	1658	EQC 2:99
Burbank, John	30	1673	EQC 5:182
Burd, John	30	1665	EQC 3:262
Burditt, Thomas	44	1699	MCC folio 171
Burgess, goodwife	44	1663	EQC 3:112
Burgess, Robert	36	1657	EQC 2:29
Burgess, Robert	40	1662	EQC 2:352
Burgess, Robert	40	1662	EQC 2:356
Burgess, Robert	60	1682	EQC 8:259
Burgis, James	30	1685/6	SJC 2388
Burgis, Robert	40	1661/2	SJC 577
Burke, Samuel	17	1660	MCC folio 25
Burley, Andrew	16	1674	EQC 5:415
Burley, Andrew	25	1682	EQC 8:367
Burnam, James	30	1687	EQC WPA 47-32-4
Burnap, John	26	1681	MCC folio 96
Burnap, John	26	1683	EQC 9:45
Burnap, John	26	1683	EQC 9:46
Burnap, John	27	1683	EQC 9:44
Burnap, John	35	1691	MCC folio 143
Burnap, Joseph	18	1681	MCC folio 96
Burnap, Joseph	18	1681	MCC folio 97
Burnap, Joseph	32	1695	SJC 162388
Burnap, Mary	26	1669	EQC 4:208
Burnap, Robert	26	1656	MCC folio 15
Burnap, Robert	53	1681	MCC folio 93
Burnap, Robert	55	1682	MCC folio 101
Burnham, Abigail	19	1674	EQC 5:318
Burnham, James	20	1673	EQC 5:145
Burnham, James	20	1674	EQC 5:375
Burnham, James	21	1674	EQC 5:307
Burnham, James	22	1674	EQC 5:319
Burnham, Johanna	16	1670	EQC 4:218

Burnham, Johanna	16	1670	EQC 4:241
Burnham, John	18	1668	EQC 4:48
Burnham, John	18	1668	EQC 4:69
Burnham, John	18	1668	EQC 4:70
Burnham, John	27	1674	EQC 5:341
Burnham, John	30	1678	EQC 7:117
Burnham, John	31	1682	EQC 8:410
Burnham, John	59	1675	EQC 6:112
Burnham, John	63	1678	EQC 7:117
Burnham, John	69	1682	EQC 8:410
Burnham, John	69	1682	SJC 3138
Burnham, John	71	1685	EQC 9:462
Burnham, John	71	1685	SJC 2310
Burnham, John	81	1694	SJC 2913
Burnham, Josiah	14	1674	EQC 5:318
Burnham, Lydia	24	1668	EQC 4:83
Burnham, Lydia	24	1670	EQC 4:241
Burnham, Mary	18	1670	EQC 4:241
Burnham, Mary	18	1670	EQC 4:242
Burnham, Mary	19	1670	EQC 4:218
Burnham, Mary	20	1668	EQC 4:48
Burnham, Mary	20	1668	EQC 4:69
Burnham, Mary	20	1668	EQC 4:70
Burnham, Mary	20	1668	SJC 897
Burnham, Mary	35	1659	EQC 2:173
Burnham, Mary	45	1670	EQC 4:218
Burnham, Mary	70	1695	SJC 162347
Burnham, Thomas	25	1668	EQC 4:70
Burnham, Thomas	35	1680	EQC 8:8
Burnham, Thomas	39	1682	EQC 8:405
Burnham, Thomas	40	1658	EQC 2:142
Burnham, Thomas	50	1668	EQC 4:70
Burnham, Thomas	50	1695	SJC 3228
Burnham, Thomas	51	1695	SJC 3158
Burnham, Thomas	52	1670	SJC 999
Burnham, Thomas	55	1674	EQC 5:375
Burnham, Thomas	60	1678	EQC 6:418
Burr, John	22	1668	MCC folio 47
Burrage, Joanna	47	1671	MCC folio 57
Burrage, John	45	1662	MCC folio 31
Burrage, John	45	1662	SJC 478
Burrage, John	56	1685	SJC 2332
Burrage, William	17	1675	MCC folio 69
Burrill, Edward	19	1685	SJC 2354
Burrill, Edward	28	1657	MCC folio 20
Burrill, George	76	nd	SJC 121
Burrill, James	13	1671	EQC 4:448
Burrill, James	21	1678	EQC 7:156
Burrill, John	30	1665	EQC 3:257
Burrill, John	47	1682	EQC 8:253
Burrill, John	47	1682	EQC 8:298
Burrill, John	47	1683	EQC 9:49
Burrill, John	50	1686	EQC 9:591
Burrill, Joseph	11	1671	EQC 4:448

Burrill, Samuel	17	1671	EQC 4:448
Burrington, Thomas	28	1686	EQC WPA 46-100-2
Burron, John	28	1679	EQC 7:296
Burroughs, Thomas	16	1679	SJC 1896
Burrows, John	21	1674	EQC 5:346
Bursly, Sarah	13	1666/7	SJC 814
Burt, Edward	28	1657	MCC folio 20
Burt, Edward	31	1662	MCC folio 28
Burt, Hugh	70	1661	EQC 2:269
Burt, Thomas	25	1670	MCC folio 54
Burton, Isaac	18	1665	EQC 3:258
Burton, Isaac	50	nd	SJC 3064
Burton, John	20	1661	EQC 2:321
Burton, John	58	1666	EQC 3:368
Burton, John	75	1683	EQC 9:88
Burton, Richard	24	1684	SJC 2242
Busby, Abigail	34	1668	SJC 1911
Buse, William	25	1665	SJC 709
Bush, Edward	28	1670	EQC 4:300
Bush, Joseph	25	1681	MCC folio 95
Bushell, Stephen	27	1671	SJC 1081
Bushum, Nathaniel	50	1695	MCC folio 196
Buss, John	24	1670	MCC folio 53
Buss, John	25	1669	MCC folio 48
Buss, Joseph	29	1680	MCC folio 89
Bussey, Mary	12	1688	SJC 2504
Buswell, Isaac	79	1671	SJC 1334
Buswell, Samuel	38	1667	EQC 3:425
Buswell, Samuel	38	1667	SJC 813
Buswell, Samuel	43	1672	SJC 1563
Buswell, Sarah	45	1671	SJC 1334
Butler, Daniel	24	1666	EQC 3:373
Butler, Edward	30	1662	SJC 468
Butler, James	24	nd	SJC 1707
Butler, Jane	32	1661	SJC 874
Butler, Steven	55	1675	MCC folio 69
Butler, Susanna	30	1684	SJC 2249
Butler, Tabitha	42	1697	SJC 4451
Butler, William	21	1672	EQC 5:7
Butler, William	22	1676	EQC 6:159
Butler, William	30	1682	EQC 8:408
Butress, William	25	1663	MCC folio 34
Butterworth, Samuel	56	1665	SJC 815
Buttery, John's wife	25	1660	MCC folio 23
Button, Elizabeth	47	1669	EQC 4:154
Button, Elizabeth	60	1683	EQC 9:7
Button, Elizabeth	60	1683	EQC 9:8
Button, John	70	1668/9	SJC 913
Button, John	73	1667	MCC folio 43
Button, John	79	1673	SD 8:172
Buttrick, John	39	1692	MCC folio 173
Buttrick, John	40	1694	MCC folio 182
Buttrick, John	40	1694	SJC 3063
Buttrick, Samuel	25	1679	MCC folio 88

Buttrick, Samuel	30	1685	MCC folio 116
Buttrick, Samuel	40	1695	MCC folio 198
Buttrick, William	76	1692	MCC folio 173
Butts, Idido	22	nd	SJC 2787
Buxton, Anthony	71	1681	EQC 8:150
Buxton, Anthony	76	1677	EQC 6:284
Buxton, Elizabeth	38	1661	EQC 2:340
Buxton, John	49	1694	SJC 3212
Buzway, William	28	1679	SJC 1908
Byfield, Nathaniel	26	1679	SJC 1815
Byfield, Nathaniel	30	1682/3	SJC 2123
Byram, Nicholas	43	1694/5	SJC 3185
Cady, Elizabeth	15	1700	MCC folio 193
Cady, Nicholas	59	1678	MCC folio 81
Caine, Arthur	50	1665	EQC 3:285
Call, John	16	1674	MCC folio 67
Call, John	24	1663	MCC folio 34
Call, John	27	1663	MCC folio 34
Call, John	39	1674	MCC folio 67
Call, John	50	1685	MCC folio 116
Call, John	50	1685	SJC 2325
Call, John	56	1692	MCC folio 153
Call, Thomas	30	1691	MCC folio 157
Call, Thomas	65	1663	MCC folio 33
Calley, John	27	1691	SJC 2629
Calley, John	49	1679	EQC 7:303
Calley, Joseph	36	1680	SJC 1928
Calley, Joseph	37	1681	EQC 8:124
Callun, Thomas	32	1662	MCC folio 29
Cam, Robert	18	1677	EQC 6:333
Cam, Robert	19	1678	EQC 7:138
Camm, Robert	26	1684	SJC 2263
Campbell, Daniel	28	nd	SJC 27731
Campbell, Duncan	30	1694	SJC 3111
Canada, Hannah	25	1682	EQC 9:20
Candidge, John	18	1682	MCC folio 100
Candidge, John	21	1685	MCC folio 117
Candish, Mary	35	1679	MCC folio 88
Cane, Deborah	27	1677	MCC folio 75
Cane, Deborah	27	1677	SJC 1612
Cane, Deborah	28	1682	MCC folio 102
Cane, Roger	24	1686	SJC 2424
Cantleberry, Rebecca	20	1658	EQC 2:100
Capen, Hannah	23	1683	MCC folio 104
Capen, John	53	1666	SJC 743
Capen, John	70	1683	MCC folio 104
Card, John	21	1664	SJC 746
Caringbone, James	26	1677	MCC folio 77
Carle, Richard	70	1697	SJC 4705
Carle, Timothy	19	1678	SJC 1734
Carleton, Edward	27	nd	SJC 3579
Carleton, John	17	1678	EQC 7:96
Carleton, Joseph	18	1681	EQC 8:153
Carleton, Thomas	27	nd	SJC 3579

Carly, Jane	40	1685	MCC folio 120
Carly, William	45	1685	MCC folio 120
Carnes, Rachel	20	1660	EQC 2:208
Carpenter, Ailse	21	1671/2	SJC 1148
Carr, George	36	1679	EQC 8:37
Carr, James	25	1678	EQC 7:156
Carr, James	26	1676	EQC 6:200
Carr, James	26	1676	EQC 6:202
Carr, John	21	1656	MCC folio 12
Carr, John	22	1661	EQC 2:288
Carr, John	22	1661	EQC 2:328
Carr, John	23	1662	EQC 2:354
Carr, John	23	1662	EQC 2:355
Carr, John	23	1662	EQC 2:366
Carr, Richard	23	1682	EQC 8:430
Carr, William	28	1676	EQC 6:200
Carr, William	30	1679	EQC 7:168
Carrell, Samuel	21	1686	EQC WPA 46-20-2
Carrill, Anthony	30	1662	EQC 3:13
Carrill, Mary	35	1672	EQC 5:53
Carrill, Nathaniel	22	1685	EQC 9:466
Carrill, Nathaniel	22	1685	EQC 9:467
Carrill, Nathaniel	23	1661	EQC 2:283
Carrill, Nathaniel	23	1686	EQC 9:592
Carrington, Edward	40	1653	MCC folio 7
Carter, Anne	42	1660/1	SJC 394
Carter, Bethiah	15	1686	MCC folio 123
Carter, Bethiah	23	1669	EQC 4:207
Carter, Bethiah	39	1685	MCC folio 117
Carter, Bethiah	40	1686	MCC folio 123
Carter, Elizabeth	46	1661	MCC folio 27
Carter, Elizabeth	51	1675	MCC folio 71
Carter, James	35	1668	EQC 4:28
Carter, John	20	1677	EQC 6:282
Carter, John	32	1685	MCC folio 117
Carter, John	40	1660	MCC folio 25
Carter, John	43	1662	MCC folio 28
Carter, John	45	1665	MCC folio 39
Carter, John	47	1661	MCC folio 27
Carter, John	49	1670	MCC folio 54
Carter, John	54	1672	MCC folio 59
Carter, John	61	1686	MCC folio 128
Carter, John	65	1679	MCC folio 185
Carter, John	67	1686	MCC folio 121
Carter, Joseph	27	1673	MCC folio 62
Carter, Ralph	34	1670/1	SJC 1011
Carter, Ralph	36	1672/3	SJC 1162
Carter, Ralph	40	1679	SJC 1896
Carter, Rebecca	24	1685	MCC folio 117
Carter, Susanna	28	1670/1	SJC 1011
Carter, Susanna	46	1662	MCC folio 30
Carter, Thomas	25	1682	EQC 8:445
Carter, Thomas	26	1680	EQC 8:27
Carter, Thomas	32	1679	MCC folio 185

Carter, Thomas	36	1682	MCC folio 99
Carter, Thomas	52	1662	MCC folio 32
Carter, Thomas	74	1682	MCC folio 100
Carter, Thomas	75	1681	MCC folio 102
Carter, Thomas	75	1682	MCC folio 100
Carter, William	50	1677	EQC 6:241
Carter, William	55	1677	EQC 6:282
Carthew, John	33	1672	SCC 379
Carthew, John	33	1672	SJC 1281
Cartwright, Thomas	17	1680	EQC 7:423
Carveath, Ezekiel	30	1667	SJC 818
Cary, Jonathan	25	1673	SJC 1232
Cary, Nathaniel	22	1667	MCC folio 41
Cary, Nathaniel	36	1680	SJC 1935
Cary, Peter	30	1683	EQC 9:68
Cary, Peter	36	1680	EQC 7:334
Caryll, Nathaniel	22	1685	SJC 2345
Caryll, Nathaniel	22	1685	SJC 2345
Caryll, Samuel	21	nd	SJC 2345
Case, Humphery	55	1684	EQC 9:285
Case, Humphrey	50	1680	EQC 8:60
Casey, John	32	1670/1	SJC 1016
Casey, Rebecca	46	1681	SJC 2037
Catlan, Philip	16	1671	EQC 4:448
Cave, Thomas	40	1679	EQC 7:294
Chadwell, Abigail	45	1667	SJC 814
Chadwell, Benjamin	34	1676	EQC 6:198
Chadwell, Moses	29	1666	EQC 7:197
Chadwell, Thomas	63	1676	EQC 6:146
Chadwick, James	44	1686	EQC WPA 47-9-3
Chadwick, John	79	1680	MCC folio 90
Chadwick, Thomas	26	1674	EQC 5:443
Chadwick, Thomas	40	1685	MCC folio 115
Chadwick, Thomas	44	1685	MCC folio 115
Chadwick, William	30	1682	EQC 8:266
Chaffe, James	30	1682	EQC 9:68
Chaflin, Elizabeth	20	1695	SJC 3223
Challis, Philip	52	1669	EQC 4:100
Chamberlain, Benjamin	21	1673	MCC folio 62
Chamberlain, Jacob	23	1681	MCC folio 93
Chamberlain, John	26	1680	MCC folio 184
Chamberlain, John	27	1684	MCC folio 108
Chamberlain, John	31	1686	MCC folio 123
Chambers, Edward	29	1672	EQC 5:98
Champney, Daniel	19	1663	MCC folio 34
Champney, Samuel	33	1670	MCC folio 54
Champney, Samuel	40	1675	MCC folio 69
Champnye, Daniel	26	1672	MCC folio 59
Chandler, Bridget	40	1682	EQC 8:382
Chandler, Bridget	52	1695	MCC folio 162
Chandler, Elizabeth	22	1663/4	SJC 600
Chandler, Hannah	49	1678	EQC 7:96
Chandler, John	29	1663/4	SJC 600
Chandler, John	33	1667	EQC 3:443

Chandler, John	33	1668	SJC 905
Chandler, Mary	28	1676	MCC folio 71
Chandler, Roger	22	1662	MCC folio 30
Chandler, Thomas	14	1678	EQC 7:96
Chandler, Thomas	32	1661	EQC 2:327
Chandler, Thomas	32	1661	EQC 2:329
Chandler, Thomas	35	1662	EQC 2:354
Chandler, Thomas	37	1665	EQC 3:265
Chandler, Thomas	43	1671	EQC 4:370
Chandler, Thomas	50	1677	EQC 6:325
Chandler, Thomas	51	1678	EQC 7:96
Chandler, William	19	1678	EQC 7:95
Chandler, William	45	1681	EQC 8:82
Chandler, William	48	1664	EQC 3:161
Chandler, William	48	1664	EQC 3:213
Chandler, William	53	1669	EQC 4:215
Chandler, William	54	1671	EQC 4:372
Chandler, William	60	1676	EQC 6:227
Chandler, William	60	1677	EQC 6:332
Chandler, William	62	1678	EQC 7:156
Chanell, John	28	1665	EQC 3:282
Chaney, Anna	38	1681	EQC 8:386
Chaney, William	23	1690	MCC folio 137
Chaney, William	23	1691	MCC folio 145
Channon, John	24	1685	SJC 2354
Chantrill, John	18	1689/90	SJC 2540
Chapin, Caleb	39	1695	SJC 4190
Chapin, Josiah	46	1682	SJC 2126
Chaplin, John	19	1673	SJC 1232
Chaplin, Joseph	22	1669	EQC 4:177
Chapman, Dorothy	37	1673	EQC 5:234
Chapman, Edward	28	1666	SJC 740
Chapman, Edward	67	nd	SJC 1758
Chapman, Gilbert	22	1679	MCC folio 183
Chapman, Hope	25	1680	EQC 7:423
Chapman, John	19	1670	EQC 4:242
Chapman, Nathaniel	26	1679	EQC 7:270
Chapman, Robert	30	1662	SJC 461
Chapman, Simon	23	1672	EQC 5:36
Chapman, Simon	30	1674	EQC 5:343
Chapman, Simon	51	1695	SJC 162347
Chapman, Thomas	28	1679	MCC folio 183
Chappel, George	45	nd	SJC 2839
Chappley, Joseph	34	1680	EQC 8:34
Chard, Helling	33	1679	SJC 1767
Charles, William	74	1669	EQC 4:156
Chase, Aquila	26	1678	EQC 7:157
Chase, Aquila	48	1666	EQC 3:347
Chase, Aquila	50	1669	SJC 924
Chase, Daniel	16	1678	EQC 7:157
Chase, John	23	1678	EQC 7:157
Chase, John	25	1682	EQC 8:353
Chase, Joseph	26	1673	SJC 1229
Chase, Thomas	23	1667	EQC 3:425

Chase, Thomas	24	1678	EQC 7:157
Chater, John	40	1669	EQC 4:125
Chatwell, Nicholas	27	1671	EQC 4:404
Cheever, Bartholomew	58	1675	SJC 1405
Cheever, Bartholomew	64	1681	SJC 2010
Cheever, Bartholomew	66	1684	SJC 2228
Cheever, Daniel	[torn]	1658	MCC folio 16
Cheever, Daniel	47	1668	MCC folio 45
Cheever, Daniel	50	1691	MCC folio 149
Cheever, Daniel	61	1681	MCC folio 94
Cheever, Elizabeth	25	1690	MCC folio 136
Cheever, Ezekiel	22	1677	EQC 6:348
Cheever, Hannah	20	1690	MCC folio 136
Cheever, Israel	27	1691	MCC folio 143
Cheever, Israel	29	1691	MCC folio 149
Cheever, Lydia	54	1677	SCC 838
Cheever, Lydia	54	1677	SJC 1644
Cheever, Lydia	54	nd	SJC 26619
Cheever, Peter	32	1675	EQC 6:89
Cheever, Peter	37	1679	EQC 7:328
Cheever, Peter	37	1680	EQC 7:405
Cheichley, Richard	47	1653	EQC 1:316
Chenery, Isaac	35	1663/4	SJC 606
Chenery, John	19	1677	MCC folio 77
Chenery, Lambert	80	1673	MCC folio 63
Cheney, Anna	38	1682	EQC 8:288
Cheney, Daniel	43	1678	EQC 7:157
Cheney, Hannah	38	1682	EQC 8:262
Cheney, Nathaniel	30	1682	EQC 8:420
Cheney, Nathaniel	31	1678	EQC 7:157
Cheney, Nathaniel	38	1684	EQC 9:261
Cheney, Peter	25	1663	EQC 3:90
Cheney, Peter	39	1678	EQC 7:157
Cheny, Anna	38	1681	EQC WPA 46-9-3
Chichester, Mary	40	1662	EQC 2:389
Chick, Joshua	19	1675	SJC 1407
Chickering, Nathaniel	25	1673	SCC 351
Chickering, Nathaniel	25	1673	SJC 1341
Chickley, John	63	1671/2	SJC 1276
Chickley, Samuel	21	1683	SJC 2161
Chickley, Samuel	39	1692	SJC 4071
Child, Ephraim	61	1659	MCC folio 21
Child, John	32	1668	MCC folio 44
Child, John	36	1673	MCC folio 64
Child, John	37	1672	MCC folio 60
Child, John	40	1695	SJC 4205
Child, Richard	40	1671	MCC folio 57
Child, Richard	41	1673	MCC folio 64
Childs, John	25	1653	EQC 1:319
Chilson, John	40	1686	EQC 9:592
Chily, David	28	1678	EQC 7:157
Chisholme, Thomas	56	1660	MCC folio 25
Choate, John	32	1660	EQC 2:200
Choate, John	40	1664	EQC 3:165

Choate, John	40	1669	EQC 4:166
Choate, John	40	1674	EQC 5:319
Choate, John	40	1674	EQC 5:414
Choate, John	40	1675	EQC 6:12
Choate, John	40	1675	SJC 1400
Choate, John	46	1671	EQC 4:334
Choate, John	52	1679	EQC 7:220
Choate, John	57	1684	EQC 9:174
Choate, John	58	1683	EQC 9:122
Choate, John	60	1684	EQC 9:181
Choate, John	70	1695	SJC 162347
Chock, Peter	30	1679	EQC 8:116
Chrismas, John	23	1668	SJC 910
Christopher, Richard	40	1689/90	SJC 2604
Chubb, John	18	1669	EQC 4:125
Chubb, John	20	1673	EQC 5:146
Chubb, John	24	1678	EQC 7:22
Chubb, John	29	1684	EQC 9:209
Chubb, Mary	30	1685	SJC 2324
Chubb, Thomas	28	1678	EQC 7:22
Chubb, Thomas	36	1685	SJC 2324
Chubb, Thomas	53	1665	SJC 690
Chubb, Thomas	70	1679	EQC 7:310
Chubb, Thomas	75	1684	EQC 9:344
Chubb, Thomas	77	1685	EQC 9:439
Chubb, Thomas	77	1685	SJC 2285
Chubb, William	29	1684	EQC 9:208
Church, Jonathan	23	1684	MCC folio 104
Church, Caleb	34	1679	MCC folio 88
Church, Caleb	37	1682	MCC folio 104
Church, Garret	61	1672	MCC folio 61
Church, Garrett	51	1662	MCC folio 33
Church, Garrett	51	1662	SJC 495
Church, Gerarach	56	1668	MCC folio 45
Church, Jonathan	23	1683	MCC folio 111
Church, Richard	47	1656	MCC folio 25
Church, Richard	48	1657	EQC 7:126
Church, Samuel	26	1669	MCC folio 52
Church, Samuel	74	1673	MCC folio 62
Church, Sarah	33	1681	MCC folio 104
Church, Sarah	33	1681	MCC folio 97
Chute, James	19	1668	EQC 4:15
Chute, James	28	1686	EQC WPA 46-67-2
Chute, James	38	1686	EQC WPA 46-49-3
Clapham, Arthur	38	1662	SJC 461
Clapham, Arthur	50	1672	SJC 162109
Clapp, Noah	20	1686	MCC folio 127
Clapp, Roger	62	1671	SCC 8
Clapp, Roger	62	1671	SJC 1179
Clapp, Samuel	60	1695	SJC 4180
Clapp, William	20	1685	SJC 2354
Clark, Edward	40	1662	EQC 2:439
Clark, Hugh	68	1681	MCC folio 97
Clark, John	22	1663	EQC 3:35

Clark, John	24	1675	EQC 6:28
Clark, John	40	1683	EQC 9:220
Clark, John	45	1667	EQC 3:430
Clark, Jonathan	21	1669	EQC 4:176
Clark, Joseph	30	1685	EQC 9:545
Clark, Josiah	28	1674	EQC 5:308
Clark, Margery	80	1676	MCC folio 71
Clark, Mary	22	1675	EQC 6:28
Clark, Mary	29	1662	EQC 2:408
Clark, Mary	29	1680	EQC 7:374
Clark, Mary	40	1667	EQC 3:471
Clark, Perciful	22	1664	MCC folio 36
Clark, Sarah	15	1680	EQC 7:375
Clark, Thomas	30	1668	EQC 4:15
Clark, Thomas	31	1669	EQC 4:194
Clark, Thomas	40	1658	EQC 2:130
Clark, Thomas	42	1695	MCC folio 207
Clark, William	70	1678	EQC 7:29
Clarke, Abigail	35	1676	EQC 6:154
Clarke, Adam	17	1672	EQC 5:41
Clarke, Andrew	25	1671	SJC 1179
Clarke, Christopher	42	1660	MCC folio 25
Clarke, Christopher	62	1679	SD 11:200
Clarke, Edward	43	1664	EQC 3:184
Clarke, Edward	45	1674	EQC 5:330
Clarke, Eleanor	16	1677	EQC 6:348
Clarke, Eleanor	41	1662	MCC Harvard #2015
Clarke, Ellen	41	1662	MCC folio 30
Clarke, Francis	32	1665	SJC 705
Clarke, Freeman	17	1675	EQC 6:17
Clarke, Haniel	23	1674	EQC 5:270
Clarke, Haniel	30	1682	EQC 8:276
Clarke, Hannah	19	1682	EQC 8:295
Clarke, John	28	1653	EQC 2:94
Clarke, John	30	1671	SJC 1179
Clarke, John	33	1685	SJC 2377
Clarke, John	40	1680	SJC 2025
Clarke, John	40	1683/4	SJC 2227
Clarke, Jonas	65	1685	MCC folio 118
Clarke, Josiah	28	1674	EQC 5:305
Clarke, Josiah	36	1680	EQC 7:375
Clarke, Josiah	36	1680	SJC 1894
Clarke, Josiah	38	1682/3	SJC 2227
Clarke, Josiah	38	1683	EQC 9:17
Clarke, Margary	60	1659	MCC folio 21
Clarke, Margery	80	1676	MCC folio 71
Clarke, Mary	27	1677	EQC 6:354
Clarke, Mary	29	1680	SJC 1694
Clarke, Mary	31	1682	EQC 8:282
Clarke, Mathew	30	1657	MCC folio 19
Clarke, Mercy	40	1675	MCC folio 69
Clarke, Nathaniel	23	1686	EQC WPA 46-24-1
Clarke, Nathaniel	39	1683	EQC 9:92
Clarke, Pearson	35	1673	SJC 1216

Clarke, Richard	25	1693	MCC folio 159
Clarke, Sarah	15	1680	SJC 1894
Clarke, Thomas	25	1663	EQC 3:27
Clarke, Thomas	28	1666	EQC 3:346
Clarke, Thomas	40	1658	MCC folio 17
Clarke, Thomas	44	1683	EQC 9:114
Clarke, Thomas	48	1654	EQC 1:399
Clarke, Thomas	49	1667	EQC 3:455
Clarke, Thomas	52	1670	MCC folio 207
Clarke, Thomas	53	1673	MCC folio 62
Clarke, Thomas	63	1669	SJC 1022
Clarke, Thomas	64	1681	MCC folio 92
Clarke, Thomas	65	1682	MCC folio 101
Clarke, William	19	1689/90	SJC 2540
Clary, John	60	1672	MCC folio 60
Clay, Quentin	22	1695	SJC 3221
Cleaves, William	32	1667	EQC 3:443
Clemence, John	60	1673	EQC 5:180
Clemence, John	60	1674	EQC 5:347
Clement, Abraham	24	1682	EQC 8:266
Clement, Daniel	26	1682	EQC 8:266
Clement, John	28	1683	EQC 9:109
Clement, Nathaniel	20	1683	EQC 9:109
Clements, Abraham	17	1675	SJC 1402
Clements, Abraham	25	1684	EQC 9:254
Clements, Edward	30	1671	SCC 15
Clements, Edward	30	1671	SJC 1077
Clements, Henry	18	1670	EQC 4:264
Clements, Robert	30	1664	EQC 3:167
Clements, William	22	1682	EQC 8:416
Clements, William	23	1681	EQC 8:197
Clements, William	24	1683	EQC 9:43
Clements, William	26	1662/3	SJC 507
Clemones, Samuel	21	1691	SJC 2624
Clesby, John	58	1691/2	SJC 2650
Cleveland, Isaac	16	1685	MCC folio 117
Cleveland, Isaac	17	1686	MCC folio 123
Cleveland, Timothy	30	1685	SJC 2391
Clifford, Bridget	56	1673	SJC 1229
Clifford, Israel	25	1675	SJC 1372
Clifford, John	63	nd	SJC 2770
Clifford, John	66	1675	SJC 1372
Clifford, Mary	18	1700	SJC 4758
Clinton, Lawrence	24	1667	EQC 3:457
Clinton, Lawrence	24	1670	EQC 4:257
Clough, John	47	1673	SD 8:298
Clough, John	50	1665	SJC 1321
Clough, John	72	1670	SJC 986
Clough, John	77	1690	SJC 3039
Clough, Philram	46	1679	MCC folio 185
Clough, Samuel	30	1695	SJC 3123a
Clough, William	45	1679	MCC folio 185
Clough, William	45	1679	MCC folio 83
Clough, William	45	1679	SJC 1798

Cloutman, Thomas	35	1681	EQC 8:205
Clovard, Meder	45	1665	SJC 754
Clungen, Thomas	24	1668	EQC 4:80
Coaklie, Thomas	20	1693	MCC folio 176
Coales, Elizabeth	15	1668	MCC folio 48
Coard, Francis	22	1676	MCC folio 72
Coartman, Thomas	35	1657	SD 3:135
Coates, John	23	1682	EQC 8:343
Coates, Robert	36	1663	EQC 3:26
Coates, Thomas	20	1681	EQC 8:109
Cobbett, Samuel	32	1676/7	SJC 1560
Cobbett, Sarah	29	1684	EQC 9:191
Cobham, Josiah	70	1685/6	SJC 2384
Coburn, Edward	41	1666	EQC 3:371
Coburn, John	21	1667	EQC 3:430
Cock, Mary	39	1679	EQC 7:249
Cock, Peter	15	1680	EQC 8:26
Cockran, William	20	1685	MCC folio 117
Coddington, John	21	1676	MCC folio 71
Codner, Christopher	21	1678	SJC 1778
Codner, Christopher	21	1679	EQC 7:225
Codner, Henry	17	1669	EQC 4:162
Codner, Henry	24	1674	EQC 5:348
Codner, Joan	43	1680	EQC 8:28
Codner, John	34	1660	EQC 2:221
Codner, John	40	1665	EQC 3:257
Codner, John	40	1665	EQC 3:262
Codner, John	44	1669	EQC 4:151
Codner, John	50	1672	EQC 5:110
Codner, John	60	1680	EQC 8:29
Codner, Mary	26	1664	EQC 3:158
Codner, Peter	33	1670	MCC folio 54
Codner, Rachel	28	1675	SJC 1422
Coe, Elizabeth	21	1698	SJC 3936
Coe, John	46	1696/7	SJC 3526
Coffin, James	19	1678	EQC 7:157
Coffin, Judith	50	1679	MCC folio 86
Coffin, Peter	30	1660	EQC 3:169
Coffin, Peter	35	1666	SJC 764
Coffin, Peter	37	1668	SJC 851
Coffin, Tristram	32	1664	EQC 3:131
Coffin, Tristram	36	1668	EQC 4:12
Coffin, Tristram	39	1671	EQC 4:335
Coffin, Tristram	39	1671	EQC 4:381
Coffin, Tristram	41	1673	EQC 5:177
Coffin, Tristram	41	1673	EQC 5:178
Coffin, Tristram	44	1676	EQC 6:126
Coffin, Tristram	44	1676	EQC 6:163
Coffin, Tristram	44	1676	EQC 6:164
Coffin, Tristram	45	1677	EQC 6:259
Coffin, Tristram	47	1678	EQC 7:156
Coffin, Tristram	47	1679	MCC folio 86
Coffin, Tristram	49	1681	EQC 8:172
Coffin, Tristram	50	1682	EQC 8:243

Coffin, Tristram	50	1682	EQC 8:245
Coffin, Tristram	50	1682	EQC 8:250
Coffin, Tristram	50	1682	EQC 8:260
Coffin, Tristram	50	1682	EQC 8:265
Coffin, Tristram	50	1682	EQC 8:429
Coffin, Tristram	54	1686	EQC 9:578
Coffin, Tristram	54	1686	EQC WPA 46-118-2
Coffin, Tristram	58	nd	SJC 3325
Coffin, Tristram	63	1695	SJC 3325
Coffin, Tristram	66	1697/8	SJC 4028
Coffin, William	26	nd	SJC 2770
Coggin, Abigail	18	1691	MCC folio 157
Cogswell, Edward	24	1679	EQC 7:170
Cogswell, Esther	19	1676	EQC 6:159
Cogswell, Hester	19	1676	SJC 162146
Cogswell, John	23	1673	EQC 5:186
Cogswell, John	27	1677	EQC 6:368
Cogswell, John	27	1678	EQC 7:117
Cogswell, Margaret	25	1678	EQC 7:117
Cogswell, William	19	1679	EQC 7:170
Cogswell, William	56	1677	EQC 6:277
Cogswell, William	57	1678	EQC 6:418
Cogswell, William	70	nd	SJC 3138
Coker, Benjamin	26	1678	EQC 7:156
Coker, Joseph	38	1678	EQC 7:156
Coker, Robert	72	1678	EQC 7:156
Colburn, Alice	60	1668	EQC 4:40
Colburn, Elizabeth	40	1695	MCC folio 201
Colburn, Hannah	30	1695	MCC folio 201
Colburn, Hannah	33	1696	MCC folio 201
Colburn, John	40	1686	EQC 9:582
Colburn, Robert	60	1667	EQC 3:438
Colburn, Robert	60	1668	EQC 4:40
Colburn, Robert	65	1672	EQC 5:79
Colburn, Robert	86	1678	EQC 7:8
Colby, Isaac	24	nd	SJC 718
Colby, John	37	1673	EQC 5:155
Colby, John	39	1672	SJC 1334
Colby, Mary	20	1677/8	MCC folio 184
Colcord, Edward	62	1678	SJC 1734
Colcott, Edward	59	1674	EQC 5:405
Coldham, Clement	37	1662	EQC 3:10
Coldham, Clement	40	1666	EQC 3:327
Coldham, Clement	40	1667	EQC 3:390
Coldham, Clement	40	1667	EQC 3:431
Coldham, Clement	50	1673	EQC 5:231
Coldham, Clement	50	1673	EQC 5:250
Coldham, Clement	50	1674	EQC 5:358
Coldham, Clement	52	1676/7	SJC 1569
Coldham, Clement	52	1677	SJC 1731
Coldham, Clement	53	1677	EQC 6:333
Coldham, Clement	53	1677	SJC 1731
Coldham, Clement	55	1678	EQC 7:127
Coldham, Clement	56	1679	EQC 7:323

Coldham, Clement	56	1679	MCC folio 88
Coldham, Clement	56	1681	EQC 8:76
Coldham, Clement	57	1681	EQC 8:199
Coldham, Clement	58	1682	EQC 8:259
Coldham, Clement	58	1682	MCC folio 101
Coldham, Clement	60	1684	EQC 9:254
Coldham, Clement	60	1684	EQC 9:313
Coldham, Clement	60	1684	EQC 9:340
Coldham, Clement	60	1685	EQC 9:434
Coldham, Clement	60	1685	SJC 2344
Coldham, Thomas	25	1663	EQC 3:26
Coldham, Thomas	60	1662	EQC 3:11
Coldham, Thomas	86	1675	EQC 6:58
Cole, Ann	66	1662/3	SJC 162048
Cole, Ann	70	1665?	SJC 2233
Cole, Isaac	58	1665	MCC folio 39
Cole, Jacob	28	1670	MCC folio 54
Cole, John	53	1678	SJC 1809
Cole, Mary	17	1668	MCC folio 47
Cole, Nicholas	30	1666	EQC 3:376
Cole, Sarah	24	1683	EQC 9:19
Cole, Sarah	36	1681	EQC 8:225
Cole, Simon	22	1669	SJC 1637
Cole, Ursula	30	1662	MCC folio 31
Cole, Ursula	30	1663	MCC folio 34
Cole, Ursula	33	1665	SJC 2233
Cole, Ursula	35	1669	MCC folio 52
Colebron, William	67	1660	SD 3:386
Coleman, James	33	1675	EQC 6:68
Coleman, James	33	1675	SJC 1456
Coleman, James	34	1676	EQC 6:159
Coleman, James	35	1676	EQC 6:157
Coleman, James	43	1685	SJC 2311
Coleman, John	20	1664	EQC 3:120
Coleman, John	20	1690	SJC 2563
Coleman, John	46	1677	MCC folio 77
Coleman, Sarah	40	1685	EQC 9:463
Coleman, Sarah	40	1685	SJC 2311
Coleman, William	36	1679	SJC 1965
Coleson, Mary	30	1681	MCC folio 94
Coleworthy, Francis	46	1697	SJC 3897
Coleworthy, Gilbert	53	1694/5	SJC 3897
Coleworthy, Gilbert	53	1694/5	SJC 3899
Coller, Hannah	57	nd	SJC 3624
Coller, John	19	1652	MCC folio 1
Coller, John	25	1658	MCC folio 17
Colles, John	29	1677	MCC folio 76
Colles, John	30	1653	MCC folio 8
Colles, John	40	1662	MCC folio 31
Colles, John	57	1679	MCC folio 184
Collicott, Edward	54	1669	SD 6:96
Collicott, Richard	52	1656	EQC 2:25
Collicott, Richard	67	1670	MCC folio 54
Collicott, Richard	75	1679	SCC 1048

Collicott, Richard	77	1681	MCC folio 98
Collicott, Richard	77	1682	MCC folio 101
Collier, Anne	32	1685	EQC 9:448
Collier, Hannah	26	1679	EQC 7:238
Collier, John	24	1672	MCC folio 59
Collier, John	25	1680	EQC 7:424
Collier, John	28	1684	EQC 9:280
Collier, Moses	50	1677	SJC 1633
Collier, Moses	50	1677	SJC 1633
Collier, Moses	54	1679	MCC folio 84
Collier, Peter	30	1682	EQC 8:348
Collier, William	85	1668	SJC 857
Collins, Edward	46	1659	MCC folio 21
Collins, Edward	57	1660	MCC folio 25
Collins, Francis	45	1666	SJC 762
Collins, Henry	26	1683	EQC 9:89
Collins, Henry	42	1673	EQC 5:184
Collins, Henry	55	1662	EQC 3:11
Collins, James	20	1664	EQC 3:158
Collins, James	50	1675	EQC 6:78
Collins, John	24	1660	EQC 2:258
Collins, John	28	1664	EQC 3:158
Collins, John	28	nd	SJC 98533
Collins, John	30	1662	EQC 2:352
Collins, John	30	1665	EQC 3:257
Collins, John	30	1666	EQC 3:350
Collins, Joan	38	1674	EQC 5:268
Collins, John	54	1658	EQC 2:64
Collins, John	60	1670/1	SJC 1016
Collins, Joseph	34	1676/7	SJC 1560
Collins, Joseph	45	1694	SJC 4114
Collins, Martha	71	1681	MCC folio 96
Collins, Martha	75	1684	MCC folio 113
Collins, Martha	84	1693	MCC folio 206
Collins, Martha	84	1693	SJC 3925
Collins, Mehitable	22	1660	EQC 2:258
Collins, Rose	23	1685	SJC 2375
Collins, Samuel	20	1656	MCC folio 14
Collson, Adam	39	1681	MCC folio 96
Collson, Mary	30	1681	MCC folio 96
Colman, James	43	1685	EQC 9:463
Colman, Thomas	60	1662	EQC 2:436
Coman, Arthur	31	1677	MCC folio 76
Combs, Mighell	28	1662	EQC 2:391
Combs, Mihill	31	1663	EQC 3:108
Combs, Mitchell	46	1678	EQC 7:148
Comeg, David	32	1670	MCC folio 55
Comer, Richard	26	1684	EQC 9:250
Comes, Sarah	17	1684	EQC 9:319
Comie, David	30	1663	MCC folio 34
Comie, Thomas	16	1689	MCC folio 133
Comly, Humphrey	60	1674	MCC folio 66
Commue, Peter	25	1671	EQC 4:434
Commy, John	20	1685	MCC folio 112

Conant, James	27	1695	MCC folio 162
Conant, John	30	1682	EQC 8:397
Conant, Lot	50	1674	EQC 5:431
Conant, Roger	85	1677	EQC 7:321
Conant, Roger	86	1678	EQC 7:50
Conant, Roger	87	1680	EQC 7:390
Condey, Rebecca	30	1660	EQC 2:208
Condey, Samuel	33	1664	EQC 3:157
Conney, John	44	1672	SJC 1163
Connor, Robert	25	1675	MCC folio 69
Converse, Edward	27	1683	EQC 9:46
Converse, Edward	68	1658	MCC folio 16
Converse, Edward	71	1660	MCC folio 25
Converse, Edward	71	1660	MCC folio 33
Converse, Edward	73	1661/2	MCC folio 28
Converse, Elizabeth	50	1668	MCC folio 48
Converse, James	22	1667	MCC folio 43
Converse, James	24	1670	MCC folio 53
Converse, James	25	1670	MCC folio 54
Converse, James	31	1677	MCC folio 74
Converse, James	32	1682	MCC folio 101
Converse, James	36	1657	MCC folio 20
Converse, James	36	1682	MCC folio 98
Converse, James	37	1684	MCC folio 109
Converse, James	39	1660	MCC folio 25
Converse, James	40	1685	MCC folio 115
Converse, James	40	1685	MCC folio 115
Converse, James	40	1685	MCC folio 117
Converse, James	40	1685	MCC folio 120
Converse, James	40	1685	SJC 2325
Converse, James	41	1662	MCC folio 28
Converse, James	44	1665	MCC folio 39
Converse, James	50	1670	MCC folio 54
Converse, James	50	1671	MCC folio 59
Converse, James	52	1696	MCC folio 206
Converse, James	56	1676	MCC folio 71
Converse, James	61	1681	MCC folio 102
Converse, James	63	1685	MCC folio 115
Converse, James	64	1684	MCC folio 109
Converse, James	70	1691	MCC folio 167A
Converse, Josiah	33	1681	MCC folio 102
Converse, Josiah	52	1671	MCC folio 59
Converse, Josiah	59	1677	MCC folio 71
Converse, Josias	40	1657	MCC folio 16
Converse, Josias	40	1657	MCC folio 20
Converse, Josias	41	1660	MCC folio 25
Converse, Josias	53	1672	MCC folio 59
Converse, Sarah	21	1671	MCC folio 74
Conway, Allen	63	1678	MCC folio 80
Cook, Hannah	4	1662	EQC 2:423
Cook, Henry	8	1662	EQC 2:423
Cook, Isaac	22	1662	EQC 2:423
Cook, John	20	1668	EQC 4:54
Cook, John	30	1678	EQC 7:113

Cook, Judith	18	1662	EQC 2:423
Cook, Martha	12	1662	EQC 2:423
Cook, Mary	12	1662	EQC 2:423
Cook, Rachel	16	1662	EQC 2:423
Cook, Samuel	20	1662	EQC 2:423
Cooke, Edmund	22	1676	SJC 1592
Cooke, George	25	1673	SJC 1245
Cooke, Hannah	23	1660	MCC folio 26
Cooke, Isaac	30	1678	EQC 7:32
Cooke, Isaac	38	1678	EQC 7:141
Cooke, Isaac	40	1680	EQC 7:424
Cooke, Isaac	42	1683	EQC 9:54
Cooke, Isaac	42	1683	EQC 9:55
Cooke, James	22	1675	EQC 6:79
Cooke, John	28	1675	EQC 6:89
Cooke, John	30	1678	EQC 7:108
Cooke, John	30	1678	EQC 7:141
Cooke, John	30	1678	EQC 7:4
Cooke, John	30	1678	EQC 7:55
Cooke, John	30	1679	EQC 7:252
Cooke, Joseph	36	1677	MCC folio 76
Cooke, Joseph	41	1680	MCC folio 106
Cooke, Joseph	50	1658	MCC folio 17
Cooke, Joseph	76	1677	MCC folio 78
Cooke, Martha	29	1677	MCC folio 75
Cooke, Martha	30	1677	MCC folio 78
Cooke, Richard	47	1658	SJC 290
Cooke, Richard	47	nd	SJC 962
Cooke, Richard	48	1658	EQC 2:128
Cooke, Richard	53	1663/4	SJC 606
Cooke, Richard	54	1665	SJC 705
Cooke, Richard	55	nd	SJC 721
Cooke, Richard	57	1665	SJC 2233
Cooke, Richard	60	1671	SJC 1276
Cooke, Richard	60	1671	SJC 2997
Cooke, Richard	62	1673	MCC folio 65
Cooke, Richard	62	1673	SJC 1221
Cooke, Robert	46	1681	MCC folio 95
Cooke, Samuel	25	1682	MCC folio 101
Cooke, Steven	32	1679	EQC 7:263
Cooke, Thomas	31	1653	EQC 2:95
Cookery, Henry	24	1684	MCC folio 111
Coolidge, John	40	1674	MCC folio 63
Coolidge, Mary	40	1681	MCC folio 97
Coolidge, Nathaniel	42	1678	MCC folio 81
Coolidge, Simon	30	1662	MCC folio 31
Coolidge, Steven	25	1674	MCC folio 63
Cooly, Charles	23	1683[/4]	SJC 2177
Cooly, Eliakim	28	1677	MCC folio 77
Cooly, Obadiah	31	1677	MCC folio 77
Coombes, John	20	1683	MCC folio 103
Coombs, Bathsheba	45	1682	EQC 8:341
Cooper, John	52	1670	MCC folio 61
Cooper, Josiah	29	1662	MCC folio 28

Cooper, Josiah	29	1662	MCC folio 35
Cooper, Nathan	49	nd	SJC 2802
Cooper, Thomas	20	1671	MCC folio 56
Cooper, Thomas	21	1670	MCC folio 55
Cooper, Thomas	25	1679	EQC 7:327
Cooper, Thomas	42	1671	SD 7:244
Cooper, Timothy	19	1667	EQC 3:422
Cooper, William	22	nd	SJC 3671
Corey, Giles	55	1672	EQC 5:54
Corey, Jonathan	30	1677	MCC folio 77
Corey, Jonathan	44	1690	MCC folio 134
Corey, Mary	43	1672	EQC 5:53
Corey, Mary	50	1680	EQC 7:423
Corliss, George	71	1679	SJC 1840
Corliss, George	78	1685	EQC 9:544
Corliss, John	21	1669	EQC 4:193
Corliss, John	21	1669	SJC 1009
Cornelius, John	25	1676	EQC 6:148
Corning, Samuel	62	1678	EQC 7:11
Corwin, George	30	1668	EQC 4:85
Corwin, George	56	1667	EQC 3:439
Corwin, George	63	1674	EQC 5:273
Corwin, George	65	1677	EQC 6:241
Corwin, George	68	1679	EQC 7:295
Corwin, George	70	1682	EQC 8:322
Corwin, Jonathan	34	1675	EQC 6:45
Corwin, Jonathan	43	1684	EQC 9:280
Cotrell, Henry	28	1694	SJC 3123e
Cottle, Edward	40	1668	EQC 4:29
Cottle, Edward	50	1667	EQC 3:422
Cotton, Anne	13	1674	EQC 5:413
Cotton, Prudence	37	1675	EQC 6:15
Cotton, Seaborn	34	1667	EQC 3:397
Cotton, Seaborne	35	1669	EQC 4:112
Cotton, William	19	1673	MCC folio 62
Cotton, William	48	1661	EQC 2:284
Cotton, William	50	1661	EQC 2:287
Couch, Samuel	36	1684	SJC 2197
Counts, Edward	41	1679	MCC folio 185
Courser, John	32	1673	SD 8:173
Courser, William	56	1663	MCC folio 35
Cousens, Thomas	30	1679/80	SCC 1110
Cousins, Isaac	67	1679	EQC 7:254
Covell, Philip	23	1686	MCC folio 123
Cowdrey, Nathaniel	21	1683	EQC 9:45
Cowdrey, Nathaniel	26	1655/6	MCC folio 15
Cowdrey, William	54	1652	MCC folio 1
Cowdrey, William	58	1661	MCC folio 28
Cowdrey, William	72	1674	MCC folio 70
Cowdrey, William	73	1677	EQC 6:300
Cowdrey, William	78	1681	MCC folio 92
Cowdrey, William	82	1684	EQC 9:341
Cowdrey, William	82	1684	MCC folio 199
Cowell, Eleanor	15	1694	SJC 3015

Cowell, Eleanor	18	1697	SJC 4005
Cowell, Mary	54	1697	SJC 4374
Cowes, Giles	27	1672	EQC 5:8
Cox, Edward	20	1673	SJC 1245
Cox, Elizabeth	21	1698	MCC folio 169
Cox, Robert	40	1672	SCC 378
Cox, Robert	43	1673	EQC 5:226
Coye, Martha	14	1665	EQC 3:274
Coye, Mathew	33	1655	EQC 1:382
Coye, Richard	15	1665	EQC 3:274
Coye, Richard	35	1661	EQC 2:294
Crabtree, Hester	16	1662	SJC 874
Crackbone, Benjamin	37	1668	MCC folio 48
Crackbone, Gilbert	40	1652/3	SJC 168
Craft, Benjamin	14	1697/8	SJC 4405
Craft, John	37	1668	SJC 905
Craft, Moses	28	1668	SJC 905
Crafts, William	60	1674	EQC 5:317
Cragborn, Benjamin	38	1664	MCC folio 36
Craggen, Sarah	38	1672	MCC folio 60
Craggen, Sarah	53	1682	MCC folio 101
Crague, John	20	1653	MCC folio 5
Crandall, Walter	21	1680	MCC folio 183
Cravit, Mordecai	50	1674	EQC 5:420
Crawford, Gideon	44	1698	SJC 4534
Crayen, John	50	1676	MCC folio 71
Crayen, Sarah	49	1676	MCC folio 71
Creacy, John	25	1685	EQC 9:459
Creeke, Deborah	25	1667	SJC 818
Creeke, Edward	25	1667	SJC 821
Creeke, Edward	29	1670	SJC 1016
Creeke, James	21	1680	SJC 1894
Creel, John	25	1660	MCC folio 25
Cressey, Michael	30	1658	EQC 2:107
Cressey, Mighill	40	1669	EQC 4:144
Crichly, Richard	65	1670	SJC 1015
Crick, James	21	1680	EQC 7:372
Crispe, Benjamin	70	1677	MCC folio 74
Crispe, Benjamin	77	1683	MCC folio 104
Crispe, Deliverance	20	1670	MCC folio 55
Crispe, Richard	55	1695	SJC 3310
Croade, Frances	50	1681	EQC 8:224
Croade, Frances	52	1685	EQC 9:442
Croade, John	21	1684	EQC 9:397
Croade, John	30	nd	SJC 2818
Croade, John	30	nd	SJC 2833
Croade, John	37	1660[/1]	SJC 391
Croade, Richard	46	1675	EQC 6:106
Croade, Richard	48	1676	EQC 6:239
Croade, Richard	49	1676	EQC 6:195
Croade, Richard	52	1681	EQC 8:124
Croade, Richard	55	1684	EQC 9:178
Croade, Richard	55	1684	EQC 9:198
Croade, Richard	56	1685	EQC 9:442

Croade, Richard	57	1685	EQC 9:440
Croade, Richard	58	1686	EQC 9:589
Crocker, James	16	1688	SJC 2504
Crocker, Robert	32	1663	MCC folio 34
Crocker, Sarah	28	1670	EQC 4:286
Crocker, Sarah	31	1673	EQC 5:199
Crockett, Edward	33	1681	SJC 2022
Crockett, Joseph	42	1694	SJC 3006
Crocum, John	25	1672	SJC 1163
Crocum, John	27	1674	SJC 1348
Crofts, Anna	60	1667	EQC 3:461
Crofts, Anne	80	1682	EQC 8:290
Crofts, William	60	1676	EQC 6:145
Crofts, William	70	1682	EQC 8:290
Cromwell, Dorothy	57	1662	EQC 2:444
Cromwell, John	15	1670	MCC folio 55
Cromwell, John	22	1679	MCC folio 185
Cromwell, John	35	1671	EQC 4:389
Cromwell, Philip	32	1666	SJC 764
Cromwell, Philip	48	1660	EQC 2:219
Cromwell, Philip	50	1664	EQC 3:217
Cromwell, Philip	57	1674	EQC 5:266
Cromwell, Thomas	42	1666	EQC 3:420
Cromwell, Thomas	43	1660	EQC 2:206
Cromwell, Thomas	55	1678	EQC 6:410
Cromwell, Thomas	65	1686	EQC 9:580
Croply, John	21	nd	SJC 25906
Crosby, Anthony	23	1660	EQC 2:229
Crosby, Anthony	35	1671	SJC 162102
Crosby, Anthony	35	1671/2	SCC 86
Crosby, Hannah	18	1690	MCC folio 136
Crosby, Hannah	20	1690	MCC folio 136
Crosby, Joseph	14	1683	MCC folio 102
Crosby, Joseph	25	1665	EQC 3:256
Crosby, Simon	19	1683	MCC folio 102
Crosby, Simon	42	1679	MCC folio 87
Crosby, Simon	54	1692	MCC folio 154
Crosby, Thomas	17	1683	MCC folio 102
Crosby, Thomas	24	1689	MCC folio 133
Crosby, Thomas	24	1690	MCC folio 140
Cross, Anna	21	1671	EQC 4:335
Cross, Mary	27	1680	EQC 7:375
Cross, Robert	21	1663	EQC 3:88
Cross, Robert	21	1667	EQC 3:396
Cross, Robert	24	1666	EQC 3:373
Cross, Robert	25	1667	EQC 3:458
Cross, Robert	27	1668	EQC 4:78
Cross, Robert	33	1676	EQC 6:157
Cross, Robert	34	1676	EQC 6:197
Cross, Robert	39	1682	EQC 8:315
Cross, Robert	40	1677	EQC 6:366
Cross, Robert	48	1685	EQC 9:464
Cross, Robert	50	1695	SJC 162347
Cross, Robert	50	nd	SJC 2827

Cross, Robert	52	1695	SJC 3138
Cross, Robert	55	1668	EQC 4:48
Cross, Robert	55	1668	EQC 4:80
Cross, Robert	63	1675	EQC 6:112
Cross, Robert	70	1682	EQC 8:410
Cross, Robert	70	1682	SJC 3138
Cross, Stephen	26	1673	EQC 5:186
Cross, Stephen	31	1678	EQC 7:93
Cross, Stephen	48	1695	SJC 3138
Cross, Steven	16	1663	EQC 3:87
Cross, Steven	17	1667	EQC 3:396
Cross, Steven	21	1668	EQC 4:50
Cross, Steven	23	1668	EQC 4:79
Cross, Steven	27	1675	EQC 6:17
Crossman, Robert	50	nd	SJC 25600
Croswell, Priscilla	53	1695	SJC 3413
Croswell, Thomas	47	1682	MCC folio 100
Crouch, David	33	1691[/2]	SJC 98524
Crouch, Elizabeth	26	1689	MCC folio 135
Crouch, Hannah	11	1677	MCC folio 78
Crouch, Jonathan	33	1689	MCC folio 135
Crouch, Jonathan	36	1694	MCC folio 186
Crouch, Joseph	22	1691	MCC folio 146
Crouch, Mary	17	1669	MCC folio 52
Crouch, Widow	52	1676	MCC folio 72
Crouch, William	36	1663	MCC folio 34
Crouder, Elizabeth	25	1679	MCC folio 85
Crowe, Christopher	52	1681	SJC 2022
Crowell, Deliverance	30	1669	EQC 4:216
Crowne, William	50	1668	EQC 4:2
Croy, Peter	20	1673	SJC 1254
Cuffe, Thomas	15	1694	SJC 2915
Culiver, Anthony	50	1671	SJC 1290
Cummings, Isaac	65	1666	EQC 3:312
Cummings, Isaac	72	1673	EQC 5:134
Cummings, John	18	1675	EQC 6:80
Cummings, John	40	1673	EQC 5:134
Cummings, John	40	1674	EQC 5:422
Cummings, John	47	1678	EQC 6:425
Cummings, John	50	1679	EQC 7:300
Cummings, John	50	1681	MCC folio 96
Cunniball, John	44	1694	SJC 3024
Cunningham, John	12	1679	MCC folio 85
Currier, Richard	47	1664	EQC 3:253
Currier, Richard	59	1676	EQC 6:128
Currier, Richard	65	1682	EQC 8:251
Currier, Richard	66	1682	EQC 8:374
Currier, Thomas	20	1691/2	SJC 162278
Curry, Francis	20	1660	MCC folio 25
Curry, James	73	1673	MCC folio 64
Curry, Jonathan	25	1673	MCC folio 64
Curtin, John	23	1684	EQC 9:205
Curtis, Alice	50	1680	EQC 7:401
Curtis, Ephraim	25	1667/8	MCC folio 44

Curtis, Ephraim	26	1668	MCC folio 50
Curtis, Ephraim	26	1669	MCC folio 52
Curtis, Johanna	53	1677	EQC 6:295
Curtis, John	24	1668	MCC folio 50
Curtis, John	24	1673	EQC 5:215
Curtis, John	30	1677	MCC folio 76
Curtis, Joseph	20	1667/8	MCC folio 44
Curtis, Joseph	21	1668	MCC folio 44
Curtis, Joseph	21	1668	MCC folio 50
Curtis, William	16	1679	EQC 7:251
Curtis, William	17	1680	EQC 7:401
Curtis, William	34	1666	EQC 3:420
Curtis, William	35	1666	SJC 762
Curtis, William	37	1666	EQC 3:420
Curtis, William	37	1668	EQC 4:75
Curtis, William	40	1671	EQC 4:434
Curtis, William	40	1671	EQC 4:434
Curtis, William	40	1681	EQC 8:205
Curtis, Zachariah	22	1673	EQC 5:215
Curtis, Zacheus	28	1674[/5]	SJC 1397
Curtis, Zacheus	28	1675	EQC 6:5
Curtis, Zacheus	29	1675	EQC 6:37
Curtis, Zacheus	29	1675	EQC 6:55
Curtis, Zacheus	53	1672	EQC 5:28
Curtis, Zachias	22	1669	EQC 4:177
Curwin, George	55	1672	EQC 5:12
Cutler, Frances	56	1691	MCC folio 148
Cutler, Gershom	35	1691	MCC folio 147
Cutler, Gershom	36	1691	MCC folio 173
Cutler, Hepzibah	20	1691	MCC folio 140
Cutler, Hepzibah	20	1691	MCC folio 173
Cutler, John	27	1677	MCC folio 74
Cutler, John	28	1679	MCC folio 83
Cutler, John	29	1679	MCC folio 86
Cutler, John	46	1675	MCC folio 69
Cutler, John	60	1690	MCC folio 138
Cutler, Nathaniel	16	1675	MCC folio 70
Cutler, Nathaniel	27	1691	MCC folio 147
Cutler, Nathaniel	32	1691	MCC folio 140
Cutler, Richard	73	1691	MCC folio 146
Cutler, Ruth	19	1689	MCC folio 134
Cutler, Samuel	21	1682	EQC 8:357
Cutler, Sarah	17	1691	MCC folio 148
Cutler, Sarah	18	1683	EQC 9:49
Cutler, Thomas	40	1675	MCC folio 74
Cutler, Timothy	33	1686	MCC folio 123
Cutter, Elizabeth	39	1657	MCC folio 18
Cutter, Gershom	32	1686	MCC folio 127
Cutter, Gershom	35	1692	MCC folio 146
Cutter, Hepsibah	20	1691	MCC folio 140
Cutter, Nathaniel	21	1685	MCC folio 117
Cutter, Rebecca	33	1695	MCC folio 198
Cutter, Richard	60	1679	MCC folio 84
Cutter, Richard	60	1679	SJC 1799

Cutter, Richard	73	1691	MCC folio 173
Cutting, Sarah	46	1671	MCC folio 59
Dainell, Teague	29	1678	EQC 6:437
Dakin, Joseph	30	1700	SJC 4788
Daland, Benjamin	20	1678	EQC 7:21
Dallin, John	49	1675[/6]	SJC 1390
Dalton, Samuel	30	1679	EQC 7:290
Dalton, Samuel	38	1668	SJC 1372
Dalton, Samuel	38	1673	EQC 5:242
Dalton, Samuel	42	1671	SJC 1078
Dalton, Samuel	42	1671	SJC 1100
Dalton, Samuel	43	1673	SJC 1187
Damerill, John	22	1657	MCC folio 19
Damerill, John	22	1657	MCC folio 20
Damfort, Sarah	26	1684	EQC 9:238
Damfort, Sarah	30	1684	EQC 9:237
Damion, John	63	1683	MCC folio 104
Damon, John	74	1695	MCC folio 181
Dana, Benjamin	26	1685	MCC folio 120
Dana, Daniel	27	1691	MCC folio 157
Dana, Naomy	21	1691	MCC folio 157
Dane, Elizabeth	36	1681	MCC folio 95
Dane, George	40	1677	EQC 6:354
Dane, Hannah	66	1695	MCC folio 162
Dane, John	24	1668	EQC 4:4
Dane, John	27	1671	EQC 4:331
Dane, John	32	1677	EQC 6:276
Dane, John	52	1665	EQC 3:243
Dane, John	57	1670	EQC 4:257
Dane, John	60	1674	EQC 5:307
Dane, John	62	1674	EQC 5:414
Dane, John	64	1676	EQC 6:238
Dane, John	66	1679	EQC 7:270
Dane, Philemon	27	1674	EQC 5:321
Dane, Thomas	17	1681	MCC folio 95
Danford, William	30	1678	EQC 7:157
Danforth, Jonathan	17	1676	MCC folio 71
Danforth, Jonathan	17	1676	MCC folio 73
Danforth, Jonathan	18	1677	MCC folio 76
Danforth, Jonathan	23	1682	MCC folio 100
Danforth, Jonathan	27	1681	MCC folio 93
Danforth, Jonathan	49	1677	MCC folio 76
Danforth, Jonathan	50	1676	MCC folio 73
Danforth, Jonathan	50	1677	EQC 6:325
Danforth, Jonathan	58	1680	EQC 8:16
Danforth, Mary	62	1686	MCC folio 127
Danforth, Thomas	54	1677	MCC folio 75
Danforth, Thomas	60	1682	MCC folio 100
Danforth, Thomas	71	1695	MCC folio 180
Danforth, William	22	1663	EQC 3:86
Daniel, John	31	1679	SJC 1917
Daniel, Joseph	31	1672	MCC folio 61
Daniel, Nehemiah	47	1673	MCC folio 62
Daniel, Robert	60	1652	MCC folio 1

Daniel, Thomas	37	1674	SJC 162147
Danton, John	16	1681	MCC folio 96
Danvers, Elizabeth	25	1660	MCC folio 25
Darlin, Thomas	20	1684?	SJC 2244
Darling, George	50	1670	EQC 4:255
Darling, George	60	1677	EQC 6:361
Darling, George	66	1681	EQC 8:180
Darling, George	66	1681	EQC 8:198
Darling, Thomas	21	1684	EQC 9:250
Darvall, William	25	1668	SJC 873
Dassett, Joseph	18	1684/5	MCC folio 113
Daston, Lydia	55	1681	MCC folio 96
Daston, Sarah	27	1681	MCC folio 96
Davenport, Richard	58	1664	EQC 3:206
Daves, John	22	1678	EQC 7:22
Daves, Judith	20	1681	EQC 8:217
Davie, Humphrey	44	1670	SJC 985
Davie, Humphrey	45	1670	SJC 985
Davie, Rodger	23	1677	SJC 1686
Davis, Anthony	25	1668[/9]	SJC 911
Davis, Barnabas	22	1663	SJC 573
Davis, Barnabas	60	1660	MCC folio 26
Davis, Barnabas	60	1660	MCC folio 29
Davis, Barnabee	60	1659	MCC folio 21
Davis, Benjamin	22	1671	SJC 1290
Davis, Benjamin	40	1690	MCC folio 137
Davis, Constance	12	1686	EQC 9:604
Davis, Cornelius	25	1678	EQC 7:156
Davis, Elisha	14	1685	EQC 9:436
Davis, Elisha	15	1684/5	SJC 2338
Davis, Emmanuel	24	1679	SJC 1984
Davis, Ephraim	23	1678	EQC 7:156
Davis, Ephraim	40	nd	SJC 1414
Davis, Hopewell	40	1686	MCC folio 121
Davis, Hopewell	44	1691	MCC folio 148
Davis, James	20	1678	EQC 7:157
Davis, James	23	1692	MCC folio 154
Davis, James	29	1667/8	MCC folio 47
Davis, James	35	1672	EQC 5:50
Davis, James	49	1684	MCC folio 108
Davis, Jeremiah	28	1678	EQC 7:156
Davis, John	25	1680	EQC 8:21
Davis, John	30	1672	EQC 5:63
Davis, John	30	1678	EQC 7:156
Davis, John	39	1681	EQC 8:103
Davis, John	43	1694	SJC 3153
Davis, John	60	1668	EQC 4:42
Davis, Joseph	30	1664[/5]	SJC 721
Davis, Joseph	31	1679	MCC folio 89
Davis, Joseph	32	1668/9	SJC 913
Davis, Mary	24	1666	MCC folio 42
Davis, Nathaniel	35	1679	SJC 1798
Davis, Nathaniel	72	1685/6	MCC folio 122
Davis, Patience	20	1660	MCC folio 25

Davis, Robert	21	1687	EQC WPA 47-50-1
Davis, Samuel	28	1664	EQC 3:212
Davis, Samuel	33	1657	EQC 2:29
Davis, Sarah	30	1681	EQC 8:103
Davis, Sarah	33	1680	EQC 8:103
Davis, Sarah	35	1681	EQC 8:145
Davis, Simon	29	1691	MCC folio 141
Davis, Simon	45	1681	MCC folio 95
Davis, Stephen	17	1680	EQC 8:70
Davis, Thomas	26	1674	EQC 5:288
Davis, Thomas	30	1691	MCC folio 148
Davis, Thomas	66	1669	EQC 4:192
Davis, Timothy	27	1693	SJC 2989
Davis, William	45	1662[/3]	SJC 98507
Davis, William	49	1665[/6]	SJC 2233
Davis, William	72	1678	MCC folio 185
Davis, Zachariah	29	1678	EQC 7:156
Davison, Daniel	18	1682	EQC 9:1
Davison, Daniel	40	1670	EQC 4:223
Davison, John	14	1683	EQC 9:2
Davison, Margret	47	1680	EQC 7:362
Davison, William	18	1686	EQC 9:581
Davril, Robert	42	1681	MCC folio 96
Dawes, Ambrose	41	1683	SJC 2224
Dawes, Mary	44	1685[/6]	SJC 2388
Dawes, Samuel	21	1685	SJC 2294
Dawes, Susanna	54	nd	SJC 26619
Dawes, Susanna	60	1683	SD 12:364
Dawes, Susanna	70	1693/4	SJC 3126
Dawes, William	46	1665	SJC 721
Dawes, William	58	1677	SJC 1753
Dawes, William	62	1679/80	SCC 1128
Dawes, William	62	1679/80	SJC 1833
Dawes, William	64	1683	SD 12:364
Dawes, William	73	1692	SJC 3893
Dawes, William	77	1696	SJC 162398
Dawes, William	77	1696	SJC 3470
Dawson, Henry	29	1684	SJC 2217
Day, Anthony	36	1660	EQC 2:237
Day, Anthony	37	1663	EQC 3:43
Day, Anthony	40	1664	EQC 3:186
Day, Anthony	43	1667	EQC 3:431
Day, Anthony	56	1679	EQC 7:200
Day, Edward	27	nd	SJC 2788
Day, Joseph	25	1674	EQC 5:346
Day, Mary	70	1669	SJC 964
Day, Robert	77	1681	EQC 8:110
Day, Robert	77	1681	SJC 2008
Day, Sarah	19	1670	EQC 4:242
Day, Sarah	24	1671	EQC 4:342
Day, Steven	62	1656	MCC folio 11
Day, Thomas	17	1668	EQC 4:89
Day, Thomas	30	1682	EQC 8:367
Day, Timothy	26	1682	EQC 8:295

Day, William	38	1678	SJC 1734
Daydie, William	72	1677	MCC folio 75
Dayes, Emmanuel	22	1684	EQC 9:209
Deacon, John	73	1673	SJC 1225
Deakin, Thomas	56	1679	MCC folio 85
Dean, John	35	1685	SJC 2370
Dean, Joseph	60	nd	SJC 28113
Dean, Thomas	27	1665[/6]	SJC 722
Dean, William	30	1685	SJC 2370
Dean, William	39	1690	SJC 2561
Deane, Daniel	26	1656	MCC folio 17
Deane, Daniel	26	1658	EQC 2:112
Deane, Daniel	54	1686	MCC folio 121
Deane, Elizabeth	31	1674	EQC 5:355
Deane, Elizabeth	40	1681	EQC 8:225
Deane, George	40	1679	EQC 7:307
Deane, George	40	1682	EQC 8:341
Deane, John	26	1670	EQC 4:223
Deane, John	60	1622	EQC 2:395
Deane, Roger	44	1685	EQC WPA 46-41-1
Dearborn, Dorithy	71	1671	SJC 1100
Dearborn, John	20	1667	SJC 834
Deare, Edward	17	1682	EQC 8:286
Deare, Edward	40	1682	EQC 8:314
Deare, Edward	42	1682	EQC 8:287
Deare, Elizabeth	15	1678	EQC 7:37
Deare, Elizabeth	18	1682	EQC 8:286
Deare, John	40	1684	EQC 9:205
Death, John	27	1694	SJC 3171
Debeck, James	24	1672[/3]	SJC 1194
Decker, John	32	1678	EQC 7:157
Defew, Benjamin	26	1684	EQC 9:324
Defew, Richard	30	1684	EQC 9:324
DelaHay, Gabreell	31	1684	SJC 2251
Delare, Michael	18	1665	EQC 3:285
Dellow, William	30	1658	EQC 2:113
Deloway, William	50	1676/7	SCC 766
Deloway, William	50	1676[/7]	SJC 1569
Dence, Richard	60	1672	SCC 214
Dence, Richard	60	1672[/3]	SJC 1471
Denison, John	20	1687	EQC WPA 47-50-3
Denning, Henry	30	1667	SJC 909
Denning, William	27	1667	SJC 909
Dennis, James	29	1670	EQC 4:286
Dennis, James	30	1671	EQC 4:400
Dennis, James	30	1672	EQC 5:92
Dennis, James	30	1673	EQC 5:199
Dennis, James	35	1677	EQC 6:293
Dennis, James	35	1677	EQC 6:362
Dennis, James	35	1678	EQC 7:109
Dennis, James	35	1678	EQC 7:4
Dennis, James	36	1678	EQC 7:119
Dennis, James	38	1680	EQC 7:388
Dennis, James	38	1680	EQC 8:28

Dennis, James	42	1685	EQC 9:570
Dennis, Mary	33	1677	EQC 6:309
Dennis, Thomas	40	1680	EQC 7:374
Dent, John	24	1684	EQC 9:251
Derby, Charles	13	1682	EQC 8:341
Derby, Eleazer	37	1699	SJC 3874
Derby, Lucretia	42	1685	EQC WPA 46-41-1
Derby, Roger	43	1687	MCC folio 127
Derrick, Michael	18	1674	EQC 5:346
deSattay, Gabriel	31	1684	SJC 2251
Deven, John	40	1661	EQC 2:342
Devereux, Ann	20	1667	EQC 3:414
Devereux, Ann	43	1664	EQC 3:158
Devereux, Ann	46	1667	EQC 3:414
Devereux, Ann	62	1685	EQC 9:465
Devereux, Annn	54	1675	EQC 6:19
Devereux, Elizabeth	18	1682	EQC 8:357
Devereux, goodwife	60	1684	EQC 9:241
Devereux, Humphrey	18	1673	EQC 5:247
Devereux, Humphrey	19	1675	EQC 6:19
Devereux, Humphrey	24	1682	EQC 8:357
Devereux, Humphrey	25	1680	EQC 8:41
Devereux, Humphrey	25	1681	EQC 8:174
Devereux, John	30	1683	EQC 9:52
Devereux, John	50	1669	EQC 4:114
Devereux, John	50	1670	EQC 4:313
Devereux, John	55	1672	EQC 5:110
Devereux, John	60	1675	EQC 6:19
Devereux, John	60	1681	EQC 8:180
Devereux, John	64	1679	EQC 7:200
Devereux, John	70	1684	EQC 9:241
Devereux, John	70	1685	EQC 9:465
Devereux, John	70	1685	SJC 2334
Devereux, Robert	22	1683	EQC 9:52
Dewrell, Nicholas	21	1677	EQC 6:241
Dexter, Bridget	50	1662	MCC folio 31
Dexter, Richard	30	1666	MCC folio 42
Deyser, Elizabeth	48	1679	EQC 7:253
Dicer, William	40	1677	EQC 6:354
Dickerman, Ann	58	1691	MCC folio 157
Dickerman, Thomas	35	1658/9	MCC folio 24
Dickerman, Thomas	40	1671	MCC folio 58
Dickerson, James	29	1670	EQC 4:219
Dickerson, John	22	1667	EQC 3:425
Dickinson, Hezekiah	29	1677	MCC folio 77
Dickinson, John	17	1676[/7]	SJC 1569
Dickinson, John	17	1676[/7]	SJC 162159
Dickinson, Thomas	55	1692/3	SJC 3301
Dickson, Goodman	44	1659	MCC folio 21
Dickson, William	68	1681	MCC folio 92
Didson, Hugh	21	1689	MCC folio 133
Dill, Abraham	29	1689	SJC 2552
Dill, Mary	22	1673	EQC 5:180
Dill, Mary	22	1673	EQC 5:181

Dille, John	21	1664	EQC 3:154
Dillinton, Elizabell	24	1659	MCC folio 23
Dillo, William	45	1678	EQC 7:121
Dimont, Edward	39	1681	EQC 8:102
Dimont, Johanna	44	1672	EQC 5:8
Dinsley, Fathergone	27	1668	MCC folio 45
Dispaw, Henry	35	1681	EQC 8:116
Divan, John	35	1685	EQC 9:465
Divan, John	35	1685	SJC 2345
Dix, Esther	40	1670	MCC folio 54
Dix, John	19	1692	MCC folio 172
Dix, John	41	1692	MCC folio 172
Dix, Ralph	52	1673	MCC folio 62
Dix, Ralph	63	1682	SD 12:214
Dix, Robert	50	1672	MCC folio 59
Dix, William	68	1679	MCC folio 84
Dixey, William	50	1657	EQC 7:127
Dixey, William	62	1669	EQC 4:175
Dixey, William	70	1680	EQC 7:389
Dixey, William	72	1679	EQC 7:311
Dixon, William	68	1679	SJC 1799
Dodd, John	28	1661	EQC 2:343
Doden, Alexander	40	1678	EQC 7:92
Dodge, Edward	50	1695	SJC 3239
Dodge, Elizabeth	26	1675	EQC 6:49
Dodge, Francis	50	1692	MCC folio 154
Dodge, John	16	1679	EQC 7:292
Dodge, John	17	1679	EQC 7:293
Dodge, John	17	1680	EQC 8:22
Dodge, John	22	1661	EQC 2:323
Dodge, John	40	1679	EQC 7:311
Dodge, John	46	1678	SJC 1770
Dodge, John	46	1682	EQC 8:323
Dodge, John	47	1679	EQC 7:293
Dodge, John	48	1680	EQC 7:390
Dodge, John	49	1680	EQC 8:22
Dodge, John	60	nd	SJC 2828
Dodge, Josias	15	1680	EQC 8:21
Dodge, Mary	45	1680	EQC 7:391
Dodge, William	30	1671	EQC 4:332
Dodge, William	30	1671	EQC 4:332
Dodge, William	30	1675	EQC 6:49
Dodge, William	30	1676	EQC 6:146
Dodge, William	30	1677	EQC 6:242
Dodge, William	30	1677	EQC 6:244
Dodge, William	70	1679	EQC 7:181
Dodge, William	76	1680	EQC 8:7
Doggett, Joseph	51	1698/9	SJC 3834
Dolbeare, Edmond	40	1687	EQC WPA 47-100-1
Dole, John	26	1674	EQC 5:417
Dole, John	26	1674	EQC 5:419
Dole, John	27	1676	EQC 6:164
Dole, John	31	1681	EQC 8:77
Dole, John	31	1681	EQC 8:78

Dole, John	33	1682	EQC 8:293
Dole, Joseph	22	1678	EQC 7:156
Dole, Joseph	24	1682	EQC 8:293
Dole, Mary	37	1700	SJC 4841
Dole, Patience	50	1700	SJC 3579
Dole, Richard	28	1681	EQC 8:78
Dole, Richard	29	1681	EQC 8:172
Dole, Richard	29	1681	EQC 8:173
Dole, Richard	31	1683	EQC 9:86
Dole, Richard	46	1670	EQC 4:228
Dole, Richard	50	1674	EQC 5:330
Dole, Richard	52	1675	EQC 6:120
Dole, Richard	52	1675	EQC 6:120
Dole, Richard	52	1676	EQC 6:121
Dole, Richard	52	1676	EQC 6:125
Dole, Richard	52	1676	EQC 6:148
Dole, Richard	52	1676	EQC 6:163
Dole, Richard	52	1676	EQC 6:164
Dole, William	21	1680	EQC 8:66
Dole, William	21	1681	EQC 8:172
Dole, William	21	1681	EQC 8:173
Dole, William	32	1673	SJC 1223
Dolhoff, Christian	32	1671	SJC 1100
Dolibear, Edward	29	1671	SJC 1071
Doling, Margat	11	1679	EQC 7:251
Doliver, Joseph	40	1669	EQC 4:155
Doney, goodwife	30	1682	EQC 8:373
Doney, John	40	1682	EQC 8:373
Donill, Mary	35	1682	EQC 8:281
Donill, Michael	36	1681	EQC 8:189
Donill, Michael	36	1681	MCC folio 101
Donning, Mary	31	1670	EQC 4:281
Dorman, Amos	23	1695	SJC 3326
Dorman, Ephraim	30	1675	EQC 6:37
Dorman, Martin	21	1680	SJC 1887
Dorman, Mary	26	1679	EQC 7:301
Dorman, Thomas	45	1686	EQC 9:606
Dorman, Thomas	78	1670	EQC 4:250
Dorman, Timothy	21	1686	EQC 9:606
Dosett, John	42	1682	MCC folio 103
Dotey, Isaac	18	nd	SJC 3630
Dotey, Isaac	19	nd	SJC 3630
Dotey, James	64	1694	SJC 3460
Dotey, John	30	nd	SJC 3630
Doudey, Robert	17	1677[/8]	SJC 1683
Doule, William	32	1673	EQC 5:131
Doule, William	32	1673	EQC 5:196
Dounar, Joseph	36	1677	EQC 6:254
Dounter, William	40	1671	EQC 4:430
Dounton, Elizabeth	22	1685	EQC 9:446
Dounton, John	27	1683	EQC 9:45
Dounton, Rebecca	40	1675	EQC 6:38
Dounton, Rebecca	45	1676	EQC 6:171
Dounton, Rebecca	52	1686	EQC WPA 46-92-1

Dounton, Rebecca	54	1685	EQC 9:447
Dounton, William	[ ]4	1684	EQC 9:282
Dounton, William	48	1678	EQC 7:33
Dounton, William	53	1681	EQC 8:74
Dounton, William	56	1684	EQC 9:280
Dounton, William	57	1686	EQC WPA 46-92-1
Douse, Edward	64	1679	MCC folio 184
Douse, Jonathan	19	1679	MCC folio 183
Douse, Joseph	20	1674	MCC folio 66
Douse, Joseph	24	1679	MCC folio 184
Douse, Nathaniel	20	1679	MCC folio 184
Douster, John	27	1670	EQC 4:300
Dove, Daniel	20	1682	EQC 8:341
Dove, Daniel	20	1682	EQC 8:343
Dove, Daniel	20	1685	EQC 9:449
Dove, Mathew	69	1680	EQC 7:424
Dow, Dorcas	24	1672	EQC 5:46
Dow, Henry	35	1669	EQC 4:185
Dow, Henry	40	1674	EQC 5:294
Dow, Sarah	34	1680	EQC 7:375
Dow, Sarah	34	1680	SJC 1894
Dow, Thomas	23	1677	EQC 6:251
Dowding, Joseph	25	1696	SJC 3320
Dowding, Leonard	29	1671	SJC 1071
Dowe, Thomas	30	1672	EQC 5:46
Dower, Thomas	60	1676	MCC folio 74
Downe, Edmund	30	1663	SJC 571
Downe, Richard	40	1675	SJC 1416
Downe, William	20	1681	SJC 2021
Downer, Joseph	40	1678	EQC 7:157
Downes, John	40	1669	EQC 4:157
Downes, Thomas	30	1672	SD 6:280
Downing, Dorman	52	1671	SJC 1023
Downing, John	45	1687	EQC WPA 47-57-3
Downing, John	50	1671	SJC 1023
Downing, Mackam	50	1683	EQC 9:46
Downing, Mary	37	1675	EQC 6:18
Downing, Richard	27	1664	EQC 3:157
Downing, Richard	54	1693	SJC 4114
Downing, Sarah	18	1677	EQC 6:287
Downing, William	24	1664	EQC 3:165
Downs, Richard	40	1675	EQC 6:67
Downy, John	22	1665	EQC 3:255
Dows, John	22	1671	MCC folio 56
Dowse, Benjamin	28	1677	MCC folio 75
Dowse, Lawrence	71	1684	MCC folio 110
Dowse, Samuel	33	1676	MCC folio 73
Drake, Abraham	46	1666	SJC 823
Drake, John	48	1684	SJC 2210
Drake, John	50	1683	SJC 2160
Drake, Nathaniel	60	1674	SJC 1566
Drake, Thomas	49	1677/8	SJC 1689
Draper, Adam	26	1659	MCC folio 24
Draper, Debora	11	1654/5	MCC folio 13

Draper, Miriam	54	1676	MCC folio 72
Draper, Richard	40	1693	MCC folio 159
Dresser, John	61	1668	EQC 4:71
Drew, John	21	1684	SJC 2391
Drew, John	40	1684	EQC 9:188
Drew, Rosemon	22	1673	MCC folio 63
Drewry, Hugh	57	1674[/5]	SJC 1432
Drewry, Mary	54	1677	SJC 1644
Drinker, Elizabeth	29	1683	MCC folio 104
Drinker, Elizabeth	60	1683	MCC folio 104
Drinker, John	48	1673	SJC 1249
Driver, Robert	65	1657	EQC 7:129
Driver, Sarah	15	nd	SJC 3037
Drury, Hugh	63	1681	MCC folio 93
Drury, Mary	54	1677	SCC 839
Dudley, Biles	22	1671	SJC 1100
Dudley, Biles	23	1671/2	SJC 1100
Dudley, Elizabeth	15	1668	EQC 4:31
Dudley, Elizabeth	16	1668	EQC 4:31
Dudley, Elizabeth	43	1671	SJC 1100
Dudley, James	26	1666	MCC folio 40
Dudley, John	55	1671	MCC folio 55
Dudley, Paul	26	1677	SJC 1613
Due, Mercy	32	nd	SJC 3759
Duell, James	64	1667	SCC 105
Duer, Ann	45	1665[/6]	SJC 162070
Duerell, James	64	1667	SJC 1143
Duggles, Alexander	50	1683	EQC 9:46
Duggles, Alexander	51	1681	EQC 8:198
Dummer, Jeremy	24	1670/1	SJC 1043
Dummer, Richard	28	1678	EQC 7:156
Dunbar, Robert	25	1659	SJC 347
Duncan, Adam	20	1679	SCC 1087
Duncan, Adam	20	1679	SJC 1919
Duncan, Ann	23	1683	EQC 9:144
Duncan, Ann	26	1683	EQC 9:143
Duncan, John	30	1676	MCC folio 73
Duncan, Peter	37	1666	EQC 3:328
Duncan, Peter	45	1674	EQC 5:287
Duncan, Peter	50	1681	EQC 8:228
Dunham, Alexander	26	1667	SJC 834
Dunkin, Peter	50	1680?	SJC 4054
Dunsdell, Adam	43	1691	SJC 4066
Dunsdell, John	21	1691/2	SJC 98524
Dunsdell, William	47	1662	SJC 520
Dunster, Jonathan	35	1691	MCC folio 148
Dunster, Jonathan	35	1692	MCC folio 173
Dunster, Jonathan	36	1691	MCC folio 143
Dunton, Samuel	66	1684	MCC folio 199
Durell, Nicholas	24	1680	EQC 7:343
Durgey, William	32	1666	EQC 3:372
Durgey, William	48	1680	EQC 7:380
Durgey, William	50	1684	EQC 9:259
Durgey, William	50	1684	SJC 2243

Durgey, William	52	1684	EQC 9:181
Durgey, William	52	1684	EQC 9:191
Duston, Josiah	66	1669	MCC folio 52
Duston, Sarah	27	1681	MCC folio 96
Dutch, Abigail	32	1682	EQC 8:281
Dutch, Benjamin	15	1679/80	SJC 1894
Dutch, Benjamin	15	1680	EQC 7:374
Dutch, Benjamin	21	1686	EQC WPA 47-15-3
Dutch, Elizabeth	22	1670	EQC 4:242
Dutch, Grace	42	1658	EQC 2:68
Dutch, Grace	50	1664	EQC 3:137
Dutch, Hezekiah	18	1664	EQC 3:120
Dutch, John	20	1666	EQC 3:349
Dutch, John	27	1675	EQC 6:12
Dutch, John	34	1680	EQC 7:374
Dutch, Mary	15	1664	EQC 3:119
Dutch, Mary	36	1665	EQC 3:245
Dutch, Mary	53	1680	EQC 7:375
Dutch, Mathew	26	1679	EQC 7:238
Dutch, Osmond	60	1663	EQC 3:41
Dutch, Robert	26	1675	EQC 6:17
Dutch, Robert	35	1658	EQC 2:64
Dutch, Robert	45	1666	EQC 3:349
Dutch, Robert	45	1667	EQC 3:390
Dutch, Robert	50	1675	EQC 6:13
Dutch, Samuel	18	1663	EQC 3:41
Dutch, Samuel	24	1676	EQC 6:197
Dutch, Samuel	28	1679	EQC 7:177
Dutch, Susannah	28	1678	EQC 7:148
Dutch, Susannah	28	1679	EQC 7:251
Dutton, Mary	17	1668	MCC folio 44
Dutton, Thomas	19	1668	MCC folio 44
Dutton, Thomas	26	1677	MCC folio 78
Dutton, Thomas	39	1658	MCC folio 17
Dutton, Thomas	40	1661	MCC folio 27
Dutton, Thomas	40	1662	MCC folio 28
Dutton, Thomas	47	1668	MCC folio 44
Dwight, Timothy	26	nd	SJC 2026
Dwight, Timothy	30	1681[/2]	SJC 2058
Dwinnell, Myhill	23	1668	EQC 4:6
Dyer, Barret	24	nd	SJC 3667
Dyer, Edward	22	1686	EQC WPA 47-15-2
Dyer, Mary	32	1675	EQC 6:35
Dyer, Mary	32	1677	MCC folio 75
Dymond, John	24	1670	EQC 4:264
Dymond, Thomas	28	1670	EQC 4:264
Dyver, Giles	35	1675	SJC 1407
Eager, William	60	1690	MCC folio 132
Eager, Zachary	25	1691	MCC folio 149
Eames, Elizabeth	32	1693	MCC folio 158
Eames, Margaret	19	1686	MCC folio 128
Eames, Martha	19	1686	MCC folio 121
Eames, Robert	59	1684	MCC folio 109
Eames, Thomas	34	1652	MCC folio 7

Eames, Thomas	46	1663	MCC folio 33
Eames, Thomas	48	1667	MCC folio 43
Eames, Thomas	60	1676	MCC folio 84
Earle, Frances	44	1652	MCC folio 7
Earle, Robert	24	1662[/3]	SJC 507
Earle, Robert	41	1676	SJC 1562
East, Francis	70	1671/2	SJC 1092
Eastman, Benjamin	38	1692	SJC 3152
Eastman, John	30	1672	SJC 1563
Eastman, Philip	23	1668	MCC folio 43
Eastman, Philip	43	1688	MCC folio 148
Eastman, Roger	60	1671	EQC 4:348
Eastman, Roger	60	1671	SJC 1334
Eastman, Roger	62	1673	SJC 1563
Eastman, Sarah	50	1671	EQC 4:348
Eastman, Sarah	50	1671	SJC 1334
Eastman, Sarah	50	nd	SJC 2772
Eaton, Anna	20	1691	MCC folio 150
Eaton, Benoni	23	1662	MCC folio 30
Eaton, Benoni	45	1684	MCC folio 111
Eaton, Christian	25	1691	MCC folio 150
Eaton, Elizabeth	27	1670	MCC folio 54
Eaton, Johanath	27	1683	EQC 9:45
Eaton, John	22	1658	EQC 2:112
Eaton, John	22	1658	EQC 2:130
Eaton, John	26	1675	MCC folio 70
Eaton, John	33	1670	MCC folio 54
Eaton, John	40	1660	EQC 2:231
Eaton, John	52	1672	SJC 1563
Eaton, Joseph	20	1674	MCC folio 67
Eaton, Joseph	24	1685	EQC 9:526
Eaton, Joseph	40	1695	SJC 3239
Eaton, Joshua	29	1683	EQC 9:46
Eaton, Martha	57	1685	EQC 9:526
Eaton, Mary	21	1691	MCC folio 150
Eaton, Thomas	21	1682	EQC 8:276
Eaton, William	16	1668/9	MCC folio 52
Eaton, William	25	1691	MCC folio 150
Eaton, William	54	1658	EQC 2:112
Eaton, William	54	1658	EQC 2:130
Eaton, William	60	1667	EQC 3:455
Eburne, Mary	15	1662	EQC 2:446
Eburne, Samuel	22	1661	EQC 2:321
Eburne, Samuel	50	1661	EQC 2:341
Eburne, Samuel	56	1667	EQC 3:413
Eburne, Samuel	58	1669	EQC 4:116
Eburne, Samuel	68	1678	EQC 7:141
Eburne, Samuel	70	1684	EQC 9:345
Eccles, Richard	40	1654	EQC 1:335
Eccles, Richard	60	1680	MCC folio 106
Eddy, John	60	1698	SJC 4714
Eddy, John	62	1700[/1]	SJC 4605
Eddy, John	77	1673	MCC folio 66
Edenden, Edmund	70	1670	SJC 986

Edes, Edward	16	1697	SJC 4367
Edes, John	27	1679	MCC folio 83
Edgcom, John	26	1679/80	SCC 1110
Edgcomb, Nicholas	76	1670	SJC 1046
Edgcomb, Nicholas	76	nd	SJC 1046
Edgerton, Peter	25	1673[/4]	SJC 1341
Edgerton, Peter	28	1675	SJC 1424
Edmands, Mary	50	1685	MCC folio 114
Edminster, John	26	1663[/4]	SJC 632
Edminster, John	40	1673	SJC 1249
Edminster, Prudence	15	1682	MCC folio 99
Edminster, Sarah	43	1682	MCC folio 99
Edmonds, Daniel	49	1679	MCC folio 87
Edmonds, John	59	1695	MCC folio 179
Edmonds, John	59	1695	MCC folio 204
Edmonds, Joseph	19	1663	SJC 571
Edmunds, Elizabeth	39	1682	MCC folio 99
Edmunds, Joseph	17	1660	EQC 2:229
Edmunds, William	42	1659	EQC 2:185
Edmunds, William	47	1657	EQC 7:129
Edsall, Samuel	18	1653	EQC 1:317
Edsall, Samuel	37	1671	SCC 169
Edsell, Elizabeth	47	nd	SJC 26619
Edsell, Samuel	37	1671	SJC 1290
Edsell, Thomas	18	1661	MCC folio 26
Edsell, Thomas	33	1665	SJC 721
Edson, Richard	35	1681	MCC folio 96
Edward, Mathew	49	1681	MCC folio 93
Edwards, Abiah	22	1673	SCC 280
Edwards, Abiah	22	1673	SJC 1245
Edwards, Benjamin	18	1680	EQC 8:21
Edwards, Benjamin	21	1683	EQC 9:14
Edwards, Eleanor	60	1680	EQC 8:18
Edwards, James	31	1668	EQC 4:42
Edwards, John	30	1676	EQC 6:146
Edwards, John	30	1680	EQC 8:22
Edwards, John	37	1680	EQC 8:21
Edwards, John	40	1672	EQC 5:31
Edwards, John	40	1674	EQC 5:305
Edwards, John	50	1679	EQC 7:268
Edwards, John	53	1695	SJC 3239
Edwards, Martha	25	1658	MCC folio 17
Edwards, Mary	42	1685	EQC 9:530
Edwards, Mathew	25	1658	EQC 2:112
Edwards, Mathew	25	1658	EQC 2:130
Edwards, Mathew	29	1661	EQC 2:294
Edwards, Mathew	29	1662	MCC folio 29
Edwards, Mathew	34	1668	MCC folio 47
Edwards, Mathew	42	1674	EQC 5:276
Edwards, Mathew	45	1678	MCC folio 78
Edwards, Mathew	46	1678	EQC 7:9
Edwards, Mathew	47	1679	EQC 7:207
Edwards, Mathew	49	1681	MCC folio 92
Edwards, Mathew	50	1682	MCC folio 101

Edwards, Rise	65	1680	EQC 8:22
Edwards, Roger	22	1684	SJC 2242
Edwards, Roger	34	1665	SJC 705
Edwards, Thomas	30	1684	EQC 9:203
Edwards, William	32	1670	EQC 4:254
Edwards, William	32	1670	EQC 4:255
Edwards, William	32	1670	EQC 4:255
Eger, Ruth	33	1674	MCC folio 67
Ela, Daniel	26	1665[/6]	SJC 322
Ela, Daniel	30	1664	EQC 3:125
Ela, Daniel	30	1664	EQC 3:162
Ela, Daniel	37	1670	SJC 1009
Ela, Daniel	40	1674	SJC 1389
Ela, John	16	1685	EQC 9:545
Ela, John	18	1686	EQC WPA 47-25-1
Eldridge, Susanna	23	1684	SJC 2245
Eleison, Thomas	66	1676	MCC folio 84
Elery, William	30	1674	EQC 5:267
Elford, Tristram	40	1664	EQC 3:186
Elias, William	3 [inquest]	nd	SJC 2238
Elkins, Christopher	25	1667	SJC 824
Elkins, Thomas	64	1659	SJC 1046
Ellice, Richard	70	1692	MCC folio 173
Ellingwood, Eleanor	33	1669	EQC 4:216
Ellingwood, Mary	14	1678	EQC 7:52
Ellingwood, Ralph	60	1669	EQC 4:216
Elliot, John	18	1685	MCC folio 112
Elliot, John	36	1668	SJC 866
Elliot, John	41	1673	SJC 1225
Elliot, John	50	1683	SJC 2145
Elliott, Joseph	31	1679	EQC 7:254
Elliott, Robert	44	1676	EQC 6:185
Elliott, Thomas	26	1681	EQC 8:124
Elliott, Thomas	26	1682	EQC 8:412
Elliott, Thomas	26	1682	EQC 8:415
Ellis, Constant	20	1684	EQC 9:203
Ellis, Constant	20	1684	EQC 9:204
Ellis, Malachi	63	nd	SJC 26128
Ellis, Margaret	23	1680[/1]	SJC 1972
Ellis, Matthias	70	nd	SJC 24811
Ellis, Richard	62	1682	SJC 2126
Ellis, Robert	20	1696	SJC 3752
Ellis, Sarah	21	1683	EQC 9:5
Ellis, Sarah	66	1696	SJC 4372
Ellis, Thomas	37	1670	EQC 4:255
Ellis, Thomas	40	1672	EQC 5:92
Ellistone, George	40	1685	SJC 2321
Ellithorp, Nathaniel	55	1686	EQC 9:613
Elred, Lemuel	32	1652	MCC folio 7
Elsly, Barbary	50	1663	EQC 3:53
Elson, James	32	1675	SCC 664
Elwell, Isaac	20	1662	EQC 2:442
Elwell, Isaac	24	1666	EQC 3:328
Elwell, Isaac	25	1667	EQC 3:447

Elwell, Isaac	32	1675	EQC 6:77
Elwell, Joseph	16	1664	EQC 3:119
Elwell, Joseph	23	1672	EQC 5:67
Elwell, Samuel	63	1672	EQC 5:67
Ely, Daniel	23	1656	EQC 2:17
Elyathrop, John	44	1686	EQC WPA 46-60-3
Emerson, John	24	1679	MCC folio 86
Emerson, Joseph	28	1681	EQC 8:165
Emerson, Nathaniel	28	1659	EQC 2:184
Emerson, Samuel	17	1681	EQC 8:92
Emery, George	53	1662	EQC 2:444
Emery, John	22	1678	EQC 7:156
Emery, John	24	1682	EQC 8:299
Emery, John	32	1679	MCC folio 86
Emery, John	35	1662	EQC 3:14
Emery, John	42	1670	EQC 4:226
Emery, John	42	1670	EQC 4:228
Emery, John	45	1675	EQC 6:66
Emery, John	51	1678	EQC 7:156
Emery, John	54	1682	EQC 8:299
Emery, John	54	1682	EQC 8:300
Emery, John	70	1669	EQC 4:215
Emery, John	73	1671	EQC 4:433
Emery, John	80	1678	EQC 7:156
Emery, John	81	1679	EQC 7:194
Emery, John	82	1680	EQC 8:172
Emery, Jonathan	27	1678	EQC 7:156
Emery, William	25	1658	EQC 2:71
Emery, William	28	1653	EQC 2:96
Emmons, Benjamin	26	1673	EQC 5:189
Emmons, Joseph	17	1694/5	SJC 4131
Emmons, Joseph	34	1683	EQC 9:52
Emmons, Joseph	34	1684	EQC 9:248
Emmons, Obadiah	38	1670	SJC 1016
Emmons, Samuel	39	1680[/1]	SJC 1956
Emmons, Thomas	30	1691	MCC folio 140
Endicott, Elizabeth	60	1674	EQC 5:323
Endicott, William	23	1680	SJC 162193
Endicott, Zerubbabel	39	1674	EQC 5:324
Endicott, Zerubbabel	39	1674	EQC 5:325
Endicott, Zerubbabel	39	1674	SJC 1725
Endicott, Zerubbabel	43	1678	EQC 7:135
English, James	45	1657	SJC 269
English, James	63	1694/5	SJC 4131
English, Philip	23	1674	SJC 1360
English, Philip	27	1678	EQC 7:111
English, William	23	1659	MCC folio 24
Ephraim, Peter	40	1681	MCC folio 94
Ephraim, Peter	43	1681	MCC folio 101
Epps, Daniel	36	1685	EQC 9:449
Epps, Daniel	50	1675	EQC 6:10
Epps, Daniel	50	1675	EQC 6:85
Epps, Daniel	52	1676	EQC 6:221
Epps, Daniel	52	1677	EQC 6:247

Epps, Daniel	52	1678	EQC 6:419
Epps, Daniel	53	1678	EQC 6:418
Epps, Daniel	54	1678	EQC 7:117
Epps, Daniel	54	1678	EQC 7:93
Epps, Joseph	24	1678	EQC 6:408
Esset, William	49	1676	EQC 6:201
Est, William	21	1679	MCC folio 184
Esty, Isaac	65	1695	SJC 162358
Esty, Isaac	65	1695	SJC 3326
Evans, Agnes	30	1669[/70]	SJC 1022
Evans, Daniel	20	1677	EQC 6:332
Evans, David	25	1684	SJC 2251
Evans, Johannah	60	1677	SJC 1718
Evans, Richard	45	1685	MCC folio 116
Evans, Thomas	35	1685	MCC folio 116
Evans, William	40	1666	EQC 3:312
Evans, William	46	1667	EQC 3:390
Eve, Jasper	24	1680	SJC 1935
Eveleth, Susannah	50	1657	EQC 2:36
Everden, Jonathan	40	1694	SJC 4113
Everett, John	26	1673	EQC 5:131
Everett, John	26	1673[/4]	SJC 1223
Everett, Samuel	45	1685	SJC 2370
Everill, James	70	1673	MCC folio 64
Everill, James	76	1679	SD 11:200
Everill, James	78	1681	SD 12:106
Everton, Funnell	30	1694	SJC 3098
Everton, Ruth	25	1691	MCC folio 141
Facer, Johannah	57	1685	MCC folio 117
Fackner, Martha	16	1669	MCC folio 52
Fairbanks, Edward	23	1684	SJC 2217
Fairbanks, Jabez	20	1690	MCC folio 136
Fairfax, John	18	1680	EQC 8:59
Fairfield, Daniel	38	1676	SCC 739
Fairfield, Daniel	38	1676	SJC 1575
Fairfield, Daniel	43	1678	SJC 1729
Fairfield, Daniel	47	1685	SJC 2375
Fairfield, John	28	1669	EQC 4:180
Fairfield, Ruth	45	1685[/6]	SJC 2388
Fairfield, Sarah	43	1682	EQC 8:435
Fairfield, Walter	40	1673	EQC 5:175
Fairfield, Walter	40	1675	EQC 6:7
Fairfield, Walter	45	1677	EQC 6:368
Fairfield, Walter	45	1677	SJC 1731
Fairfield, Walter	45	1678	EQC 6:419
Fairfield, Walter	46	1678	EQC 7:9
Fairfield, Walter	46	1678	EQC 7:93
Fairfield, Walter	47	1678	EQC 7:111
Fairfield, Walter	47	1678	EQC 7:9
Fairfield, Walter	47	1679	EQC 8:160
Fairfield, Walter	48	1679	EQC 7:207
Fairfield, Walter	48	1679	EQC 7:292
Fairfield, Walter	48	1680	EQC 7:385
Fairfield, Walter	49	1681	EQC 8:162

Fairfield, Walter	49	1681	EQC 8:163
Fairfield, Walter	50	1682	EQC 8:435
Fairfield, Walter	51	1682	EQC 8:324
Fairfield, Walter	53	1685	EQC 9:440
Fairfield, Walter	53	1685	EQC 9:523
Fairfield, Walter	53	1685	SJC 2285
Fairfield, Walter	53	1686	EQC 9:584
Fairfield, Walter	62	nd	SJC 3138
Fairfield, Walter	63	1695	SJC 3239
Fairfield, Walter	63	1695	SJC 3326
Fairweather, Charles	33	1684	SJC 2251
Fairweather, John	29	1664	SD 4:227
Fairweather, John	41	1675	EQC 6:85
Fairweather, John	45	1679	EQC 7:261
Fairweather, John	45	1679[/80]	SJC 1837
Fairweather, John	49	1683[/4]	SJC 2224
Fannen, William	27	1669	EQC 4:180
Fannen, William	30	1676	EQC 6:189
Farley, Michael	20	1681	SJC 2008
Farley, Michael	21	1681	EQC 8:111
Farley, Michael	21	1681	SJC 2008
Farmer, Edward	30	1677	MCC folio 77
Farmer, Edward	42	1690	MCC folio 138
Farmer, John	26	1675	SJC 1390
Farmer, Mary	38	1679	MCC folio 87
Farmer, Mary	45	1690	MCC folio 138
Farmer, Mary	62	1699	MCC folio 170
Farnsworth, Rebecca	22	1681	MCC folio 97
Farnum, Ralph	30	1667	EQC 3:471
Farnum, Thomas	24	1657	EQC 2:39
Farr, Benjamin	33	1684	EQC 9:325
Farr, George	63	1657	EQC 7:127
Farr, Thomas	50	1669	EQC 4:209
Farrar, Johanna	40	1669	MCC folio 49
Farrar, John	70	1682	MCC folio 100
Farrar, Thomas	65	1678	EQC 7:26
Farrington, Edmund	67	1661	EQC 2:288
Farrington, John	26	nd	SJC 2769
Farrington, Mary	27	1685	SJC 2370
Farrington, Mary	55	1685	SJC 2370
Farrington, Mathew	15	1666	EQC 3:348
Farris, Johanna	34	1662	MCC folio 30
Farro, Ann	40	1658	EQC 2:118
Farum, John	40	1681	EQC 8:83
Farwell, John	30	1669	MCC folio 48
Farwell, John	50	1658	MCC folio 20
Farwell, Sarah	42	1685	MCC folio 112
Faulkner, David	33	1653	EQC 2:92
Fawckner, David	33	1653	SJC 225
Faxton, Josiah	20	1680	SJC 1975
Fay, John	33	1681	MCC folio 93
Feather, Endeger	40	1676	MCC folio 72
Felch, George	40	1654	MCC folio 9
Felch, Hannah	40	1668	MCC folio 47

Fellows, Ephraim	27	1668	EQC 4:15
Fellows, Ephraim	32	1671	EQC 4:422
Fellows, Ephraim	33	1674	EQC 5:312
Fellows, Samuel	27	1679	EQC 7:280
Fellows, Samuel	61	1679	EQC 7:279
Fellows, William	50	1659	EQC 2:170
Fellows, William	50	1659	SJC 351
Felt, Elizabeth	50	1662	MCC folio 31
Felt, George	80	1681	MCC folio 100
Felt, George	80	1681	MCC folio 90
Felton, Benjamin	64	1668	EQC 4:53
Felton, Benjamin	69	1673	EQC 5:171
Felton, Benjamin	69	1673	SJC 1226
Felton, Elizabeth	21	1676	EQC 6:171
Felton, John	32	1679	EQC 7:167
Felton, Mary	35	1661	EQC 2:340
Felton, Nathaniel	26	1682	EQC 8:344
Felton, Nathaniel	50	1666	EQC 3:380
Felton, Nathaniel	54	1670	EQC 4:279
Felton, Nathaniel	57	1673	EQC 5:171
Felton, Nathaniel	57	nd	SJC 1226
Felton, Nathaniel	62	1678	EQC 7:15
Felton, Nathaniel	64	1680	EQC 7:424
Felton, Nathaniel	65	1681	EQC 8:74
Felton, Nathaniel	67	1682	EQC 8:394
Felton, Nathaniel	68	1684	EQC 9:345
Felton, Nathaniel	70	1686	EQC 9:579
Fenten, Jonathan	20	1675	EQC 6:86
Fergeson, John	22	1677	SJC 3349
Fernside, John	60	1671	SD 7:244
Fernside, John	60	nd	SJC 1044
Ferris, Richard	30	1662	EQC 2:391
Fesey, Solomon	26	1677	SJC 1621
Feward, Hough	20	1656	MCC folio 15
Fickett, Mary	22	1684	EQC 9:399
Field, Mary	51	1677	EQC 6:294
Field, Samuel	24	1677	MCC folio 77
Fifield, Giles	46	1675	SJC 1381
Fifield, Mary	50	1672/3	SJC 1229
Fifield, William	50	1672/3	SJC 1229
Fillebrowne, Annah	34	1674	MCC folio 67
Fillebrowne, Thomas	16	1674	MCC folio 67
Fillebrowne, Thomas	32	1691	MCC folio 156
Fillebrowne, Thomas	33	1691	MCC folio 173
Fillebrowne, Thomas	44	1677	MCC folio 74
Fillebrowne, Thomas	53	1686	MCC folio 121
Fillebrowne, Thomas	53	1686	MCC folio 128
Fillebrowne, Thomas	56	1690	MCC folio 148
Fillebrowne, Thomas	60	1691	MCC folio 148
Finney, Josiah	35	nd	SJC 3630
Firmaes, Benjamin	30	1654	SD 2:27
Firman, John	31	1678	EQC 7:157
Fisher, Anthony	43	1667	SJC 2233
Fisher, Daniel	51	1669/70	SJC 966

Fisher, David	49	1667	SJC 2233
Fisher, Esther	54	1685?	SJC 2370
Fisher, George	26	1680	SJC 1935
Fiske, David	30	1654	EQC 1:335
Fiske, David	45	1669	MCC folio 52
Fiske, David	45	1670	MCC folio 53
Fiske, David	46	1670	MCC folio 53
Fiske, David	46	1670	SJC 964
Fiske, David	59	1682	MCC folio 100
Fiske, David	62	1685	MCC folio 112
Fiske, David	62	1685	MCC folio 117
Fiske, David	63	1685	MCC folio 117
Fiske, David	64	1690	MCC folio 148
Fiske, David	67	1691	MCC folio 148
Fiske, David	67	1691	MCC folio 163
Fiske, David	67	1691	MCC folio 173
Fiske, David	76	1691	MCC folio 146
Fiske, David	76	1691	MCC folio 156
Fiske, David	76	1691	MCC folio 163
Fiske, David	76	1691	MCC folio 173
Fiske, Elizabeth	23	1677	EQC 6:299
Fiske, Johanna	35	1667	EQC 3:457
Fiske, John	19	1674	EQC 5:310
Fiske, John	22	1670	MCC folio 46
Fiske, John	29	1668	MCC folio 49
Fiske, John	30	1679	MCC folio 84
Fiske, John	43	1682	MCC folio 100
Fiske, Joseph	38	1689	SJC 2541
Fiske, Mary	17	1678	MCC folio 80
Fiske, Nathaniel	30	1684	MCC folio 110
Fiske, Samuel	24	1674	EQC 5:276
Fiske, Samuel	30	1675	EQC 6:31
Fiske, Samuel	33	1680	EQC 8:9
Fiske, Samuel	33	1680	SJC 1967
Fiske, Sarah	26	1678	MCC folio 80
Fiske, Thomas	20	1674	EQC 5:267
Fiske, Thomas	29	1682	EQC 8:436
Fiske, Thomas	34	1664	EQC 3:208
Fiske, Thomas	40	1670	EQC 4:308
Fiske, Thomas	40	1673	EQC 5:175
Fiske, Thomas	43	1674	EQC 5:276
Fiske, Thomas	49	1679	EQC 7:207
Fiske, Thomas	49	1679	EQC 7:292
Fiske, Thomas	49	1680	EQC 8:9
Fiske, Thomas	49	1680	SJC 1967
Fiske, Thomas	50	1680	EQC 8:27
Fiske, Thomas	54	1686	EQC 9:584
Fiske, Thomas	63	nd	SJC 2828
Fiske, William	36	1679	EQC 7:292
Fiske, William	40	1682	EQC 8:384
Fitch, Jeremiah	49	1673	SD 8:173
Fitch, Joseph	40	1679	MCC folio 88
Fitch, Joseph	40	1679	SJC 2025
Fitch, Samuel	24	1670	MCC folio 54

Fitch, Thomas	33	1691	SJC 2629
Fitch, Zachariah	67	1696	MCC folio 199
Fitts, ---	68	1674	EQC 5:307
Fitts, Abram	21	1678	EQC 6:418
Fitts, Zachary	40	1661	MCC folio 28
Flack, Samuel	50	1671	SJC 1071
Flagg, Gershom	20	1689	MCC folio 134
Flagg, Gershom	32	1674	MCC folio 71
Flagg, Hannah	44	1691	MCC folio 143
Flagg, John	18	1691	MCC folio 140
Flagg, John	42	1685	MCC folio 114
Flake, Samuel	45	1668	SJC 905
Flander, Richard	40	1679	EQC 7:305
Flanders, Naomi	24	1683	EQC 9:65
Flegg, Bartholomew	23	1672	MCC folio 60
Flegg, Elaine	16	1672	MCC folio 60
Flegg, Eleazer	28	1685	SJC 2383
Flegg, Gershom	29	1677	SJC 1581
Flegg, John	26	1670	MCC folio 46
Flegg, John	28	1672	MCC folio 60
Flegg, Michael	22	1672	MCC folio 60
Flegg, Rebecca	36	1680	MCC folio 89
Flegg, Thomas	26	1672	MCC folio 60
Flegge, Eleazer	24	1681	MCC folio 96
Flemming, John	18	1660	MCC folio 25
Flemming, Robert	20	1666	SJC 740
Fletcher, Joseph	26	1662	EQC 2:411
Fletcher, Joseph	35	1667	SJC 813
Flint, Alice	70	1678	EQC 6:439
Flint, Edward	29	1667	EQC 3:440
Flint, Edward	46	1685	EQC 9:438
Flint, Edward	47	1684	EQC 9:345
Flint, Edward	47	1685	EQC 9:442
Flint, Hannah	22	1672	EQC 5:53
Flint, John	20	1681	EQC 8:223
Flint, John	47	1682	MCC folio 103
Flint, Jonathan	16	1681	EQC 8:156
Flint, Jonathan	16	1681	EQC 8:156
Flint, Jonathan	16	1681	EQC 8:224
Flint, Joseph	14	1674	EQC 5:428
Flint, Thomas	33	1679	EQC 7:295
Flint, Thomas	50	1695	SJC 3236
Flint, William	58	1661	EQC 2:321
Flint, William	62	1665	EQC 3:256
Flood, James	46	1690	MCC folio 132
Flood, John	32	1683	SJC 2374
Flood, John	37	1674	SJC 1397
Flood, John	38	1676	SJC 1438
Flood, John	42	1679	SJC 1827
Flood, John	45	1681	SJC 2018
Flood, John	59	1695	SJC 3258
Floyd, Elizabeth	26	1696/7	MCC folio 204
Floyd, John	30	1667	EQC 3:441
Floyd, John	32	1668	EQC 4:32

Floyd, John	33	1673	MCC folio 65
Floyd, John	33	1681	EQC 8:198
Floyd, John	37	1675	EQC 6:4
Floyd, John	42	1679	EQC 7:198
Floyd, John	44	1680	MCC folio 89
Floyd, John	45	1681	EQC 8:138
Floyd, John	45	1684	MCC folio 109
Floyd, John	59	1695	MCC folio 179
Floyd, John	59	1695	MCC folio 204
Floyd, Jon.	45	1681	EQC 8:118
Floyd, Jon.	50	1686	EQC WPA 46-91-2
Fofsee, Thomas	40	1686	EQC WPA 46-68-2
Fogotie, Philip	20	1662	MCC folio 28
Foller, James	23	1671	EQC 4:331
Follinsby, Thomas	41	1678	EQC 7:156
Foote, Isaac	38	1682	EQC 8:413
Foote, Jonathan	39	1675	MCC folio 70
Foote, Samuel	32	1669	EQC 4:100
Force, Nathaniel	23	nd	SJC 2691
Ford, Catharine	19	1691	MCC folio 157
Ford, Ellen	38	1667	SJC 815
Ford, James	26	1667	EQC 3:457
Ford, James	27	1670	EQC 4:218
Ford, James	28	1668	EQC 4:69
Ford, James	29	1671	EQC 4:331
Ford, John	33	1670	EQC 4:285
Ford, Martin	20	1681	EQC 8:92
Ford, Mary	35	1676	MCC folio 72
Ford, Mary	39	1683	MCC folio 104
Ford, Nathaniel	21	1678	SJC 1722
Ford, William	35	1669	SJC 980
Forrad, Edmund	23	1670	EQC 4:297
Forsdick, Samuel	24	1680	SJC 1935
Forstall, Robert	19	1675	SJC 1425
Forster, Joseph	30	1684/5	SJC 2285
Fosci, Thomas	30	1677	EQC 6:366
Fosdick, Mary	19	1696	MCC folio 201
Fosdick, Mary	30	1660	MCC folio 25
Fosdick, Samuel	14	1669	MCC folio 52
Fosdick, Samuel	26	1681	MCC folio 104
Fosdick, Samuel	26	1681	MCC folio 97
Fosdick, Sarah	70	1660	MCC folio 25
Fosdick, Steven	70	1653	MCC folio 7
Fosey, Thomas	17	1660	MCC folio 26
Fosket, John	40	1678	MCC folio 185
Foskett, John	46	1682	MCC folio 100
Foskett, Thomas	20	1681	MCC folio 102
Foss, John	30	1666	SJC 823
Foster, Elizabeth	21	1674	EQC 5:413
Foster, Elizabeth	30	1668	EQC 4:49
Foster, Hannah	29	1681	SJC 26559
Foster, Hester	37	1695	MCC folio 162
Foster, Hopestill	29	1673	SJC 2120
Foster, Isaac	23	1679	EQC 7:203

Foster, Jacob	23	1686	EQC 9:605
Foster, John	19	1685	MCC folio 114
Foster, John	42	1675	SJC 1503
Foster, John	67	1684/5	SJC 2285
Foster, John	67	1685	EQC 9:439
Foster, Joseph	30	1682	MCC folio 98
Foster, Joseph	30	1685	EQC 9:439
Foster, Reginald	40	1676	EQC 6:160
Foster, Reynold	67	nd	SJC 2827
Foster, Richard	24	1685	MCC folio 114
Foster, Robert	19	1675	SJC 1425
Foster, Samuel	31	1682	MCC folio 98
Foster, Samuel	45	1668	MCC folio 49
Foster, Samuel	45	1695	MCC folio 207
Foster, Samuel	49	1670	MCC folio 53
Foster, Samuel	49	1689	MCC folio 133
Foster, Thomas	21	1686	MCC folio 120
Foster, Thomas	66	1679	MCC folio 87
Foster, William	29	1656	SD 2:307
Foster, William	74	1692	MCC folio 153
Fowar, Hannah	39	1681	MCC folio 96
Fowle, Abraham	30	1685	MCC folio 117
Fowle, Abram	24	1671	MCC folio 56
Fowle, Anna	29	1669	MCC folio 52
Fowle, James	30	1681	MCC folio 93
Fowle, James	40	1685	MCC folio 117
Fowle, John	15	1685	MCC folio 117
Fowle, John	34	1671	MCC folio 57
Fowle, John	36	1674	MCC folio 66
Fowle, John	40	1679	MCC folio 87
Fowle, John	40	1681	SJC 2029
Fowle, Peter	21	1691	MCC folio 148
Fowle, Peter	35	1681	SJC 2029
Fowle, Peter	49	1690	MCC folio 132
Fowle, Samuel	19	1664	SJC 665
Fowler, Giles	25	1668	EQC 4:27
Fowler, James	40	1685	SJC 2377
Fowler, Joseph	19	1672	EQC 5:33
Fowler, Joseph	31	1672	EQC 5:69
Fowler, Joseph	32	1686	EQC 9:584
Fowler, Joseph	38	1664	SJC 2828
Fowler, Philip	21	1670	EQC 4:242
Fowler, Philip	25	1674	EQC 5:286
Fowler, Philip	26	1675	EQC 6:12
Fowler, Philip	30	1684	EQC 9:319
Fowler, Philip	32	1679	EQC 7:269
Fowler, Philip	33	1680	EQC 8:41
Fowler, Philip	33	1682	EQC 8:280
Fowler, Philip	33	1682	EQC 8:283
Fowler, Philip	35	1684	EQC 9:175
Fowler, Philip	35	1684	EQC 9:179
Fowler, Philip	35	1684	EQC 9:189
Fowler, Philip	36	1683	EQC 9:223
Fowler, Philip	36	1683	EQC 9:225

Fowler, Philip	37	1685	EQC 9:463
Fowler, Philip	37	nd	SJC 162153
Fowler, Philip	44	nd	SJC 2820
Fowler, Philip	80	1671/2	SJC 1102
Fowler, Thomas	20	1686	EQC 9:600
Fowler, Thomas	26	1662	EQC 2:381
Fowler, Thomas	33	1669	EQC 4:119
Fowler, Thomas	37	1673	EQC 5:183
Fowler, Thomas	39	1674	EQC 5:401
Fowler, Thomas	40	1676	EQC 6:160
Fox, Ann	40	1681	EQC 8:191
Fox, Jabez	29	1677	MCC folio 78
Fox, Jabez	34	1682	MCC folio 101
Fox, Jabez	34	1682	MCC folio 98
Fox, Susanna	50	1691	MCC folio 145
Fox, Thomas	70	1677	MCC folio 76
Fox, Thomas	75	1682	MCC folio 101
Fox, William	30	1679	SJC 1793
Foxwell, John	30	1669	SJC 1046
Foxwell, Philip	17	1668	SJC 1046
Foxwell, Philip	32	1684	SJC 2268
Foy, Nathaniel	35	1685	MCC folio 120
Foye, John	28	1697	SJC 4383
Frances, Stephen	40	1684	MCC folio 114
Francis, Alice	57	1666	MCC folio 42
Francis, John	33	1686	MCC folio 120
Francis, John	38	1686	MCC folio 127
Francis, Mary	27	nd	SJC 2941
Franklin, Henry	29	nd	SJC 2756
Franklin, Henry	30	1691	SJC 2629
Franklin, William	18	1695	SJC 3123g
Franks, John	20	1684	SJC 2273
Franks, John	32	1669	EQC 4:100
Frary, Theophilus	45	1675	SJC 1405
Frary, Theophilus	49	1678	SJC 1908
Frary, Theophilus	50	1679	SJC 1908
Frary, Theophilus	54	1683	SJC 2145
Frary, Theophilus	60	1691/2	SJC 98524
Frasee, Thomas	33	1679	EQC 7:263
Fraser, Collins	22	1684	EQC 9:237
Frayle, Samuel	27	1679	EQC 7:166
Frayle, Samuel	34	1682	EQC 9:21
Frayle, Samuel	34	1683	EQC 9:19
Freak, John	33	1669/70	SD 6:155
Freake, John	30	1665	SJC 705
Freake, John	31	1666	SJC 828
Freake, John	32	1668	SJC 911
Freame, Thomas	30	1680	EQC 8:37
Freeman, Joseph	36	1681	MCC folio 93
Freezes, James	27	1668	SJC 924
Freezes, James	37	1678	EQC 7:157
Freezes, James	38	1679	EQC 8:37
Freezes, James	40	1682	EQC 8:353
Freezes, James	40	1682	EQC 8:429

French, Edward	22	1694	SJC 3150
French, Hannah	15	1682	EQC 8:330
French, Hannah	36	1677	SJC 1689
French, Jacob	19	1660	MCC folio 25
French, John	15	1685	SJC 2354
French, John	40	1673	MCC folio 62
French, John	48	1682	EQC 8:329
French, John	52	1685	MCC folio 116
French, John	52	1685	SJC 2327
French, Philip	33	1671	SD 7:196
French, Richard	27	1652/3	SJC 168
French, Stephen	34	1694	SJC 3113
French, Stephen	52	1691/2	SJC 2650
French, Thomas	22	1658	EQC 2:140
French, Thomas	32	1667	EQC 3:398
French, Thomas	47	1683	EQC 9:16
French, Thomas	48	1684	EQC 9:191
Friend, Anna	22	1680	EQC 7:401
Friend, Hannah	20	1679	EQC 7:238
Friend, James	39	1681	EQC 8:146
Friend, James	40	1681	EQC 8:162
Frink, John	26	1668	EQC 4:15
Frink, John	26	1668	EQC 4:8
Frink, John	27	1668	EQC 5:416
Friyll [Frizzell?], Samuel	33	1682	EQC 8:394
Frost, Ephraim	34	1682	MCC folio 101
Frost, Ephraim	38	1685	MCC folio 116
Frost, Ephraim	43	1690	MCC folio 132
Frost, Ephraim	43	1690	MCC folio 156
Frost, Ephraim	43	1691	MCC folio 146
Frost, Ephraim	43	1691	MCC folio 163
Frost, Ephraim	43	1691	MCC folio 173
Frost, George	35	1675	MCC folio 69
Frost, Hannah	28	1673	MCC folio 62
Frost, James	18	1683	MCC folio 108
Frost, James	30	1677	MCC folio 77
Frost, John	33	1670	EQC 4:325
Frost, Joseph	36	1677	MCC folio 78
Frost, Joseph	40	1678	MCC folio 84
Frost, Joseph	43	1683	MCC folio 90
Frost, Joseph	51	1691	MCC folio 150
Frost, Nicholas	28	1676	SJC 1526
Frost, Samuel	30	1670	MCC folio 54
Frothingham, Nathaniel	32	1674	MCC folio 66
Frothingham, Peter	38	1674	MCC folio 66
Frothingham, Ruth	25	1674	MCC folio 66
Frothingham, Samuel	25	1674	MCC folio 66
Frothingham, Samuel	31	1679	MCC folio 185
Frothingham, Samuel	31	1679	MCC folio 83
Frothingham, Samuel	33	1681	MCC folio 102
Frothingham, Samuel	34	1682	MCC folio 100
Froud, James	30	1666	SJC 762
Fry, George	58	1673/4	SD 8:392
Fryer, George	23	1667	SD 5:181

Fryer, Nathaniel	40	1668	SJC 983
Fryer, Nathaniel	51	1676	SJC 1592
Fuller, Anne	79	1662	EQC 2:429
Fuller, Benjamin	19	1684	EQC 9:341
Fuller, Benjamin	22	1680	EQC 7:424
Fuller, Benjamin	25	1685	EQC 9:483
Fuller, Edward	28	1684	EQC 9:340
Fuller, Elisha	25	1684	EQC 9:340
Fuller, Elisha	25	1684	EQC 9:340
Fuller, Elisha	25	1684	EQC 9:341
Fuller, Elizabeth	17	1673	EQC 5:230
Fuller, James	14	1659	EQC 2:185
Fuller, James	22	1668	EQC 4:4
Fuller, James	22	1668	EQC 4:84
Fuller, James	23	1670	EQC 4:253
Fuller, James	25	1674	EQC 5:319
Fuller, James	25	1674	EQC 5:321
Fuller, James	47	1695	SJC 3223
Fuller, James	48	1695	SJC 3230
Fuller, John	23	1671	MCC folio 56
Fuller, John	23	1671	MCC folio 58
Fuller, John	24	1668	EQC 4:3
Fuller, John	30	1651	EQC 1:241
Fuller, John	30	1679	MCC folio 84
Fuller, John	33	1681	MCC folio 95
Fuller, John	39	1660	EQC 2:199
Fuller, John	40	1656	MCC folio 12
Fuller, John	46	1664	MCC folio 36
Fuller, John	50	1671	EQC 4:384
Fuller, John	53	1673	MCC folio 64
Fuller, John	56	1671	MCC folio 56
Fuller, John	56	1671	MCC folio 56
Fuller, John	56	1672	MCC folio 59
Fuller, John	56	1672	MCC folio 60
Fuller, John	60	1680	SJC 1973
Fuller, John	64	1685	SJC 2340
Fuller, Jonathan	27	1679	MCC folio 84
Fuller, Jonathan	31	1681	MCC folio 95
Fuller, Joseph	30	1682	MCC folio 100
Fuller, Nathaniel	40	1695	SJC 3228
Fuller, Susan	17	1668	EQC 4:4
Fuller, Susannah	19	1668	EQC 4:84
Fuller, Thomas	17	1674	EQC 5:321
Fuller, Thomas	17	1674	EQC 5:414
Fuller, Thomas	58	1674	SJC 1397
Fuller, Thomas	58	1684	EQC 9:312
Fuller, Thomas	66	1685	MCC folio 115
Fulsham, Israel	25	1671	SJC 1078
Fulsham, Israel	30	1671	SJC 1078
Fulsham, Mary	54	1671	SJC 1100
Fulsham, Nathaniel	27	1671	SJC 1078
Fulsham, Peter	22	1671	SJC 1078
Fulsham, Samuel	32	1671/2	SJC 1100
Funnell, John	57	1664	EQC 3:217

Funnell, John	63	1669/70	SJC 1009
Furbush, John	34	1661	EQC 2:291
Furbush, John	40	1667	EQC 3:314
Furbush, John	40	1669	EQC 4:145
Furbush, John	40	1670	EQC 4:255
Furbush, John	40	1671	EQC 4:412
Furgeson, Richard	17	1683	MCC folio 103
Furman, Thomas	40	1679	EQC 7:167
Furnace, Ann	30	1665	SJC 28948
Furnace, Ann	30	1665	SJC 728
Furnen, William	26	1683	EQC 9:5
Gage, Daniel	30	1669	EQC 4:117
Gage, John	50	1659	EQC 2:169
Gage, John	58	1662	EQC 2:365
Gage, Josiah	21	1669	EQC 4:117
Gage, Josiah	28	1677	EQC 6:253
Gage, Josiah	32	1680	EQC 8:16
Gage, Josiah	35	1683	EQC 9:8
Gage, Josiah	37	1686	EQC 9:603
Gage, Josiah	39	1687	EQC WPA 47-27-3
Gage, Josiah	39	1687	EQC WPA 47-28-3
Gage, Nathaniel	20	1665	EQC 3:228
Gage, Nathaniel	23	1669	EQC 4:159
Gage, Thomas	37	1694	SJC 2920
Gaines, Mary	40	1680	EQC 7:372
Gale, Amberus	44	1672	EQC 5:110
Gale, Bartholomew	25	1666	EQC 3:376
Galley, John	70	1676	EQC 6:147
Galley, John	78	1683	EQC 9:150
Gallison, Clement	26	1683	EQC 9:57
Gallop, Mary	20	1671	SJC 1179
Gallop, Samuel	36	1664	SJC 746
Galloway, Hugh	22	1679	EQC 7:251
Gammig, John	37	1680	EQC 8:90
Ganson, Benjamin	36	1677	EQC 6:354
Gardiner, Anna	32	1658	MCC folio 17
Gardiner, Hannah	19	1675	MCC folio 71
Gardiner, Hannah	19	1675	SJC 1581
Gardiner, Hannah	19	1676	MCC folio 72
Gardiner, Henry	17	1676	MCC folio 71
Gardiner, Isaac	50	1670	SJC 1016
Gardiner, John	21	1676	MCC folio 72
Gardiner, John	28	1685	SJC 2354
Gardiner, John	45	1670	EQC 4:286
Gardiner, Peter	45	1665	SJC 680
Gardiner, Rachel	18	1681	SJC 2010
Gardiner, Richard	39	1658	MCC folio 17
Gardiner, Richard	40	1661	MCC folio 27
Gardiner, Richard	42	1662	MCC folio 35
Gardiner, Richard	52	1672	MCC folio 59
Gardiner, Richard	52	1673	MCC folio 62
Gardiner, Richard	52	1673	MCC folio 65
Gardiner, Richard	52	1674	MCC folio 66
Gardiner, Samuel	40	1667	EQC 3:419

Gardiner, Samuel	43	1670	EQC 4:286
Gardiner, Samuel	45	1672	EQC 5:111
Gardiner, Samuel	46	nd	SJC 2818
Gardiner, Samuel	48	1677	EQC 6:243
Gardiner, Samuel	50	1680	EQC 7:347
Gardiner, Samuel	50	1680	EQC 7:389
Gardiner, Samuel	50	1680	EQC 7:389
Gardiner, Samuel	53	1681	EQC 8:108
Gardiner, Samuel	59	nd	SJC 2770
Gardiner, Sarah	20	1689	SJC 2536
Gardiner, Susannah	20	1681	SJC 2010
Gardiner, Susannah	33	1681	SJC 3126
Gardiner, Thomas	17	1661	EQC 2:320
Gardiner, Thomas	23	1667	SJC 905
Gardiner, Thomas	30	1680	EQC 7:389
Gardiner, Thomas	30	1680	EQC 7:390
Gardiner, Thomas	38	1684	EQC 9:183
Gardiner, Thomas	47	1665	SJC 680
Gardiner, Thomas	50	1668	SJC 905
Gardiner, Thomas	56	1672	SJC 1221
Gardiner, Thomas	69	1661	EQC 2:321
Gardner, Samuel	50	1680	EQC 7:390
Gardner, Samuel	59	1685/6	EQC WPA 46-23-2
Gare, Deborah	33	1680	EQC 8:22
Garfield, Benjamin	35	1679	MCC folio 84
Garfield, Benjamin	41	1684	MCC folio 110
Garfield, Benjamin	52	1695	MCC folio 179
Garfield, Edward	17	1681	MCC folio 95
Garfield, Edward	94	1670	SJC 2997
Garfield, Joseph	30	1668	MCC folio 45
Garfield, Joseph	30	1668	MCC folio 50
Garfield, Joseph	47	1685	MCC folio 114
Garman, Jane	25	1694	SJC 4104
Garrard, James	30	1672	SJC 1135
Gary, Stephen	28	1679	MCC folio 83
Gary, Steven	38	1690	MCC folio 137
Gaskill, Samuel	57	nd	SJC 2770
Gates, Mary	15	1691	MCC folio 151
Gates, Sarah	17	1691	MCC folio 151
Gates, Sarah	46	1691	MCC folio 151
Gates, Stephen	44	1678	MCC folio 80
Gates, Stephen	57	1691	MCC folio 151
Gates, Stephen	69	1673	MCC folio 57
Gatliffe, Jonathan	16	1684/5	MCC folio 113
Gatliffe, Jonathan	16	1684/5	SJC 2331
Gaud, John	33	nd	SJC 3547
Gay, Hugh	19	1681	EQC 8:194
Gay, Hugh	21	1683	EQC 9:89
Gay, Samuel	28	1667	SJC 830
Geake, George	31	1664	EQC 3:155
Geare, Deborah	26	1680	EQC 8:18
Geare, John	40	1695	SJC 3316
Geare, Thomas	33	1679	EQC 7:293
Geare, Triphenie	72	1674	EQC 5:311

Gedney, Bartholomew	38	1678	EQC 6:438
Gedney, Bartholomew	38	1678	EQC 7:33
Gedney, Bartholomew	38	1678	EQC 7:56
Gedney, John	64	1668	EQC 4:53
Geerish, Thomas	16	1658	MCC folio 17
Gell, John	40	1662	EQC 2:411
Gendall, Walter	35	1676	SJC 1526
George, Elizabeth	13	1690	MCC folio 139
George, Elizabeth	29	1669	SJC 1022
George, Elizabeth	35	1690	MCC folio 139
George, James	60	1693	SJC 3039
George, John	24	1678	MCC folio 185
George, Richard	50	1668	EQC 4:31
George, Richard	58	1676	SJC 1569
George, Richard	63	1683	EQC 9:45
George, Samuel	20	1695	SJC 3148
George, Thomas	52	1695	MCC folio 204
Gerrard, Andrew	26	1690	MCC folio 135
Gerrish, Benjamin	24	1678	EQC 7:245
Gerrish, Elizabeth	22	1676	EQC 6:125
Gerrish, Elizabeth	22	1676	EQC 6:148
Gerrish, Elizabeth	22	1676	EQC 6:149
Gerrish, Joseph	29	1679	EQC 7:236
Gerrish, Moses	20	1676	EQC 6:125
Gerrish, Moses	20	1676	EQC 6:149
Gerrish, Moses	20	1676	EQC 6:164
Gerrish, Moses	22	1678	EQC 6:444
Gerrish, Moses	23	1678	EQC 7:156
Gerrish, Moses	23	1679	EQC 7:224
Gerrish, Moses	26	1682	EQC 8:245
Gerrish, Moses	28	1684	EQC 9:237
Gerrish, Moses	29	1684	EQC 9:349
Gerrish, William	27	1675/6	SCC 662
Gerrish, William	64	1685	EQC 9:475
Getch, Thomas	30	1664	EQC 3:217
Getchell, Bethia	13	1684	EQC 9:279
Getchell, Dorcas	50	nd	SJC 2772
Getchell, Elizabeth	26	1683	EQC 9:148
Getchell, Elizabeth	26	1683/4	SJC 2244
Getchell, Elizabeth	26	1684	EQC 9:240
Getchell, James	60	1672	EQC 5:42
Getchell, Jeremiah	27	1675	EQC 6:78
Getchell, Jeremiah	30	1684	EQC 9:240
Getchell, Jeremiah	35	1683	EQC 9:148
Getchell, John	25	1670	EQC 4:282
Getchell, John	50	1670	EQC 4:282
Getchell, John	53	1669	EQC 4:145
Getchell, John	53	1669	EQC 4:156
Getchell, John	60	1679	EQC 7:298
Getchell, John	64	1677	EQC 6:363
Getchell, John	76	1684	EQC 9:278
Getchell, Jonathan	34	1680	EQC 7:422
Getchell, Jonathan	34	1680	EQC 7:423
Getchell, Joseph	26	1678	EQC 7:113

Getchell, Joseph	26	1678	EQC 7:141
Getchell, Joseph	28	1679	EQC 7:330
Getchell, Joseph	28	1680	EQC 7:346
Getchell, Joseph	28	1680	EQC 7:423
Getchell, Joseph	28	1680	EQC 8:13
Getchell, Joseph	30	1681	EQC 8:108
Getchell, Joseph	30	1681	EQC 8:109
Getchell, Joseph	30	1681	EQC 8:127
Getchell, Joseph	30	1681	EQC 8:174
Getchell, Joseph	32	1681	EQC 8:188
Getchell, Joseph	33	1683	EQC 9:110
Getchell, Samuel	30	1669	EQC 4:162
Getchell, Samuel	40	1680	EQC 8:43
Getchell, Samuel	40	1682	EQC 8:378
Getchell, Wiborough	50	1669	EQC 4:115
Getchell, Wiborough	50	1670	EQC 4:313
Getchell, Wiborough	65	1681	EQC 8:145
Getchell, Wiborough	66	1680	EQC 7:423
Getchell, Wiborough	67	1679	EQC 7:298
Getchell, Wiborough	70	1682	EQC 8:345
Getchell, Wiborough	70	1683	EQC 9:148
Getchell, Wiborough	70	1683	EQC 9:63
Getchell, Wiborough	70	1684	EQC 9:280
Geyles, Eleazer	45	1686	EQC WPA 46-24-2
Ghent, Thomas	37	1679	SJC 1833
Ghent, Thomas	37	1679/80	SCC 1129
Gibard, Martha	21	1670	EQC 4:242
Gibbes, Mathew	58	1673	MCC folio 64
Gibbon, Edmund	26	1667	SJC 911
Gibbs, Benjamin	36	1672	SJC 1162
Gibbs, Benjamin	36	1673	EQC 5:189
Gibbs, Benjamin	37	1672	SJC 1341
Gibbs, Ebenezer	36	1673	MCC folio 65
Gibbs, Elizabeth	24	1676	EQC 6:151
Gibbs, Matthew	58	1673	SJC 1214
Gibbs, Robert	32	1665/6	SJC 2233
Gibbs, Robert	33	1672	EQC 5:8
Gibbs, Robert	35	1668	SJC 911
Gibson, James	22	1681	MCC folio 95
Gibson, Samuel	30	1677	MCC folio 78
Gibson, Samuel	38	1685	MCC folio 113
Gibson, Sarah	15	1684	MCC folio 111
Giddings, George	40	1658	EQC 2:142
Giddings, George	59	1667	EQC 3:396
Giddings, James	27	1668	EQC 4:69
Giddings, James	40	1684	EQC 9:175
Giddings, John	21	1659	EQC 2:143
Giddings, John	21	1659	EQC 2:172
Giddings, John	46	1684	EQC 9:173
Giddings, Samuel	25	1670	EQC 4:218
Giddings, Samuel	39	1683	EQC 9:123
Giddings, Samuel	39	1684	EQC 9:174
Giddings, Sarah	40	1684	EQC 9:173
Giddings, Susannah	34	1684	EQC 9:207

Giddings, Thomas	23	1659	EQC 2:172
Giddings, Thomas	25	1658	EQC 2:142
Giddings, Thomas	33	1671	EQC 4:422
Giddings, Thomas	34	1672	EQC 5:13
Giddings, Thomas	37	1673	EQC 5:228
Gidney, Bartholomew	30	1670	EQC 4:265
Gidney, Susanna	37	1683	EQC 9:49
Gifford, John	26	nd	SJC 3525
Gifford, John	40	1665	SD 4:328
Gifford, John	60	1684	SJC 2391
Gifford, Samuel	26	1693/4	SJC 2989
Gifford, William	40	1693	SJC 2989
Gifford, William	40	nd	SJC 27518
Gilbert, Ann	22	1681	EQC 8:194
Gilbert, Ann	22	1681	EQC 8:227
Gilbert, Hannah	24	1670	EQC 4:264
Gilbert, John	17	1674	EQC 5:310
Gilbert, Martha	19	1668	EQC 4:84
Gilbert, Martha	20	1680	EQC 7:374
Gilbert, Martha	20	1680	SJC 1894
Gilbert, William	38	1683	MCC folio 106
Gilbird, Charles	25	1684	EQC 9:287
Gilbird, John	16	1674	EQC 5:267
Gilbird, John	17	1674	EQC 5:276
Gilbird, John	20	1677	EQC 6:277
Gile, Sarah	16	1674	EQC 5:397
Giles, Thomas	17	1695	MCC folio 198
Gill, John	60	nd	SJC 2878
Gill, Obadiah	49	1696	MCC folio 211
Gill, Thomas	30	1678	SJC 1722
Gill, Thomas	47	1682	SJC 3349
Gill, Thomas	61	1677	SJC 1633
Gillam, Benjamin	45	1653	EQC 2:94
Gillam, Benjamin	45	nd	SJC 225
Gillam, Benjamin	57	1661	SJC 418
Gillam, Benjamin	57	1662	SJC 874
Gillam, Joseph	34	1677	EQC 6:329
Gilligan, Alexander	80	1684	EQC 9:240
Gilligan, Elizabeth	26	1682	EQC 8:340
Gilligan, Frances	23	1666	EQC 3:420
Gilman, Elizabeth	30	1671	SJC 1100
Gilman, Elizabeth	33	1671	SJC 1100
Gilman, John	27	1678	EQC 6:414
Gilman, Moses	46	1678	EQC 6:423
Gimble, John	23	1686	SJC 2424
Girdler, Deborah	34	1681	EQC 8:104
Girdler, Deborah	36	1685	EQC 9:468
Gittings, George	57	1668	SJC 931
Gittings, George	60	1670	SJC 999
Gittings, James	27	1668	SJC 897
Glading, John	37	1678	EQC 7:157
Glasier, Goodwife	21	1662	MCC folio 34
Glasier, John	19	1656	MCC folio 11
Glazer, John	43	1676	MCC folio 71

Glazier, Elizabeth	33	1676	MCC folio 71
Gleason, John	20	1668	MCC folio 47
Gleason, John	27	1671	MCC folio 59
Gleason, Joseph	18	1660	MCC folio 25
Gleason, Joseph	40	1682	MCC folio 106
Gleason, Susanna	55	1671	SCC 115
Gleason, Susanna	55	nd	SJC 1052
Gleason, Susanna	58	1674	MCC folio 67
Gleason, Thomas	23	1664	MCC folio 36
Gleason, Thomas	40	1658	MCC folio 17
Gleason, Thomas	52	1662	MCC folio 32
Gleason, Thomas	52	1663	MCC folio 35
Gleason, Thomas	61	1670	MCC folio 54
Gleason, Thomas	66	1676	SJC 1799
Gleason, William	22	nd	SJC 1052
Gleason, William	23	1671	MCC folio 59
Gleason, William	35	1685	MCC folio 120
Glover, John	21	1656	EQC 2:12
Glover, John	27	1665	EQC 3:276
Glover, John	30	1669	EQC 4:102
Glover, John	36	1664	SJC 648
Glover, John	36	1673	EQC 5:171
Glover, John	36	1673	SJC 1226
Glover, John	53	1681	SJC 162210
Glover, Mary	20	1684	SJC 2246
Glover, Stephen	56	1679	SJC 2011
Glover, Steven	38	1663	EQC 3:41
Glover, William	22	1686	EQC WPA 46-132-2
Gloyd, John	25	1678	EQC 7:124
Gloyd, John	25	1678	EQC 7:135
Gloyd, John	25	1678	EQC 7:147
Gloyd, John	25	1678	EQC 7:89
Gloyd, Mary	21	1678	EQC 7:147
Goage, Joane	21	1677	SJC 1682
Goble, Alice	17	1690	MCC folio 145
Goble, Daniel	25	1690	MCC folio 145
Goble, John	43	1667	SD 5:181
Goble, Mary	14	1673	MCC folio 62
Goble, Thomas	19	1673	MCC folio 62
Goble, Thomas	24	1678	MCC folio 82
Goble, Thomas	29	1684	MCC folio 107
Goble, Thomas	37	1668	MCC folio 50
Goble, Thomas	40	1673	MCC folio 62
Goble, Thomas	45	1678	MCC folio 81
Goble, Thomas	53	1684	MCC folio 107
Goble, Thomas	53	1684	MCC folio 108
Goddan, William	65	1663	MCC folio 35
Goddard, Giles	32	1680	SJC 1916
Goddard, John	23	1665	MCC folio 39
Goden, Henry	32	1674	MCC folio 63
Godew, William	65	1663	MCC folio 35
Godfrey, Andrew	22	1678	EQC 7:156
Godfrey, John	27	1676	SCC 743
Godfrey, John	27	1676	SJC 1498

Godfrey, John	30	1661	EQC 2:288
Godfrey, John	40	1660	EQC 2:250
Godfrey, Mary	39	1675	EQC 6:71
Godfrey, Mary	41	1676	EQC 6:204
Godfrey, Peter	30	1662	EQC 2:355
Godfrey, Peter	40	1671	EQC 4:382
Godfrey, Peter	40	1675	EQC 6:71
Godfrey, Peter	48	1678	EQC 7:156
Godfrey, Samuel	20	1685	SJC 2346
Godsoe, Elizabeth	24	1684	EQC 9:281
Godsoe, William	29	1681	EQC 8:110
Godsoe, William	29	1681	EQC 8:71
Godsoe, William	30	1681	EQC 8:215
Godsoe, William	34	1684	EQC 9:250
Godsoe, William	34	1684	EQC 9:276
Goff, Abiah	16	1662	MCC folio 28
Goff, Anthony	29	1685	MCC folio 120
Goff, Philip	39	1690	MCC folio 136
Goff, Samuel	33	1663	MCC folio 35
Goff, Samuel	49	1677	MCC folio 78
Goff, Samuel	64	1691	MCC folio 146
Goff, Samuel	64	1691	MCC folio 156
Goff, Samuel	64	1691	MCC folio 173
Goffe, Samuel	27	1655	MCC folio 12
Gold, Mary	21	1682	EQC 8:353
Gold, Nathan	64	1682	EQC 8:374
Goldthwait, Samuel	37	1676	EQC 6:193
Golifer, Anthony	64	1685	SD 13:408
Gooch, Lydia	28	1672	SJC 1126
Good, Elizabeth	28	1686	MCC folio 127
Goodale, Robert	89	1679	EQC 7:295
Goodale, Zachariah	45	1685	EQC 9:439
Goodale, Zachariah	45	1685	SJC 2285
Goodale, Zachary	30	1676	EQC 6:191
Goodale, Zachary	40	1679	EQC 7:295
Goodhue, Joseph	38	1677	EQC 6:276
Goodhue, Joseph	43	1683	EQC 9:121
Goodhue, Joseph	44	1684	EQC 9:210
Goodhue, Joseph	55	1695	SJC 3228
Goodhue, Sarah	37	1677	EQC 6:277
Goodhue, William	15	1658	EQC 2:139
Goodhue, William	37	1684	EQC 9:174
Goodhue, William	40	1685	EQC 9:464
Goodhue, William	40	1685	SJC 2311
Goodhue, William	56	1672	EQC 5:38
Goodhue, William	72	1685	EQC 9:463
Goodin, Timothy	19	1684	MCC folio 107
Goodin, William	69	1665	MCC folio 38
Gooding, Jane	35	1685	MCC folio 114
Goodman, Richard	23	1680	SJC 1909
Goodridge, Benjamin	36	1678	EQC 7:157
Goodridge, Jeremiah	27	1664	EQC 3:196
Goodridge, Jeremiah	42	1678	EQC 7:157
Goodridge, Jeremiah	47	1684	EQC 9:220

Goodridge, Jeremiah	50	1686	EQC WPA 46-126-1
Goodridge, Joseph	39	1678	EQC 7:157
Goodridge, Joseph	44	1684	EQC 9:327
Goodridge, Joseph	59	1697	SJC 3784
Goodridge, Mary	46	1686	EQC WPA 46-121-1
Goodridge, Robert	26	1672	MCC folio 65
Goodridge, Robert	26	1672	SJC 1221
Goodridge, Thomas	41	1673	SCC 405
Goodridge, Thomas	41	1673	SJC 1270
Goodridge, William	18	1684	EQC 9:220
Goodwin, Christopher	35	1682	MCC folio 99
Goodwin, Christopher	40	1691	MCC folio 157
Goodwin, Edard	48	1668	SJC 924
Goodwin, Edward	39	1669	SJC 924
Goodwin, Marcey	25	1678	MCC folio 78
Goodwin, Richard	40	1695	SJC 3148
Goodwin, William	20	1686	EQC WPA 46-20-2
Goodwin, William	20	nd	SJC 2770
Goodwin, William	64	1662	SJC 789
Goodwin, William	65	1663	MCC folio 35
Goose, John	36	1679	SJC 1819
Goose, William	36	1668	MCC folio 44
Gordin, Alexander	40	1678	EQC 7:6
Gore, John	31	1666	EQC 3:302
Gorman, Jane	25	1694	SJC 4104
Gorum, John	45	1666	SJC 857
Gory, Mary	50	1676	EQC 6:190
Gott, Charles	30	1669	EQC 4:97
Gott, Charles	36	1674	EQC 5:309
Gott, Charles	40	1679	EQC 8:160
Gott, Charles	40	1680	SJC 1967
Gott, Charles	41	1680	EQC 8:22
Gott, Charles	41	1680	EQC 8:27
Gott, Charles	41	1680	EQC 8:9
Gott, Charles	41	1680	SJC 1967
Gott, Charles	42	1681	EQC 8:163
Gott, Charles	45	1683	EQC 9:131
Gott, Daniel	14	1682	EQC 8:296
Gott, Daniel	24	1669	EQC 4:97
Gott, Daniel	34	1679	MCC folio 86
Gott, Daniel	36	1682	EQC 8:258
Gott, Daniel	36	1682	EQC 8:296
Gott, Elizabeth	22	1668	EQC 4:9
Gott, Elizabeth	36	1682	EQC 8:296
Gott, widow	66	1668	EQC 4:9
Gould, Daniel	20	1676	MCC folio 72
Gould, Daniel	20	1676	MCC folio 74
Gould, Henry	30	1678	EQC 6:408
Gould, Joanna	67	1676	MCC folio 72
Gould, Johanna	50	1658	MCC folio 17
Gould, John	20	1676	SJC 1562
Gould, John	26	1676	MCC folio 72
Gould, John	26	1676	MCC folio 74
Gould, John	28	1665	EQC 3:259

Gould, John	36	1698	SJC 3778
Gould, John	40	1658	EQC 2:130
Gould, John	47	1658	EQC 2:111
Gould, John	47	1658	MCC folio 17
Gould, John	48	1658	EQC 2:112
Gould, John	60	nd	SJC 3582a
Gould, John	66	1676	MCC folio 72
Gould, Samuel	21	1679	MCC folio 87
Gould, Sarah	35	1677	EQC 6:353
Gould, Sarah	38	1679	EQC 7:299
Gould, Sarah	39	1680	EQC 8:2
Gould, Sarah	39	1680	SJC 1951
Gould, Thomas	21	1680	SJC 162193
Gould, Thomas	25	nd	SJC 2770
Gould, Thomas	32	1693	SJC 3125
Gould, Thomas	45	1652	MCC folio 7
Gould, Thomas	48	1678	EQC 7:90
Gould, Thomas	50	1680	EQC 7:426
Gould, Thomas	53	1683	EQC 9:21
Gould, Zacheus	72	1661	EQC 2:268
Goulding, Peter	18	1681	SJC 2065
Goulding, Peter	33	1665	SJC 714
Goulding, Peter	48	1683	SJC 2224
Goult, Deborah	15	1660	EQC 2:214
Goult, Rebecca	19	1660	EQC 2:214
Goult, Sarah	13	1660	EQC 2:214
Gourding, Lot	32	1679	EQC 7:302
Gourding, Lot	32	1679	EQC 7:303
Gourding, Lott	40	1690	SJC 2572
Gove, Edward	28	1667	EQC 3:452
Gove, Edward	38	1678	EQC 6:392
Gove, Edward	38	1678	EQC 7:6
Gove, Edward	38	1678	EQC 7:92
Gove, John	48	1680	MCC folio 101
Gove, John	50	1685	MCC folio 119
Gove, John	60	1691	MCC folio 146
Gove, John	60	1691	MCC folio 163
Gove, Mary	40	1686	MCC folio 127
Gover, Tamsin	35	1676	EQC 6:149
Gover, Tomasin	37	1677	SCC 805
Grafes, Samuel	26	1683	EQC 9:113
Grafton, John	15	1679	EQC 7:307
Grafton, John	17	1680	SJC 1953
Granger, John	24	1678	EQC 7:156
Granger, John	26	1681	EQC 8:81
Grant, Abigail	26	1661	MCC folio 26
Grant, Caleb	32	1672	MCC folio 61
Grant, Christopher	23	1672	MCC folio 61
Grant, Christopher	26	1677	MCC folio 74
Grant, Christopher	48	1658	MCC folio 17
Grant, Christopher	60	1674	MCC folio 66
Grant, Edward	35	1667	SJC 909
Grant, Edward	40	1673	SJC 1216
Grant, Elizabeth	18	1685	SJC 2370

Grant, Fran.	42	1679	EQC 7:307
Grant, Johanna	45	1672	EQC 5:8
Grant, John	22	1681	EQC 8:92
Grant, John	50	1667	MCC folio 43
Grant, Joseph	20	1669	MCC folio 52
Grant, Joseph	20	1672	MCC folio 61
Grant, Joseph	23	1671	MCC folio 56
Grant, Robert	35	1674	MCC folio 63
Grant, Thomas	28	1657	MCC folio 20
Grant, Thomas	30	1664	EQC 3:142
Grant, Thomas	30	1667	EQC 3:388
Graves, Abraham	22	1673	EQC 5:128
Graves, Benjamin	30	1679	MCC folio 87
Graves, Elizabeth	30	1673	EQC 5:128
Graves, Elizabeth	37	1677	EQC 6:300
Graves, Elizabeth	37	1678	EQC 7:24
Graves, Elizabeth	39	1680	EQC 7:360
Graves, Francis	26	1684	EQC 9:174
Graves, Johanna	22	1682	EQC 8:281
Graves, John	24	1675	EQC 6:86
Graves, John	24	1675	SJC 162144
Graves, Joseph	26	1668	MCC folio 50
Graves, Mark	35	1657	EQC 7:128
Graves, Mark	39	1662	EQC 2:412
Graves, Mark	45	1665	EQC 3:274
Graves, Mark	48	1671	EQC 4:338
Graves, Mark	49	1673	EQC 5:128
Graves, Mark	55	1677	EQC 6:300
Graves, Mark	55	1678	EQC 7:24
Graves, Mary	15	1670	EQC 4:258
Graves, Mary	38	1691	MCC folio 141
Graves, Richard	50	1663	SJC 573
Graves, Richard	60	1680	MCC folio 91
Graves, Samuel	38	1660	EQC 2:248
Graves, Samuel	38	1666	EQC 3:304
Graves, Samuel	38	1666	EQC 3:373
Graves, Samuel	54	1681	EQC 8:153
Gray, Abigail	21	1677	EQC 6:298
Gray, Abigail	24	1679	EQC 7:302
Gray, Abigail	24	1679	SJC 1826
Gray, Elizabeth	58	1685	EQC 9:524
Gray, James	22	1675	MCC folio 69
Gray, Joseph	27	1680	EQC 7:345
Gray, Joseph	27	1680	EQC 7:347
Gray, Robert	22	1680	EQC 7:330
Gray, Samuel	28	1679	EQC 7:301
Gray, Samuel	29	1680	EQC 7:401
Grealy, Philip	40	1686	EQC WPA 46-125-3
Greely, Andrew	35	1685	EQC 9:544
Greely, Andrew	52	1672	SJC 1563
Greely, Andrew	52	1679	EQC 7:288
Greely, Andrew	68	1683	EQC 9:108
Greely, Andrew	74	1692	SJC 3039
Greely, Benjamin	25	1682	EQC 8:276

Greely, Benjamin	28	1687	EQC WPA 47-28-3
Greely, John	22	1694	SJC 3150
Greely, Philip	32	1679	SJC 1796
Greely, Philip	45	1692	SJC 3152
Greely, Philip	48	1695	SJC 162371
Greely, Philip	48	1695	SJC 3782
Greely, Philip	49	1697	SJC 3485
Green, Daniel	18	1697/8	SJC 4705
Green, Edward	18	1685	MCC folio 117
Green, Henry	54	1673	SJC 1229
Green, Henry	54	1682	EQC 8:403
Green, Henry	57	1695	MCC folio 179
Green, Hester	21	1676	EQC 6:149
Green, Jacob	36	1657	MCC folio 20
Green, James	48	1659	SJC 393
Green, John	19	1664	EQC 3:211
Green, John	20	1665	EQC 3:334
Green, John	47	1684	EQC 9:182
Green, John	49	1685	MCC folio 117
Green, John	49	1685	MCC folio 118
Green, John	63	1695	MCC folio 179
Green, John	63	1696/7	MCC folio 204
Green, Nathaniel	15	1674	MCC folio 67
Green, Nathaniel	16	1676	MCC folio 71
Green, Nathaniel	22	1681	MCC folio 92
Green, Nathaniel	24	1683	MCC folio 103
Green, Nathaniel	33	1691	MCC folio 143
Green, Nathaniel	39	1667	EQC 3:466
Green, Percival	15	1676	MCC folio 71
Green, Richard	25	1695	SJC 3123b
Green, Richard	39	1667	EQC 3:465
Green, Ruth	16	1677	MCC folio 78
Green, Samuel	18	1681	MCC folio 94
Green, Samuel	20	1683	MCC folio 103
Green, Samuel	22	1685	MCC folio 113
Green, Samuel	25	1689	MCC folio 134
Green, Samuel	30	1698	MCC folio 164
Green, Samuel	76	1691	MCC folio 149
Green, William	30	1680	SJC 1956
Green, William	58	1695	MCC folio 179
Green, William	58	1695	MCC folio 204
Green, William	58	1695	SJC 3258
Green, William	60	1696/7	MCC folio 204
Greene, Abraham	16	1660	EQC 2:228
Greene, Charles	30	1680	EQC 7:336
Greene, Elizabeth	21	1661	MCC folio 29
Greene, Henry	38	1664	MCC folio 36
Greene, Henry	40	1660	EQC 2:230
Greene, Henry	46	1673	MCC folio 65
Greene, Isaac	15	1660	EQC 2:228
Greene, Jacob	30	1653	MCC folio 7
Greene, Jacob	35	1660	MCC folio 25
Greene, Jacob	36	1657	MCC folio 20
Greene, James	50	1660	MCC folio 25

Greene, James	50	1660	MCC folio 29
Greene, James	60	1660	MCC folio 26
Greene, Johanna	59	1659	EQC 2:172
Greene, John	17	1666	EQC 3:333
Greene, John	20	1666	EQC 3:330
Greene, John	54	1682	EQC 8:403
Greene, Mary	32	1670	MCC folio 55
Greene, Nathaniel	50	1672	MCC folio 61
Greene, Richard	34	1653	EQC 2:95
Greene, Thomas	62	1662	MCC folio 32
Greene, William	20	1672	MCC folio 59
Greene, William	35	1670	MCC folio 55
Greenland, John	45	1690	MCC folio 138
Greenland, John	50	1657	MCC folio 18
Greenland, John	60	1662	MCC folio 31
Greenland, John	60	1665	MCC folio 40
Greenland, John	60	1666	MCC folio 40
Greenland, John	60	1669	MCC folio 52
Greenleaf, Edmund	20	nd	SJC 2762
Greenleaf, Elizabeth	38	1669	EQC 4:136
Greenleaf, Enoch	42	1697	SJC 4365
Greenleaf, Enoch	50	1666	MCC folio 41
Greenleaf, John	26	1697	SJC 28619
Greenleaf, Sarah	7	nd	SJC 3562
Greenleaf, Stephen	26	1678	EQC 7:156
Greenleaf, Stephen	29	1681	EQC 8:128
Greenleaf, Stephen	30	1682	EQC 8:429
Greenleaf, Stephen	31	1683	EQC 9:92
Greenleaf, Stephen	45	1675	EQC 6:11
Greenleaf, Stephen	50	1678	EQC 7:157
Greenleaf, Stephen	50	1679	EQC 7:164
Greenleaf, Stephen	51	1680	EQC 7:387
Greenleaf, Steven	23	1653	EQC 1:277
Greenleaf, Steven	35	1664	EQC 3:187
Greenleaf, Steven	47	1676	EQC 6:165
Greenough, William	40	1667	SJC 1911
Greenough, William	43	1671	SD 7:196
Greenough, William	43	1684	MCC folio 111
Greenough, William	45	1672	SD 8:35
Greenwood, Nathaniel	40	1673	SJC 1216
Greenwood, Nathaniel	50	1682	MCC folio 101
Greggs, Steven	25	1664	EQC 3:155
Gregory, Jonas	42	1683	EQC 9:121
Gregory, Jonas	42	1683	EQC 9:122
Gregory, Jonas	56	nd	SJC 2827
Gregory, Jones	24	1682	EQC 8:309
Gregory, Richard	24	1667	SD 5:181
Grelah, Andrew	60	1683	EQC 9:109
Gretian, Dorothy	40	1680	SJC 2055
Gretian, Thomas	42	1680	SJC 2028
Gretian, Thomas	42	1680	SJC 2055
Grice, William	30	1679	EQC 7:177
Gridley, Benoni	15	1679	SJC 1833
Gridley, Benoni	15	1679/80	SCC 1129

Gridley, Benoni	21	1685?	SJC 2385
Gridley, Joseph	33	1662	SJC 508
Gridley, Joseph	35	1663	MCC folio 34
Gridley, Joseph	51	1680	SJC 2016
Gridley, Joseph	56	1685?	SJC 2388
Gridley, Mary	47	1677	SD 11:9
Gridley, Richard	59	1660	SD 3:382
Gridley, Richard	60	1662	SJC 508
Gridley, Richard	65	1667	SJC 1911
Gridley, Richard	68	1670/1	SD 7:100
Gridley, Richard	74	1674	SD 8:439
Griffen, John	24	1665	EQC 3:276
Griffin, Humphrey	53	1658	EQC 2:139
Griffin, James	33	1691	MCC folio 157
Griffin, John	20	1661	EQC 2:274
Griffin, John	24	1659	EQC 2:148
Griffin, John	28	1670	SJC 976
Griffin, John	37	1678	EQC 6:423
Griffin, Joseph	25	1679	SJC 1819
Griffin, Mary	36	1677	SJC 1707
Griffin, Matthew	30	1663	SJC 573
Griffin, Nathaniel	30	1680	EQC 8:68
Griffin, Priscilla	27	1691	MCC folio 157
Griffin, Samuel	28	1686	MCC folio 121
Griffin, Samuel	28	1686	MCC folio 128
Griffin, Sgt.	25	1685	MCC folio 118
Griffin, Shemuel	24	1669	MCC folio 50
Griffin, Thomas	17	1677	EQC 6:332
Griffing, Humphrey	53	1658	EQC 2:142
Griffing, Humphrey	53	1659	EQC 2:173
Griffing, John	24	1666	EQC 3:308
Griffing, John	28	1669	EQC 4:154
Griffing, John	30	1671	EQC 4:373
Griffing, John	37	1675	EQC 6:10
Griffing, John	40	1680	EQC 8:69
Griffing, John	42	1683	EQC 9:7
Griggs, Elizabeth	50	1675	EQC 6:78
Griggs, Joseph	43	1668	SJC 905
Griggs, Stephen	40	1679	EQC 7:307
Grimes, George	25	1677	MCC folio 77
Grimes, George	26	1674	MCC folio 66
Grimes, George	29	1678	MCC folio 80
Grimes, George	29	1679	MCC folio 87
Grimes, George	35	1685	MCC folio 120
Grimes, George	38	1684	MCC folio 107
Grimes, George	40	1685	MCC folio 120
Gross, Christopher	30	1664	SJC 746
Gross, Elizabeth	26	1680	EQC 7:371
Gross, Elizabeth	26	1680	SJC 1894
Gross, Mathew	25	1655	SD 2:166
Gross, Mercy	19	1694/5	SJC 4132
Groundell, Judith	21	1669	EQC 4:116
Grounden, Judith	18	1669	EQC 4:108
Grounden, Judith	20	1667	EQC 3:415

Grounden, Judith	23	1670	EQC 4:297
Grout, John	37	1652	MCC folio 7
Grout, John	68	1684	SD 13:344
Grout, John	80	1695	MCC folio 179
Grove, Edward	40	1666	EQC 3:380
Grove, Edward	56	1683	EQC 9:28
Grove, Hannah	19	1674	EQC 5:291
Grove, John	27	1669	EQC 4:195
Grover, Edmund	60	1660	EQC 2:220
Grover, Edmund	70	1671	EQC 4:332
Grover, Edmund	78	1678	EQC 9:54
Grover, John	43	1671	EQC 4:332
Grover, John	45	1672	EQC 5:112
Grover, John	53	1681	EQC 8:190
Grover, Lazarus	55	1696	SJC 3413
Grover, Nehemiah	30	1677	EQC 6:349
Grover, Nehemiah	38	1684	EQC 9:207
Grover, Tomasin	37	1677	SJC 1635
Grover, William	46	1668	SJC 910
Grow, John	29	1671	EQC 4:422
Guest, Thomas	79	1694	SJC 3104
Guile, John	20	1674	EQC 5:314
Guile, John	23	1678	EQC 7:157
Guile, Samuel	24	1674	EQC 5:314
Guill, Samuel	16	1665	EQC 3:277
Guinne, John	45	1682	SJC 2120
Gunnison, Elihu	21	1680	SJC 1941
Guppy, Elizabeth	72	1678	MCC folio 185
Guppy, Elizabeth	72	1679	MCC folio 83
Guppy, John	25	1674	EQC 5:360
Guppy, John	40	1663	MCC folio 35
Guppy, John	50	1667	MCC folio 43
Guppy, John	50	1670	MCC folio 54
Guppy, John	60	1678	MCC folio 185
Guppy, John	60	1679	MCC folio 83
Guppy, Reuben	60	1665	EQC 3:276
Guppy, Reuben	73	1678	EQC 7:25
Guppy, Reuben	85	1684	EQC 9:273
Guppy, Reuben	85	1684	EQC 9:344
Guppy, Reuben	86	1685	EQC 9:438
Gutterson, Elizabeth	18	1677	EQC 6:277
Guttridge, Jeremiah	47	1683	EQC 9:58
Guttridge, Robert	48	nd	SJC 2898
Guy, Hugh	18	1681	EQC 8:194
Guy, John	14	1685	MCC folio 113
Guy, John	22	1666	MCC folio 42
Gyles, Eliezer	45	nd	SJC 2770
Gyles, James	42	1668	SJC 889
Gyles, Thomas	29	1668	SJC 889
Hack, William	36	1697	SJC 3530
Hacker, Anthony	48	1657	EQC 2:29
Hackett, Rebecca	15	1685	EQC 9:534
Hackett, Sarah	18	1663	SJC 1972
Hackett, William	22	1663	SJC 612

Haddon, Jarret	63	1668	SJC 931
Haddon, Jarrett	60	1668	EQC 4:26
Haddon, Jarrett	69	1674	EQC 5:401
Hadley, John	27	1680	EQC 7:371
Hadley, Mary	18	1675	EQC 6:116
Hadsell, Charles	46	1664	SJC 746
Hage, James	54	1665	EQC 3:265
Hage, James	55	1665	EQC 3:266
Haines, Jonathan	36	1682	EQC WPA 46-10-1
Haines, Sarah	26	1682	EQC WPA 46-10-1
Haines, Thomas	32	1683	EQC 9:49
Hakes, Adam	50	1658	EQC 2:112
Hakes, Adam	50	1658	EQC 2:129
Hale, Apphia	17	1659	EQC 2:176
Hale, John	18	1680	EQC 7:422
Hale, John	21	1656	MCC folio 16
Hale, John	42	1678	EQC 7:43
Hale, John	46	1683	EQC 9:25
Hale, John	48	1683	EQC 9:108
Hale, John	48	1683	EQC 9:249
Hale, Mary	25	1681	SJC 2010
Hale, Samuel	22	1667/8	MCC folio 47
Hale, Sarah	44	1680	EQC 7:422
Hale, Thomas	25	1676	MCC folio 71
Hale, Thomas	48	1681	EQC 8:171
Hale, Thomas	67	1671	EQC 4:432
Hall, Christopher	44	1680	MCC folio 91
Hall, Elizabeth	25	1679/80	SJC 1836
Hall, George	47	1672	SJC 1163
Hall, goodwife	37	1681	EQC 8:215
Hall, Honor	21	1681	MCC folio 104
Hall, Honor	21	1681	MCC folio 97
Hall, John	18	1669	SJC 1022
Hall, John	25	1686	MCC folio 123
Hall, John	39	1668	MCC folio 45
Hall, John	50	1685?	SJC 2354
Hall, John	52	1690	MCC folio 138
Hall, John	53	1685	SJC 2354
Hall, Martha	75	1691	MCC folio 146
Hall, Martin	50	1670	SJC 1077
Hall, Nathaniel	25	1691	MCC folio 146
Hall, Nathaniel	30	1695	MCC folio 162
Hall, Paul	32	1668	SJC 873
Hall, Ralph	50	1679	MCC folio 83
Hall, Ralph	53	1672	EQC 5:99
Hall, Ralph	59	1678	EQC 7:31
Hall, Richard	42	1656	MCC folio 12
Hall, Richard	65	1685	SD 13:408
Hall, Samuel	31	1697	MCC folio 205
Hall, Sarah	33	1678	MCC folio 80
Hall, Steven	28	1668	MCC folio 45
Hall, Susanna	33	1690	MCC folio 139
Hall, Thomas	27	1679/80	SJC 1836
Hall, Thomas	27	nd	SJC 26473

Hall, Thomas	42	1700	SJC 4794
Hall, William	25	1684	SJC 2203
Hallam, John	18	1680	EQC 8:7
Halle, John	17	1678	EQC 7:157
Halle, John	42	1678	EQC 7:156
Halle, Sarah	33	1680	EQC 7:355
Halle, Sarah	43	1679	EQC 7:317
Halle, Thomas	19	1678	EQC 7:157
Halle, Thomas	45	1678	EQC 7:156
Halle, Thomas	74	1678	EQC 7:156
Hallfull, George	43	1686	EQC WPA 46-102-1
Hallowell, Richard	27	1679	SJC 1842
Halsall, George	43	1678	EQC 7:27
Halsall, George	43	1683	EQC 9:46
Halsall, George	43	1684	EQC 9:254
Halsey, George	43	1660	SJC 2103
Halsey, James	29	1673	SJC 1216
Halsey, John	40	nd	SJC 2802
Hambleton, Mary	51	1680	SJC 1958
Hamblett, Jacob	30	1686	MCC folio 123
Hamblett, Jacob	31	1677	MCC folio 76
Hamblett, Jacob	42	1685	MCC folio 117
Hamblett, Mary	26	1677	MCC folio 76
Hamblett, William	63	1677	MCC folio 78
Hamersley, Thomas	49	1669	SJC 1022
Hamilton, John	30	1666	MCC folio 40
Hamilton, John	30	1666	MCC folio 41
Hammond, Abigail	18	1677	MCC folio 74
Hammond, John	40	1673	MCC folio 63
Hammond, John	43	1673	MCC folio 62
Hammond, John	50	1677	MCC folio 77
Hammond, John	50	1678	MCC folio 81
Hammond, Lawrence	46	1684	MCC folio 185
Hammond, Lawrence	48	1686	MCC folio 122
Hammond, Sarah	35	1673	MCC folio 62
Hammond, Thomas	35	1692	MCC folio 172
Hamon, Nathaniel	20	1663	SJC 606
Hampton, Elizabeth	21	nd	SJC 818
Hampton, William	32	nd	SJC 818
Hancock, George	27	1675	MCC folio 69
Hancock, John	19	1689	SJC 2536
Hancock, Nathaniel	40	1681	MCC folio 94
Hands, John	31	1685	SJC 2391
Hanford, Nathaniel	50	1665	EQC 3:256
Hanforth, Nathaniel	54	1663	EQC 3:31
Hanforth, Nathaniel	54	1663	SJC 577
Hanforth, Nathaniel	72	1679	EQC 7:196
Harbard, Henry	60	1667	MCC folio 41
Harbert, Ellinor	60	1663	MCC folio 33
Harding, Abigail	23	1684	SJC 2242
Harding, John	20	1663	SJC 606
Harding, Peter	36	1689	SJC 2541
Hardy, George	17	1678	EQC 7:157
Hardy, James	24	1684	EQC 9:398

Hardy, John	16	1662	EQC 2:351
Hardy, Joseph	26	1681	EQC 8:207
Hardy, Joseph	48	1668	SJC 911
Hardy, William	17	1679	MCC folio 85
Hardy, William	18	1683	MCC folio 103
Harker, Anthony	65	1673	SJC 2120
Harker, Elizabeth	17	1669	EQC 4:216
Harker, John	20	1663	SJC 600
Harker, William	65	1661	EQC 2:303
Harlock, Bethiah	32	1672	SJC 1165
Harlock, Bethiah	32	1672/3	SCC 208
Harndoll, Richard	30	1675	MCC folio 70
Harridine, Edward	50	1678	EQC 6:415
Harrindin, Elizabeth	28	1671	SJC 1148
Harrington, Daniel	35	1692	MCC folio 172
Harrington, Joseph	19	1679	MCC folio 84
Harrington, Susan	26	1657	MCC folio 18
Harrington, Susannah	17	1666	MCC folio 40
Harrington, Susannah	39	1671	MCC folio 59
Harris, Bernard	29	1664	SJC 746
Harris, George	46	nd	SJC 2769
Harris, Hannah	21	1678	MCC folio 78
Harris, Hannah	30	1677	EQC 6:349
Harris, Henry	24	1673	SJC 1257
Harris, James	23	1666	SJC 754
Harris, James	23	1666	SJC 754
Harris, Jane	17	nd	SJC 2010
Harris, John	18	1661	EQC 2:323
Harris, John	30	1678	MCC folio 184
Harris, John	30	1680	EQC 7:375
Harris, John	40	1681	EQC 8:102
Harris, Joseph	24	1673	MCC folio 64
Harris, Joseph	26	1692	MCC folio 154
Harris, Joseph	30	1660	EQC 2:220
Harris, Martha	35	1664	EQC 3:136
Harris, Nicholas	22	1669	SJC 980
Harris, Richard	24	nd	SJC 1787
Harris, Richard	27	1677	EQC 6:348
Harris, Richard	35	1684	EQC 9:274
Harris, Samuel	25	1669	EQC 4:216
Harris, Thomas	24	1697	MCC folio 208
Harris, Thomas	27	1691	MCC folio 157
Harris, Thomas	40	1658	EQC 2:113
Harris, Timothy	17	1676	EQC 6:206
Harrison, Erasmus	26	1694/5	SJC 3101
Harrison, John	58	1668	SJC 911
Harrison, William	18	1666	EQC 3:347
Harrison, William	21	1672	MCC folio 65
Harrison, William	8	1666	EQC 3:348
Hart, Elizabeth	35	1658	EQC 2:129
Hart, Isaac	40	1658	EQC 2:111
Hart, Isaac	40	1658	EQC 2:129
Hart, Isaac	40	1658	MCC folio 17
Hart, Isaac	70	1678	EQC 7:240

Hart, Jonathan	40	1685	EQC 9:538
Hart, Lawrence	29	1680	EQC 7:397
Hart, Samuel	31	1678	EQC 6:397
Hart, Samuel	48	1694	SJC 3223
Hart, Samuel	51	1672	EQC 5:63
Hart, Samuel	52	1673	EQC 5:193
Hart, Samuel	62	1683	EQC 9:50
Hart, Sarah	23	1677	EQC 6:287
Hartshorn, Benjamin	28	1683	EQC 9:19
Hartshorn, John	29	1680	EQC 8:16
Hartshorn, Thomas	40	1654	MCC folio 9
Hartwell, Samuel	24	1679	MCC folio 88
Hartwell, Samuel	34	1679	MCC folio 88
Harvey, John	40	1670	SJC 983
Harvey, Richard	22	1675	SJC 1632
Harvey, Thomas	27	1663	EQC 3:40
Harwood, Emme	54	1683	EQC 9:21
Harwood, John	27	1653	EQC 2:92
Harwood, Jonathan	17	1683	EQC 9:19
Harwood, Martha	16	1669	MCC folio 52
Harwood, Rachel	56	1677	SCC 839
Harwood, Rachel	56	1677	SJC 1644
Harwood, Rachel	67	1684	SJC 2228
Harwood, Robert	24	1668	SJC 910
Harwood, Thomas	57	1684	SJC 2228
Haselton, Ellen	25	1666	EQC 3:338
Haselton, Gershom	18	1681	EQC 8:215
Haselton, John	24	1682	EQC 8:300
Haselton, Robert	23	1681	EQC 8:215
Haselton, Samuel	34	1681	EQC 8:215
Haselton, Samuel	34	1682	EQC 8:300
Haskell, Elizabeth	45	1668	EQC 4:2
Haskell, Mark	26	1677	EQC 6:243
Haskell, Mark	26	1677	EQC 6:244
Haskell, Richard	46	1662	MCC folio 35
Haskell, Roger	22	1680	EQC 7:390
Haskell, Roger	50	1664	EQC 3:221
Haskell, Stephen	38	1675	SJC 1503
Haskell, Stephen	43	1678	EQC 9:54
Haskell, Steven	37	1671	EQC 4:434
Haskell, William	15	1661	EQC 2:324
Haskell, William	21	1666	EQC 3:327
Haskell, William	42	1661	EQC 2:323
Haskell, William	48	1668	EQC 4:70
Haskell, William	48	1668	EQC 4:70
Haskell, William	55	1672	EQC 5:111
Haskell, William	55	1672	EQC 5:47
Haskell, William	55	1675	EQC 6:49
Haskell, William	58	1677	EQC 6:242
Haskell, William	58	1677	EQC 6:243
Hasket, Mary	16	1687	EQC WPA 47-59-3
Hasket, Sarah	14	1687	EQC WPA 47-59-3
Haskett, Steven	37	1671	EQC 4:430
Haskett, Steven	38	1675	EQC 6:9

Haskin, Susannah	22	1670	EQC 4:216
Haskings, Roger	34	1677	EQC 6:349
Haskins, Nicholas	38	1678	SJC 1734
Hasleton, David	50	nd	SJC 3579
Hassall, Richard	40	1662	MCC folio 32
Hasten, Samuel	21	1658	MCC folio 16
Hasting, Elizabeth	37	1684	MCC folio 111
Hasting, John	21	1661	MCC folio 27
Hasting, John	29	1669	SJC 964
Hasting, John	43	1683	MCC folio 103
Hasting, Martha	30	1694	SJC 162313
Hasting, Samuel	47	1683	MCC folio 103
Hasting, Thomas	25	1677	SJC 1586
Hasting, Walter	60	1691	MCC folio 163
Hasting, Walter	60	1691	MCC folio 35
Hastings, Benjamin	12	1671	MCC folio 59
Hastings, John	17	1671	MCC folio 59
Hastings, Martha	30	1694	MCC folio 186
Hastings, Nathaniel	19	1681	MCC folio 92
Hastings, Thomas	77	1681	MCC folio 97
Hastings, Walter	30	1662	MCC folio 32
Hastings, Walter	60	1691	MCC folio 146
Hastings, Walter	60	1691	MCC folio 149
Hastings, Walter	60	1691	MCC folio 173
Hatch, Jonathan	40	1694	SJC 2989
Hatch, Joseph	36	1694	SJC 2989
Hathaway, John	67	1696/7	SJC 3396
Hatherly, Thomas	37	1668	SJC 910
Hatherly, Thomas	38	1672	SCC 162
Hatherly, Thomas	38	1672	SJC 1163
Hatherly, Thomas	50	1681	SJC 2010
Hathord, William	34	1684	EQC 9:248
Haughton, Robert	28	1668	SJC 910
Haulie, Joseph	18	1672	MCC folio 59
Haven, Elizabeth	29	1685	EQC 9:525
Haven, Joseph	43	1682	EQC 8:250
Haven, Richard	29	1681	EQC 8:123
Haven, Richard	30	1683	EQC 9:43
Haven, Richard	30	1683	EQC 9:45
Haven, Richard	30	1683	EQC 9:50
Haven, Richard	33	1685	EQC 9:434
Haven, Richard	33	1685	SJC 2344
Haven, Richard	33	1685	SJC 2345
Haven, Richard	34	1685	EQC 9:526
Haven, Richard	38	1690	MCC folio 132
Haven, Richard	40	1666	EQC 3:345
Haven, Richard	60	1683	EQC 9:50
Haven, Richard	64	1682	EQC 8:258
Haven, Susannah	37	1661	EQC 2:286
Haviland, Leonard	30	1672	EQC 5:6
Hawke, Sarah	59	1679	MCC folio 88
Hawkes, John	33	nd	SJC 726
Hawkes, Sarah	39	1679	SJC 2025
Hawkins, Gamaliel	20	1684	EQC 9:397

Hawkins, James	56	1659/60	SD 3:344
Hawkins, Mary	66	1682	SJC 2120
Hawkins, William	44	1680	EQC 7:395
Hawks, Adam	18	1683	EQC 9:45
Hawks, John	33	1666	EQC 3:306
Hawks, John	34	1668	EQC 4:32
Hawthorne, Ebenezer	20	1677	EQC 6:368
Hawthorne, Ebenezer	39	1692	MCC folio 154
Hawthorne, Eleazer	32	1669	EQC 4:151
Hawthorne, Esther	27	1692	MCC folio 154
Hawthorne, J.	19	1691	MCC folio 148
Hawthorne, John	20	1662	SJC 561
Hawthorne, John	24	1665	SJC 716
Hawthorne, John	31	1673	EQC 5:211
Hawthorne, John	38	1659/60	SJC 350
Hawthorne, John	42	1665	EQC 3:298
Hawthorne, John	49	1671	EQC 4:383
Hawthorne, Nathaniel	21	1682	EQC 8:258
Hawthorne, Nathaniel	21	1682	EQC 8:259
Hawthorne, Nathaniel	24	1663	EQC 3:169
Hawthorne, Sarah	36	1659/60	SJC 350
Hawthorne, Sarah	58	1683	EQC 9:65
Hawthorne, William	17	1689	MCC folio 131
Hawthorne, William	27	1673	EQC 5:210
Hawthorne, William	32	1678	EQC 7:26
Hawthorne, William	51	1658	EQC 2:128
Hayden, John	27	1667	SJC 828
Hayden, Samuel	19	1678	MCC folio 82
Hayle, Mary	50	1656	SD 4:217
Hayle, Thomas	50	1660	EQC 2:206
Haylett, Edmund	26	1652	MCC folio 4
Hayman, John	40	1654	SJC 236
Hayman, John	59	1670	EQC 4:265
Haynes, Jonathan	33	1679	SJC 1870
Haynes, Jonathan	35	1682	EQC 8:261
Haynes, Jonathan	36	1682	EQC 8:387
Haynes, Nicholas	30	1672	SJC 1288
Haynes, Sarah	26	1682	EQC 8:387
Haynes, Thomas	19	1670	EQC 4:219
Hayward, John	23	1664	MCC folio 36
Hayward, John	27	1667	MCC folio 45
Hayward, John	29	1670	MCC folio 53
Hayward, John	30	1670	MCC folio 53
Hayward, John	33	1672	SD 8:29
Hayward, John	34	1674	SCC 455
Hayward, John	39	1679	MCC folio 87
Hayward, John	45	1684/5	SD 13:253
Hayward, Joseph	25	1667/8	MCC folio 45
Hayward, Nathaniel	33	1675	EQC 6:102
Hayward, Nathaniel	37	1679	EQC 7:311
Hayward, Simeon	19	1667/8	MCC folio 45
Hayward, Thomas	26	1679	EQC 7:307
Haywood, Anthony	42	1682	SJC 2123
Haywood, John	30	1675	SJC 2013

Haywood, John	40	1680	SJC 1916
Haywood, Margery	20	1696	SJC 4342
Haywood, Robert	55	1665	SJC 721
Haywood, Robert	60	1663	SJC 669
Haywood, Sarah	32	1676	MCC folio 71
Haywood, Thomas	37	1680	EQC 7:426
Haywood, William	58	1666	SJC 1885
Hazeltine, John	16	1674	EQC 5:270
Hazeltine, John	40	1663	EQC 3:37
Hazeltine, Robert	16	1674	EQC 5:270
Hazeltine, Robert	20	1677	EQC 6:252
Hazeltine, Samuel	23	1669	EQC 4:192
Hazeltine, Samuel	26	1674	EQC 5:270
Hazeltine, Samuel	29	1678	EQC 6:421
Hazelton, David	18	1663	EQC 3:37
Heald, Gershom	22	1691	MCC folio 141
Heald, John	24	1691	MCC folio 141
Heald, John	48	1681	MCC folio 95
Heale, Arthur	21	nd	SJC 1972
Heale, Timothy	21	1659	MCC folio 21
Heall, Mary	74	1680	EQC 7:395
Healy, Sarah	52	1681	MCC folio 94
Healy, Sarah	52	1682	MCC folio 101
Healy, William	24	1677	MCC folio 75
Healy, William	63	1677	MCC folio 78
Healy, William	64	1677	MCC folio 76
Healy, William	71	1681	MCC folio 94
Hear, Joan	25	nd	SJC 25884
Hear, Thomas	26	nd	SJC 818
Hearson, Thomas	43	1666	EQC 3:350
Hearsy, William	21	1671	SCC 20
Heart, Elizabeth	35	1658	EQC 2:112
Heart, Elizabeth	35	1658	EQC 2:65
Heary, William	21	1671	SJC 1081
Heath, Bartholomew	41	1657	EQC 2:27
Heath, William	26	1691	SJC 2610
Heaton, Jabez	32	1665	SJC 711
Hebert, David	36	1674	SCC 495
Heddan, Andrew	40	1662	EQC 3:22
Hedge, John	45	1657	EQC 2:43
Hedges, Humphrey	52	1673	MCC folio 64
Heill, Tommos	50	1679	EQC 7:260
Heines, Robert	70	1680	EQC 8:66
Heiney, Mathew	20	1689	MCC folio 134
Helemsby, William	37	1690	MCC folio 145
Helman, John	20	1679	EQC 7:327
Heman, Samuel	20	1659	MCC folio 21
Hemingway, John	54	1695/6	SJC 4225
Hemingway, John	54	1696	SJC 3323
Henchman, Ann	30	1672	SJC 1162
Henchman, Ann	30	1672/3	SCC 196
Henchman, Hannah	20	1672	SJC 1162
Henchman, Hannah	20	1672/3	SCC 196
Henderson, Mary	17	1688	EQC WPA 47-123-4

Hendrick, Daniel	70	1685	EQC 9:544
Hendrick, John	33	1682	EQC 8:353
Henfield, Edmund	23	1679	EQC 7:326
Henly, George	40	1672	SJC 1148
Henshaw, Joshua	35	1680	SJC 1964
Henshaw, Thomas	25	1676	MCC folio 72
Henshaw, Thomas	33	1684	MCC folio 107
Hensher, Thomas	28	1681	MCC folio 93
Herbert, John	28	1672	EQC 5:48
Herod, Em	50	1678	EQC 7:148
Herod, John	40	1678	EQC 7:148
Herrick, Edith	60	1672	EQC 5:112
Herrick, Elizabeth	20	1669	EQC 4:104
Herrick, Henry	28	1669	EQC 4:103
Herrick, Henry	30	1672	EQC 5:24
Herrick, John	19	1669	EQC 4:104
Herrick, John	28	1678	EQC 7:156
Herrick, John	29	1679	EQC 7:182
Herrick, John	36	1699	SJC 3963
Herrick, Lydia	26	1669	EQC 4:104
Herrick, Zachariah	48	1681	EQC 8:191
Herrick, Zachariah	30	1669	EQC 4:104
Herrick, Zachary	26	1661	EQC 2:243
Herrick, Zachary	43	1680	EQC 8:22
Herrick, Zachary	44	1679	SJC 1770
Hett, Eliphelet	22	1661	MCC folio 29
Hett, John	50	1661	MCC folio 28
Hett, Thomas	50	1661	MCC folio 29
Hewes, Abel	74	1678	EQC 7:156
Hewes, Alice	60	1685	SJC 2377
Hewes, James	44	1680	SJC 1953
Hewes, James	45	1684	SJC 2208
Hewes, Joshua	59	1670	SJC 1014
Hewes, Mary	9	nd	SJC 27945
Hewes, Thomas	22	1671	SJC 1100
Hewes, Thomas	29	1676	SJC 1562
Hewett, Rebecca	22	1676	EQC 6:150
Hewin, Jacob	16	1695	SJC 4180
Heydon, Joshua	19	1667/8	MCC folio 47
Hibbard, Robert	21	1669	EQC 4:180
Hibbard, Robert	55	1671	EQC 4:332
Hibbard, Robert	58	1673	EQC 6:247
Hibner, Nathaniel	28	1666	MCC folio 41
Hickcock, Edward	20	1659	EQC 2:172
Hickock, Edward	20	1658	EQC 2:141
Hicks, Goodman	44	1677	MCC folio 76
Hicks, Hannah	54	1700	SJC 4677
Hicks, Mary	35	nd	SJC 754
Hicks, Peter	18	1680	EQC 8:30
Hicks, Richard	40	nd	SJC 754
Hicks, Zachary	52	1682	MCC folio 101
Hicks, Zachary	52	1682	MCC folio 102
Hicks, Zechariah	33	1691	MCC folio 143
Hicks, Zechariah	47	1675	MCC folio 69

Hidden, Andrew	40	1662	EQC 2:397
Hidden, Andrew	55	1678	EQC 7:83
Hidden, Andrew	55	1679	EQC 7:208
Hidden, Andrew	55	1679	SJC 1792
Hidden, Margret	15	1674	EQC 5:443
Hide, Richard	60	1677	EQC 6:363
Hides, Eliezer	22	1686	MCC folio 123
Hides, Job	30	1673	MCC folio 63
Hides, Job	37	1679	MCC folio 84
Hides, Jonathan	47	1673	MCC folio 63
Hides, Jonathan	60	1682	MCC folio 100
Hides, Samuel	42	1652	MCC folio 7
Higginson, John	63	1679	MCC folio 86
Hildreth, Dorothy	19	1696	MCC folio 201
Hildreth, James	20	1651	MCC folio 2
Hill, Abraham	20	1665	EQC 3:298
Hill, Abraham	22	1695	MCC folio 180
Hill, Abraham	38	1683	MCC folio 103
Hill, Abraham	38	1686	MCC folio 120
Hill, Abraham	40	1655	MCC folio 13
Hill, Abraham	45	1660	MCC folio 26
Hill, Ann	50	1671	EQC 4:381
Hill, Charles	20	1666	EQC 3:420
Hill, Elizabeth	38	1674	EQC 5:291
Hill, Hannah	19	1674	MCC folio 67
Hill, Isaac	45	1690	MCC folio 138
Hill, Isaac	55	1696/7	MCC folio 204
Hill, John	20	1651	EQC 1:213
Hill, John	40	1679	SCC 1099
Hill, John	40	nd	SJC 24623
Hill, John	42	1677	EQC 6:349
Hill, John	42	1677	EQC 6:373
Hill, John	54	1694	SJC 3126
Hill, Joseph	44	1691/2	SJC 2653
Hill, Joseph	47	1694	SJC 3897
Hill, Nathaniel	48	1689	MCC folio 133
Hill, Roger	50	1679	EQC 7:251
Hill, Sarah	16	1665	EQC 3:298
Hill, Thomas	15	1682	MCC folio 100
Hill, Thomas	50	1672	SJC 1165
Hill, Thomas	50	1672/3	SCC 207
Hill, Thomas	64	1680	SJC 1891
Hill, William	45	1691	SJC 2629
Hill, William	45	1693	SJC 2756
Hill, Zebulon	25	1680	EQC 7:424
Hilliard, Edward	22	1683	SJC 2151
Hilliard, Edward	34	1662	EQC 3:14
Hilliard, Philip	25	1686	EQC WPA 46-78-3
Hillman, Hannah	25	1671	SJC 1148
Hillman, Hannah	31	1676/7	SJC 1544
Hillman, John	47	1698	SJC 4714
Hills, Ann	58	1678/9	SJC 1791
Hills, Ann	58	1679	EQC 7:165
Hills, Ann	72	1695	SJC 3214

Hills, Ebenezer	19	1678	EQC 7:157
Hills, Ebenezer	23	1681	EQC 8:199
Hills, Joseph	23	1661	MCC folio 28
Hills, Joseph	32	1662	MCC folio 32
Hills, Joseph	60	1662	MCC folio 33
Hills, Joseph	60	1662	SJC 472
Hills, Joseph	69	1671	EQC 4:356
Hills, Joseph	70	1674	MCC folio 65
Hills, Joseph	70	1676	EQC 6:126
Hills, Sarah	30	1653	MCC folio 8
Hillyard, Edward	41	1671	EQC 4:432
Hilston, Nowell	22	1685	MCC folio 118
Hilton, Charles	37	1679	EQC 7:216
Hilton, Katherine	71	1671	SJC 1100
Hilton, William	44	1676	SJC 1474
Hilton, William	56	1675	MCC folio 70
Hincher, Thomas	25	1676	MCC folio 74
Hincher, Thomas	34	1685	MCC folio 117
Hincher, Thomas	35	1686	MCC folio 123
Hinchman, Nathaniel	23	1685	MCC folio 117
Hinchman, Thomas	34	1670	MCC folio 53
Hinchman, Thomas	50	1681	MCC folio 98
Hinckes, John	23	1672	SJC 1894
Hindaraks, Jotham	30	1681	EQC 8:183
Hines, William	25	1681	SJC 2055
Hirst, William	30	1682	EQC 8:413
Hitchcock, Jerusha	18	1672	MCC folio 60
Hitchins, Daniel	50	1683	EQC 9:43
Hoall, John	23	1685	MCC folio 117
Hoar, Daniel	22	1672	MCC folio 60
Hoar, Dorcas	39	1673	EQC 5:216
Hoar, goodwife	34	1670	EQC 4:217
Hoar, Hannah	35	1683	SJC 2198
Hoar, John	47	1663	SJC 1276
Hoar, John	47	1663	SJC 669
Hoar, John	56	1671	SJC 1276
Hoar, Thomas	24	1666	EQC 3:334
Hoar, William	23	1684	EQC 9:208
Hoar, William	35	1670	EQC 4:217
Hoar, William	56	1684	EQC 9:208
Hoaten, Mary	15	1670	EQC 4:219
Hobart, Caleb	48	1680	SJC 1916
Hobbs, Josiah	40	1690	MCC folio 137
Hobbs, Thomas	54	1679	EQC 7:205
Hobbs, Thomas	55	1679	EQC 7:262
Hobbs, Thomas	58	1680	EQC 8:21
Hobbs, Thomas	60	1687/8	SJC 2476
Hobbs, Thomas	64	1685	EQC 9:457
Hobbs, William	28	1669	EQC 4:111
Hobby, William	32	1667/8	MCC folio 47
Hobby, William	33	1666	SJC 1016
Hobby, William	59	1693	SD 14:239
Hobson, Tho.	64	1654	MCC folio 9
Hodges, Anthony	60	1690	MCC folio 135

Hodges, Henry	60	nd	SJC 24777
Hodges, Humphrey	52	1673	SJC 1212
Hodges, Samuel	18	1690	MCC folio 136
Hodges, Thomas	32	1673	SJC 1245
Hodgkins, Christopher	28	1695	SJC 3223
Hodgneff, William	28	1670	SJC 1009
Hodgskins, Grace	20	1673	EQC 5:143
Hoeg, John	35	1678	EQC 7:157
Hoeman, Edward	35	1676	EQC 6:167
Hoggman, Mary	40	1681	MCC folio 94
Holbrook, John	45	1665	SJC 815
Holbrook, John	49	1667	SJC 909
Holbrook, John	55	1675	SJC 1403
Holbrook, John	56	1675	SJC 1418
Holbrook, Peter	41	1700	SJC 4703
Holbrook, Thomas	24	1653	MCC folio 8
Holbrook, Thomas	77	1666	SJC 815
Hold, Gershom	45	1692	MCC folio 173
Holden, Justinian	32	1676	MCC folio 71
Holden, Mary	32	1676	MCC folio 71
Holden, Mary	45	1692	MCC folio 153
Holdsworth, Joseph	21	1663	SJC 602
Holdsworth, Joseph	25	1666	SJC 911
Holiman, Edward	23	1670	EQC 4:267
Holland, James	17	1671	MCC folio 56
Holland, James	17	1684	MCC folio 111
Holland, James	30	1684	MCC folio 56
Holland, John	35	1683	SJC 2151
Holland, John	40	1675	SJC 1422
Holland, Joseph	24	1683	MCC folio 103
Holland, Nathaniel	40	1674	MCC folio 63
Holland, Nathaniel	60	1691	MCC folio 151
Holland, Thomas	22	1657	MCC folio 19
Holledge, Richard	38	1653	EQC 1:316
Hollingsworth, Eleanor	50	1684	EQC 9:396
Hollingsworth, Eleanor	53	1684	EQC 9:396
Hollingsworth, Eleanor	56	1679	EQC 7:238
Hollingsworth, William	40	1668	EQC 4:175
Hollingwood, Mary	20	1674	EQC 5:348
Holloway, Adam	20	1679	MCC folio 87
Holloway, Joseph	35	1670	EQC 4:304
Holloway, William	72	1658/9	SD 3:193
Holman, Abraham	58	1682	MCC folio 100
Holman, Jeremiah	16	1686	MCC folio 128
Holman, Jeremiah	55	1686	MCC folio 120
Holman, Jeremiah	55	1686	MCC folio 121
Holman, John	43	1679	EQC 7:260
Holman, Rachel	24	1676/7	SJC 1544
Holman, Samuel	30	1680	SJC 1916
Holman, Thomas	28	1672	SD 6:280
Holman, Thomas	45	1685	SD 13:408
Holmes, Elisha	26	nd	SJC 3630
Holmes, Hester	23	1674	EQC 5:419
Holmes, John	35	1675	EQC 6:101

Holmes, John	39	1678	EQC 7:112
Holmes, Joseph	23	1685	SJC 2354
Holmes, Joseph	25	1685	SJC 2354
Holmes, Joseph	44	1678	SJC 1908
Holmes, Joseph	46	1679	SJC 1908
Holmes, Joseph	47	1681	SJC 2056
Holmes, Joseph	49	1683/4	SJC 2188
Holmes, Joseph	49	1685	SJC 2332
Holmes, Mary	18	1685	SJC 2354
Holmes, Michael	24	1672	SJC 1221
Holmes, Nathaniel	21	1685	SJC 2354
Holmes, Richard	53	1664	EQC 3:124
Holmes, Richard	60	1674	EQC 5:277
Holmes, Richard	70	1680	EQC 8:35
Holmes, William	37	1690	MCC folio 137
Holmsby, William	37	1690	MCC folio 145
Holmsby, William	37	1691	MCC folio 143
Holsell, George	58	1672	SD 6:329
Holt, Elizabeth	20	1657	EQC 2:40
Holt, Martha	44	1666	EQC 3:325
Holt, Mary	18	1657	EQC 2:39
Holt, Nicholas	63	1671	EQC 4:370
Holt, Samuel	29	1669	EQC 4:150
Holton, James	25	1677	MCC folio 75
Holton, William	84	1690	SJC 3301
Homan, Edward	43	1684	EQC 9:239
Homan, Solomon	23	1694/5	SJC 3148
Homer, Mary	27	1694	MCC folio 160
Honeywell, Israel	30	1685	EQC 9:528
Honeywell, Israel	30	1686	EQC WPA 47-13-4
Honeywell, Richard	31	1676	SJC 1526
Honeywell, Richard	50	1664	EQC 3:211
Hoogman, Thomas	35	1675	EQC 6:217
Hoon, Priscilla	30	1681	EQC 8:225
Hooper, Christian	32	1678	EQC 6:387
Hooper, Elizabeth	72	1677	EQC 6:363
Hooper, George	40	1680	SJC 1887
Hooper, John	35	1672	SJC 1163
Hooper, John	35	1678	EQC 6:387
Hooper, John	36	1677	EQC 6:362
Hooper, Robert	50	1670	EQC 4:254
Hooper, Robert	50	1670	EQC 4:255
Hooper, Robert	60	1672	EQC 5:92
Hooper, Robert	64	1677	EQC 6:363
Hooper, William	17	1665	EQC 3:289
Hopkins, Charles	38	1672	SJC 1165
Hopkinson, Caleb	30	1681	EQC 8:214
Hopkinson, Caleb	32	1682	EQC 8:300
Hopkinson, John	17	1663	EQC 3:23
Hopkinson, John	28	1675	EQC 6:15
Hopper, Robert	62	1669	EQC 4:108
Horne, Deacon	72	1674	EQC 5:360
Horne, John	40	1685	SJC 2285
Horne, John	60	1662	EQC 2:389

Horne, John	74	1675	EQC 6:39
Horne, John	81	1684	EQC 9:345
Horne, Mary	18	1675	EQC 6:39
Horne, Thomas	24	1684	EQC 9:319
Horrell, goodwife	70	1678	EQC 7:54
Hosmer, James	34	1670	MCC folio 53
Houchin, Jeremy	53	1668	SJC 924
Hough, Atherton	19	1696	SJC 4372
Houghton, Ralph	47	1671	MCC folio 56
Houghton, Ralph	54	1678	MCC folio 80
Houghton, Robert	40	1699/1700	MCC folio 192
Houlden, Martha	68	1659	MCC folio 21
Houlden, Richard	50	1658	MCC folio 16
Houlden, Richard	51	1661	MCC folio 27
Houlding, Jonathan	66	1678	MCC folio 84
Houlton, Joseph	48	1669	EQC 4:109
Hovey, Daniel	17	1659	EQC 2:184
Hovey, Daniel	22	1695	SJC 3223
Hovey, Daniel	40	1684	EQC 9:259
Hovey, Daniel	42	1660	EQC 2:200
Hovey, Daniel	48	1666	EQC 3:313
Hovey, Daniel	60	1678	EQC 7:87
Hovey, Daniel	64	1683	EQC 9:103
How, Abraham	20	1669	EQC 4:177
How, Abraham	30	1681	EQC 8:189
How, Abraham	30	1681	MCC folio 101
How, Abraham	34	1686	EQC 9:605
How, Abraham	35	1686	EQC 9:607
How, Elizabeth	50	1664	EQC 3:161
How, James	30	1666	EQC 3:326
How, James	30	167	EQC 3:161
How, James	34	1669	EQC 4:177
How, James	34	1669	EQC 4:177
How, James	48	1682	EQC 8:405
How, James	61	1666	EQC 3:312
How, James	80	1681	EQC 8:189
How, James	80	1681	MCC folio 101
How, John	23	1663	EQC 3:85
How, John	23	nd	SJC 503
How, John	30	1670	EQC 4:219
How, John	30	1674	EQC 5:353
How, John	30	1674	SJC 1397
How, John	30	1675	EQC 6:4
How, John	33	1674	EQC 5:422
How, John	33	1675	EQC 6:33
How, John	33	1675	SJC 1400
How, John	35	1675	EQC 6:7
How, John	36	1677	EQC 6:355
How, John	46	1686	EQC 9:606
How, John	56	1695	SJC 162358
How, John	56	1695	SJC 3326
How, Josiah	29	1681	MCC folio 93
How, Samuel	26	1679	MCC folio 88
How, Sarah	20	1664	EQC 3:161

How, Thomas	27	1685	MCC folio 114
Howard, John	23	1684	MCC folio 116
Howard, John	30	1675/6	SCC 670
Howard, Nathaniel	38	1679	MCC folio 87
Howard, Robert	16	1669	MCC folio 51
Howard, Robert	60 or 63	1663	SJC 1276
Howard, Tabitha	52	1674	EQC 5:267
Howard, William	52	1661	EQC 2:268
Howard, William	56	1665	EQC 3:260
Howard, William	57	1666	EQC 3:323
Howell, Abraham	26	1658	EQC 2:112
Howell, Abraham	26	1658	MCC folio 17
Howell, Abraham	27	1658	MCC folio 17
Howell, John	37	1669	SJC 1046
Howell, John	40	1670	SJC 162087
Howell, Lawrence	44	1659	MCC folio 23
Howen, Anna	30	1671	SJC 1148
Howen, Anna	34	1671	SJC 1148
Howen, Johanna	30	1671	SJC 1148
Howes, William	22	nd	SJC 2754
Howland, Jabez	36	1680	SJC 1915
Howland, John	16	1683	EQC 9:63
Howlet, John	32	1675	SJC 1458
Howlett, Thomas	52	1658	EQC 2:146
Howlett, Thomas	60	1665	EQC 3:259
Howlett, Thomas	60	1666	EQC 3:312
Howlett, William	27	1678	EQC 6:425
Howlett, William	29	1679	EQC 7:300
Hownsell, Edward	26	1679	SCC 1111
Hows, goodwife	25	1677	MCC folio 77
Hows, John	18	1674	MCC folio 63
Hows, John	23	1676	MCC folio 77
Hows, John	23	1677	MCC folio 77
Hoyt, John	40	1680	EQC 8:37
Hoyt, John	46	1684	EQC 9:324
Hubbard, Anne	54	1662	SJC 468
Hubbard, James	27	1660	MCC folio 26
Hubbard, James	27	1660	SJC 386
Hubbard, James	48	1676	SJC 1799
Hubbard, James	48	1679	MCC folio 84
Hubbard, Jeremy	28	1660	EQC 2:205
Hubbard, John	30	1679/80	SJC 1910
Hubbard, Richard	40	1671	SJC 1334
Hubbard, Richard	45	1679	EQC 7:167
Hubbard, William	40	1665	EQC 3:234
Hubbard, William	40	1665	SJC 717
Hud, Richard	32	1653	EQC 2:92
Hud, Richard	32	1653	SJC 225
Hudson, Daniel	18	1670	MCC folio 53
Hudson, Daniel	35	1658	MCC folio 17
Hudson, Daniel	61	1678	MCC folio 80
Hudson, Francis	48	1663	MCC folio 34
Hudson, John	57	1670	EQC 4:282
Hudson, Jonathan	40	1661	EQC 2:286

Hudson, Jonathan	44	1661	EQC 2:284
Hudson, Mary	50	1670	EQC 4:281
Hudson, Mary	50	1670	EQC 4:287
Hudson, Samuel	21	1670	EQC 4:281
Hudson, Samuel	24	1674	EQC 5:347
Hudson, Thomas	17	1690	MCC folio 131
Hudson, Thomas	18	1690	MCC folio 145
Hudson, William	43	1667	MCC folio 43
Hues, Abel	64	1666	EQC 3:347
Hues, George	32	1690	MCC folio 136
Hues, Lydia	58	1690	MCC folio 136
Huffey, Daniel	40	1683	EQC 9:103
Huggins, Bridget	44	1660	EQC 2:230
Huggins, John	26	1678	EQC 7:157
Huggins, Martha	16	1672	EQC 5:34
Hughs, John	23	1677	MCC folio 76
Huit, Thomas	20	1680	SCC 1089
Hukar, Ruth	31	1671	MCC folio 74
Hull, Edith	17	1677	EQC 6:281
Hull, George	42	1695	SJC 3239
Hull, John	57	1681	SJC 2060
Hull, Naomi	20	1661	EQC 2:296
Humphreys, Edward	34	1675	EQC 6:18
Humphreys, Edward	44	1684	EQC 9:239
Humphreys, Elizabeth	20	1674	EQC 6:18
Humphreys, Elizabeth	23	1678	EQC 7:24
Humphreys, Joseph	21	1662	EQC 2:352
Hunt, Ann	52	1673	EQC 5:225
Hunt, Ebetth	43	1677	SJC 1689
Hunt, Elizabeth	14	1674	EQC 5:413
Hunt, Elizabeth	30	1673	EQC 5:156
Hunt, Elizabeth	36	1673	EQC 5:187
Hunt, Elizabeth	37	1674	EQC 5:412
Hunt, Elizabeth	40	1678	EQC 7:86
Hunt, Elizabeth	55	1654/5	MCC folio 13
Hunt, Isaac	23	1670	MCC folio 55
Hunt, John	25	1672	SJC 1194
Hunt, John	35	1683	SJC 2187
Hunt, Samuel	15	1673	EQC 5:156
Hunt, Samuel	46	1678	EQC 7:86
Hunt, Sarah	25	1695	SJC 3230
Hunt, William	65	1667	MCC folio 44
Hunting, Samuel	43	1686	MCC folio 125
Hunting, Samuel	46	1690	MCC folio 138
Huntings, Hannah	28	1669	SJC 966
Huntings, Samuel	29	1669	SJC 966
Huntley, John	40	1663	SJC 600
Huntoon, Mordecai	17	1658	EQC 2:134
Huper, William	30	1677	EQC 6:349
Hurd, Jacob	27	1679	MCC folio 184
Hurd, Jacob	27	1681	MCC folio 102
Hurd, Jacob	28	1683	MCC folio 104
Hurd, Jacob	37	1688	SJC 4767
Hurd, Jacob	37	1689	MCC folio 134

Hurd, Jacob	37	1693	MCC folio 156
Hurd, Joseph	33	1679	EQC 7:260
Hurd, Joseph	36	1681	MCC folio 95
Hurry, John	23	1690	MCC folio 137
Hutchins, John	65	1669	EQC 4:193
Hutchins, John	65	1669	SJC 1009
Hutchins, Joseph	32	1668	EQC 4:33
Hutchins, Nicholas	35	1673	EQC 5:185
Hutchins, Nicholas	42	1679	EQC 7:253
Hutchinson, Edward	43	1656	SJC 262
Hutchinson, Edward	56	1669	SD 6:47
Hutchinson, Edward	61	1674	EQC 5:376
Hutchinson, Elisha	17	1658	EQC 2:128
Hutchinson, Francis	36	1666	EQC 3:306
Hutchinson, John	23	1666	EQC 3:307
Hutchinson, Joseph	27	1660	EQC 2:206
Hutchinson, Joseph	30	1663	EQC 3:118
Hutchinson, Joseph	36	1669	EQC 4:194
Hutchinson, Joseph	37	1671	EQC 4:452
Hutchinson, Joseph	46	1681	EQC 8:120
Hutchinson, Joseph	48	1683	EQC 9:54
Hutchinson, Nathaniel	45	1679	MCC folio 87
Hutchinson, Nathaniel	45	1682	MCC folio 100
Hutchinson, Nathaniel	46	1690	MCC folio 132
Hutchinson, Nathaniel	48	1681	MCC folio 102
Hutchinson, Nathaniel	52	1685/6	MCC folio 122
Hutchinson, Nathaniel	52	1686	MCC folio 127
Hutchinson, Richard	58	1660	EQC 2:206
Hutchinson, Richard	70	1674/5	SJC 1503
Hutchinson, Richard	80	1682	EQC 9:55
Hutchinson, Samuel	40	1658	EQC 2:112
Hutchinson, Samuel	40	1658	EQC 2:129
Hutchison, Elizabeth	63	1670	MCC folio 54
Hutton, John	20	1683	EQC 9:14
Hutton, Richard	19	1680	EQC 8:9
Hutton, Richard	19	1680	SJC 1967
Hutton, Richard	40	1664	EQC 3:208
Hutton, Richard	40	1666	EQC 3:371
Hutton, Richard	55	1679	EQC 7:292
Hutton, Richard	58	1681	EQC 8:160
Hutton, Richard	59	1680	EQC 8:18
Hutton, Richard	59	1680	EQC 8:26
Hutton, Richard	59	1680	EQC 8:27
Hutton, Richard	60	1681	EQC 8:163
Hutton, Richard	60	1682	EQC 8:384
Hutton, Richard	60	1683	EQC 9:113
Hutton, Richard	60	1685	EQC 9:457
Hutton, Richard	62	1682	EQC 8:436
Hutton, Richard	63	1684	EQC 9:204
Hutton, Richard	63	1686	EQC 9:584
Hutton, Richard	70	1693/4	SJC 2942
Huxtable, Christopher	40	1686	EQC WPA 46-87-2
Huxtable, Christopher	40	1686	EQC WPA 46-88-3
Hydes, Job	30	1673	MCC folio 64

Hyland, Deborah	60	1662	SJC 874
Ierson, Edward	57	1657	EQC 7:128
Ierson, Edward	62	1662	EQC 2:352
Illsley, William	32	1681	EQC WPA 46-8-3
Ilsley, Elisha	30	1678	EQC 7:157
Ilsley, Isaac	26	1678	EQC 7:156
Ilsley, John	50	1659	EQC 2:229
Ilsley, Joseph	27	1678	EQC 7:157
Ilsley, Joseph	28	1680	EQC 8:173
Ilsley, William	28	1678	EQC 7:156
Ilsley, William	70	1678	EQC 7:157
Ilsly, John	60	1673	SJC 1321
Indicott, Mary	12	1679	EQC 7:251
Ingalls, Elizabeth	42	1689	SJC 2541
Ingalls, Francis	60	1662	EQC 3:10
Ingalls, Francis	60	1662	MCC folio 32
Ingalls, Henry	27	1657	EQC 2:40
Ingalls, Henry	30	1662	EQC 2:353
Ingalls, Robert	20	1673	EQC 5:186
Ingalls, Robert	35	1686	EQC WPA 46-145-2
Ingalls, Robert	62	1684	EQC 9:245
Ingalls, Robert	62	1684	EQC 9:314
Ingalls, Robert	62	1684	EQC 9:317
Ingalls, Samuel	27	1681	EQC 8:124
Ingalls, Samuel	30	1664	EQC 3:165
Ingersoll, George	61	1678	EQC 7:14
Ingersoll, George	61	1678	SJC 1725
Ingersoll, Hannah	46	1683	EQC 9:48
Ingersoll, John	39	1683	EQC 9:163
Ingersoll, John	55	1678	EQC 7:14
Ingersoll, John	55	1678	SJC 1725
Ingersoll, Nathaniel	40	1674	SJC 1503
Ingersoll, Nathaniel	41	1674	EQC 6:9
Ingersoll, Nathaniel	42	1675	EQC 6:8
Ingersoll, Nathaniel	45	1678	EQC 7:13
Ingersoll, Nathaniel	50	1683	EQC 9:47
Ingersoll, Nathaniel	54	1678	SJC 1725
Ingersoll, Nathaniel	60	1694	SJC 3212
Ingerson, John	50	1674	EQC 5:325
Ingerson, John	50	1674	SJC 1503
Ingerson, Nathaniel	41	1674	EQC 5:324
Ingle, Bernard	57	1664	MCC folio 36
Inglesby, Ebenezer	23	1680	SJC 1916
Inglesby, Ebenezer	31	1691	MCC folio 145
Inglesby, John	64	167	SJC 2016
Ireland, John	26	1672	MCC folio 65
Ireland, William	56	1680	MCC folio 91
Ireson, Edward	70	1671	EQC 4:411
Ireson, Edward	70	1672	EQC 5:108
Irons, Rebecca	18	1662	SJC 532
Irons, Thomas	42	1683	SJC 2224
Isset, William	49	1676	EQC 6:199
Ive, Elizabeth	30	1681	MCC folio 104
Ives, Elizabeth	23	1680	EQC 7:400

Ives, Martha	72	1678	MCC folio 81
Ives, Thomas	20	1668	EQC 4:39
Ives, Thomas	26	1674	EQC 5:266
Ives, Thomas	28	1675	EQC 6:13
Ives, Thomas	30	1677	EQC 6:354
Ivory, Mary	42	1681	EQC 8:124
Ivory, Mary	43	1682	EQC 8:290
Ivory, Mary	44	1683	EQC 9:65
Jackman, James	22	1678	EQC 7:157
Jackman, James	60	1678	EQC 7:157
Jackman, Richard	19	1678	EQC 7:157
Jackson, Edmund	65	1674	SJC 1432
Jackson, Eleanor	58	1660	EQC 2:258
Jackson, George	50	1696	SJC 3483
Jackson, Hester	17	1661	SJC 874
Jackson, John	21	1655	EQC 1:391
Jackson, John	24	1671	MCC folio 58
Jackson, John	25	1671	MCC folio 59
Jackson, John	25	1672	MCC folio 59
Jackson, John	30	1660	EQC 2:238
Jackson, John	30	1660	EQC 2:257
Jackson, John	30	1677	MCC folio 76
Jackson, John	45	1691	MCC folio 140
Jackson, John	45	1691	MCC folio 146
Jackson, John	45	1691	MCC folio 173
Jackson, John	60	1671/2	SJC 1092
Jackson, Margaret	30	1676	SJC 1526
Jackson, Margaret	50 or 60	1677	MCC folio 78
Jackson, Mary	24	1671	SJC 1148
Jackson, Nathaniel	30	nd	SJC 3630
Jackson, Samuel	18	1684	EQC 9:289
Jackson, Sarah	28	1677	MCC folio 76
Jackson, Susanna	21	1660	EQC 2:238
Jacob, John	45	1675	SJC 1422
Jacob, Joseph	17	1673	EQC 5:146
Jacob, Joseph	22	1678	EQC 7:120
Jacob, Joseph	22	1679	EQC 7:219
Jacob, Samuel	22	1661	EQC 2:267
Jacob, Sarah	30	1678	EQC 7:38
Jacob, Tamsen	63	1682	MCC folio 101
Jacob, Thomas	18	1659	EQC 2:171
Jacob, Thomas	20	1661	EQC 2:267
Jacob, Thomas	38	1678	EQC 7:121
Jacob, Thomas	38	1679	EQC 7:220
Jacob, Thomas	39	1679	EQC 7:219
Jacob, Thomas	40	1684	EQC 9:204
Jacobs, George	30	1679	EQC 7:308
James, Erasmus	27	1662	EQC 2:442
James, Erasmus	30	1665	EQC 3:269
James, Erasmus	34	1669	EQC 4:107
James, Erasmus	34	1669	EQC 4:116
James, Erasmus	34	1669	EQC 4:191
James, Erasmus	34	1670	EQC 4:298
James, Erasmus	36	1669	EQC 4:151

James, Erasmus	36	1671	EQC 4:378
James, Erasmus	38	1673	EQC 5:182
James, Erasmus	41	1677	EQC 6:362
James, Erasmus	49	1654	EQC 1:330
James, Erasmus	50	1684	EQC 9:250
James, James	33	1685	MCC folio 117
James, Jane	53	1654	EQC 1:330
James, Jane	64	1667	EQC 3:444
James, Mary	33	1683	EQC 9:63
James, Mary	33	1684	EQC 9:250
James, Peter	23	1680	SJC 1935
James, William	35	1676	SJC 1718
Jameson, William	40	1685	MCC folio 116
Jameson, William	40	1686	MCC folio 123
Jaques, Henry	45	1664	EQC 3:131
Jaques, Henry	56	1676	EQC 6:128
Jaques, Henry	56	1676	EQC 6:162
Jaques, Henry	60	1678	EQC 7:156
Jaques, Henry	60	1679	SJC 1791
Jaques, Henry	63	1682	EQC 8:243
Jaques, Richard	22	1678	EQC 7:157
Jaques, Stephen	17	1678	EQC 7:157
Jaquith, Henry	56	1676	EQC 6:227
Jaquith, Henry	60	1679	EQC 7:165
Jaquith, Richard	21	1671	EQC 7:163
Jarman, William	38	1682	EQC 8:338
Jarvis, Andrew	42	1663	EQC 3:88
Jeffrey, George	40	1669	EQC 4:127
Jeffulls, Aaron	62	1683	SJC 2224
Jefts, Robert	15	1669	MCC folio 52
Jeggles, Thomas	48	1670	EQC 4:265
Jeggles, Thomas	57	1679	EQC 7:306
Jeggles, Thomas	60	1682	EQC 8:412
Jeggles, Thomas	60	1682	EQC 8:413
Jemmison, John	25	1673	SJC 1270
Jemson, John	24	1664	EQC 3:213
Jemson, John	25	1673	SCC 405
Jenison, Samuel	42	1685	MCC folio 115
Jenison, Samuel	42	1685	SJC 2348
Jenison, Samuel	44	1686	MCC folio 125
Jenkins, Joel	58	1684	MCC folio 109
Jenkins, Rowland	20	nd	SJC 2770
Jenks, John	17	1678	EQC 7:28
Jenks, John	22	1683	EQC 9:43
Jenks, Joseph	76	1678	EQC 7:28
Jenks, Joseph	81	1681	EQC 8:197
Jenks, Samuel	28	1685	SJC 2345
Jenner, David	27	1691	MCC folio 148
Jennings, Richard	42	1689	SJC 2552
Jephson, John	45	1655	SD 2:167
Jepson, John	36	1698	SJC 4700
Jersey, Nicholas	23	1691	SJC 2597
Jewell, Samuel	30	1675	MCC folio 69
Jewett, Abraham	30	1665	EQC 3:240

Jewett, Hannah	18	1681	EQC 8:145
Jewett, Hannah	36	1691	MCC folio 149
Jewett, Jeremiah	30	1670	EQC 4:260
Jewett, Jeremiah	30	1670	SJC 999
Jewett, Jeremiah	32	1669	EQC 4:176
Jewett, Jeremy	17	1680	EQC 8:34
Jewett, John	37	1674	EQC 5:394
Jewett, John	37	1674	SJC 1389
Jewett, John	40	1682	EQC 8:404
Jewett, John	43	1680	EQC 8:34
Jewett, John	43	1680	EQC 8:35
Jewett, Maximillion	68	1674	EQC 5:393
Jewett, Nehemiah	22	1665	EQC 3:257
Jewett, Nehemiah	30	1674	EQC 5:393
Jewett, Nehemiah	30	1674	SJC 162131
Jewett, Nehemiah	31	1674	EQC 5:394
Jewett, Nehemiah	43	1686	EQC 9:585
Jimson, John	29	1669	EQC 4:118
Johns, Thomas	29	1667	EQC 3:455
Johnson, Alexander	25	1696	MCC folio 208
Johnson, Benjamin	40	1697/8	SJC 4428
Johnson, Bethiah	23	1683	MCC folio 104
Johnson, Bethiah	36	1676	MCC folio 74
Johnson, Bethiah	47	1683	MCC folio 104
Johnson, Daniel	29	1680	EQC 8:104
Johnson, Daniel	29	1681	EQC 8:102
Johnson, Daniel	33	1684	EQC 9:325
Johnson, Daniel	34	1684	EQC 9:341
Johnson, Edward	26	1675	MCC folio 69
Johnson, Edward	30	1653	MCC folio 8
Johnson, Edward	40	1661	MCC folio 29
Johnson, Edward	40	1662	MCC folio 31
Johnson, Edward	40	1692	MCC folio 146
Johnson, Edward	60	1660	MCC folio 25
Johnson, Edward	60	1660	MCC folio 29
Johnson, Edward	60	1662	MCC folio 29
Johnson, Edward	62	1659	MCC folio 24
Johnson, Edward	65	1664	MCC Harvard #2584
Johnson, Edward	65	1665	MCC folio 39
Johnson, Edward	69	1668	MCC folio 44
Johnson, Edward	69	1691	MCC folio 167A
Johnson, Edward	72	1671	MCC folio 59
Johnson, Edward	82	1678	SJC 3006
Johnson, Elizabeth	31	1669	EQC 4:147
Johnson, Francis	59	1667	EQC 3:417
Johnson, Francis	66	1672	EQC 5:115
Johnson, Francis	67	1674	EQC 5:282
Johnson, Francis	67	1674	SJC 1323
Johnson, Francis	82	nd	SJC 2770
Johnson, Hannah	38	1668	MCC folio 50
Johnson, Isaac	12	1679/80	SJC 1836
Johnson, Isaac	22	1671	MCC folio 57
Johnson, Isaac	35	1686	MCC folio 125
Johnson, Isaac	44	1694	MCC folio 160

Johnson, James	48	1662	EQC 2:434
Johnson, James	50	1653	SJC 277
Johnson, James	62	1673	SJC 1432
Johnson, John	16	1675	EQC 6:15
Johnson, John	17	1676	MCC folio 74
Johnson, John	19	1676	MCC folio 74
Johnson, John	23	1682	MCC folio 100
Johnson, John	24	1690	MCC folio 136
Johnson, John	25	1683	MCC folio 104
Johnson, John	27	1685	MCC folio 120
Johnson, John	33	1671	MCC folio 62
Johnson, John	36	1673	MCC folio 64
Johnson, John	36	1673	SJC 1232
Johnson, John	37	1672	MCC folio 59
Johnson, John	39	1676	MCC folio 71
Johnson, John	40	1695	SJC 3123d
Johnson, John	44	1671/2	SJC 1097
Johnson, John	45	1684	MCC folio 109
Johnson, John	48	1673	SJC 1257
Johnson, John	49	1684	MCC folio 109
Johnson, John	50	1685	MCC folio 114
Johnson, John	50	1686	MCC folio 123
Johnson, John	53	1685	MCC folio 115
Johnson, John	57	1686	MCC folio 125
Johnson, John	64	1692	MCC folio 174
Johnson, John	67	1671	EQC 4:372
Johnson, Jonah	28	1677	EQC 6:349
Johnson, Jonathan	25	1666	MCC folio 40
Johnson, Jonathan	50	1692	MCC folio 174
Johnson, Joseph	14	1679/80	SJC 1836
Johnson, Joseph	14	nd	SJC 26669
Johnson, Joseph	24	1691	MCC folio 167A
Johnson, Joseph	27	1665	EQC 3:277
Johnson, Joseph	28	1681	SJC 2010
Johnson, Joseph	33	1685	SJC 2377
Johnson, Katherin	58	1684	MCC folio 110
Johnson, Martha	30	1681	EQC 8:103
Johnson, Mary	48	1662	MCC folio 30
Johnson, Mathew	25	1692	MCC folio 174
Johnson, Mathew	39	1672	MCC folio 59
Johnson, Mathew	40	1673	MCC folio 62
Johnson, Mathew	44	1676	MCC folio 71
Johnson, Mathew	44	1677	MCC folio 72
Johnson, Mathew	47	1679	MCC folio 87
Johnson, Mathew	53	1685	MCC folio 115
Johnson, Mathew	55	1685	MCC folio 115
Johnson, Mathew	57	1691	MCC folio 167A
Johnson, Mathew	61	1695	MCC folio 197
Johnson, Mathew	67	1691	MCC folio 167A
Johnson, Matthew	44	1677	SJC 1581
Johnson, Return	25	1678	EQC 7:96
Johnson, Richard	51	1663	EQC 3:32
Johnson, Richard	51	1663	SJC 577
Johnson, Samuel	20	1692	MCC folio 174

Johnson, Samuel	24	1675	SJC 1422
Johnson, Samuel	27	1670	EQC 4:309
Johnson, Samuel	30	1675	EQC 6:10
Johnson, Samuel	34	1685	SJC 2377
Johnson, Samuel	35	1675	EQC 6:16
Johnson, Samuel	35	1675	SJC 1560
Johnson, Samuel	35	1676	SJC 1569
Johnson, Samuel	35	1678	EQC 7:30
Johnson, Samuel	36	1684	SJC 2228
Johnson, Samuel	39	1682	EQC 8:253
Johnson, Samuel	40	1684	EQC 9:338
Johnson, Samuel	40	1686	EQC 9:591
Johnson, Samuel	41	1685	SJC 2340
Johnson, Samuel	43	1690/1	SJC 2596
Johnson, Simon	39	1681	SJC 2031
Johnson, Solomon	59	1686	MCC folio 125
Johnson, Stephen	21	1661	EQC 2:288
Johnson, Stephen	36	1677	EQC 6:325
Johnson, Steven	29	1671	EQC 4:338
Johnson, Susan	66	1664	MCC Harvard #2584
Johnson, Susan	71	1668	MCC folio 44
Johnson, Susannah	77	1676	MCC folio 74
Johnson, Susannah	80	1676	MCC folio 71
Johnson, Susannah	83	1675	MCC folio 71
Johnson, Susannah	83	1675	SJC 162162
Johnson, Thomas	27	1661	EQC 2:289
Johnson, Thomas	28	1661	EQC 2:329
Johnson, Thomas	28	1662	EQC 2:367
Johnson, Thomas	30	1665	EQC 3:265
Johnson, Thomas	32	1665	SJC 725
Johnson, Thomas	32	nd	SJC 322
Johnson, Thomas	38	1671	EQC 4:338
Johnson, Timothy	17	1661	EQC 2:275
Johnson, William	20	1690	MCC folio 136
Johnson, William	22	1684	MCC folio 107
Johnson, William	27	1657	MCC folio 20
Johnson, William	28	1686	MCC folio 121
Johnson, William	28	1691	MCC folio 167A
Johnson, William	29	1658	MCC folio 17
Johnson, William	31	1679	MCC folio 87
Johnson, William	33	1661	MCC folio 27
Johnson, William	38	1658	MCC folio 16
Johnson, William	44	1673	MCC folio 62
Johnson, William	46	1675	MCC folio 70
Johnson, William	46	1676	MCC folio 71
Johnson, William	48	1676	MCC folio 74
Johnson, William	51	1679	MCC folio 87
Johnson, William	54	1657	MCC folio 18
Johnson, William	57	1668	MCC folio 45
Johnson, William	62	1691	MCC folio 148
Johnson, William	62	1691	MCC folio 157
Johnson, William	63	1693	MCC folio 175
Johnson, William	64	1695	MCC folio 195
Johnson, William	67	1695	MCC folio 210

Johnson, Zachariah	33	1679	MCC folio 184
Johnson, Zachariah	33	1679	MCC folio 85
Johnston, Katharine	25	1684	MCC folio 109
Johnston, Mathew	51	1684	MCC folio 109
Jones, Edward	40	1668	MCC folio 48
Jones, Grace	25	1666	EQC 3:334
Jones, Griffin	35	1681	EQC 8:102
Jones, Henry	32	1697	SJC 3489
Jones, Hugh	25	1661	EQC 2:322
Jones, Hugh	40	1678	EQC 7:113
Jones, Hugh	40	1680	EQC 7:424
Jones, Hugh	46	1683	EQC 9:55
Jones, Isaac	55	1683	MCC folio 104
Jones, John	22	1676	EQC 6:119
Jones, John	22	1676	EQC 6:121
Jones, John	22	1676	MCC folio 72
Jones, John	38	1679	MCC folio 184
Jones, Josiah	25	1669	MCC folio 51
Jones, Josiah	26	1669	MCC folio 51
Jones, Mary	29	1680	EQC 7:419
Jones, Mary	32	1662	SJC 470
Jones, Mary	47	1675	SJC 1412
Jones, Morgan	28	1664	SJC 648
Jones, Nathaniel	23	1691	MCC folio 141
Jones, Rebecca	25	1671	MCC folio 57
Jones, Robert	27	1680	SJC 1887
Jones, Robert	29	1662	EQC 3:2
Jones, Robert	63	1694/5	SJC 3782
Jones, Sarah	28	1678	MCC folio 78
Jones, Thomas	24	1669	MCC folio 52
Jones, Thomas	28	1680	SJC 1926
Jones, Thomas	34	nd	SJC 3632
Jones, Thomas	35	1654	MCC folio 10
Jones, Thomas	35	1677	MCC folio 78
Jones, Thomas	60	1663	SJC 162051
Jones, Thomas	67	1666	EQC 3:327
Jones, Thomas	68	1667	EQC 3:390
Jones, William	46	1671	MCC folio 59
Joslyn, Peter	33	1699	MCC folio 192
Joy, Deborah	27	1652	EQC 1:264
Joy, Ephraim	28	1677	SJC 1633
Joy, Joseph	32	1677	SJC 1633
Joy, Peter	40	1677	EQC 6:376
Joy, Samuel	21	nd	SJC 2762
Joy, Thomas	54	1665	SJC 726
Joy, Thomas	54	1666	EQC 3:306
Joy, Thomas	66	1676	EQC 6:219
Joyliffe, John	57	1673	MCC folio 65
Joyliffe, John	57	1693	SJC 1221
Joyliffe, John	64	1681	EQC 8:115
Joyliffe, John	65	1681	EQC 8:116
Judkins, Hannah	19	1696	SJC 3535
Judkins, Joel	24	1671	SJC 1100
Judkins, Thomas	32	1663	EQC 3:44

Judkins, Thomas	50	1679	EQC 7:200
Judkins, Thomas	50	1679	SJC 2011
Juell, Samuel	28	1673	SJC 1232
Kaley, John	41	1683	EQC 9:87
Kay, Stephen	30	1694	SJC 3123f
Kebby, Edward	60	1667	MCC folio 43
Kebby, Elisha	21	1667	MCC folio 43
Kebby, Elisha	28	1676	EQC 6:190
Keen, William	20	1681	SJC 2037
Keen, William	35	1694	SJC 4116
Kell[ ], James	33	1691	MCC folio 148
Kellam, John	23	1680	SJC 1953
Kellam, William	29	1685	SJC 2345
Kelling, Hannah	42	1686	MCC folio 125
Kellom, John	19	1678	EQC 7:22
Kellond, John	23	1680	SJC 1953
Kellond, Thomas	26	1663	SJC 561
Kellond, Thomas	42	1678/9	SJC 1756
Kelly, John	40	1684	EQC 9:256
Kelso, William	26	1681	SJC 2010
Kelton, John	30	1691	SJC 2596
Kemball, Benjamin	45	1680	EQC 8:91
Kemball, Joseph	18	1680	EQC 7:343
Kemble, Henry	40	1674	MCC folio 67
Kemble, Thomas	56	1676	EQC 6:198
Kemble, Thomas	56	1679	EQC 7:291
Kemble, Thomas	62	1684	SD 13:121
Kempthorn, Mary	43	1671	MCC folio 57
Kempton, Ephraim	30	1679	EQC 7:328
Kendall, Frances	48	1662	MCC folio 28
Kendall, Frances	50	1671	MCC folio 59
Kendall, Frances	62	1679	MCC folio 87
Kendall, Frances	65	1684	MCC folio 109
Kendall, Francis	50	1671	MCC folio 59
Kendall, Francis	57	1672	MCC folio 60
Kendall, Francis	65	1684	MCC folio 115
Kendall, John	39	1685	MCC folio 118
Kendall, Rebecca	40	1660	MCC folio 23
Kendall, Rebecca	49	1668	MCC folio 48
Kendall, Rebecca	62	1681	MCC folio 94
Kendrick, John	50	1683	EQC 9:221
Kennett, Richard	40	1691	MCC folio 141
Kennison, Abel	47	1680	MCC folio 183
Kenny, Henry	55	1679	EQC 7:310
Kenny, John	22	1674	EQC 5:428
Kenny, John	36	1672	SD 6:280
Kent, Cornelius	25	1670	EQC 4:224
Kent, Joanna	65	1686	EQC WPA 46-21-1
Kent, Joanna	65	nd	SJC 2770
Kent, John	27	1691	MCC folio 157
Kent, John	28	1674	EQC 5:411
Kent, John	30	1675	EQC 6:78
Kent, John	34	1678	EQC 7:157
Kent, John	36	1681	EQC 8:76

Kent, John	36	1681	EQC 8:78
Kent, John	37	1678	EQC 7:157
Kent, Steven	60	1667	EQC 3:454
Kent, William	37	1673	SJC 1216
Kerly, William	45	1666	MCC folio 40
Kerly, William	46	1667	MCC folio 44
Kery, Peter	34	1678	EQC 7:118
Keser, George	65	1678	EQC 7:126
Kettle, Hester	60	1666/7	SJC 814
Kettle, James	20	1685	EQC 9:459
Kettle, John	25	1691	MCC folio 148
Kettle, Richard	72	1677	MCC folio 74
Kettle, Samuel	47	1690	MCC folio 131
Kettle, Samuel	47	1690	MCC folio 150
Keyes, Joseph	30	1698	MCC folio 167
Keyes, Samuel	20	1663	SJC 721
Keyes, Samuel	28	1671	SJC 1276
Keyes, Solomon	60	1692	MCC folio 154
Keyes, Solomon	60	1695	MCC folio 207
Kezer, Benjamin	20	1678	EQC 7:114
Kezer, Eleazer	18	1665	EQC 3:283
Kezer, Elijah	18	1665	EQC 3:269
Kezer, George	50	1664	EQC 3:158
Kezer, George	64	1675	EQC 6:77
Kezer, John	14	1665	EQC 3:269
Kezer, John	17	1665	EQC 3:283
Kiats, Richard	41	1691	SJC 98524
Kibbee, Edward	80	1680	SJC 1973
Kidder, Anna	50	1677	MCC folio 78
Kidder, James	22	1676	MCC folio 73
Kidder, Nathaniel	26	1686	MCC folio 123
Kilby, John	30	nd	SJC 2898
Kilby, Sarah	55	1697/8	SJC 4451
Kilcup, William	50	1656	SD 2:295
Killam, Daniel	33	1686	EQC 9:584
Killam, John	22	1677	EQC 6:277
Killam, John	52	1679	EQC 7:207
Killam, Joseph	16	1677	EQC 6:277
Killam, Lot	40	1678	EQC 7:8
Killam, Thomas	23	1677	EQC 6:277
Killam, William	24	1685	EQC 9:465
Killam, William	25	1686	EQC 9:591
Kimball, Benjamin	23	1660	EQC 2:231
Kimball, Benjamin	24	1660	EQC 2:229
Kimball, Benjamin	32	1669	EQC 4:117
Kimball, Benjamin	37	1674	EQC 5:270
Kimball, Benjamin	45	1682	EQC 8:273
Kimball, Caleb	33	1672	EQC 5:12
Kimball, Caleb	40	1679	EQC 7:269
Kimball, Ebenezer	18	1686	EQC WPA 47-18-2
Kimball, Henry	22	1677	EQC 6:252
Kimball, Henry	38	1670	EQC 4:303
Kimball, Henry	53	1669	EQC 4:180
Kimball, Henry	56	1674	EQC 5:275

Kimball, John	30	1676	EQC 6:158
Kimball, John	35	1666	EQC 3:325
Kimball, John	37	1686	EQC 9:606
Kimball, John	40	1677	MCC folio 76
Kimball, John	40	nd	SJC 1738
Kimball, John	47	1683	EQC 9:224
Kimball, John	50	1683	EQC 9:225
Kimball, John	53	1683	EQC 9:223
Kimball, John	56	1692	MCC folio 172
Kimball, Joseph	18	1679	EQC 7:310
Kimball, Mary	45	1680	SJC 1932
Kimball, Mercy	30	1674	EQC 5:270
Kimball, Richard	15	1658	EQC 2:138
Kimball, Richard	20	1681	EQC 8:216
Kimball, Richard	50	1675	EQC 6:31
Kimball, Thomas	17	1681	EQC 8:216
Kimball, Thomas	25	1682	EQC 8:436
Kimball, Thomas	26	1660	EQC 2:229
Kimball, Thomas	26	1661	EQC 2:275
Kimball, Thomas	30	1665	EQC 3:278
Kimball, Thomas	32	1666	EQC 3:325
Kimball, Thomas	49	1670	SJC 1276
Kimball, Thomas	53	1674/5	SJC 1458
Kimball, Thomas	53	1675	SJC 1390
Kindricke, John	50	1683	SJC 2227
King, Abraham	28	1679	EQC 7:326
King, Anne	50	1679	EQC 7:249
King, Daniel	27	1659	EQC 2:193
King, Daniel	50	1686	EQC WPA 46-83-4
King, Daniel	55	1657	EQC 7:129
King, Ebenezer	23	1676	SJC 1562
King, James	18	1670	EQC 4:242
King, John	57	1657	MCC folio 19
King, Mark	28	1660	EQC 2:203
King, Ralph	18	1685	EQC 9:521
King, Ralph	22	1661	EQC 2:287
King, Ralph	35	1675	EQC 6:10
King, Ralph	40	1679	EQC 7:252
King, Ralph	42	1681	EQC 8:122
King, Ralph	42	1682	EQC 8:403
King, Ralph	43	1682	EQC 8:397
King, Ralph	46	1684	EQC 9:317
King, Richard	19	1696	SJC 3377
King, Samuel	28	nd	SJC 2770
King, William	53	1680	EQC 8:74
King, William	53	1681	EQC 8:73
Kingman, Henry	70	1665	SJC 815
Kingsberry, John	28	1694	SJC 3153
Kingsbury, Eleazer	26	1671	SD 7:185
Kingsbury, Henry	54	1669	EQC 4:117
Kinnekim, John	24	1695	MCC folio 177
Kinnicut, Roger	33	1669	MCC folio 52
Kirbe, William	74	1679	MCC folio 89
Kirk, Elizabeth	20	1688	EQC WPA 47-151-1

Kirtland, John	52	1661	EQC 2:303
Kirtland, Mary	27	1681	EQC 8:103
Kirtland, Nathaniel	34	1681	EQC 8:124
Kitchin, Elizabeth	52	1675	EQC 6:98
Kitchin, Elizabeth	53	1676	EQC 6:171
Kitchin, John	42	1661	EQC 2:321
Kitchin, Robert	29	1684	EQC 9:178
Kittell, John	32	1655	EQC 1:390
Kittle, John	32	1657	EQC 2:38
Knap, John	43	1667	MCC folio 44
Knap, John	48	1673	MCC folio 64
Knap, John	50	1674	MCC folio 63
Knap, Joseph	30	1685	MCC folio 115
Knapp, James	50	1677	MCC folio 77
Kneeland, Edward	35	1680	SJC 1967
Kneeland, John	52	1684	SJC 2228
Kneeland, Mary	22	1691	MCC folio 141
Knight Philip	23	1668	EQC 4:74
Knight, Abigail	15	1679	MCC folio 85
Knight, Barshua	40	1664	EQC 3:134
Knight, Charles	21	1661	EQC 2:320
Knight, Charles	35	1678	EQC 7:141
Knight, Charles	35	1679	EQC 7:297
Knight, Charles	35	1679	EQC 7:305
Knight, Charles	35	1680	SJC 2011
Knight, Daniel	30	1655	MCC folio 12
Knight, Dinah	15	1676	MCC folio 71
Knight, Dinah	16	1676	MCC folio 71
Knight, Eliza	13	1668	EQC 4:74
Knight, Elizabeth	17	1671	EQC 4:432
Knight, Elizabeth	17	1675	MCC folio 71
Knight, Elizabeth	17	1675	MCC folio 72
Knight, Elizabeth	17	1675	SJC 1581
Knight, Jacob	24	1669	EQC 4:208
Knight, Jacob	29	1674	EQC 5:379
Knight, Jacob	36	1681	EQC 8:103
Knight, John	18	1666	SJC 762
Knight, John	19	1679	EQC 7:200
Knight, John	19	1679	EQC 7:257
Knight, John	30	1678	EQC 7:157
Knight, John	34	1668	MCC folio 52
Knight, John	45	1666	SJC 762
Knight, John	45	1669	EQC 4:111
Knight, John	46	1679	MCC folio 85
Knight, John	47	1669	EQC 4:207
Knight, John	47	1681	MCC folio 93
Knight, John	48	1671	EQC 4:332
Knight, John	50	1673	EQC 5:224
Knight, John	50	1675	EQC 6:11
Knight, John	51	1676	EQC 6:125
Knight, John	51	1676	EQC 6:128
Knight, John	51	1676	EQC 6:165
Knight, John	51	1676	SJC 1481
Knight, John	55	1684	MCC folio 111

Knight, John	55	1684	MCC folio 183
Knight, John	64	1679	MCC folio 85
Knight, Jonathan	24	1666	EQC 3:323
Knight, Jonathan	26	1668	EQC 4:74
Knight, Jonathan	38	1680	EQC 7:392
Knight, Jonathan	38	1680	EQC 7:392
Knight, Jonathan	38	1680	SJC 1884
Knight, Joseph	25	1677	EQC 6:254
Knight, Joseph	26	1678	EQC 7:156
Knight, Joseph	29	1682	EQC 8:283
Knight, Joseph	33	1678	SJC 1908
Knight, Joseph	35	1659	MCC folio 21
Knight, Mary	11	1668	EQC 4:74
Knight, Mary	32	1679	MCC folio 85
Knight, Mary	50	1675	EQC 6:77
Knight, Philip	31	1668	MCC folio 47
Knight, Philip	46	1663	MCC folio 34
Knight, Philip	52	1666	EQC 3:323
Knight, Rebecca	17	1668	EQC 4:74
Knight, Richard	17	1683	EQC 9:87
Knight, Richard	42	1653	MCC folio 7
Knight, Richard	50	1675	SJC 1422
Knight, Richard	53	1676	MCC folio 74
Knight, Richard	63	1677	SJC 1753
Knight, Richard	69	1671	EQC 4:432
Knight, Richard	70	1673	EQC 5:224
Knight, Richard	73	1675	EQC 6:66
Knight, Richard	75	1677	EQC 6:321
Knight, Richard	77	1678	EQC 7:157
Knight, Richard	78	1680	EQC 8:172
Knight, Robert	16	1679	EQC 7:201
Knight, Robert	16	1679	EQC 7:257
Knight, Robert	16	1679	EQC 7:297
Knight, Robert	50	1675	EQC 6:77
Knight, Robert	54	1668	EQC 4:34
Knight, Robert	55	1669	EQC 4:156
Knight, Robert	55	1669	EQC 4:174
Knight, Robert	58	1673	EQC 5:129
Knight, Robert	65	1680	EQC 7:387
Knight, Ruth	34	1685	MCC folio 116
Knight, Sarah	16	1663	EQC 3:51
Knight, William	33	1686	EQC WPA 46-88-2
Knights, Michael	39	1668	MCC folio 48
Knoher, George	55	1666	MCC folio 40
Knop, James	53	1678	MCC folio 81
Knop, John	23	1685	MCC folio 115
Knop, John	58	1681	MCC folio 97
Knop, John	63	1686	MCC folio 121
Knop, John	63	1686	MCC folio 125
Knop, Joseph	30	1685	SJC 2348
Knott, Eleanor	3mo	1684	EQC 9:292
Knott, Mary	6	1684	EQC 9:292
Knott, Richard	35	1677	EQC 6:369
Knott, Richard	36	1679	MCC folio 86

Knott, Richard	8	1684	EQC 9:292
Knowling, Thomas	26	1672	MCC folio 65
Knowling, Thomas	26	1672	SJC 1221
Knowlton, Hannah	35	1682	EQC 8:282
Knowlton, John	14	1683	EQC 9:222
Knowlton, John	14	1684	EQC 9:203
Knowlton, John	23	1669	EQC 4:142
Knowlton, John	25	1683	EQC 9:113
Knowlton, John	28	1684	EQC 9:189
Knowlton, John	29	1674	EQC 5:319
Knowlton, John	34	1681	EQC 8:87
Knowlton, Joseph	25	1674	EQC 5:415
Knowlton, Joseph	34	1684	EQC 9:331
Knowlton, Thomas	27	1668	EQC 4:83
Knowlton, Thomas	27	1668	EQC 4:84
Knowlton, Thomas	28	1670	EQC 4:279
Knowlton, Thomas	31	1674	EQC 5:321
Knowlton, Thomas	32	1674	EQC 5:414
Knowlton, Thomas	36	1678	EQC 7:120
Knowlton, Thomas	38	1679	EQC 7:220
Knowlton, Thomas	42	1686	EQC 9:584
Knowlton, William	26	1669	EQC 4:142
Knowlton, William	30	1674	EQC 5:415
Knowlton, William	31	1674	EQC 5:319
Knowlton, William	34	1678	EQC 7:120
Knowlton, William	35	1680	EQC 8:9
Knowlton, William	36	1679	EQC 7:219
Knowlton, William	36	1679	EQC 7:258
Knowlton, William	36	1680	EQC 8:21
Knowlton, William	36	1680	EQC 8:22
Knowlton, William	36	1681	EQC 8:87
Knowlton, William	38	1679	EQC 7:292
Knowlton, William	50	1695	SJC 3239
Lackins, Timothy	21	1672	MCC folio 60
Lahagoe, James	36	1684	SJC 2251
Lake, Lancelott	31	1680	EQC 8:30
Lake, Lancelott	31	1680	SJC 1971
Lake, Robert	22	1681	EQC 8:102
Lake, Thomas	22	1668	EQC 4:30
Lake, Thomas	43	1658	EQC 2:92
Lake, Thomas	55	1671	SJC 1290
Lake, William	38	1675	EQC 6:45
Lakin, John	67	1694	MCC folio 182
Lakin, John	67	nd	SJC 3063
Lakin, William	70	1694	MCC folio 182
Lakin, William	70	nd	SJC 3063
Lambe, Caleb	36	1675	EQC 6:53
Lambert, Daniel	26	1684	EQC 9:344
Lambert, Daniel	26	1685	EQC 9:470
Lambert, Daniel	26	1685	SJC 2339
Lambert, John	27	1686	EQC WPA 46-92-3
Lambert, John	30	1662	EQC 2:397
Lambert, John	30	1662	EQC 2:398
Lambert, John	34	1662	EQC 3:22

Lambert, John	48	1677	EQC 6:354
Lambert, John	55	1685	EQC 9:482
Lambert, Mary	15	1673	SJC 1254
Lambert, Mary	15	1682	EQC 8:340
Lambert, Mary	16	1674	EQC 5:415
Lambert, Sarah	12	1673	SJC 1254
Lamberton, Deliverance	17	1654/5	MCC folio 13
Lambord, Margaret	40	1679	EQC 7:269
Lamprey, Henry	50	1667	EQC 3:410
Lamprey, Henry	82	1677	SJC 1753
Lamson, John	39	1682	EQC 8:281
Lamson, Joseph	18	1676	MCC folio 73
Lamson, Martha	34	1682	EQC 8:280
Lamson, Samuel	32	1681	MCC folio 96
Lamstone, John	40	1698/9	MCC folio 209
Lancaster, Joseph	26	1666	EQC 3:365
Lander, John	38	1681	EQC 8:126
Lander, John	42	1684	EQC 9:280
Lander, John	43	1684	EQC 9:398
Lane, Job	52	1673	MCC folio 62
Langburn, John	34	1667	SJC 841
Langdon, Mary	44	1695	MCC folio 197
Langdon, Philip	48	1695	SJC 3203
Langdon, Phillip	48	1695	MCC folio 197
Langford, John	20	1668	SJC 889
Langley, John	63	1691	MCC folio 156
Laraby, William	45	1668	SJC 910
Larcom, Mordecai	55	1684	EQC 9:248
Larcom, Mordicah	30	1695	SJC 3239
Larcomb, Elizabeth	40	1673	EQC 5:217
Largin, Sarah	19	1669	MCC folio 52
Larkin, Edward	23	1691	MCC folio 148
Larkin, John	38	1689	SJC 2553
Larrimore, Thomas	30	1695	SJC 3123f
Larrimore, Thomas	31	1694/5	SJC 162352
Larrimore, Thomas	31	1694/5	SJC 3101
Larrimore, Thomas	31	1694/5	SJC 3123g
Larrimore, Thomas	34	nd	SJC 3547
Lasher, Stephen	28	1668/9	SD 6:133
Lathrop, Benjamin	25	1653	MCC folio 7
Lathrop, Benjamin	30	1661	MCC folio 36
Lathrop, Benjamin	35	1662	MCC folio 31
Lathrop, Benjamin	58	1681	MCC folio 184
Lathrop, Hannah	21	1676/7	MCC folio 77
Lattimore, Christopher	43	1661	EQC 2:291
Lattimore, Christopher	50	1674	EQC 5:283
Lattimore, Christopher	52	1674	EQC 5:348
Lattimore, Christopher	58	1679	MCC folio 86
Lattimore, Christopher	60	1680	EQC 7:353
Lattimore, Christopher	64	1684	EQC 9:241
Lattimore, Hugh	23	1680	EQC 7:352
Laughton, Thomas	56	1664	EQC 3:158
Laughton, Thomas	75	1684	EQC 9:341
Lavistone, John	22	1679	MCC folio 87

Lawkings, Thomas	46	1654	MCC folio 13
Lawrence, Daniel	24	1689	MCC folio 135
Lawrence, George	40	1674	MCC folio 70
Lawrence, George	40	1677	MCC folio 77
Lawrence, George	40	1678	MCC folio 81
Lawrence, Hannah	20	1680	MCC folio 184
Lawrence, Hannah	20	1681	MCC folio 104
Lawrence, John	10	1674	MCC folio 67
Lawrence, John	35	1655/6	SJC 236
Lawrence, John	35	1656/7	MCC folio 19
Lawrence, John	36	1654	MCC folio 10
Lawrence, Joseph	25	1679	SJC 1827
Lawrence, Judah	17	1677	MCC folio 77
Lawrence, Robert	28	1664	EQC 3:211
Lawrence, Robert	32	1671	EQC 4:420
Lawson, Christopher	55	1671	EQC 4:385
Lawson, Christopher	65	1680/1	SJC 2014
Lawson, Elizabeth	40	nd	SJC 913
Lawson, John	27	1692	SJC 4085
Lawson, John	28	1695	SJC 162362
Laynton, Katherine	20	1680	EQC 7:375
Laynton, Katherine	20	1680	SJC 1894
Layton, Rebecca	23	1673	EQC 5:251
Layton, Thomas	60	1665	SJC 764
Leach, John	63	1681	EQC 8:74
Leach, John	69	1685	EQC 9:439
Leach, Lawrence	85	1662	EQC 2:428
Leach, Richard	50	1669	EQC 4:111
Leach, Richard	60	1678	EQC 7:15
Leach, Richard	67	1685	EQC 9:438
Leach, Robert	20	1673	EQC 5:215
Leach, Robert	58	1673	EQC 5:215
Leach, Robert	65	1666	MCC folio 40
Leach, Samuel	39	1672	EQC 5:67
Leads, Mary	29	1672	SJC 1281
Leargen, Henry	47	1668	SJC 913
Leaver, Thomas	30	1678	EQC 7:84
Leaver, Thomas	67	1682	EQC 8:268
Ledge, John	47	1657	EQC 7:129
Lee, George	40	1666	SJC 740
Lee, John	33	1678	EQC 6:404
Lee, John	34	1679	EQC 7:305
Lee, John	34	1680	EQC 7:362
Lee, John	36	1681	EQC 8:164
Lee, John	60	1658	EQC 2:146
Lee, John	67	1669	EQC 4:157
Lee, Joseph	30	1678	EQC 6:404
Lee, Joseph	30	1678	EQC 6:419
Lee, Joseph	30	1678	EQC 6:419
Lee, Joseph	30	1678	SJC 1731
Lee, Joseph	32	1679	MCC folio 87
Lee, Mary	37	1700	SJC 4704
Lee, Rebecca	28	1681	MCC folio 104
Lee, Richard	21	1682	EQC 8:338

Lee, Richard	30	1694	SJC 2915
Lee, Richard	38	1682	EQC 8:377
Lee, Samuel	16	1685	SJC 2325
Lee, Thomas	33	1681	SJC 2057
Leech, Ambrose	60	1676	SJC 1498
Leech, Robert	27	1679	EQC 7:296
Leeds, Abigail	35	1679	EQC 7:269
Leeke, William	30	nd	SJC 1049
Leffingwell, Isabel	50	1668	MCC folio 48
Leffingwell, Michael	85	1684	MCC folio 109
Leffingwell, Michael	85	1684	MCC folio 115
Leffingwell, Thomas	30	1681	MCC folio 93
Leffingwell, Thomas	38	1685	MCC folio 115
Leffingwell, Thomas	38	1689	MCC folio 134
Leffingwell, Thomas	40	1690	MCC folio 167A
Legg, Elizabeth	57	1665	EQC 3:284
Legg, Elizabeth	58	1668	EQC 4:42
Legg, John	21	1665	EQC 3:284
Legg, John	28	1673	EQC 5:179
Legg, John	28	1673	EQC 5:180
Legg, John	35	1680	EQC 7:386
Legg, John	47	1657	EQC 7:128
Legg, John	60	1670	EQC 4:221
Legg, John	60	1671	EQC 4:412
Legg, John	65	nd	SJC 26488
Legg, Samuel	37	1679	SJC 1789
Legge, John	29	1674	EQC 5:256
Legge, John	58	1666	EQC 3:368
Legroo, Philip	16	1677	EQC 6:346
Leigh, John	24	1668	EQC 4:83
Leigh, John	24	1668	EQC 4:84
Leigh, John	70	1654	EQC 1:336
Leigh, Thomas	70	1650	EQC 1:188
Lemar, Samuel	24	1691	MCC folio 148
Lemmon, John	52	1675	SJC 1425
Lemmon, Samuel	25	1692	MCC folio 154
Lensey, Eleazer	35	1681	EQC 8:102
Lensey, Eleazer	35	1681	EQC 8:124
Leonard, Elisha	24	1685	EQC 9:449
Leonard, Henry	40	1660	EQC 2:211
Leonard, James	52	1695	SJC 3299
Leonard, John	29	1697	SJC 3530
Leonard, Mary	32	1657	EQC 2:58
Leonard, Mary	49	1674	EQC 5:352
Leonard, Mary	49	1674	EQC 5:354
Lesenby, Henry	18	1663	EQC 3:50
Lesson, Nicholas	60	1678	EQC 7:5
Lesson, Nicholas	60	1678	EQC 7:92
Letherland, William	62	1670/1	SD 7:87
Letherland, William	62	1670/1	SJC 1092
Letherland, William	68	1676	SJC 1565
Letherland, William	69	1677	SJC 1626
Letherland, William	75	1683	SJC 2198
Leverett, Hudson	23	1664	SJC 754

Leverett, Hudson	25	1665	SJC 826
Leverett, Hudson	32	1672	SCC 139
Leverett, Hudson	32	1672	SJC 1194
Leverett, Hudson	36	1675	SCC 593
Leverett, Hudson	36	1675	SJC 1398
Leverett, Hudson	40	1680	SJC 2016
Leverett, Hudson	49	1689	SJC 2549
Leverett, John	47	1663	SJC 580
Levitt, Hezron	30	1674	SJC 1566
Levitt, John	28	1665	SJC 709
Levitt, Thomas	60	1676	SJC 1566
Lewes, James	23	1655	SJC 257
Lewin, Edward	23	1682	EQC 8:413
Lewin, John	21	1668	SJC 889
Lewis, Christopher	30	1677	MCC folio 75
Lewis, John	19	1679	EQC 7:252
Lewis, John	21	1684	EQC 9:317
Lewis, John	24	1684	EQC 9:246
Lewis, John	34	1666	EQC 3:345
Lewis, John	40	1677	EQC 6:360
Lewis, John	40	1678	EQC 7:26
Lewis, John	40	1679	EQC 7:252
Lewis, John	42	1657	MCC folio 20
Lewis, John	44	1678	MCC folio 80
Lewis, John	49	1682	MCC folio 101
Lewis, John	51	1684	EQC 9:246
Lewis, John	51	1684	EQC 9:314
Lewis, John	51	1684	EQC 9:316
Lewis, John	51	1684	EQC 9:317
Lewis, John	57	1673	EQC 5:178
Lewis, Joseph	37	1680	MCC folio 89
Lewis, Mary	43	1695	SJC 4189
Lewis, Thomas	60	1698	SJC 3726
Lewis, Thomas	63	1694	SJC 2989
Lian, Thomas	25	1674	EQC 6:19
Liberte, James	25	nd	SJC 1001
Lidget, Peter	44	1673	MCC folio 65
Lidgett, Peter	38	1672	EQC 5:9
Lidgett, Peter	44	1673	SJC 1221
Lightfoot, William	23	1658	EQC 2:97
Lightfoot, William	33	1665	EQC 3:257
Lighton, Sarah	19	1681	EQC 8:278
Lighton, Sarah	19	1682	EQC 8:279
Lilboure, Elizabeth	23	1668	EQC 4:15
Lilley, Samuel	22	1685	SD 13:382
Lillie, Samuel	26	1690	MCC folio 131
Lilly, Edward	19	1684	SJC 2196
Lilly, Edward	50	1679	SJC 1800
Lilly, Samuel	30	nd	SJC 2807
Lilly, Samuel	31	1696	MCC folio 199
Lilly, Samuel	31	1696	MCC folio 209
Lilly, Samuel	31	1696	SJC 162407
Lilly, Samuel	31	1696	SJC 3697
Lincoln, Daniel	42	1663	SJC 659

Lind, Enoch	17	1666	SD 5:53
Lindall, Timothy	35	1677	EQC 6:280
Linde, John	43	1669	MCC folio 53
Linde, Joseph	46	1681	MCC folio 100
Linde, Joseph	46	1682	MCC folio 102
Linde, Joseph	47	1684	MCC folio 111
Line, John	23	1673	EQC 5:231
Line, John	24	1674	EQC 5:321
Lines, Thomas	50	1667	MCC folio 41
Linkhorn, William	23	1667	EQC 3:390
Linsey, Eleazer	35	1681	EQC 8:124
Linsey, Eleazer	44	1687	EQC WPA 47-66-3
Linsey, Mary	35	1681	EQC 8:104
Linsey, Sarah	30	1681	EQC 8:102
Linsey, Sarah	30	1681	EQC 8:225
Linsford, Francis	60	1662	EQC 2:442
Liscum, John	44	1677	SD 10:249
Little, Joseph	25	1678	EQC 7:156
Little, Mary	25	1672	SJC 1148
Little, Moses	19	1676	EQC 6:188
Little, Moses	21	1678	EQC 7:157
Little, Robert	32	1673	MCC folio 64
Little, Robert	32	1673	SJC 1221
Littlehale, John	23	1675	EQC 6:32
Livermore, Daniel	16	1691	MCC folio 151
Livermore, Nathaniel	32	1683	MCC folio 104
Livermore, Samuel	13	1691	MCC folio 151
Lloyd, Hannah	24	1680	MCC folio 183
Lloyd, Hannah	27	1684	MCC folio 109
Lloyd, James	27	1679	SD 11:255
Loader, John	22	1683/4	SJC 2244
Loader, John	28	1688	EQC WPA 47-123-4
Loader, Mary	20	1685	SJC 2375
Lobdall, Isaac	40	1672	SJC 1163
Lochan, Allexander	25	1679	MCC folio 85
Lock, William	27	1657	MCC folio 20
Lock, William	28	1657	MCC folio 20
Lock, William	29	1659	MCC folio 21
Lock, William	30	1658	MCC folio 16
Lock, William	31	1661	MCC folio 27
Lock, William	33	1662	MCC folio 29
Lock, William	50	1656	MCC folio 16
Lock, William	61	1691	MCC folio 167A
Lock, William	64	1695	MCC folio 197
Locker, George	40	1698	SJC 3778
Locker, Henry	16	1671	MCC folio 58
Locker, Henry	60	1668	MCC folio 50
Locker, Henry	69	1677	MCC folio 76
Locker, John	30	1682	MCC folio 106
Lockhart, George	21	1678	EQC 7:136
Lockhart, George	21	1678	EQC 7:147
Loe, John	18	1681	EQC 8:152
Logan, Alexander	25	1679	MCC folio 185
Logia, Mary	29	1677	EQC 6:295

Lomar, Stephen	37	1689	SJC 2520
Long, Abiel	29	1678	EQC 7:156
Long, Elizabeth	70	1673	MCC folio 64
Long, Hannah	22	1681	MCC folio 104
Long, Hannah	22	1681	MCC folio 97
Long, John	47	1676	MCC folio 72
Long, John	49	1677/8	MCC folio 185
Long, Michael	30	1653	MCC folio 8
Long, Michael	40	1657	MCC folio 20
Long, Michael	68	1681	MCC folio 104
Long, Michael	68	1681	MCC folio 97
Long, Richard	30	1685	EQC 9:526
Long, Richard	30	1686	EQC WPA 46-125-2
Long, Richard	40	nd	SJC 2762
Long, Robert	32	1653	EQC 1:288
Long, Robert	58	1678	EQC 7:157
Long, Ruth	24	1681	MCC folio 104
Long, Ruth	24	1681	MCC folio 97
Long, Shubael	17	1678	EQC 7:156
Long, William	34	1681	SJC 2029
Long, Zachariah	31	1667	SJC 909
Long, Zachariah	53	1684	MCC folio 111
Longfellow, William	26	1677	EQC 6:357
Longfellow, William	27	1678	EQC 7:156
Longfellow, William	28	1679	EQC 7:317
Longfellow, William	30	1683	EQC 9:10
Longfellow, William	31	1683	EQC 9:236
Longfellow, William	31	1684	EQC 9:237
Longhorne, Richard	45	1662	EQC 2:361
Longhorne, Richard	49	1667	EQC 3:437
Longhorne, Sarah	14	1674	EQC 5:344
Longhorne, Sarah	63	1685	MCC folio 116
Longhorne, Thomas	40	1662	MCC folio 29
Longhorne, Thomas	48	1669	MCC folio 53
Longhorne, Thomas	48	1669	SJC 964
Longhorne, Thomas	50	1671	MCC folio 58
Longhorne, Thomas	60	1677	MCC folio 76
Longhorne, Thomas	60	1677	MCC folio 78
Longhorne, Thomas	64	1681	MCC folio 92
Longley, Anna	16	1663	EQC 3:34
Longley, Annah	16	1663	SJC 577
Longley, Cicely	40	1691	MCC folio 148
Longley, Cicely	40	1691	MCC folio 163
Longley, Cicely	40	1691	MCC folio 173
Longley, John	23	1663	EQC 3:38
Longley, John	23	1663	EQC 3:46
Longley, John	23	1663	SJC 577
Longley, John	25	1663	EQC 3:25
Longley, John	42	1678	SJC 1722
Longley, John	42	1681	EQC 8:124
Longley, John	42	1681	EQC 8:124
Longley, John	53	1691	MCC folio 156
Longley, Mary	19	1663	EQC 3:32
Longley, Mary	19	1663	EQC 3:34

Longley, Mary	19	1663	SJC 577
Longley, Sicely	40	1691	MCC folio 145
Longley, Stephen	45	nd	SJC 1964
Longley, William	47	1661	EQC 2:284
Longley, William	48	1663	EQC 3:26
Lopez, Jacobus	40	1689	SJC 2539
Lord, Hannah	30	1669	MCC folio 51
Lord, Hannah	37	1675	EQC 6:85
Lord, Hannah	37	1675	SJC 162144
Lord, Jane	55	1684	EQC 9:275
Lord, Jane	56	1680	EQC 7:330
Lord, Jeane	15	1682	EQC 8:340
Lord, John	40	1677	MCC folio 78
Lord, Joseph	17	1679	EQC 7:252
Lord, Joseph	18	1680	EQC 7:331
Lord, Joseph	19	1681	EQC 8:110
Lord, Joseph	20	1682	EQC 8:342
Lord, Nathaniel	17	1674	EQC 5:375
Lord, Nathaniel	20	1674	EQC 5:306
Lord, Robert	26	1684	EQC 9:255
Lord, Robert	31	1664	EQC 3:122
Lord, Robert	34	1666	EQC 3:324
Lord, Robert	34	1666	EQC 3:372
Lord, Robert	37	1669	EQC 4:154
Lord, Robert	39	1662	SJC 561
Lord, Robert	39	1671	EQC 4:345
Lord, Robert	40	1673	EQC 5:196
Lord, Robert	40	1673	SJC 1234
Lord, Robert	41	1663	SJC 561
Lord, Robert	43	1675	EQC 6:12
Lord, Robert	47	1678	EQC 6:419
Lord, Robert	47	1679	EQC 7:218
Lord, Robert	47	1679	EQC 7:262
Lord, Robert	47	1679	EQC 7:270
Lord, Robert	48	1680	EQC 8:35
Lord, Robert	48	1680	EQC 8:9
Lord, Robert	49	1681	EQC 8:113
Lord, Robert	50	1662	EQC 2:396
Lord, Robert	50	1682	EQC 8:245
Lord, Robert	51	1683	EQC 9:95
Lord, Robert	52	1684	EQC 9:189
Lord, Robert	52	1684	EQC 9:257
Lord, Robert	57	1660	EQC 2:230
Lord, Robert	58	1662	EQC 2:349
Lord, Robert	59	1662	EQC 2:434
Lord, Robert	60	1663	SJC 577
Lord, Robert	62	1665	EQC 3:236
Lord, Robert	63	1666	EQC 3:303
Lord, Robert	63	1666	EQC 3:325
Lord, Robert	64	1667	EQC 3:425
Lord, Robert	64	1667	SJC 794
Lord, Robert	67	1670	EQC 4:253
Lord, Robert	70	1674	EQC 5:286
Lord, Robert	75	1676	EQC 6:162

Lord, Robert	75	1678	EQC 7:117
Lord, Robert	76	1679	EQC 7:220
Lord, Robert	79	1682	EQC 8:410
Lord, Robert	87	1687	EQC WPA 47-50-2
Lord, Samuel	20	1660	EQC 2:253
Lord, Samuel	42	1682	MCC folio 100
Lord, Thomas	40	1673	SJC 1249
Lord, Thomas	43	1676	MCC folio 73
Lord, Thomas	46	1679	MCC folio 185
Lord, William	60	1680	EQC 7:330
Lord, William	77	1654	EQC 1:380
Loren, John	24	1664	MCC folio 36
Lorphlyn, Peter	40	1672	SJC 1353
Lorphlyn, Peter	40	1674	SJC 1350
Lorphlyn, Peter	43	1678	MCC folio 79
Lorphlyn, Peter	43	1678	SJC 1732
Lorton, John	24	1691	MCC folio 146
Lorton, John	24	1691	MCC folio 156
Lorton, John	24	1691	MCC folio 163
Lorton, John	24	1691	MCC folio 173
Love, Bridget	84	1672	EQC 5:24
Lovejoy, Christopher	16	1678	EQC 7:96
Lovejoy, John	38	1659	SJC 322
Lovejoy, John	40	1662	EQC 2:438
Lovejoy, John	47	1669	EQC 4:150
Lovejoy, John	49	1671	EQC 4:338
Lovejoy, John	49	1671	EQC 4:371
Lovejoy, John	59	1681	EQC 8:83
Lovejoy, William	21	1678	EQC 7:96
Lovell, Thomas	65	1686	EQC WPA 46-67-1
Loveran, Thomas	30	1668	MCC folio 49
Loveran, Thomas	30	1677	MCC folio 74
Loveran, Thomas	40	1677	MCC folio 77
Loveran, Thomas	45	1685	MCC folio 115
Loverin, John	17	1680	EQC 7:361
Lovett, Bethiah	39	1678	EQC 7:53
Lovett, Bethiah	40	1683	EQC 9:107
Lovett, Joanna	50	1670	MCC folio 53
Lovett, John	32	1670	EQC 4:217
Lovett, John	40	1678	EQC 7:53
Lovett, John	45	1683	EQC 9:88
Lovett, Martha		1670	MCC folio 53
Lovett, Mary	50	1673	EQC 5:217
Lovewell, Hannah	18	1674	EQC 5:306
Lovrett, Margret	22	1677	SJC 1682
Low, David	24	1694	SJC 3223
Low, John	20	1683	EQC 9:221
Low, John	20	1683	SJC 2227
Low, John	43	1678	EQC 7:88
Low, Martha	27	1668	EQC 4:50
Low, Martha	27	1668	EQC 4:80
Low, Martha	28	1669	EQC 4:125
Low, Sarah	23	1660	EQC 2:200
Low, Thomas	36	1676	EQC 6:159

Low, Thomas	37	1669	EQC 4:156
Low, Thomas	55	1660	EQC 2:200
Low, Thomas	63	1695	SJC 162357
Lowden, James	38	1686	MCC folio 122
Lowden, James	43	1691	MCC folio 157
Lowden, James	44	1691	MCC folio 146
Lowden, James	44	1694	MCC folio 186
Lowden, John	21	1684	MCC folio 184
Lowden, John	22	1663	MCC folio 34
Lowden, Richard	40	1655	MCC folio 12
Lowden, Richard	60	1675	MCC folio 69
Lowden, Richard	61	1676	MCC folio 73
Lowden, Richard	64	1679	MCC folio 87
Lowden, Richard	64	1682	MCC folio 100
Lowden, Richard	65	1679	MCC folio 86
Lowden, Richard	65	1679	MCC folio 86
Lowden, Richard	65	1681	MCC folio 102
Lowden, Richard	66	1683	MCC folio 90
Lowden, Richard	66	1684	MCC folio 108
Lowden, Richard	68	1684	MCC folio 184
Lowell, Benjamin	37	1678	EQC 7:156
Lowell, Gideon	22	1695	SJC 3148
Lowell, John	36	1665	SJC 815
Lowell, John	40	1667	SJC 815
Lowell, John	42	1664	SJC 648
Lowell, John	63	1684	EQC 9:246
Lowell, John	63	1684	EQC 9:317
Lowell, John	63	1692	SJC 3893
Lowell, Margaret	70	1676	EQC 6:204
Lowell, Margaret	74	1678	EQC 7:159
Lowell, Margaret	74	1678	EQC 7:164
Lowell, Margaret	74	1678	SJC 1791
Lowell, Margaret	74	1678	SJC 26657
Lowell, Percival	29	1667	EQC 4:14
Lowell, Percival	29	1683	EQC 9:167
Lowell, Percival	30	1669	EQC 4:127
Lowell, Percival	30	1671	EQC 4:379
Lowell, Percival	30	1671	SJC 1791
Lowell, Percival	40	1678	EQC 7:156
Lowell, Richard	72	1674	EQC 5:330
Lowell, Richard	76	1678	EQC 7:156
Lowell, Ruth	24	1674	EQC 5:419
Lowell, Samuel	19	1664	EQC 3:127
Lowell, Samuel	29	1676	EQC 6:200
Lowell, Samuel	29	1676	EQC 6:201
Lowell, Samuel	29	1676	EQC 6:204
Lowell, Samuel	30	1678	EQC 6:413
Lowell, Thomas	20	1671	EQC 4:382
Lowell, Thomas	24	1676	EQC 6:121
Lowell, Thomas	27	1678	EQC 7:156
Lowell, Thomas	27	1680	EQC 7:397
Lowler, John	27	1682	MCC folio 101
Lucas, Henry	18	1678	EQC 7:157
Lucas, Thomas	24	1677	SJC 1686

Ludden, James	74	1685	SD 13:350
Luddington, Ellen	40	1659	MCC folio 24
Luddington, John	17	1657	MCC folio 25
Luddington, Thomas	20	1657	MCC folio 25
Luddington, William	50	1657	MCC folio 18
Luddington, William	51	1659	MCC folio 24
Luddington, William	51	1659	MCC folio 25
Ludkin, Aaron	58	1676	MCC folio 73
Ludkin, Aaron	64	1679	MCC folio 88
Luffort, Lewis	54	1686	EQC 9:584
Luist, Robert	39	1691	SJC 2600
Luke, John	22	1668	MCC folio 49
Lummas, Edward	58	1662	EQC 2:350
Lummas, Edward	64	1670	EQC 4:260
Lummas, Edward	64	1670	SJC 999
Lummas, Mary	66	1672	EQC 5:39
Lummas, Nathaniel	21	1662	EQC 2:350
Lummas, Samuel	40	1684	EQC 9:188
Lummas, Samuel	45	1686	EQC 9:584
Lun, Nicholas	40	1674	MCC folio 66
Lunnen, John	50	1677	MCC folio 77
Lunt, Daniel	27	1668	EQC 4:13
Lunt, Daniel	34	1676	EQC 6:162
Lunt, Daniel	35	1676	EQC 6:163
Lunt, Daniel	36	1678	EQC 7:156
Lunt, Daniel	36	1678	EQC 7:31
Lunt, Henry	28	nd	SJC 3633
Lyde, Edward	20	1681/2	SD 12:158
Lyde, Edward	23	1685	SJC 2337
Lyford, Francis	38	1680	EQC 8:59
Lynde, Joseph	33	1671	EQC 4:452
Lynde, Simon	43	1666	SJC 822
Lynde, Simon	46	1670	SJC 1276
Lynde, Thomas	55	1671	MCC folio 61
Lyndes, Joseph	47	1684	MCC folio 183
Lynds, Thomas	33	1679	SJC 1837
Lynds, Thomas	75	1690	MCC folio 132
Lyng, Winifreet	17	1656	SD 4:217
Maber, Richard	18	1664	EQC 3:217
Maber, Richard	40	1685	EQC 9:440
MacCarty, Thaddeus	30	1670	SJC 1011
MacCarty, Thaddeus	33	1672	SJC 1194
MacGinnes, Rose	30	1685	MCC folio 120
Machee, Daniel	35	1672	MCC folio 59
MacIntire, Robert	24	1653/4	SJC 225
MacIntosh, Jane	48	1685	SJC 2370
MacIntyre, Robert	24	1653	EQC 2:97
MacMallen, Alistair	42	1673	SJC 1226
MacMallen, Elizabeth	32	1673	SJC 1226
MacMillan, Alistair	30	1661	EQC 1:339
MacMillan, Alistair	35	1669	EQC 4:98
MacMillan, Alistair	42	1673	EQC 5:171
MacMillan, Elizabeth	32	1673	EQC 5:171
MacPherson, Angus	30	1663	SJC 632

Maddock, John	29	1692	MCC folio 172
Maginne, Daniel	30	1682	MCC folio 101
Mainard, John	62	1692	MCC folio 174
Major, George	31	1678	EQC 7:156
Majory, Martin	20	1679	EQC 7:248
Makepeace, Thomas	70	1662	MCC folio 28
Makepeace, Thomas	70	1662	MCC folio 35
Maloone, John	46	1691	MCC folio 156
Maloone, Owen	30	1690	MCC folio 136
Man, Deborah	34	1683	SJC 2145
Man, Hannah	30	1680	EQC 7:395
Man, Henry	30	1656	SJC 248
Man, Mary	36	1671	SJC 1281
Man, Robert	35	1671	MCC folio 57
Man, Robert	62	1696	SJC 3255
Mander, Thomas	25	1676	MCC folio 74
Mander, Thomas	28	1680	EQC 7:352
Mandor, James	30	1686	EQC WPA 46-99-1
Mandor, Walter	34	1686	EQC WPA 46-99-1
Manning, Ann	43	1670	MCC folio 54
Manning, Daniel	21	1669	EQC 4:154
Manning, Dorothy	51	1665	SJC 690
Manning, Elizabeth	50	1680	EQC 7:404
Manning, George	28	1672	SJC 1194
Manning, Jacob	18	1679	EQC 7:303
Manning, Jacob	19	1680	EQC 7:344
Manning, Jacob	22	1684	EQC 9:392
Manning, Jacob	25	1688	EQC WPA 47-123-4
Manning, John	22	1681	EQC 8:227
Manning, Mary	14	nd	SJC 1972
Manning, Nicholas	27	1671	EQC 4:434
Manning, Samuel	18	1662	MCC folio 31
Manning, Sarah	18	1684	EQC 9:392
Manning, Thomas	26	1671	EQC 4:342
Manning, Thomas	31	1680	EQC 7:336
Manning, Thomas	35	1681	EQC 8:193
Manning, Thomas	35	1681	EQC 8:194
Manor, John	42	1673	MCC folio 65
Manse, Peter	16	1683	SJC 2175
Mansell, William	16	1681	SJC 2026
Manser, Elizabeth	13	1684	MCC folio 109
Manser, Elizabeth	27	1680	MCC folio 184
Mansfield, Andrew	38	1661	EQC 2:269
Mansfield, Andrew	40	1665	EQC 3:256
Mansfield, Andrew	46	1667	EQC 3:444
Mansfield, Andrew	49	1670	EQC 4:308
Mansfield, Andrew	50	1669	EQC 4:189
Mansfield, Andrew	52	1673	EQC 5:193
Mansfield, Andrew	60	1682	EQC 8:256
Mansfield, Andrew	60	1682	EQC 8:257
Mansfield, Andrew	60	1682	MCC folio 101
Mansfield, Andrew	60	1683	EQC 9:50
Mansfield, Andrew	61	1682	EQC 8:398
Mansfield, John	20	1678	EQC 7:114

Mansfield, John	44	1663	EQC 3:26
Mansfield, John	44	1663	EQC 3:31
Mansfield, John	44	1663	SJC 162057
Mansfield, John	44	1668	SJC 577
Mansfield, John	46	1665	EQC 3:283
Mansfield, John	68	1665	SJC 2233
Mansfield, Joseph	22	1678	EQC 7:29
Mansfield, Joseph	25	1682	EQC 8:256
Mansfield, Joseph	26	1682	EQC 8:253
Mansfield, Joseph	26	1683	EQC 9:49
Mansfield, Lydia	15	1678	EQC 6:388
Mansfield, Mary	48	1663	EQC 3:112
Mansfield, Mary	58	1665	SJC 2233
Mansfield, Samuel	19	1673	EQC 5:251
Mansfield, William	27	1673	EQC 5:228
Manto, George	30	1694	SJC 3098
Manus, William	20	1663	SJC 632
Maplesden, Thomas	23	1691	MCC folio 143
Marble, Elizabeth	40	1652	MCC folio 7
Marble, Gershom	23	1685	MCC folio 118
Marble, Gershom	23	1685	SJC 2389
Marble, Nicholas	40	1669	EQC 4:114
Marble, Nicholas	50	1674	EQC 5:321
Marble, Nicholas	71	1691	SJC 3138
Marble, Nicholas	72	nd	SJC 3138
Marble, Samuel	23	1671	EQC 4:422
Marble, William	36	1653	MCC folio 7, 8
March, Anne	70	1667	SJC 814
March, George	32	1678	EQC 7:157
March, Hugh	22	1678	EQC 7:156
March, Hugh	22	1695/6	SJC 3680
March, Hugh	27	1683	EQC 9:91
March, Hugh	54	1675	EQC 6:116
March, Hugh	54	1675	EQC 6:79
March, Hugh	54	1676	EQC 6:164
March, Hugh	55	1676	EQC 6:128
March, Hugh	55	1676	EQC 6:201
March, Hugh	55	1676	SJC 1481
March, Hugh	56	1678	EQC 7:157
March, Hugh	62	1682	EQC 8:283
March, James	13	1676	EQC 6:200
March, James	18	1682	EQC 8:260
March, James	19	1683	EQC 9:17
March, James	20	1683	EQC 9:249
March, Jemima	24	1683	EQC 9:10
March, John	16	1674	EQC 5:314
March, John	20	1678	EQC 7:131
March, John	23	1680	EQC 8:69
March, John	23	1681	EQC WPA 46-8-2
March, John	23	1682	EQC 8:261
March, John	23	1682	EQC 8:293
March, John	23	1682	EQC 8:387
March, John	24	1683	EQC 9:10
Marchant, goodwife	50	1664	EQC 3:141

Mare, Henry	38	1672	SJC 1281
Mare, Henry	38	1673/4	SCC 379
Mare, John	25	1667	SJC 824
Mare, Sarah	15	1676	EQC 6:149
Marion, Isaac	28	1681	MCC folio 93
Marion, John	25	1676	SJC 1575
Marion, John	54	1676	SJC 1575
Marke, Patrick	42	1673	SJC 1214
Marke, Patrick	55	1686	MCC folio 122
Marke, Roger	35	1678	EQC 7:96
Markham, Daniel	25	1668	MCC folio 50
Markham, Daniel	25	1670	MCC folio 54
Markham, Richard	31	1684	SJC 2259
Marks, Noyes	40	1685	MCC folio 114
Markum, Daniel	25	1670	MCC folio 53
Marrit, John	44	1672	MCC folio 61
Marrit, John	50	1679	MCC folio 85
Marrow, Daniel	29	1691	MCC folio 147
Marsh, Benjamin	16	1680	EQC 7:401
Marsh, John	30	1679	SJC 1919
Marsh, John	32	1679	SCC 1088
Marsh, John	32	1679	SJC 1919
Marsh, Mary	30	1678	EQC 7:135
Marsh, Mary	30	1685	SJC 2332
Marsh, Onesipherus	50	1684	EQC 9:187
Marsh, Samuel	24	1676	EQC 6:239
Marsh, Samuel	27	1680	EQC 7:424
Marsh, Theophilus	67	1692	MCC folio 154
Marshall, Benjamin	21	1668	EQC 4:67
Marshall, Benjamin	24	1674	EQC 5:341
Marshall, Benjamin	25	1676	EQC 6:200
Marshall, Edmund	23	1668	EQC 4:67
Marshall, Edmund	23	1668	EQC 4:80
Marshall, Edmund	26	1674	EQC 5:339
Marshall, Edmund	26	1674	EQC 5:341
Marshall, Edmund	27	1676	EQC 6:201
Marshall, Edmund	29	1678	EQC 7:156
Marshall, Edmund	29	1679	EQC 7:167
Marshall, Edmund	34	1682	EQC 8:377
Marshall, Edmund	70	1668	EQC 4:81
Marshall, Edward	26	1667	EQC 3:455
Marshall, Edward	44	1683	EQC 9:45
Marshall, Henry	21	1685	SJC 2389
Marshall, James	18	1677	SJC 1621
Marshall, John	15	1661	MCC folio 26
Marshall, Joseph	22	1694	SJC 3038
Marshall, Joseph	38	1684	EQC 9:174
Marshall, Mary	17	1682	EQC 8:417
Marshall, Mary	17	1684	EQC 9:254
Marshall, Millicent	67	1668	EQC 4:81
Marshall, Rebecca	63	1683	EQC 9:148
Marshall, Robert	30	nd	SJC 26680
Marshall, Sarah	20	1668	EQC 4:80
Marshall, Thomas	37	1653	EQC 2:92

Marshall, Thomas	39	1658	EQC 2:93
Marshall, Thomas	45	1661	MCC folio 28
Marshall, Thomas	58	1674	EQC 5:387
Marshall, Thomas	58	1674	EQC 5:398
Marshall, Thomas	65	1680	SJC 1973
Marshall, Thomas	66	1681	EQC 8:121
Marshall, Thomas	66	1682	EQC 8:401
Marshall, Thomas	66	1682	EQC 8:403
Marshall, Thomas	67	1680	EQC 7:396
Marshall, Thomas	67	1683	EQC 9:44
Marshall, William	33	1685	MCC folio 118
Marshall, William	38	1678	MCC folio 81
Marshall, William	45	1685	MCC folio 118
Marston, Benjamin	33	1685	EQC 9:521
Marston, Ephraim	34	1678	EQC 7:107
Marston, John	33	1669	EQC 4:144
Marston, John	33	1674	EQC 5:356
Marston, John	37	1678	EQC 7:32
Marston, John	40	1679	EQC 7:245
Marston, John	50	1666	EQC 3:324
Marston, John	57	1673	EQC 5:171
Marston, John	65	1680	EQC 8:74
Marston, John	65	1681	EQC 8:73
Marston, Mannassah	34	1678	EQC 7:246
Marston, Mannassah	34	1679	EQC 7:252
Marston, Mannassah	36	1678	EQC 7:109
Marston, Mannassah	40	1685	EQC 9:524
Marston, Mercy	30	1679	EQC 7:251
Marston, William	52	1674	EQC 5:356
Martin, Charles	50	1681	SJC 2057
Martin, George	56	1674	SJC 1563
Martin, John	16	1664	MCC folio 36
Martin, John	25	1673	MCC folio 65
Martin, John	30	1672	EQC 5:109
Martin, John	40	1680	EQC 7:335
Martin, John	40	1680	EQC 7:335
Martin, Peter	21	1694	SJC 4124
Martin, Richard	27	1674	EQC 5:402
Martin, Robert	33	1666	EQC 3:350
Martin, Samuel	17	1661	EQC 2:309
Martin, Samuel	18	nd	SJC 2769
Martin, Samuel	27	1672	EQC 5:20
Martin, William	24	1677	MCC folio 79
Martine, Sarah	26	1659	EQC 2:172
Marvell, Nichols	60	1684	EQC 9:207
Maryon, John	25	1676	SCC 740
Maskell, Eleanor	55	1680	EQC 7:405
Maskell, John	25	1680	EQC 7:347
Maskell, John	29	1680	EQC 7:346
Maskell, John	34	1685	EQC 9:473
Maskell, John	34	1686	EQC WPA 46-80-2
Maskell, Thomas	27	1684	EQC 9:392
Mason, Arthur	44	1674	SD 8:406
Mason, Arthur	47	1676	MCC folio 72

Mason, Arthur	47	1676	MCC folio 76
Mason, Arthur	47	1676	SJC 1638
Mason, Elias	60	1679	SJC 1767
Mason, Francis	26	1676	SJC 1592
Mason, Jacob	46	1691/2	SJC 98524
Mason, John	20	1673	SJC 1228
Mason, John	23	1669	MCC folio 52
Mason, John	24	1680	SJC 1913
Mason, John	44	1669	EQC 4:114
Mason, John	49	1691	SJC 98524
Mason, John	64	1687	EQC WPA 47-64-2
Mason, Joseph	43	1691	MCC folio 151
Mason, Joseph	45	1692	MCC folio 172
Mason, Richard	30	1668	SJC 905
Mason, Sarah	24	1667	SJC 821
Mason, Thomas	43	1695	SJC 3101
Massey, Jeffery	82	1674	EQC 5:282
Massey, Jeffrey	60	1669	EQC 4:103
Massey, Jeffrey	70	1661	EQC 2:323
Massey, Jeffrey	73	1664	EQC 3:207
Massey, Jeffrey	82	1674	EQC 5:325
Massey, Jeffry	82	1674	SJC 1503
Massey, John	36	1666	SJC 762
Massey, John	37	1669	EQC 4:98
Massey, John	41	1672	EQC 5:68
Massey, John	47	1678	EQC 7:108
Massey, John	47	1678	EQC 7:79
Massey, John	49	1680	EQC 7:389
Massey, John	49	1680	EQC 7:390
Massey, John	49	1680	EQC 7:391
Massey, John	53	1683	EQC 9:110
Massey, John	54	1685	EQC 9:440
Massey, John	54	1685	SJC 2285
Massey, John	84	1684	EQC 9:343
Massey, Sarah	38	1678	EQC 7:79
Massiloway, Daniel	33	1678	EQC 7:156
Massure, John	19	1677	EQC 6:347
Masters, Nathaniel	47	1678	EQC 7:106
Maston, John	23	1664	EQC 3:217
Mathees, Daniel	17	1663	EQC 3:33
Mather, Richard	26	1681	SJC 2024
Mathes, Rebecca	13	1691	MCC folio 157
Mathew, Jerome	36	1665	SJC 728
Mathews, Daniel	20	1665	EQC 3:283
Mathews, Daniel	30	1675	SJC 1374
Mathews, Daniel	30	1680	SJC 1940
Mathews, Daniel	32	1680	SJC 1943
Matson, Jane	34	1682	SJC 2224
Matson, John	46	1682	SJC 2224
Matson, Joshua	43	1683	SJC 2224
Matson, Mary	18	1685	MCC folio 115
Matson, Philip	20	1675	EQC 6:17
Matson, Thomas	38	1673	EQC 5:226
Matson, Thomas	39	1672	SJC 1194

Matson, Thomas	43	1677	SCC 803
Matson, Thomas	43	1677	SJC 1582
Matson, Thomas	47	1681	EQC 8:115
Matson, Thomas	49	1682	SJC 2224
Matson, Thomas	50	1663	SJC 607
Matson, Thomas	73	1674	SJC 1432
Mattock, Samuel	49	1680	SJC 162193
Mattooson, Nathaniel	43	1671	SJC 1073
Maule, Thomas	32	1680	EQC 7:423
Maule, Thomas	40	1685	EQC 9:432
Maverick, Elias	75	1680	MCC folio 89
Maverick, Eunice	43	1671	EQC 4:389
Maverick, Moses	18	1677	SCC 859
Maverick, Moses	18	1677	SJC 1789
Maverick, Moses	50	1662	EQC 2:442
Maverick, Moses	54	1665	EQC 3:282
Maverick, Moses	55	1667	EQC 3:418
Maverick, Moses	57	1668	EQC 4:30
Maverick, Moses	57	1669	EQC 4:115
Maverick, Moses	58	1669	EQC 4:155
Maverick, Moses	60	1671	EQC 4:389
Maverick, Moses	62	1672	EQC 5:110
Maverick, Moses	62	1672	EQC 5:115
Maverick, Moses	62	1673	EQC 5:130
Maverick, Moses	66	1677	EQC 6:362
Maverick, Samuel	63	1665	SD 4:328
Maxey, Alexander	45	1678	EQC 7:8
Maxey, Alexander	45	1679	EQC 7:205
Maxfields, John	35	1665	MCC folio 39
May, Thomas	40	1673	MCC folio 62
Mayfield, John	25	1664	SJC 648
Maynard, John	60	1690	MCC folio 140
Mayo, John	32	1691	SJC 2627
Mayo, Joseph	45	1695	SJC 3150
McCarter, John	38	1686	EQC WPA 46-99-3
McCarty, Thaddeus	33	1672/3	SCC 138
McCollum, James	36	1666	MCC folio 42
McCollum, Robert	17	1681	MCC folio 184
McKay, Daniel	27	1665	SJC 680
Meachum, Jeremiah	43	nd	SJC 2770
Meade, Isaac	40	1682	MCC folio 101
Meade, Israel	40	1681	MCC folio 94
Meade, Israel	40	1682	MCC folio 101
Meade, Richard	65	1671	SJC 1053
Meade, Richard	65	1671	SJC 2997
Meader, John	40	1677	SJC 1679
Meads, Israel	45	1686	MCC folio 127
Meager, John	26	1664	EQC 3:209
Mearo, Henry	46	1671	MCC folio 58
Meddlecott, Richard	38	1682	SJC 2121
Meek, Elizabeth	37	1685	EQC 9:521
Meek, Richard	40	1685	EQC 9:521
Megrigo, Elizabeth	25	1690	MCC folio 163
Mekings, Thomas	18	1660	EQC 2:219

Melinges, Simon	25	1663	MCC folio 35
Mellows, Simon	27	1663	MCC folio 35
Melot, Augustine	22	1674	SCC 454
Melvin, John	28	1684	MCC folio 108
Mentor, Thomas	22	1674	EQC 5:414
Mercer, Richard	29	1669	SJC 924
Merifield, Benjamin	32	1691	SJC 98514
Merifield, Henry	66	1685	SD 13:408
Merifield, John	15	nd	SJC 28636
Merifield, John	26	1670	SJC 993
Merifield, Margret	65	1685	SD 13:408
Merke, Patrick	42	1673	MCC folio 64
Merlote, Bartholomew	25	1690	MCC folio 135
Merrick, Hannah	22	1682	EQC WPA 46-10-4
Merrick, Hannah	26	1686	EQC WPA 46-118-1
Merrick, Isaac	19	1684	EQC 9:242
Merrick, James	27	1679	EQC WPA 46-11-2
Merrick, James	31	1682	EQC WPA 46-10-4
Merrick, Joseph	18	1678	EQC 7:156
Merrick, Joseph	23	1684	EQC 9:242
Merrick, Joseph	25	1686	EQC WPA 46-118-2
Merrick, Margaret	63	1686	EQC WPA 46-118-2
Merrill, Abel	14	1658	EQC 2:139
Merrill, Abel	32	1678	EQC 7:157
Merrill, Abraham	41	1678	EQC 7:156
Merrill, Daniel	34	1678	EQC 7:157
Merrill, John	19	1682	EQC 8:267
Merrill, Nathaniel	17	1682	EQC 8:267
Merrill, Nathaniel	40	1678	EQC 7:157
Merritt, Deborah	21	1677	SJC 4595
Merritt, Elizabeth	6	1677	SJC 4595
Merritt, Henry	14	1677	SJC 4595
Merritt, Henry	19	1684	SJC 2259
Merritt, John	16	1677	SJC 4595
Merritt, John	29	1672	EQC 5:110
Merritt, John	35	1680	EQC 7:331
Merritt, Jonathan	12	1677	SJC 4595
Merritt, Mary	9	1677	SJC 4595
Merritt, Nicholas	59	1672	EQC 5:110
Merrow, Daniel	28	1691	MCC folio 140
Merrow, Daniel	28	1691	MCC folio 143
Merrow, Henry	60	1681	MCC folio 94
Merrow, James	40	1681	MCC folio 94
Merry, Mary	18	1691	MCC folio 140
Messenger, Ebenezer	18	1683	SJC 2160
Messenger, Henry	17	1670	SJC 1015
Messenger, John	27	1668	SJC 905
Messenger, Simeon	25	1670	SJC 1015
Messenger, Simeon	27	1668	SJC 905
Metcalf, Joseph	22	1682	EQC 8:404
Metcalf, Joseph	60	1665	EQC 3:326
Metcalf, Sarah	23	1674	MCC folio 68
Metup, Daniel	42	1683	MCC folio 104
Michel, John	35	1686	EQC WPA 46-118-4

Michell, John	25	1676	EQC 6:189
Michell, John	26	1677	EQC 6:254
Michell, Mary	62	1698	MCC folio 169
Michelson, Mary	19	1674	MCC folio 66
Michelson, Thomas	28	1685	SJC 2326
Mico, John	25	1691	SJC 2629
Middleton, Richard	49	1691	SJC 2738
Middleton, William	30	1670	SJC 993
Midreke, James	40	1653	MCC folio 7
Mighill, Elizabeth	46	1681	EQC 8:98
Mighill, John	30	1664	EQC 3:187
Mighill, John	42	1678	EQC 7:157
Mighill, John	44	1679	EQC 7:318
Mighill, Samuel	51	1681	EQC 8:98
Mighill, Thomas	30	1677	SJC 1689
Miles, Edward	54	1668	SJC 905
Miles, Mary	60	1691	MCC folio 157
Milford, Thomas	35	1682	EQC 8:445
Mill, Mary	52	1685	MCC folio 114
Millard, Thomas	40	1640	SD 1:51
Miller, Isaac	25	1695	MCC folio 196
Miller, John	22	1661	EQC 2:324
Miller, Joseph	64	1682	MCC folio 100
Miller, Mary	44	1682	MCC folio 100
Miller, Paul	32	1685	SJC 2386
Miller, Peter	55	1686	EQC WPA 46-92-4
Miller, Richard	20	1669	EQC 4:105
Miller, William	26	1666	EQC 7:197
Millerd, Joseph	25	1686	MCC folio 127
Millett, Thomas	34	1667	EQC 3:431
Mills, Edward	23	1655/6	MCC folio 12
Mills, Edward	24	1655	MCC folio 14
Mills, John	49	1682	SJC 2126
Mills, Samuel	66	1685	MCC folio 114
Milman, Abraham	30	1677	SCC 804
Milman, Abraham	30	1677	SJC 1635
Milton, Christopher	30	1666	EQC 3:346
Milton, Christopher	31	1668	SJC 924
Milton, Richard	24	1663	SJC 593
Milton, Robert	19	1672	SJC 1163
Minot, Elizabeth	23	1698	SJC 4279
Minot, James	42	1672	SJC 1281
Minot, John	38	1663	SJC 606
Minot, Samuel	44	1680	SJC 1891
Mirick, Hannah	21	1676/7	SJC 1549
Mirick, Hannah	22	1682	EQC 8:261
Mirick, Hannah	25	1682	EQC 8:263
Mirick, Hopestill	50	1669	MCC folio 52
Mirick, Isaac	17	1681	MCC folio 100
Mirick, Isaac	17	1681	MCC folio 184
Mirick, James	27	1679	EQC 7:318
Mirick, James	28	1679	MCC folio 85
Mirick, James	31	1682	EQC 8:261
Mirick, James	31	1682	EQC 8:262

Mirick, James	31	1682	EQC 8:265
Mirick, James	43	1694/5	SJC 4118
Mirick, James	52	1664	EQC 3:196
Mirick, John	25	1678	MCC folio 78
Mirick, John	46	1660	MCC folio 26
Mirick, Joseph	19	1680	EQC 7:355
Mirick, Margaret	53	1682	EQC 8:262
Mirick, Margaret	56	1677	MCC folio 78
Mitchell, Alexander	29	1695	SJC 3310
Mitchell, Hannah	30	1686	EQC WPA 46-120-1
Mitchell, John	28	1678	EQC 7:157
Mitchell, Mary	48	1683	EQC 9:90
Mitchell, Mary	50	1685	SJC 2391
Mitchell, Mary	62	1698	SJC 3936
Mitchell, Thomas	25	1655/6	SJC 236
Mitchell, Thomas	26	1657	SJC 270
Mitchell, William	24	1678	EQC 7:157
Mitchell, William	24	1679	MCC folio 85
Mitchelson, Edward	75	1678	EQC 7:6
Mitchelson, Mary	30	1684/5	MCC folio 113
Mitchelson, Thomas	28	1685	MCC folio 113
Mixer, Isaac	62	1692	MCC folio 172
Mochen, Christopher	27	1686	MCC folio 128
Mogridge, Robert	30	1691	SJC 2600
Mogridge, Robert	35	1692/3	SJC 2756
Mollom, George	42	1663	SJC 558
Mongey, Martha	38	1671	EQC 4:400
Mongey, Walter	30	1665	EQC 3:262
Monk, George	45	1690/1	SJC 2596
Monroe, William	20	1661	MCC folio 28
Monroe, William	56	1691	MCC folio 146
Moody, Caleb	31	1668	SJC 924
Moody, Caleb	41	1678	EQC 7:156
Moody, Caleb	57	nd	SJC 3039
Moody, Daniel	17	1678	EQC 7:157
Moody, Daniel	22	1685	EQC 9:534
Moody, Daniel	32	1694	SJC 162328
Moody, Eliezer	30	1691	SJC 2640
Moody, Elizabeth	18	1685	EQC 9:535
Moody, Ingram	16	1677	EQC 6:361
Moody, William	17	1678	EQC 7:157
Moore, Benjamin	21	1667	MCC folio 41
Moore, Enoch	37	1677	MCC folio 79
Moore, Enoch	37	1677	SJC 1732
Moore, Enoch	43	1685	MCC folio 118
Moore, Enoch	57	1677	SJC 1732
Moore, Francis	36	1668	SJC 889
Moore, Francis	61	1682	MCC folio 101
Moore, Jeremiah	19	1668	EQC 4:83
Moore, John	26	1672	SD 7:335
Moore, John	33	1682	EQC 8:417
Moore, John	33	1684	EQC 9:254
Moore, John	40	1665	SJC 680
Moore, Jonas	33	1662	EQC 2:387

Moore, Jonas	33	1662	EQC 2:401
Moore, Jonas	40	1667	SJC 909
Moore, Jonathan	37	1683	EQC 9:86
Moore, Joseph	34	1682	MCC folio 106
Moore, Thomas	52	1679	SJC 1911
Moore, William	20	1663	SJC 648
Moore, William	33	1666	SJC 764
Moore,Thomas	42	1667	SJC 1911
Moores, Constance	27	1678	EQC 7:138
Moores, Contance	32	1684	EQC 9:237
Moores, Edmund	27	1678	EQC 7:157
Moores, Edward	64	1678	EQC 7:156
Moores, Jacob	32	1677	MCC folio 76
Moores, Jonathan	28	1674	EQC 5:344
Moores, Jonathan	32	1678	EQC 7:157
Moores, Jonathan	37	1683	EQC 9:87
Moores, Sarah	29	1683	EQC 9:237
More, Caleb	30	1678	EQC 7:148
More, Henry	42	1657	SJC 478
More, John	16	1661	MCC folio 27
More, John	33	1681	EQC 8:197
More, Thomas	42	1667	SCC 1030
Moreing, Joseph	24	1681	EQC 8:83
Morgan, Benjamin	20	1669	EQC 4:136
Morgan, Elizabeth	34	1684	EQC 9:248
Morgan, Francis	28	1671	SJC 1137
Morgan, Moses	15	1672	EQC 5:24
Morgan, Robert	70	1671	EQC 4:332
Morgan, Robert	70	1671	EQC 4:346
Morgan, Rogert	18	1670	EQC 4:217
Morgan, Samuel	28	1665	EQC 3:261
Morgan, Samuel	32	1669	EQC 4:191
Morgan, Samuel	36	1674	EQC 5:348
Morgan, Samuel	47	1684	EQC 9:248
Morgan, William	21	1681	EQC 8:114
Moring, Joseph	22	1678	EQC 7:156
Morren, William	24	1677	SJC 1732
Morrill, Abraham	30	1684	EQC 9:394
Morrill, Abraham	30	1684	EQC 9:396
Morrill, Isaac	22	1669	EQC 4:100
Morrill, Isaac	40	1685	EQC 9:545
Morrill, Jacob	32	1680	EQC 8:68
Morrill, Jacob	35	1684	EQC 9:324
Morrill, Jacob	35	1684	EQC 9:394
Morrill, Jacob	35	1684	EQC 9:396
Morrill, Jacob	38	1685	EQC 9:545
Morrill, John	35	1667	EQC 3:430
Morrill, John	40	1668	EQC 4:6
Morrill, Mary	30	1677	EQC 6:347
Morrill, Moses	25	1680	EQC 8:68
Morris, David	18	1658	MCC folio 16
Morris, Dorcas	23	1665/6	SCC 914
Morris, Dorcas	23	1665/6	SJC 741
Morris, Elizabeth	19	1663	EQC 3:112

Morris, Elizabeth	20	1665	EQC 3:283
Morris, Evan	66	1674	EQC 5:396
Morris, Evan	66	1675	EQC 6:4
Morris, Thomas	13	1665	EQC 3:283
Morris, William	45	1659/60	MCC folio 25
Morse, Anthony	45	1677	EQC 6:255
Morse, Anthony	60	1668	EQC 4:12
Morse, Anthony	60	1674	EQC 5:330
Morse, Anthony	72	1678	EQC 7:156
Morse, Benjamin	37	1678	EQC 7:157
Morse, Francis	31	1673	SJC 1221
Morse, Francis	51	1694/5	SJC 4118
Morse, Francis,	31	1673	MCC folio 65
Morse, goodwife	65	1680	EQC 7:355
Morse, Henry	42	nd	SJC 325
Morse, Jeremiah	20	1674	MCC folio 63
Morse, Jeremiah	23	1674	MCC folio 63
Morse, Jeremiah	23	1677	MCC folio 77
Morse, Jeremy	63	1684	MCC folio 111
Morse, Johannah	20	1682	EQC 8:263
Morse, Jonathan	22	1666	MCC folio 40
Morse, Joseph	30	1670	SJC 983
Morse, Joseph	40	1678	EQC 7:157
Morse, Joshua	23	1679	EQC 7:316
Morse, Joshua	27	1682	EQC 8:262
Morse, Joshua	27	1682	EQC 8:289
Morse, Joshua	29	1682	EQC 8:420
Morse, Samuel	58	1699	SJC 4696
Morse, William	64	1678	EQC 7:156
Morse, William	65	1680	EQC 7:355
Morse, William	67	1682	EQC 8:263
Morse, William	67	1682	EQC 8:289
Mortimer, Edward	23	1675	SCC 614
Mortimer, Edward	23	1675	SJC 1042
Mortimer, Edward	28	nd	SJC 2045
Morton, Richard	40	1677	MCC folio 77
Morton, Thomas	30	nd	SJC 3630
Mosely, Samuel	26	1668	EQC 4:5
Mosely, Samuel	36	1675	SJC 1422
Moss, Benjamin	25	1694	SJC 3153
Moss, Mary	28	1678	EQC 7:52
Moss, William	53	1667	SJC 813
Mould, Edward	38	1668	SJC 910
Mould, Edward	46	1678	EQC 6:410
Mould, Thomas	33	1681	EQC 8:174
Mould, Thomas	35	1682	EQC 8:258
Mould, Thomas	38	1685	EQC 9:449
Moulton, James	44	1681	EQC 8:146
Moulton, James	46	1682	EQC 8:384
Moulton, James	65	1669	EQC 4:97
Moulton, Jane	45	1654	MCC folio 9
Moulton, John	25	1678	EQC 7:147
Moulton, John	25	1678	EQC 7:90
Moulton, John	26	1659	MCC folio 24

Moulton, John	27	1660	MCC folio 25
Moulton, Mary	26	1678	EQC 7:147
Moulton, Mary	30	1683	EQC 9:20
Moulton, Robert	33	1678	EQC 7:91
Moulton, Robert	34	1680	EQC 7:423
Moulton, Robert	39	1683	EQC 9:20
Moulton, Samuel	38	1681	EQC 8:146
Mountfort, Benjamin	30	1675	SJC 1417b
Mountfort, Edmund	35	1668/9	SJC 913
Mountfort, Henry	29	1668/9	SJC 913
Mountfort, Henry	32	1672	SD 8:35
Mountfort, Ruth	50	nd	SJC 2941
Mousall, Elizabeth	28	1663	SJC 573
Mousall, Elizabeth	30	1663	MCC folio 34
Mousall, John	20	1686	MCC folio 123
Mousall, John	27	1694	MCC folio 186
Mousall, John	33	1663	MCC folio 34
Mousall, John	49	1679	MCC folio 185
Mousall, John	50	1679	MCC folio 87
Mousall, John	52	1681	MCC folio 102
Mousall, John	56	1685/6	MCC folio 122
Mousall, John	60	1690	MCC folio 132
Mousall, John	63	1658	MCC folio 16
Mousall, John	64	1694	MCC folio 186
Mousall, John	66	1661/2	MCC folio 28
Mousall, Mary	24	1681	MCC folio 93
Mousall, Ralph	27	1694	MCC folio 186
Mousall, Thomas	27	1661	MCC folio 36
Mouscool, Elizabeth	34	1669	MCC folio 52
Moussett, Katherine	32	1694	SJC 2911
Mowry, Katherine	17	1654	EQC 1:330
Muddley, Christopher	18	1693	MCC folio 176
Mudge, Mary	18	1669	MCC folio 52
Mudge, Thomas	25	1668	MCC folio 47
Mudgins, Christopher	28	1686	MCC folio 127
Muffet, William	18	1682	EQC 8:284
Muffet, William	19	1682	EQC 8:303
Mulberry, Ann	17	1694	SJC 3015
Munden, Deborah	50	1680	SJC 162196
Mundey, Steven	36	1680	SJC 1879
Mungay, Walter	46	1678	EQC 7:306
Munkon, William	60	1696	MCC folio 206
Munning, George	58	16571	MCC folio 19
Munning, Johanna	35	1657	MCC folio 19
Munrow, William	60	1696/7	SJC 3925
Murah, Henry	26	1691	MCC folio 145
Murdo, John	30	1692/3	SJC 2740
Murphy, Brime	60	1677	SCC 1102
Murphy, Brime	60	1677	SJC 1636
Murray, William	26	1682	EQC 8:413
Mushat, Margaret	60	1685	SJC 2377
Musket, John	20	1675	SJC 1425
Mussabin, Sarah	33	1694	SJC 162343
Muzzey, Benjamin	20	1655	EQC 1:381

Muzzey, Benjamin	30	1661	EQC 2:326
Muzzey, Benjamin	30	1662	MCC folio 31
Muzzey, Benjamin	33	1691	MCC folio 143
Muzzey, Benjamin	46	1676	SCC 761
Muzzey, Benjamin	46	1676	SJC 1569
Muzzey, Benjamin	46	1680	EQC 8:34
Muzzey, Benjamin	47	1676	SJC 1438
Muzzey, Benjamin	48	1678	EQC 7:33
Muzzey, Benjamin	50	1682	EQC 8:403
Muzzey, Benjamin	59	1690	MCC folio 138
Muzzey, John	19	1683	MCC folio 109
Muzzey, Joseph	40	1667	EQC 3:426
Muzzey, Joseph	50	1678	EQC 7:157
Muzzey, Joseph	50	1680	EQC 8:34
Muzzey, Richard	27	nd	SJC 3614
Muzzey, Robert	19	1684	MCC folio 109
Mynate, Mary	45	1685	EQC 9:475
Myrick, James	30	1682	EQC 8:387
Myrick, James/Jonas	40	1653	MCC folio 8
Nash, James	19	1698	SJC 4529
Nash, James	60	1667	SJC 828
Nash, Joseph	38	1683/4	SJC 2188
Nash, Joshua	19	1652	EQC 1:263
Nash, Joshua	38	1672	SD 8:29
Naylor, Edward	30	1672/3	SCC 138
Naylor, Edward	38	1672/3	SJC 1194
Naylor, Edward	38	1674	MCC folio 66
Naylor, Edward	43	1677	SJC 1679
Nealand, Edward	25	1668	EQC 4:3
Nealand, Edward	30	1673	EQC 5:229
Neale, Henry	35	1654	MCC folio 1
Neale, Jeremiah	34	1679	EQC 7:250
Neale, Jeremiah	34	1679	EQC 7:308
Neale, Jeremiah	39	1685	EQC 9:440
Neale, Jeremiah	40	1685	EQC 9:438
Neale, Jeremiah	40	1685	EQC 9:442
Neale, Jeremiah	40	1685	SJC 2285
Neale, Jeremiah	41	nd	SJC 2770
Neale, Jeremiah	50	1695	SJC 162383
Neale, Jeremith	25	1670	EQC 4:278
Neale, Jeremy	38	1684	EQC 9:397
Neale, Jeremy	39	1684	EQC 9:344
Neale, John	21	1661	MCC folio 27
Neale, Joseph	33	nd	SJC 2770
Neck, Christopher	41	1674	EQC 5:281
Neck, John	20	1671	EQC 4:376
Neck, William	40	1672	EQC 5:110
Neck, William	42	1674	EQC 5:348
Needham, Ann	44	1678	EQC 7:147
Needham, Anthony	36	1667	EQC 3:418
Needham, Anthony	46	1678	EQC 7:148
Needham, Anthony	46	1678	EQC 7:89
Needham, Anthony	48	1679	EQC 7:312
Needham, Anthony	56	1686	EQC WPA 46-92-4

Needham, Anthony	57	1686	EQC WPA 46-23-4
Needham, Anthony	57	nd	SJC 2770
Needham, Daniel	40	1681	EQC 8:145
Needham, Ezekiel	28	1672	EQC 5:116
Needham, Ezekiel	30	1676	EQC 6:198
Needham, Ezekiel	30	1678	EQC 7:26
Needham, Ezekiel	32	1679	EQC 7:252
Needham, Ezekiel	36	1678	EQC 7:30
Needham, Ezekiel	38	1684	EQC 9:316
Needham, Grace	60	1678	SJC 1729
Needham, Joseph	35	1674	EQC 6:19
Needham, Joseph	37	1674	EQC 6:19
Needham, Ruth	40	1681	EQC 8:145
Neeland, Edward	35	1680	EQC 8:9
Neeland, Edward	35	1683	EQC 9:112
Neeland, Edward	35	1683	EQC 9:225
Neeland, Edward	35	1684	EQC 9:191
Neeland, Edward	38	1678	EQC 7:37
Neff, William	24	1664	EQC 3:127
Neff, William	24	1664	SJC 665
Negus, Jonathan	56	1657	EQC 7:127
Nelson, Elizabeth	48	1684	EQC 9:174
Nelson, Elizabeth [sic] Henry	60	1669/70	SD 6:156
Nelson, Philip	19	1678	EQC 7:97
Nelson, Philip	31	1667	EQC 3:390
Nelson, Philip	39	1664	EQC 3:124
Nelson, Philip	40	1674	EQC 5:393
Nelson, Philip	40	1674	SJC 1389
Nelson, Philip	40	1675	SJC 1791
Nelson, Philip	40	1676	EQC 6:204
Nelson, William	31	1666	EQC 3:372
Nelson, William	33	1669	EQC 4:105
Nelson, William	35	1668	EQC 4:70
Nerlen, Edward	35	1680	SJC 1967
Never, Richard	30	1676	MCC folio 74
Nevinson, Elizabeth	40	1680	MCC folio 89
Newall, John	35	1673	EQC 5:186
Newall, Thomas	35	1666	EQC 3:346
Newall, Thomas	36	1690	MCC folio 138
Newbury, Sarah	66	1685	MCC folio 119
Newbury, Trial	26	1676/7	MCC folio 75
Newby, Mary	34	1680	EQC 8:30
Newcomb, Frances	70	1668	SJC 931
Newcomb, John	48	1682	SJC 2126
Newcum, Andrew	32	1672	EQC 5:7
Newell, Esther	26	1683	EQC 9:148
Newell, John	27	1683	EQC 9:147
Newgate, John	72	1653	SJC 286
Newgate, Joseph	26	1656	SD 2:295
Newhall, John	28	1684	EQC 9:339
Newhall, Joseph	24	1683	EQC 9:148
Newhall, Joseph	25	1684	EQC 9:246
Newhall, Nathaniel	22	1684	EQC 9:339
Newhall, Thomas	18	1672	EQC 5:59

Newhall, Thomas	27	1681	EQC 8:199
Newhall, Thomas	51	1682	MCC folio 101
Newhall, Thomas	54	1685	SJC 2340
Newly, Judah	17	1679	SJC 1919
Newman, Robert	17	1667	EQC 3:414
Newman, Thomas	25	1696	SJC 3378
Newman, Thomas	35	1680	SJC 1909
Newmarch, John	16	1662	EQC 2:351
Newmarch, John	60	1675	EQC 6:67
Newmarch, John	60	1682	EQC 8:270
Newmarch, John	70	1683	SJC 2227
Newmarch, John	70	1684	EQC 9:220
Newmarch, Thomas	24	1673	EQC 5:226
Newmarch, Thomas	35	1683	EQC 9:16
Newsham, William	22	1680	EQC 8:30
Newton, John	30	1671	MCC folio 58
Newton, John	39	1671	MCC folio 58
Nichols, Edward	28	1681	EQC 8:238
Nichols, Frances	28	1678	EQC 7:56
Nichols, Hannah	18	1665	EQC 3:258
Nichols, James	60	1685	MCC folio 114
Nichols, John	20	1660	EQC 2:204
Nichols, John	22	1662	EQC 2:388
Nichols, John	24	1665	EQC 3:258
Nichols, Lydia	20	1665	EQC 3:258
Nichols, Mary	21	1663	MCC folio 34
Nichols, Nathaniel	30	1685	MCC folio 118
Nichols, Nathaniel	30	1685	SJC 2389
Nichols, Philip	20	1681	EQC 8:283
Nichols, Randall	73	1686	MCC folio 122
Nichols, Thomas	23	1684	EQC 9:198
Nichols, William	100	nd	SJC 3064
Nichols, William	63	1662	EQC 2:388
Nichols, William	70	1672	EQC 5:29
Nicholson, Edmund	16	1660	EQC 2:207
Nicholson, Joseph	20	1661	EQC 2:291
Nicholson, Joseph	27	1670	EQC 4:297
Nicholson, Thomas	15	1669	EQC 4:151
Nick, William	35	1661	EQC 2:291
Nick, William	35	1669	EQC 4:116
Nick, William	35	1669	EQC 4:116
Nick, William	38	1670	EQC 4:222
Nick, William	40	1670	EQC 4:280
Nick, William	40	1672	EQC 5:115
Nick, William	42	1674	EQC 5:338
Nims, Mehitable	31	1698	SJC 3718
Nivear, Thomas	25	1676	MCC folio 74
Nixon, Mathew	50	1674	EQC 5:348
Noble, Martha	14	1687	EQC WPA 47-28-2
Noll, Alsue	19	1663/4	MCC folio 36
Norcross, Richard	23	1685	MCC folio 115
Norcross, Richard	23	1685	SJC 2348
Norcross, Richard	60	1681	MCC folio 97
Norcross, Richard	71	1695	MCC folio 179

Norcross, Richard	71	nd	SJC 3175
Norden, Nathaniel	35	1685	MCC folio 114
Norman, John	47	1685	EQC 9:442
Norman, John	57	1695	SJC 3665
Norman, Richard	49	1672	EQC 5:5
Norman, Richard	50	1674	EQC 5:256
Norman, Richard	50	1674	EQC 5:348
Norman, Richard	50	1674	EQC 5:430
Norman, Richard	50	1678	EQC 7:108
Norman, Richard	50	1678	EQC 7:4
Norman, Richard	57	1680	EQC 7:386
Norman, Robert	40	1669	EQC 4:156
Norman, Thomas	28	1672	SJC 1194
Norman, Thomas	38	1679	EQC 7:167
Norman, William	36	1672	SCC 190
Norman, William	36	1672	SJC 1153
Norris, Richard	50	1664	MCC folio 36
Northend, Ezekiel	40	1662	EQC 2:397
Northend, Ezekiel	41	1663	EQC 3:30
Northend, Ezekiel	45	1667	EQC 3:426
Northend, Ezekiel	50	1672	EQC 5:17
Northend, Ezekiel	50	1682	EQC 8:269
Northey, John	65	1672	EQC 5:110
Northey, John	66	1677	EQC 6:363
Norton, George	21	1662	EQC 2:389
Norton, John	35	1671	EQC 4:430
Norton, John	40	1678	EQC 7:56
Norton, John	48	1686	EQC WPA 46-23-1
Norton, Nathaniel	23	1662	EQC 2:389
Norton, Priscilla	18	1687	EQC WPA 47-52-3
Norton, William	40	1666	EQC 3:372
Norton, William	50	1658	EQC 2:138
Nowell, Hannah	18	1676/7	SJC 1549
Nowell, Robert	34	1680	EQC 8:26
Noyes, Cutting	29	1678	EQC 7:156
Noyes, Cutting	32	1682	EQC 8:283
Noyes, Hannah	20	1663	EQC 3:53
Noyes, James	21	1678	EQC 7:157
Noyes, James	29	1658	MCC folio 16
Noyes, John	33	1678	EQC 7:157
Noyes, Joseph	26	1663	EQC 3:67
Noyes, Nicholas	55	1671	EQC 4:433
Noyes, Nicholas	63	1679	EQC 7:165
Noyes, Nicholas	63	1679	SJC 1791
Noyes, Thomas	19	1682	EQC 8:284
Noyes, Thomas	30	1678	EQC 7:156
Noyes, Thomas	30	1679	MCC folio 86
Noyes, Thomas	38	1686	EQC WPA 46-126-1
Noyes, William	20	1674	EQC 5:355
Noyes, William	25	1678	EQC 7:156
Noyes, William	28	1682	EQC 8:245
Nurse, Benjamin	20	1686	EQC WPA 46-31-2
Nurse, Frances	45	1666	EQC 3:378
Nurse, Frances	58	1678	EQC 7:119

Nurse, Frances	60	1680	EQC 7:426
Nurse, Samuel	29	1681	EQC 8:121
Nurse, Samuel	29	1681	SJC 2018
Nurse, Samuel	35	1686	EQC WPA 46-31-2
Nutting, John	42	1667	MCC folio 43
Oakes, Edward	56	1660	MCC folio 25
Oakes, Edward	58	1662	MCC folio 30
Oakes, Edward	68	1672	SJC 1214
Oakes, Edward	68	1673	MCC folio 64
Oakes, John	25	1689/90	SJC 2541
Oakes, John	28	nd	SJC 2769
Oakes, Urion	18	1676	MCC folio 73
Oakman, Elias	23	1667	SJC 824
Oakman, Mary	45	1679	SJC 1828
Oakman, Samuel	25	nd	SJC 236
Oakman, Samuel	34	1664	SJC 652
Oarum, William	23	1675	SJC 1402
Oates, John	18	1683	EQC 9:145
Oates, John	24	1672	MCC folio 65
Obbison, William	36	1681	SJC 2029
Ockinton, Thomas	66	nd	SJC 25547
Odell, Benoni	17	nd	SJC 2770
Odell, Regnall	23	nd	SJC 2037
Odell, Regnall	40	1697	SJC 4312
Odlin, John	72	1674/5	SJC 1432
Odlin, Richard	29	1680	SJC 1935
Ogrado, Charles	60	1689	SJC 3006
Oldam, John	33	1686	MCC folio 120
Oliver, Daniel	21	1684	SJC 2271
Oliver, James	30	1691	MCC folio 143
Oliver, James	35	1655	EQC 1:398
Oliver, James	35	1655	EQC 1:399
Oliver, James	44	1664	SJC 754
Oliver, James	44	1664	SJC 754
Oliver, James	51	1672	SJC 1221
Oliver, James	55	1676	MCC folio 72
Oliver, James	55	1676	MCC folio 76
Oliver, James	56	1676	SD 9:432
Oliver, James	57	1676	MCC folio 74
Oliver, James	64	1682	EQC 8:353
Oliver, John	19	1662/3	SD 4:88a
Oliver, John	19	1663	SJC 570
Oliver, John	27	1640	SD 1:51
Oliver, Joseph	23	1668	SJC 905
Oliver, Nathaniel	20	1671/2	SD 7:275
Oliver, Peter	44	nd	SJC 520
Oliver, Peter	48	1666	SJC 754
Oliver, Peter	50	1668	SJC 905
Oliver, Thomas	22	1668	MCC folio 45
Onge, Isaac	25	1661	EQC 2:286
Onge, Isaac	27	1663	MCC folio 35
Onge, Simon	50	1672	MCC folio 59
Onge, Simon	50	1672	MCC folio 60
Onge, Simon	50	1672	MCC folio 64

Onion, Sarah	21	1671	SD 7:185
Ordway, Abner	58	1669	EQC 4:180
Ordway, Ann	50	1679/80	SJC 1870
Ordway, Hannah	31	1684	EQC 9:203
Ordway, James	26	1678	EQC 7:156
Ordway, James	45	1669	EQC 4:178
Ordway, James	54	1677	EQC 6:260
Ordway, James	60	1678	EQC 7:156
Ordway, James	61	1680	EQC 8:173
Ordway, James	64	1681	EQC 8:172
Ordway, James	64	1681	EQC 8:173
Ordway, John	20	1678	EQC 7:156
Ormsby, John	20	1662	EQC 2:411
Ormsby, John	21	1662	EQC 2:411
Ormsby, Richard	52	1660	EQC 2:230
Orne, John	40	1685	EQC 9:440
Orne, Sarah	24	1694	SJC 3037
Orris, Elizabeth	57	1678	SJC 2016
Orton, Hannah	28	1694	SJC 3015
Orton, Thomas	62	1675	MCC folio 69
Osborn, Alexander	35	1683	EQC 9:48
Osborn, William	24	1668	MCC folio 48
Osborn, William	33	1679	EQC 7:166
Osborn, William	36	1683	EQC 9:55
Osgood, Christopher	27	1671	EQC 4:422
Osgood, Elizabeth	72	1687	EQC WPA 47-51-3
Osgood, Hannah	30	1671	EQC 4:422
Osgood, John	37	1669	EQC 4:118
Osgood, John	40	1677	EQC 6:325
Osgood, John	46	1676	EQC 6:229
Osgood, John	46	1676/7	SJC 1554
Osgood, John	48	1677	EQC 6:324
Osgood, John	48	1677	EQC 6:325
Osgood, John	54	1650	EQC 1:239
Osgood, John	54	1685	EQC 9:545
Osgood, John	55	1686	EQC 9:607
Osgood, Sgt.	30	1661	EQC 2:288
Osgood, Stephen	22	1661	EQC 2:288
Osgood, Steven	18	1657	EQC 2:40
Osgood, Steven	33	1672	EQC 5:31
Osgood, Susanna	30	1682	EQC 8:382
Osgood, William	21	1694/5	SJC 3782
Osgood, William	21	1695	SJC 3782
Osgood, William	35	1685	EQC 9:534
Osgood, William	60	1669	EQC 4:100
Overman, Thomas	39	1672/3	SCC 206
Overman, Thomas	39	1672/3	SJC 1165
Overy, Alexander	50	1667	SJC 818
Overy, Mary	48	1667	SJC 818
Owen, William	20	1685	EQC 9:530
Owens, Thomas	35	1678	EQC 7:21
Oxman, William	35	1669	EQC 4:168
Oxman, William	35	1669	EQC 4:91
Paddy, Thomas	24	1673	SJC 1216

Pagan, John	26	1677	EQC 6:332
Page, Edward	30	1663/4	SJC 591
Page, George	28	1669	SJC 1046
Page, George	29	1670	SJC 1046
Page, George	36	1678	EQC 7:34
Page, John	36	1660	MCC folio 25
Page, John	38	1667	MCC folio 43
Page, John	48	1678	MCC folio 80
Page, Nicholas	23	nd	SJC 26762
Page, Nicholas	24	1663	SJC 571
Page, Nicholas	30	1665	SJC 705
Page, Nicholas	30	1666/7	SJC 791
Page, Nicholas	31	1668	SJC 983
Page, Robert	59	1660	SJC 378
Page, Thomas	18	1656	MCC folio 14
Page, Thomas	23	1670	EQC 4:243
Pahey, Samuel	34	1691	MCC folio 151
Paine, Edward	19	1679	MCC folio 184
Paine, Elizabeth	30	1669	MCC folio 52
Paine, Elizabeth	60	1698	MCC folio 169
Paine, Elizabeth	60	1698	SJC 3936
Paine, John	34	1666	SJC 754
Paine, Joseph	22	1649	SD 1:109
Paine, Katherine	22	1681	SJC 2003
Paine, Mary	22	nd	SJC 4849
Paine, Steven	26	1662	MCC folio 31
Paine, Steven	28	1662	MCC folio 31
Paine, Steven	41	1680	MCC folio 90
Paine, Steven	43	1677	MCC folio 75
Paine, Thomas	15	1647	SD 1:86
Palfery, Constant	36	1694	MCC folio 161
Palmer, Frances	20	1678	EQC 7:97
Palmer, John	26	1669	SJC 1088
Palmer, John	27	nd	SJC 1100
Palmer, John	30	1670	SJC 1046
Palmer, John	30	1676	EQC 6:156
Palmer, John	35	1684	EQC 9:348
Palmer, John	43	1663	MCC folio 34
Palmer, Mary	30	1685	EQC 9:524
Palmer, Pasco	37	1677	SJC 1620
Palmer, Stephen	16	1685	MCC folio 117
Palmer, Stephen	16	1686	MCC folio 123
Paney, Samuel	34	1691	MCC folio 151
Parish, John	41	1683	MCC folio 104
Parke, John	18	1673	MCC folio 60
Parke, John	18	1673	MCC folio 64
Parke, Thomas	18	1673	MCC folio 64
Parke, Thomas	20	1673	MCC folio 60
Parke, Thomas	42	1670	MCC folio 46
Parke, Thomas	50	1679	MCC folio 84
Parke, William	75	1682	MCC folio 106
Parker, Abraham	47	1699	MCC folio 207
Parker, Ann	27	1689	MCC folio 131
Parker, Benjamin	15	1651	MCC folio 2

Parker, Benjamin	25	1689	MCC folio 133
Parker, Benjamin	25	1689	MCC folio 140
Parker, Elizabeth	17	1693	SJC 162288
Parker, Hannaniah	34	1672	EQC 5:85
Parker, James	37	1657	MCC folio 20
Parker, John	25	1658	SJC 491
Parker, John	40	1678	EQC 7:91
Parker, John	45	1680	EQC 7:423
Parker, John	46	1672	MCC folio 59
Parker, John	46	1672	MCC folio 60
Parker, John	79	1664	MCC folio 36
Parker, Joseph	47	1670	MCC folio 55
Parker, Joseph	58	1683	EQC 9:104
Parker, Josiah	26	1681/2	MCC folio 98
Parker, Margaret	17	1681	MCC folio 104
Parker, Mary	18	1676/7	SJC 1554
Parker, Mary	20	1656	EQC 2:11
Parker, Mary	20	1659	EQC 2:365
Parker, Mary	20	1685	MCC folio 117
Parker, Mary	25	1678	EQC 7:124
Parker, Mary	32	1678	SJC 1733
Parker, Nathan	28	1678	EQC 7:156
Parker, Nathan	40	1662	EQC 2:404
Parker, Nathan	40	nd	SJC 322
Parker, Nathan	42	1661	EQC 2:327
Parker, Nathan	44	1665/6	SJC 725
Parker, Nathan	48	1671	EQC 4:338
Parker, Noah	34	1673	SJC 1245
Parker, Richard	76	1670	MCC folio 54
Parker, Robert	66	1670	MCC folio 61
Parker, Robert	77	1682	MCC folio 101
Parker, Robert	82	1683/4	SJC 2287
Parker, Samuel	22	1682	EQC 8:276
Parkhurst, George	78	1695	SJC 3175
Parkis, George	44?	1678	MCC folio 81
Parkis, John	34	1678	MCC folio 81
Parks, Mary	48	1691	MCC folio 142
Parks, William	61	1668	SJC 857
Parks, William	63	1670	SJC 1014
Parminter, Benjamin	50	1675	EQC 6:78
Parminter, Benjamin	57	1666	EQC 3:369
Parminter, Benjamin	60	1674	EQC 5:282
Parminter, Benjamin	60	1680	EQC 8:5
Parminter, Benjamin	60	1680	SJC 2011
Parminter, Benjamin	63	1674	EQC 5:347
Parminter, Benjamin	65	1677	EQC 6:363
Parminter, Benjamin	70	1680	EQC 8:5
Parminter, Benjamin	70	1680	SJC 2011
Parminter, Benjamin	70	1681	EQC 8:104
Parminter, Benjamin	70	1681	EQC 8:180
Parminter, Benjamin	75	1685	EQC 9:468
Parminter, John	31	1672	SJC 1163
Parminter, John	55	1665	MCC folio 38
Parminter, Mary	19	1690	MCC folio 145

Parnell, Mary	22	1666	EQC 3:420
Parris, Mary	18	nd	SJC 2839
Parser, John	40	1659	MCC folio 24
Parslow, William	38	1698/9	SJC 3834
Parsons, Elizabeth	46	1683	EQC 9:63
Parsons, Jeffery	32	1663	EQC 3:43
Parsons, Philip	43	1689/90	SJC 2541
Parsons, Thomas	23	1658	EQC 2:139
Parsons, William	60	1680	EQC 8:28
Partridge, Ann	22	1662	SJC 874
Partridge, John	28	1666	SJC 764
Partridge, John	28	1666	SJC 813
Partridge, John	38	1674	EQC 5:421
Partridge, John	38	1674	SJC 1354
Partridge, John	42	1678	SJC 1829
Partridge, John	42	1679	MCC folio 87
Partridge, Mary	32	1674	EQC 5:421
Partridge, Nehemiah	22	1666	SJC 813
Partridge, Nehemiah	29	1674	EQC 5:421
Partridge, Rachel	16	1667	EQC 3:425
Partridge, Samuel	50	1694	SJC 3301
Partridge, William	39	nd	SJC 2802
Pary, Mary	17	1677	EQC 6:348
Pasco, Hugh	44	1686	EQC WPA 46-93-1
Passmore, Richard	30	1675	EQC 6:12
Passmore, Richard	30	1675	SJC 1400
Patch, Thomas	39	1677	EQC 6:349
Patch, Thomas	40	1679	EQC 7:182
Patch, Thomas	40	1679	EQC 7:207
Patch, Thomas	41	1679	EQC 7:258
Patch, Thomas	42	1680	EQC 8:22
Patch, Thomas	42	1680	EQC 8:63
Patch, Thomas	56	nd	SJC 98534
Pateshall, Robert	55	1665	EQC 3:284
Pateshall, Robert	56	1665/6	SJC 728
Pateshall, Robert	59	1668	SJC 913
Pather, Nathaniel	34	1695	SJC 3322
Patrick, Katherine	32	1681	EQC 8:238
Patten, Justin	86	1673	SCC 378
Patten, Nathaniel	36	1681	MCC folio 94
Patten, Nathaniel	46	1690	MCC folio 173
Patten, Nathaniel	48	1691	MCC folio 146
Patten, Nathaniel	48	1691	MCC folio 163
Patten, Nathaniel	48	1691	MCC folio 173
Patterson, John	20	1679	MCC folio 85
Patteson, Joseph	18	1661	MCC folio 27
Pattey, Robert	23	1662	EQC 2:408
Pattey, Robert	23	1665	EQC 3:262
Pattishal, Robert	40	1653/4	MCC folio 12
Pattishall, Robert	40	1655	EQC 2:93
Pattishall, Robert	40	1658	EQC 2:91
Patton, David	27	1684	EQC 9:283
Paul, Dorothy	46	1685	SJC 26063
Paul, John	32	1660	EQC 2:230

Paul, John	37	1665	EQC 3:290
Paul, John	45	1671	EQC 4:383
Paul, John	55	1682	EQC 8:403
Paul, John	59	1685	EQC 9:431
Paul, John	59	1685	SJC 2345
Paul, John	69	1692	MCC folio 204
Paul, John	69	1695	MCC folio 179
Paul, Lydia	53	1692	MCC folio 204
Paul, Lydia	53	1695	MCC folio 179
Paul, Samuel	23	nd	SJC 26748
Payne, Robert	40	1677	EQC 6:283
Payne, Robert	65	1667	EQC 3:397
Payne, Robert	71	1672	EQC 5:28
Payne, Samuel	29	1677	MCC folio 78
Payne, Samuel	29	1685	EQC 9:484
Payson, John	22	1665	SJC 680
Peabody, Francis	50	1662	EQC 2:405
Peabody, Francis	63	1676	SJC 1566
Peabody, Hannah	30	1674	EQC 5:353
Peabody, John	32	1674	EQC 5:422
Peabody, John	43	1686	EQC 9:606
Peabody, Joseph	30	1675	EQC 6:37
Peach, Alice	37	1674	EQC 5:348
Peach, Alice	54	1669	EQC 4:145
Peach, Alice	70	1684	EQC 9:205
Peach, John	50	1669	EQC 4:116
Peach, John	53	1669	EQC 4:145
Peach, John	55	1669	EQC 4:145
Peach, John	59	1672	EQC 5:115
Peach, John	60	1672	EQC 5:115
Peach, John	60	1674	EQC 5:347
Peach, John	60	1677	EQC 6:362
Peach, John	74	1677	EQC 6:362
Peach, John	80	1684	EQC 9:241
Peacock, Mary	22	1662	EQC 2:402
Peacock, Samuel	23	1662	EQC 2:402
Peacock, Sarah	30	nd	SJC 28895
Peake, William	59	1665/6	SJC 725
Peall, George	35	1679	EQC 7:239
Pearce, Daniel	38	1678	MCC folio 81
Pearce, John	22	1679	EQC 7:263
Pearce, John	35	1683	MCC folio 104
Pearce, John	41	1673	SCC 405
Pearce, Jonathan	14	1676	MCC folio 71
Pearce, Mary	22	1680	EQC 7:371
Pearce, Mary	24	1682	EQC 8:282
Pearce, Mary	56	1676	MCC folio 71
Pearce, Moses	15	1682	EQC 8:282
Pearce, Moses	20	1684	EQC 9:244
Pearce, Samuel	23	1676	EQC 6:216
Pearce, Samuel	27	1680	EQC 7:371
Pearce, Samuel	27	1680	EQC 7:375
Pearce, Samuel	28	1682	EQC 8:281
Pearce, Samuel	33	1686	EQC WPA 46-68-2

Pearce, William	16	1680	EQC 7:401
Pearl, Elizabeth	35	1699	SJC 4030
Pearl, John	28	1681	SJC 2008
Pearl, John	29	1681	EQC 8:111
Pearl, John	29	1681	EQC 8:112
Pearl, John	29	1681	SJC 2008
Pearse, Daniel	27	1696	SJC 3408
Pearse, Daniel	56	nd	SJC 3579
Pearse, David	24	nd	SJC 28431
Pearse, Esther	45	1673	SJC 2120
Pearse, George	17	1678	EQC 7:157
Pearse, Jabith	31	nd	SJC 26146
Pearse, John	23	1690/1	SJC 2596
Pearse, John	40	1658	EQC 2:64
Pearse, John	41	1673/4	SJC 1270
Pearse, John	55	1670	SJC 974
Pearse, John	70	1679/80	SJC 1833
Pearse, Lucius	35	1685	SJC 2377
Pearse, Mary	14	1682	EQC 8:282
Pearse, Mary	22	1680	SJC 1894
Pearse, Moses	25	1679	SJC 1765
Pearse, Nathaniel	28	1679	SJC 1800
Pearse, Thomas	46	1665	MCC folio 39
Pearson, Elizabeth	39	1673	SJC 1228
Pearson, George	40	1670	EQC 4:303
Pearson, George	42	1672	SJC 1341
Pearson, George	43	1673	MCC folio 64
Pearson, George	43	1673	SJC 1221
Pearson, John	19	1669	EQC 4:208
Pearson, John	60	1674	MCC folio 75
Pearson, Madeline	50	1669	EQC 4:209
Pearson, Mary	24	1675	EQC 6:14
Pearson, Mary	34	1685	EQC 9:531
Pearson, Samuel	32	1682	EQC 8:275
Pease, James	50	1685	MCC folio 116
Pease, John	45	1677	EQC 6:284
Pease, John	48	1665	SJC 721
Pease, John	65	1679	SD 11:200
Pease, Nathaniel	43	1681	EQC 8:215
Pease, Robert	50	1678	EQC 7:148
Peash, John	58	1672	EQC 5:4
Peash, John	60	1672	EQC 5:4
Peasley, Joseph	26	1673	EQC 5:242
Peasley, Joseph	30	1681	EQC 8:84
Peasley, Joseph	30	1681	SJC 2009
Peasley, Joseph	33	1680	EQC 8:70
Peasley, Joseph	35	1682	EQC 8:316
Peasley, Joseph	35	1683	EQC 9:7
Peasley, Joseph	38	1686	EQC 9:604
Peason, John	55	1671	EQC 4:411
Peck, John	42	nd	SJC 2727
Peck, Thomas	48	1667	SJC 909
Peck, Thomas	54	1672	SJC 1341
Peck, Thomas	54	1673	MCC folio 64

Peck, Thomas	54	1673	SJC 1221
Pecker, James	42	1664	EQC 3:184
Pecker, James	44	1667	EQC 3:422
Pecker, James	50	1672	EQC 5:101
Pecker, James	63	1685	EQC 9:544
Pecker, Mary	68	1685	SJC 2354
Pedrick, John	25	1663	EQC 3:108
Pedrick, John	40	1664	EQC 3:156
Pedrick, John	48	1674	EQC 5:338
Pees, Mary	35	1682	EQC 8:370
Peeteter, Andrew	21	1687	EQC WPA 47-39-1
Pegea, Ann	17	1681	EQC 8:93
Pegg, Robert	36	1662	SJC 508
Peggy, Edward	30	1676	EQC 6:172
Peggy, Edward	30	1676	SJC 1567
Peirce, Elizabeth	19	1676	MCC folio 71
Peirce, Joseph	26	1672	MCC folio 61
Peirce, Mary	31	1689	MCC folio 134
Peirce, Mary	56	1676	MCC folio 71
Peirce, Nathaniel	26	1682	MCC folio 98
Peirce, Nathaniel	28	1679	SCC 1043
Peirce, Steven	36	1689	MCC folio 133
Peirce, Thomas	24	1670	MCC folio 53
Peirce, Thomas	39	1684	MCC folio 109
Peirce, Thomas	46	1690	MCC folio 167A
Peirie, Jonathan	29	1690	MCC folio 140
Peirpoint, John	51	1670	EQC 4:288
Pelton, John	30	1675	EQC 6:53
Pelton, John	34	1680	SJC 1909
Pelton, John	60	1673/4	SCC 379
Pelton, John	60	1673/4	SJC 1281
Pelton, Robert	27	1679/80	SJC 1819
Pelton, Robert	27	1679/80	SJC 1837
Pelton, Robert	27	1680	SJC 1909
Pelton, Samuel	24	1672/3	SCC 379
Pelton, Samuel	24	1672/3	SJC 1281
Pemberton, James	51	1683	MCC folio 128
Pemberton, John	21	1663	MCC folio 35
Pemberton, John	21	1666	MCC folio 35
Pemberton, John	21	1666	MCC folio 40
Pemberton, Sarah	53	1683	MCC folio 128
Pembroke, Margaret	50	1662	MCC folio 31
Pen, William	50	1659	SJC 347
Penewell, Joseph	51	1679/80	SJC 1837
Penfield, Samuel	26	1678	EQC 6:389
Pengelly, John	28	1678	EQC 7:121
Pengry, Aaron	26	1679	EQC 7:270
Pengry, John	21	1674	EQC 5:286
Pengry, John	23	1676	EQC 6:217
Pengry, Moses	24	1674	EQC 5:286
Pengry, Moses	50	1661	EQC 2:328
Pengry, Moses	57	1669	EQC 4:141
Pengry, Moses	64	1676	EQC 6:206
Pengry, Moses	66	1678	EQC 6:409

Pengry, Moses	70	1680	EQC 8:35
Pengry, Moses	72	1682	EQC 8:410
Pengry, Moses	74	1685	EQC 9:449
Pengry, Moses	74	1685	EQC 9:545
Penision, Rebecca	23	1679	EQC 7:238
Penly, Rachel	60	1677	EQC 6:354
Pennell, Joseph	50	1679/80	SJC 1819
Penniman, James	37	1670	SJC 993
Penniman, James	41	1673	SD 8:298
Penniman, Joseph	42	nd	SJC 28547
Penny, John	24	1684	MCC folio 111
Penny, Oliver	22	1676	EQC 6:199
Penticost, John	70	1679	MCC folio 184
Penticost, John	84	1686	MCC folio 122
Peppin, Samuel	32	1679	EQC 7:260
Peppin, Samuel	35	1678	EQC 7:117
Peppin, Samuel	35	1678	EQC 7:204
Peppin, Samuel	35	1678	SJC 1797
Percival, James	21	1693/4	SJC 2989
Peren, Elizabeth	40	1673	EQC 5:228
Perham, John	60	1692	MCC folio 154
Perkins, Abraham	29	1668	EQC 4:57
Perkins, Beamsly	20	1695	SJC 3223
Perkins, David	16	1668	SJC 924
Perkins, Elizabeth	25	1671	EQC 4:350
Perkins, Elizabeth	26	1683	EQC 9:144
Perkins, Hannah	16	1689	MCC folio 133
Perkins, Hannah	26	1663	MCC folio 34
Perkins, Hannah	34	1671	MCC folio 57
Perkins, Hannah	47	1686	MCC folio 124
Perkins, Hannah	48	1686	MCC folio 125
Perkins, Jacob	20	1674	EQC 5:339
Perkins, Jacob	40	1686	EQC WPA 46-69-1
Perkins, James	29	1677	EQC 6:413
Perkins, John	16	1671	EQC 4:425
Perkins, John	32	1686	EQC 9:583
Perkins, John	40	1672	SJC 1194
Perkins, John	60	1650	EQC 1:187
Perkins, Jonathan	27	1678	EQC 6:434
Perkins, Luke	25	1674	EQC 5:339
Perkins, Luke	25	1674	EQC 5:341
Perkins, Luke	40	1683	MCC folio 104
Perkins, Luke	44	1695	SJC 3223
Perkins, Luke	46	1695	SJC 3223
Perkins, Remember	23	1696	SJC 4301
Perkins, Samuel	27	1680	EQC 7:372
Perkins, Sarah	14	1671	EQC 4:425
Perkins, Sarah	33	1678	MCC folio 78
Perkins, Thomas	55	1677	SJC 162379
Perkins, Thomas	56	1677	SJC 3349
Perkins, William	19	1660	EQC 2:255
Perkins, William	64	1671	EQC 4:420
Perley, John	33	1669	EQC 4:177
Perley, Nathaniel	19	1662	EQC 3:13

Perley, Nathaniel	22	1666	EQC 3:326
Perley, Sarah	21	1669	EQC 4:177
Perley, Thomas	21	1662	EQC 3:13
Perley, Thomas	28	1669	EQC 4:177
Perley, Thomas	34	1675	EQC 6:55
Perrin, Hugh	29	1679	SJC 1787
Perrin, Noah	20	1699	SJC 3847
Perrin, William	44	1672	SJC 1163
Perry, Michael	25	nd	SJC 2798
Perry, Francis	45	1653	EQC 2:92
Perry, John	33	1677	SJC 1738
Perry, John	42	1685	MCC folio 117
Perry, John	47	1691	MCC folio 151
Perry, John	49	1692	MCC folio 172
Perry, Michael	25	1691	SJC 162269
Perry, Seth	18	1691/2	SJC 2653
Perry, Seth	32	1672/3	SJC 1162
Perry, Seth	40	1680	SJC 1919
Perry, Seth	51	1691	SJC 2596
Perry, Thomas	70	1669	EQC 4:114
Pers, Robert	38	1658	MCC folio 16
Perse, Anthony	62	1670	MCC folio 46
Perse, Daniel	40	1678	EQC 7:156
Persifild, John	18	1694	SJC 2989
Persifild, Thomas	16	1695	SJC 3322
Persifild, Thomas	16	1695	SJC 4205
Person, John	40	1656	MCC folio 15
Person, John	45	1661	MCC folio 28
Person, John	60	1675	EQC 6:35
Person, John	63	1678	EQC 7:240
Person, John	65	1680	EQC 7:352
Persons, Jeffrey	38	1675	EQC 6:116
Peter, Nathaniel	21	1684	MCC folio 107
Peters, Andrew	50	1685	EQC 9:453
Petit, Mary	19	1681	MCC folio 95
Pettingell, Mathew	30	1678	EQC 7:156
Pettingell, Mathew	33	1682	EQC 8:243
Pettingell, Mathew	33	1682	EQC 8:250
Pettingell, Mathew	34	1683	EQC 9:58
Pettingell, Richard	45	1669	EQC 4:111
Pettingell, Richard	47	1668	EQC 4:13
Pettingell, Richard	52	1673	EQC 5:244
Pettingell, Richard	54	1674	EQC 5:276
Pettingell, Richard	60	1678	EQC 7:156
Pettingell, Samuel	33	1678	EQC 7:156
Petty, Robert	23	1664	EQC 3:157
Petty, William	72	1667	SJC 815
Petty, William	72	nd	SJC 26725
Peverlo, Lazarus	20	1677	SJC 1686
Peyne, Samuel	29	1684	EQC 9:286
Pharoh, Thomas	55	1672	EQC 5:116
Phelps, Eleanor	23	1678	EQC 7:96
Phelps, John	36	1678	EQC 7:113
Phelps, John	36	1678	EQC 7:135

Phelps, John	36	1678	EQC 7:90
Phelps, John	41	1683	EQC 9:21
Phelps, William	35	1668	MCC folio 48
Philbrick, Thomas	42	1667	EQC 3:425
Philbrick, Thomas	42	1667	EQC 3:452
Philbrick, Thomas	46	1671/2	SJC 1148
Philbrick, Thomas	47	nd	SJC 26616
Philip, Andrew	20	1681	MCC folio 184
Philipbaer, Annah	50	1685	MCC folio 117
Phillips, Abigail	16	1676/7	SJC 1549
Phillips, Abigail	18	1680	EQC 7:374
Phillips, Abigail	18	nd	SJC 1894
Phillips, Andrew	19	1680	MCC folio 185
Phillips, Andrew	20	1681	MCC folio 102
Phillips, Charles	19	1681	EQC 8:224
Phillips, Charles	49	1678	EQC 7:147
Phillips, Charles	50	1678	EQC 7:113
Phillips, Eleazer	30	1685	MCC folio 114
Phillips, Eleazer	37	1692	MCC folio 153
Phillips, Jacob	18	1683	EQC 9:145
Phillips, Richard	33	1689	SJC 2552
Phillips, Theophilus	30	1668	MCC folio 45
Phillips, Thomas	47	1694	SJC 3104
Phillips, Timothy	10	1679	MCC folio 83
Phippen, Elizabeth	50	nd	SJC 2808
Phippeny, David	30	1679	EQC 7:308
Phippeny, Joseph	68	1684	EQC 9:395
Phipps, John	17	1686	MCC folio 128
Phipps, Joseph	20	1682	MCC folio 100
Phipps, Joseph	28	1690	MCC folio 134
Phipps, Joseph	30	nd	SJC 2848
Phipps, Solomon	35	1681	MCC folio 102
Phipps, Solomon	36	1682	MCC folio 100
Phipps, Solomon	39	1685	MCC folio 116
Phipps, Solomon	39	1685	SJC 2325
Pick, Sarah	35	1680	EQC 8:29
Pickard, Edmund	60	1679	EQC 7:326
Pickard, John	42	1664	EQC 3:124
Pickard, John	43	1665	EQC 3:233
Pickard, John	43	1665	SJC 717
Pickard, John	47	1668	EQC 4:71
Pickard, John	47	1668	SJC 908
Pickard, John	48	1670	EQC 4:260
Pickard, John	49	1670	EQC 4:283
Pickard, John	50	1672	EQC 5:17
Pickard, John	52	1674	EQC 5:393
Pickard, John	52	1674	SJC 1389
Pickard, John	53	1674	EQC 5:393
Pickard, John	53	1674	EQC 5:397
Pickard, John	53	1674	SJC 1389
Pickard, John	53	1675	EQC 6:27
Pickard, John	55	1676	EQC 6:217
Picke, Jonas	28	1681	MCC folio 94
Pickerell, Jonathan	40	1679	EQC 7:308

Pickering, John	35	1673	EQC 5:169
Pickering, John	35	1673	SJC 1246
Pickering, John	35	nd	SJC 2818
Pickering, John	48	1686	EQC WPA 46-24-3
Pickering, John	48	nd	SJC 2770
Pickering, Jonathan	44	1686	EQC WPA 46-24-5
Pickering, Sarah	45	1666	SJC 740
Pickett, Christopher	60	1676	EQC 6:185
Pickett, Elizabeth	60	1685/6	SJC 2388
Pickett, John	30	1689	SJC 2520
Pickett, Nichoals	33	1680	EQC 7:335
Pickett, Nicholas	28	1682	EQC 8:331
Pickett, Nicholas	33	1680	EQC 7:334
Pickett, Nicholas	33	1680	EQC 7:386
Pickman, Nathaniel	19	1695	SJC 3123
Pickman, Nathaniel	30	1678	EQC 7:80
Pickman, Nathaniel	47	1662	EQC 2:395
Pickman, Nathaniel	60	1676	EQC 6:247
Pickworth, Abigail	30	1678	EQC 7:24
Pickworth, Elias	18	1676	EQC 6:146
Pidgaway, Mary	16	1671	MCC folio 61
Pierce, Abigail	16	1669	EQC 4:195
Pierce, Benjamin	35	1684	MCC folio 110
Pierce, Daniel	43	1682	EQC 8:429
Pierce, Daniel	44	1683	EQC 9:105
Pierce, Daniel	44	1684	MCC folio 110
Pierce, Elizabeth	42	1684	MCC folio 110
Pierce, Elizabeth	74	1669	MCC folio 52
Pierce, John	27	1691	MCC folio 157
Pierce, John	40	1660	EQC 2:217
Pierce, John	50	1666	EQC 3:327
Pierce, John	61	1674	MCC folio 67
Pierce, Joseph	43	1690	MCC folio 135
Pierce, Nathaniel	27	1682	MCC folio 101
Pierce, Nathaniel	28	1684	MCC folio 107
Pierce, Nathaniel	32	1683/4	SJC 2172
Pierce, Nathaniel	33	1689	MCC folio 134
Pierce, Nathaniel	33	1689	MCC folio 134
Pierce, Nathaniel	34	1685	MCC folio 115
Pierce, Nehemiah	36	1679	EQC 7:260
Pierce, Robert	38	1656	MCC folio 16
Pierce, Robert	38	1659	MCC folio 21
Pierce, Robert	50	1663	EQC 3:35
Pierce, Robert	59	1676	MCC folio 71
Pierce, Robert	60	1671	EQC 4:333
Pierce, Robert	60	1672	EQC 5:7
Pierce, Robert	63	1675	EQC 6:67
Pierce, Ruth	24	1663	SJC 573
Pierce, Samuel	17	1669	EQC 4:195
Pierce, Samuel	27	1680	SJC 1894
Pierce, Samuel	43	1697	SJC 4005
Pierce, Samuel	45	1678	MCC folio 78
Pierce, Stephen	55	1666	EQC 3:346
Pierce, Stephen	60	1669	EQC 4:194

Pierce, Steven	34	1685	MCC folio 116
Pierce, Steven	44	1695	MCC folio 207
Pierce, Thomas	22	nd	SJC 3579
Pierce, Thomas	24	1668	MCC folio 48
Pierce, Thomas	39	1684	MCC folio 115
Pierce, Thomas	40	1685	MCC folio 115
Pierce, Thomas	52	1690/1	SJC 2596
Pierce, Thomas	53	1671	MCC folio 59
Pierce, Thomas	76	1660	MCC folio 26
Pierce, William	15	1679	EQC 7:250
Pierpoint, John	61	1679/80	SJC 2997
Pigg, Thomas	18	1653	MCC folio 8
Pike, Hugh	21	1678	EQC 7:156
Pike, John	22	1663	MCC folio 35
Pike, John	24	1667	SJC 909
Pike, John	25	1663	SJC 909
Pike, Joseph	30	1669	EQC 4:117
Pike, Joseph	37	1676	EQC 6:165
Pike, Joseph	39	1678	EQC 6:442
Pike, Joseph	39	1678	EQC 7:157
Pike, Joseph	43	1682	EQC 8:250
Pike, Joseph	43	1682	EQC 8:260
Pike, Joseph	43	1682	EQC 8:265
Pike, Joseph	43	1682	EQC 8:284
Pike, Joseph	43	1682	EQC 8:288
Pike, Morris	50	1680	EQC 7:335
Pike, Moses	20	1680	EQC 8:17
Pike, Robert	25	1685	EQC 9:535
Pike, Robert	52	1669	EQC 4:154
Pike, Robert	52	1671	EQC 4:357
Pike, Robert	63	1680	EQC 8:17
Pike, Robert	77	nd	SJC 3231
Pike, Robert	79	1695	SJC 3214
Pike, Samuel	22	1676	EQC 6:258
Pike, Samuel	23	1677	EQC 6:360
Pike, Samuel	23	1677	EQC 6:361
Pike, Samuel	27	1681	EQC 8:179
Pike, Samuel	30	1684	EQC 9:194
Pillsbury, Abel	26	1678	EQC 7:157
Pillsbury, Caleb	24	1678	EQC 7:157
Pillsbury, Deborah	28	1680	EQC 7:422
Pillsbury, Increase	18	1678	EQC 7:157
Pillsbury, Increase	21	1682	EQC 8:283
Pillsbury, Increase	23	1684	EQC 9:242
Pillsbury, Job	35	1678	EQC 7:157
Pillsbury, Mery	20	1680	EQC 7:425
Pillsbury, Moses	38	1686	EQC WPA 46-119-3
Pillsbury, William	22	1678	EQC 7:157
Pillsbury, William	71	1676	EQC 6:203
Pillsbury, William	73	1678	EQC 7:157
Pinchon, John	32	1681	EQC 8:165
Pinder, Jacob	25	1661	MCC folio 26
Pinder, John	22	1681	EQC 8:152
Pinder, John	42	1673	EQC 5:135

Pine, John	22	1676	MCC folio 71
Pingrey, Moses	72	1682	SJC 3138
Pinson, William	30	1678	EQC 7:114
Pinwell, Peter	26	1678	SJC 1756
Piper, Nathaniel	44	1670	EQC 4:280
Pipone, John	21	1672	EQC 5:92
Pisecyss, Solomon	16	1685	MCC folio 117
Pitman, James	29	1681	EQC 8:101
Pitman, Mark	40	1662	EQC 2:441
Pitman, Mark	40	1669	EQC 4:155
Pitman, Mark	48	1672	EQC 5:68
Pitman, Nicholas	29	1683	EQC 9:57
Pitman, Thomas	17	1669	EQC 4:162
Pitman, Thomas	45	1662	EQC 2:442
Pitman, Thomas	50	1672	EQC 5:42
Pitman, Thomas	55	1669	EQC 4:162
Pitman, Thomas	56	1670	EQC 4:281
Pitman, William	15	1665	EQC 3:269
Pitt, William	80	1672	EQC 5:109
Pittman, Nathaniel	19	1694	SJC 4123
Pittman, Nathaniel	19	1695	SJC 3123a
Pitts, William	29	1668	SJC 162081
Pitts, William	29	1668	SJC 924
Platts, Abel	24	1674	EQC 5:343
Platts, Abel	25	1675	EQC 6:14
Platts, Abel	30	1679	EQC 7:291
Platts, Abel	36	1686	EQC WPA 46-6-2
Platts, James	75	nd	SJC 24799
Platts, Jonathan	34	1665	EQC 3:240
Platts, Jonathan	40	1674	EQC 5:393
Platts, Jonathan	40	1674	SJC 162131
Plimble, Thomas	33	1682	SJC 2224
Plimpton, Mary	30	1677/8	SJC 1705
Plimpton, Peter	24	1677/8	SJC 1705
Plumb, Deborah	21	1678	EQC 7:51
Plumb, John	17	1669	EQC 4:193
Plumb, John	40	1670	SJC 993
Plumb, Mary	56	1685	SJC 2324
Plummer, Anne	21	1682	EQC 8:279
Plummer, Benjamin	22	1678	EQC 7:157
Plummer, Ephraim	24	1678	EQC 7:156
Plummer, Joseph	23	1678	EQC 7:157
Plummer, Joseph	50	1680	EQC 8:65
Plummer, Samuel	35	1682/3	SJC 2120
Plummer, Samuel	52	1671	EQC 4:381
Plummer, Samuel	60	1678	EQC 7:157
Plummer, Samuel	62	1680	EQC 8:66
Plummer, Samuel	65	1684	EQC 9:256
Plummer, Silvanus	20	1678	EQC 7:156
Plummer, Silvanus	25	1684	EQC 9:256
Poag, Robert	24	1677	MCC folio 77
Poate, William	40	1680	EQC 7:386
Poet, William	25	1666	EQC 3:350
Poland, John	46	1681	EQC 8:162

Pollard, James	46	1678	EQC 7:112
Pollard, William	60	1671/2	SJC 1092
Pollard, William	62	1673	SCC 309
Pollard, William	62	1673	SJC 1209
Polley, Daniel	24	1680	EQC 7:401
Polley, George	43	1668	MCC folio 47
Polley, John	35	1686	MCC folio 123
Polydore, [boy]	18	1695	SJC 4182
Pomeroy, John	38	1674	EQC 5:339
Pond, Anna	43	1685	MCC folio 114
Pond, Daniel	54	1685	MCC folio 114
Pond, Martha	18	nd	SJC 1787
Poole, Daniel	24	1680	EQC 7:331
Poole, Daniel	25	1680	EQC 7:424
Poole, Jonathan	39	1674	EQC 5:423
Poole, Margaret	60	1663	MCC folio 34
Pooly, Richard	23	1655	SJC 257
Poore, Anthony	62	1678	MCC folio 82
Poore, Edward	23	1678	EQC 7:156
Poore, Elizabeth	43	1692	MCC folio 153
Poore, Hannah	14	1663	EQC 3:23
Poore, Henry	26	1678	EQC 7:157
Poore, James	45	1664	EQC 3:156
Poore, John	20	1662	EQC 3:22
Poore, John	36	1678	EQC 7:157
Poore, John	43	1680	MCC folio 183
Poore, John	45	1682	MCC folio 99
Poore, John	46	1662	EQC 3:22
Poore, John	63	1678	EQC 7:156
Poore, Joseph	17	1678	EQC 7:156
Poore, Joseph	22	1676	EQC 6:188
Poore, Joseph	24	1678	EQC 7:156
Poore, Joseph	30	1683	EQC 9:87
Poore, Joseph	30	1695	SJC 3148
Poore, Mary	20	1683	EQC 9:87
Poore, Rebecca	50	1681	EQC 8:217
Poore, Samuel	25	1678	EQC 7:156
Poore, Samuel	40	1695	SJC 3148
Poore, Samuel	55	1678	EQC 7:156
Poore, Thomas	76	1660	MCC folio 25
Pope, Elizabeth	50	1691	MCC folio 141
Pope, Enise	17	1680	EQC 7:424
Pope, Jonathan	24	1650	SJC 1014
Pope, Thomas	44	1690	MCC folio 136
Popowne, Nicholas	23	1680	SJC 1941
Porter, Abel	60	1674/5	SJC 1432
Porter, Abel	62	1675/6	SJC 1432
Porter, Abel	62	1676	SJC 1656
Porter, Abel	67	1680	SJC 1911
Porter, Benjamin	26	1669	EQC 4:193
Porter, Benjamin	55	1695	SJC 3326
Porter, Israel	25	1669	EQC 4:144
Porter, Israel	30	1674	SJC 28631
Porter, Israel	30	1678	EQC 7:11

Porter, Israel	30	1683	EQC 9:54
Porter, Israel	33	1678	EQC 9:54
Porter, Israel	52	1695	SJC 3326
Porter, John	24	1683	EQC 9:14
Porter, John	25	1695	SJC 3236
Porter, John	48	1678	EQC 9:54
Porter, John	52	1695	SJC 3236
Porter, John	73	1669	EQC 4:110
Porter, John	79	1678	EQC 7:12
Porter, Joseph	19	1656	EQC 2:12
Porter, Joseph	23	1661	EQC 2:321
Porter, Joseph	26	1664	EQC 3:167
Porter, Joseph	40	1678	EQC 9:54
Porter, Joseph	57	1695	SJC 3326
Porter, Robert	33	1663	EQC 3:38
Post, Richard	40	1668	EQC 4:2
Potter, Anthony	40	1668	EQC 4:82
Potter, Daniel	15	1674	EQC 5:318
Potter, Edman	30	1683	EQC 9:222
Potter, Edmund	14	1668	EQC 4:83
Potter, Edmund	27	1683	EQC 9:2
Potter, Indigo	25	1662	EQC 2:391
Potter, John	16	1668	EQC 4:83
Potter, Robert	52	1682	EQC 8:259
Potter, Robert	54	1685	SJC 2340
Potter, Robert	58	1682	EQC 8:259
Potter, Sarah	19	1680	EQC 7:372
Potter, Sarah	19	1680	SJC 1894
Potts, John	22	1678	MCC folio 80
Poulter, John	23	1690	MCC folio 149
Pow, Elizabeth	30	1682	EQC 8:340
Pow, William	37	nd	SJC 2174
Powell, Felix	21	nd	SJC 26989
Powell, Mary	23	1662	EQC 2:373
Powell, Robert	40	1676	EQC 6:159
Powell, Robert	40	1676	SJC 1456
Powell, Thomas	30	1673	EQC 5:179
Powell, Thomas	30	1673	EQC 5:181
Powell, Thomas	30	1673	EQC 5:181
Powell, Thomas	50	1696	MCC folio 201
Power, Walter	27	1666	MCC folio 41
Power, Walter	37	1677	MCC folio 76
Powland, James	46	1678	EQC 7:141
Powland, John	50	1682	EQC 8:411
Powline, James	31	1665	SJC 705
Pownell, Henry	42	1695	SJC 3322
Pownell, Henry	42	1695	SJC 4205
Pownell, Henry	43	1695	SJC 4206
Pownell, Henry	45	1695	SJC 3322
Powning, Henry	48	1663/4	SJC 669
Prance, Rachel	22	1683	EQC 9:5
Prance, Rachel	22	1683	EQC 9:64
Prance, Rachel	23	1684	EQC 9:250
Pratt, Barsheba	22	1661	MCC folio 27

Pratt, Daniel	30	1690	MCC folio 139
Pratt, John	30	1666	SJC 815
Pratt, John	30	1693	MCC folio 159
Pratt, John	43	1698	MCC folio 169
Pratt, John	43	1698	SJC 3936
Pratt, John	66	1699	SJC 4696
Pratt, Ruth	28	1693	MCC folio 159
Pratt, Samuel	28	1666	SJC 815
Pratt, Sarah	33	1677/8	SJC 1689
Pratt, Thomas	39	1685	MCC folio 116
Pratt, Thomas	39	1685	SJC 2325
Pratt, Thomas	48	1696/7	MCC folio 204
Pratt, Timothy	19	1679	MCC folio 85
Pray, Quentin	61	1656	EQC 2:94
Pray, Thomas	54	1658	EQC 2:64
Prentice, James	25	1681	MCC folio 95
Prentice, James	44	1673	MCC folio 63
Prentice, James	44	1673	SJC 1185
Prentice, James	54	1682	MCC folio 100
Prentice, John	21	1677	MCC folio 74
Prentice, Solomon	39	1686	MCC folio 127
Prentice, Thomas	33	1683	MCC folio 104
Prentice, Thomas	47	1679	MCC folio 84
Prescott, John	27	1681	MCC folio 93
Prescott, John	35	1678	MCC folio 80
Prescott, John	50	1695	MCC folio 196
Prescott, Jonathan	23	1670	MCC folio 53
Prescott, Mary	66	1678	MCC folio 80
Pressy, John	44	1682	EQC 8:374
Pressy, John	55	1693	SJC 3039
Preston, Samuel	15	1666	EQC 3:325
Preston, Thomas	35	1678	EQC 7:33
Preston, Thomas	40	1683	EQC 9:55
Preston, Thomas	43	1686	EQC WPA 46-31-2
Price, Elizabeth	52	1668	EQC 4:40
Price, Elizabeth	60	1676	EQC 6:195
Price, Hannah	30	1695	SJC 3126
Price, John	19	1684	MCC folio 107
Price, John	23	1669	EQC 4:156
Price, John	25	1671	EQC 4:384
Price, John	32	1678	EQC 7:35
Price, John	33	1679	EQC 7:239
Price, John	35	1691	SJC 2709
Price, Mary	44	1684	MCC folio 107
Price, Mathew	28	1657	MCC folio 19
Price, Mathew	31	1660	EQC 2:228
Price, Mathew	37	1666	EQC 3:333
Price, Mathew	37	1667	EQC 3:421
Price, Mathew	45	1673	EQC 5:248
Price, Mathew	48	1678	EQC 7:55
Price, Richard	29	1662	EQC 2:402
Price, Richard	30	nd	SJC 754
Price, Sarah	16	1684	MCC folio 107
Price, Theodore	16	1659	EQC 2:175

Price, Thomas	25	nd	SJC 2237
Price, Walter	45	1658	EQC 2:133
Price, Walter	50	1663	SJC 561
Price, Walter	53	1667	EQC 3:417
Price, Walter	55	1668	EQC 4:53
Price, Walter	55	1669	EQC 4:115
Price, William	35	1666	MCC folio 40
Price, William	43	1673	MCC folio 62
Price, William	43	1674	MCC folio 63
Price, William	44	1672	MCC folio 60
Price, William	53	1684	MCC folio 107
Prid, William	24	1662	MCC folio 29
Prince, John	22	1662	SJC 874
Prince, John	28	1667/8	SJC 1911
Prince, Joseph	25	1671	EQC 4:434
Prince, Margaret	40	1666	EQC 3:329
Prince, Richard	59	1673	EQC 5:171
Prince, Richard	61	1675	EQC 6:98
Prince, Richard	59	1673	SJC 1226
Prince, Samuel	25	1679	EQC 7:252
Prince, Samuel	25	1679	EQC 7:253
Prince, Samuel	26	1680	EQC 7:344
Prince, Thomas	15	1666	EQC 3:329
Prince, Thomas	45	1664	EQC 3:185
Prince, Thomas	45	1664	EQC 3:186
Printer, James	43	1685	MCC folio 112
Pritchet, John	18	1663	EQC 3:85
Proctor, Benjamin	17	1668	EQC 4:15
Proctor, Benjamin	17	1678	EQC 7:147
Proctor, Benjamin	18	1678	EQC 7:135
Proctor, Benjamin	18	1678	EQC 7:136
Proctor, Benjamin	26	1686	EQC WPA 46-78-1
Proctor, Elizabeth	16	1678	EQC 7:135
Proctor, Elizabeth	16	1678	EQC 7:136
Proctor, Elizabeth	16	1678	EQC 7:147
Proctor, John	40	1676	EQC 6:191
Proctor, John	40	1678	EQC 7:147
Proctor, John	46	1678	EQC 7:114
Proctor, John	50	1683	EQC 9:54
Proctor, John	54	1686	EQC WPA 46-78-1
Proctor, John	60	nd	SJC 2827
Proctor, John	70	1671	EQC 4:330
Proctor, John	75	1667	EQC 3:397
Proctor, John	83	1671/2	SJC 1102
Proctor, Joseph	33	1684	EQC 9:174
Proctor, Martha	16	1682	EQC 8:341
Proctor, Samuel	34	1676	SCC 739
Proctor, Samuel	34	1676	SJC 1575
Proctor, William	21	1679	SJC 1793
Prosser, Roger	40	1671/2	SCC 61
Prosser, Roger	40	1671/2	SJC 1140
Proude, Abial	20	1687	EQC WPA 47-53-4
Prout, Deborah	40	1691/2	SJC 2650
Prout, Deborah	50	1694	SJC 3113

Prout, Ebenezer	34	1691	MCC folio 148
Prout, Timothy	26	1670	SJC 1016
Prout, Timothy	33	1677	SCC 793
Prout, Timothy	33	1677	SJC 1582
Prout, Timothy	40	1661	EQC 2:322
Prout, Timothy	57	1677	SJC 1582
Prower, John	30	1663/4	MCC folio 36
Pryer, Peter	27	1664	SJC 746
Pryor, Richard	40	1684	EQC 9:175
Prytherck, Richard	37	1678	EQC 7:25
Pudeater, Jacob	33	1675	EQC 6:45
Pudeter, Jacob	25	1666	SJC 762
Pudney, John	17	1680	EQC 7:426
Pudney, John	17	1681	EQC 8:145
Pudney, John	42	1678	EQC 7:135
Pudney, John	57	nd	SJC 2770
Pudney, Judith	39	1683	EQC 9:20
Puffer, Ruth	45	1699	SJC 3896
Puggy, William	46	1677	SJC 1686
Pugless, Ann	54	1672	SJC 1281
Pugless, George	60	1675/6	SJC 2013
Pulsifer, Benedict	19	1682	EQC 8:366
Pumry, Peter	21	1678	SJC 1734
Pumry, Thomas	20	1695	SJC 3316
Punchard, Francis	38	1667	SD 5:181
Punell, Robert	20	1660	EQC 2:252
Punell, Robert	20	1662	EQC 2:364
Purchase, Elizabeth	48	1677	EQC 6:361
Purchase, John	25	1667	EQC 3:456
Purchase, John	26	1668	EQC 4:31
Purchase, John	26	1668	EQC 4:32
Purchase, Oliver	48	1665	EQC 3:256
Purchase, Oliver	50	1668	EQC 4:31
Purchase, Oliver	50	1674	EQC 5:332
Purchase, Oliver	53	1674	EQC 5:374
Purchase, Oliver	54	1672	EQC 5:44
Purchase, Oliver	56	1674/5	SCC 532
Purchase, Oliver	56	1674/5	SJC 1362
Purchase, Oliver	58	1675	EQC 6:54
Purchase, Oliver	63	1680	SJC 1973
Purchase, Oliver	64	1680	EQC 8:39
Purchase, Oliver	64	1681	EQC 8:197
Purchase, Oliver	66	1682	EQC 8:404
Purchase, Oliver	66	1683	EQC 9:45
Purchase, Oliver	66	1684	EQC 9:339
Purchase, Oliver	68	1684	EQC 9:326
Purchase, Oliver	68	1685	EQC 9:434
Purchase, Oliver	68	1685	EQC 9:466
Purchase, Oliver	68	1685	SJC 2344
Purchase, Oliver	69	1685	SJC 2340
Purchase, Oliver	70	1685	EQC 9:521
Purchase, Oliver	70	1685	EQC 9:525
Purrington, John	44	1679/80	SCC 1109
Purrington, John	44	1679/80	SJC 1823

Putnam, Benjamin	32	1695	SJC 3326
Putnam, Edward	17	1672	EQC 5:28
Putnam, Edward	23	1678	EQC 7:249
Putnam, James	34	1695	SJC 3326
Putnam, John	22	1679	EQC 7:167
Putnam, John	25	1682	EQC 8:357
Putnam, John	30	1660	EQC 2:206
Putnam, John	36	1665	EQC 3:259
Putnam, John	38	1695	SJC 3236
Putnam, John	40	1669	EQC 4:110
Putnam, John	40	1669	EQC 4:110
Putnam, John	40	1669	EQC 4:144
Putnam, John	40	1671	EQC 4:343
Putnam, John	44	1673	EQC 5:131
Putnam, John	44	1673	SJC 1223
Putnam, John	45	1685	EQC 9:459
Putnam, John	50	1678	EQC 7:12
Putnam, John	50	1678	SJC 1725
Putnam, John	50	1679	EQC 7:167
Putnam, John	50	1679	EQC 7:296
Putnam, John	54	1682	EQC 8:396
Putnam, John	55	1683	EQC 9:107
Putnam, John	56	1683	EQC 9:88
Putnam, John	56	1684	EQC 9:313
Putnam, John	58	1685	EQC WPA 46-21-3
Putnam, John	59	1687	EQC WPA 47-43-2
Putnam, Jonathan	26	1686	EQC 9:606
Putnam, Jonathan	36	1695	SJC 3326
Putnam, Nathaniel	19	1675	EQC 6:8
Putnam, Nathaniel	46	1666	EQC 3:323
Putnam, Nathaniel	48	1669	EQC 4:110
Putnam, Nathaniel	50	1671	EQC 4:434
Putnam, Nathaniel	57	1678	EQC 7:12
Putnam, Nathaniel	57	1678	SJC 1725
Putnam, Nathaniel	58	1678	SJC 1859
Putnam, Nathaniel	60	1679	EQC 7:426
Putnam, Nathaniel	63	1684	EQC 9:177
Putnam, Nathaniel	65	1686	EQC WPA 46-22-1
Putnam, Nathaniel	65	nd	SJC 3639
Putnam, Nathaniel	74	1695	SJC 3326
Putnam, Nathaniel	74	nd	SJC 98534
Putnam, Samuel	22	1674/5	SJC 1503
Putnam, Samuel	22	1675	EQC 6:9
Putnam, Thomas	34	1686	EQC WPA 46-22-2
Putnam, Thomas	34	nd	SJC 2770
Putnam, Thomas	35	1687?	EQC WPA 47-42-2
Putnam, Thomas	64	1680	EQC 7:392
Putnam, Thomas	66	1682	EQC 8:323
Puttifer, Henry	35	1671	SCC 169
Puttifer, Henry	54	1671	SJC 1290
Pym, John	27	1690	MCC folio 137
Pym, John	27	1690	MCC folio 146
Pym, John	27	1691	MCC folio 143
Quarles, William	18	1665	EQC 3:244

Quarles, William	28	1676	EQC 6:221
Quarles, William	33	1680	EQC 7:362
Quarles, William	40	1684	EQC 9:209
Quash, Edmund	30	1695	SJC 3310
Quilter, Frances	40	1673	EQC 5:234
Quilter, Joseph	30	1679	EQC 7:268
Quilter, Joseph	40	1685	EQC 9:530
Quilter, Mark	42	1672	EQC 5:32
Quilter, Thomas	67	1679	EQC 7:268
Quincy, Edmund	43	1673	SJC 1342
Raddock, Henry	58	1693	MCC folio 176
Rainer, Mary	22	1668	SJC 869
Rainsbury, Rowland	46	1674	EQC 5:430
Rainsford, David	33	1678	SJC 1735
Rainsford, Edward	65	1674/5	SJC 1432
Rainsford, John	25	1660	EQC 2:204
Rainsford, Jonathan	30	1668	EQC 4:5
Rainsford, Martha	24	nd	SJC 3675
Rainsford, Priscilla	35	1691/2	SJC 98524
Rainsford, Solomon	28	1674/5	SJC 1350
Rainsford, Solomon	34	nd	SJC 2016
Rainsford, Solomon	45	1691/2	SJC 98524
Ralph, Mary	44	1685	MCC folio 117
Ramsdell, John	55	1657	EQC 2:43
Ramsey, Henry	49	1662	SJC 467
Rand, Alice	72	1667	SJC 814
Rand, Hannah	21	1681	EQC 8:102
Rand, John	27	1686	MCC folio 121
Rand, Nathaniel	44	1679	MCC folio 87
Rand, Nathaniel	45	1683	MCC folio 102
Rand, Nathaniel	47	1683	MCC folio 90
Rand, Robert	24	1681	EQC 8:102
Rand, Thomas	19	1676	MCC folio 73
Randall, John	25	1681	MCC folio 92
Randall, John	56	1678	MCC folio 81
Randall, Robert	15	1669	EQC 4:146
Randall, Sarah	20	1667	EQC 3:415
Randall, Sarah	20	1669	EQC 4:108
Randall, Stephen	44	1672	MCC folio 60
Randall, Walter	24	1670/1	SJC 1016
Randall, William	40	1661	EQC 2:328
Randall, William	48	1666	EQC 3:329
Randall, William	65	1678	EQC 7:156
Rashley, John	23	1668	SJC 889
Ravenscraft, Anthony	28	1671	EQC 4:434
Ravenscraft, Anthony	28	1671	EQC 4:434
Rawling, Ezekiel	38	1669	MCC folio 48
Rawlings, Benjamin	28	1679	EQC 7:302
Rawlings, Benjamin	28	1679	EQC 7:303
Rawlings, Nicholas	32	1678	EQC 7:156
Rawlins, Caleb	28	1678	SJC 1735
Rawson, Edward	55	1667	SD 6:174
Rawson, Edward	58	1673	MCC folio 64
Rawson, Edward	58	1673	SJC 1214

Rawson, Edward	60	1674	SJC 1389
Rawson, Edward	64	1679	EQC 7:215
Rawson, Edward	66	1681/2	SD 12:152
Rawson, Grindall	15	1674	EQC 5:306
Ray, Joshua	29	1666	EQC 3:371
Ray, Joshua	38	1669	EQC 4:111
Rayment, John	60	1680	EQC 8:7
Rayment, John	60	1682	EQC 8:323
Rayment, Thomas	43	1694	SJC 2920
Rayment, William	30	1669	EQC 4:103
Rayment, William	32	1671	EQC 4:332
Rayment, William	40	1682	EQC 8:397
Rayment, William	42	1680	EQC 7:390
Rayment, William	42	1680	EQC 8:7
Rayment, William	43	1682	EQC 8:323
Rayment, William	43	1682	EQC 8:324
Rayment, William	45	1685	EQC 9:459
Raymond, John	38	1660	EQC 2:219
Raymond, Samuel	24	1670	EQC 4:264
Rayner, Abigail	28	1693	MCC folio 177
Rayner, Thomas	22	1682	EQC 8:411
Rayner, William	45	1669	EQC 4:97
Rea, Joshua	41	1669	EQC 4:145
Rea, Joshua	50	1681	EQC 8:120
Rea, Joshua	50	1681	SJC 2018
Rea, Joshua	67	1695	SJC 3326
Read, Arabella	48	1694	MCC folio 161
Read, Edward	48	1662	EQC 2:442
Read, Edward	65	1681	EQC 8:180
Read, Edward	73	1685	EQC 9:468
Read, Elizabeth	22	1661	MCC folio 27
Read, George	33	1661	MCC folio 27
Read, George	55	1684	MCC folio 109
Read, George	58	1685	MCC folio 115
Read, Hannah	42	1685	MCC folio 115
Read, Israel	26	1668	MCC folio 47
Read, Israel	48	1686	MCC folio 123
Read, Jacob	18	1690	MCC folio 137
Read, Joane	30	1686	EQC 9:579
Read, Mary	25	1661	MCC folio 27
Read, Philip	19	1690	MCC folio 137
Read, Philip	49	1672	MCC folio 60
Read, Ralph	26	1659	MCC folio 21
Read, Ralph	29	1661	MCC folio 27
Read, Ralph	33	1668	MCC folio 48
Read, Ralph	40	1673	MCC folio 62
Read, Ralph	54	1684/5	MCC folio 116
Read, Richard	40	1672	EQC 5:92
Read, Thomas	28	1684	MCC folio 107
Read, Thomas	28	1685	MCC folio 116
Read, Thomas	32	1659	MCC folio 21
Read, William	23	1685	MCC folio 118
Reade, Edward	55	1666	EQC 3:369
Reade, Eseras	57	1657	MCC folio 20

Reade, Israel	44	1684	MCC folio 115
Reade, Israel	44	1684	MCC folio 115
Reade, Obediah	31	1671	SJC 1024
Reade, Philip	45	1669	EQC 4:207
Reading, Anne	70	1674	EQC 5:413
Redat, Mehitable	19	1665	MCC folio 38
Reddack, John	71	1681	MCC folio 93
Redden, Elizabeth	20	1677	EQC 6:299
Rede, Samuel	29	1686	MCC folio 122
Redington, Abraham	58	1673	EQC 5:134
Redington, Daniel	15	1672	EQC 5:37
Redington, Phebe	17	1672	EQC 5:36
Redknap, Joseph	60	1657	EQC 7:128
Redland, William	29	1662	MCC folio 32
Redland, William	37	1667	MCC folio 43
Redland, William	47	1679	MCC folio 184
Redman, John	40	1661	MCC folio 29
Redman, John	42	1660	EQC 2:230
Redman, John	56	1673	EQC 5:242
Redman, Sarah	43	1660	EQC 2:230
Rednap, Joseph	70	1670	EQC 4:309
Reed, Abigail	20	1684	EQC 9:250
Reed, Abigail	34	1684	EQC 9:286
Reed, Edward	60	1674	EQC 5:282
Reed, Edward	63	1677	EQC 6:362
Reed, James	21	1678	SJC 1722
Reed, John	45	1680	SJC 1887
Reed, Samuel	37	1692	MCC folio 154
Reed, William	28	1686	MCC folio 123
Reede, Samuel	25	1681	MCC folio 102
Reede, Samuel	26	1681	MCC folio 102
Reeves, John	30	1665	EQC 3:256
Reeves, William	33	1678	EQC 7:80
Reeves, William	34	1679	EQC 7:252
Remick, Jacob	31	1697/8	SJC 4705
Remick, Joshua	25	1697/8	SJC 4705
Remington, Jonathan	37	1679	MCC folio 83
Remington, Jonathan	50	1690	MCC folio 173
Remington, Jonathan	51	1691	MCC folio 146
Remington, Jonathan	51	1691	MCC folio 163
Remington, Jonathan	51	1692	MCC folio 173
Remington, Jonathan	52	1691	MCC folio 152
Remington, Martha	23	1668	MCC folio 45
Remington, Martha	33	1677	MCC folio 78
Reymer, William	35	1662	EQC 2:408
Reynolds, Alexius	25	1683	EQC 9:55
Reynolds, Edward	22	nd	SJC 2026
Reynolds, Nathaniel	47	1674	SD 8:406
Rhodes, Eleazer	30	1674	EQC 5:334
Rhodes, Eleazer	45	1686	EQC 9:591
Rhodes, Elizabeth	35	1684	EQC 9:254
Rhodes, Henry	71	1679	EQC 7:196
Rhodes, Joan	46	1676	EQC 6:150
Rhodes, John	37	1686	EQC WPA 46-88-1

Rhodes, John	40	1670	EQC 4:255
Rhodes, Joshua	37	1686	EQC 9:591
Rhodes, Josiah	30	1682	EQC 8:417
Rhodes, Josiah	30	1686	EQC 9:591
Rhodes, Josiah	33	1685	EQC 9:465
Rhodes, Josiah	33	1685	SJC 2345
Rhodes, Samuel	28	1674	EQC 5:334
Rhodes, Samuel	40	1684	EQC 9:313
Rhodes, Sarah	25	1676	EQC 6:150
Rice, Edward	34	1660	MCC folio 22
Rice, Edward	42	1666	MCC folio 40
Rice, Edward	62	1656	MCC folio 11
Rice, Edward	70	1692	MCC folio 174
Rice, Elizabeth	38	1667	MCC folio 43
Rice, Henry	50	1668	MCC folio 44
Rice, Joshua	30	1692	MCC folio 174
Rice, Nicholas	44	1671	SJC 1106
Rice, Nicholas	75	1696	SJC 3697
Rice, Peter	32	1692	MCC folio 174
Rice, Samuel	21	1681	SJC 2024
Rice, Samuel	32	1665	MCC folio 40
Rice, Samuel	32	1666	MCC folio 42
Rice, Thomas	44	1671/2	SJC 1097
Rice, Thomas	44	1675	MCC folio 65
Rice, Thomas	4x	1675	MCC folio 70
Rich, Henry	16	1671	EQC 4:434
Rich, Henry	22	1677	EQC 6:241
Rich, Henry	22	1677	EQC 6:282
Richard, Edward	35	1654	SJC 225
Richard, Edward	70	1685	SJC 2334
Richards, Anne	63	1684	EQC 9:240
Richards, Edward	40	1661	EQC 2:285
Richards, Edward	40	1661	EQC 2:331
Richards, Edward	40	1662	EQC 3:11
Richards, Edward	55	1671	EQC 4:411
Richards, Edward	55	1672	EQC 5:107
Richards, Edward	60	1674	EQC 5:317
Richards, Edward	60	1675	EQC 6:16
Richards, Edward	60	1677	EQC 6:362
Richards, Edward	65	1681	EQC 8:138
Richards, Edward	65	1681	EQC 8:178
Richards, Edward	65	1681	EQC 8:199
Richards, Edward	70	1683	EQC 9:51
Richards, Edward	70	1684	EQC 9:240
Richards, Edward	70	1684	EQC 9:338
Richards, Edward	70	1684	EQC 9:339
Richards, Edward	70	1685	EQC 9:465
Richards, Hannah	19	1662	SJC 874
Richards, John	22	1684	EQC 9:344
Richards, John	28	1677	EQC 6:280
Richards, John	30	1679	EQC 7:252
Richards, John	30	1679	EQC 7:253
Richards, John	37	1684	EQC 9:246
Richards, John	37	1684	EQC 9:317

Richards, Rice	23	nd	SJC 27519
Richards, William	21	1684	EQC 9:246
Richards, William	21	1684	EQC 9:316
Richardson, Amos	60	1679	SJC 1919
Richardson, Benjamin	18	1678	EQC 7:157
Richardson, Daniel	17	1699/1700	MCC folio 192
Richardson, Edward	27	1678	EQC 7:156
Richardson, Edward	60	1679	SJC 1719
Richardson, Edward	61	1678	EQC 7:157
Richardson, Ezekiel	23	1695	MCC folio 207
Richardson, Isaac	27	1671	MCC folio 58
Richardson, Jacob	27	1671	MCC folio 58
Richardson, John	21	1699/1700	MCC folio 192
Richardson, John	22	1661	MCC folio 27
Richardson, John	25	1664	MCC folio 36
Richardson, John	30	1671	MCC folio 58
Richardson, John	31	1678	EQC 7:156
Richardson, John	50	1690	MCC folio 138
Richardson, Jonathan	22	1691	MCC folio 140
Richardson, Joseph	21	1664	MCC folio 36
Richardson, Joseph	23	1678	EQC 7:156
Richardson, Joshua	22	1669	SJC 924
Richardson, Joshua	28	1677	EQC 6:332
Richardson, Joshua	38	1678	EQC 7:157
Richardson, Richard	58	1664	SJC 648
Richardson, Ruth	10	1656	MCC folio 11
Richardson, Samuel	20	1691	MCC folio 140
Richardson, Samuel	22	1668	MCC folio 47
Richason, Edward	60	1679	EQC 7:165
Richmond, John	67	1696/7	SJC 3396
Riddan, Thaddeus	56	1681	EQC 8:199
Riddan, Thaddeus	60	1684	EQC 9:339
Ridden, Thaddeus	49	1674	EQC 5:282
Ridgeway, John	[torn]2	1657	MCC folio 14
Ridgeway, Mary	16	1671	MCC folio 61
Ridland, Patience	54	1691	MCC folio 157
Ridley, John	39	1672	SJC 1194
Rieth, Richard	37	1674	EQC 5:357
Riggs, Thomas	32	1667	EQC 3:431
Riley, Henry	40	1674	SJC 1389
Ring, Elizabeth	15	1679	EQC 7:288
Ring, Isaac	22	1683	EQC 9:114
Ring, Isaac	23	1684	EQC 9:331
Ring, Isaac	24	1687	EQC WPA 47-32-4
Ring, Jarvis	27	1684	EQC 9:347
Ring, Jarvis	35	1694	SJC 3039
Ring, Jarvis	36	1695	SJC 162371
Ring, Jarvis	36	1695	SJC 3782
Ring, John	33	1695	SJC 162371
Ring, John	33	1695	SJC 3782
Ring, John	46	1684	EQC 9:251
Ripe, Thomas	40	1662	EQC 2:389
Riply, George	41	1685	MCC folio 117
Rise, Roger	32	1669	EQC 4:107

Rise, Roger	34	1668	EQC 4:34
Rist, Nicholas	75	1696	MCC folio 199
Rist, Nicholas	75	1696	SJC 3697
Robbens, Thomas	62	1679	EQC 7:306
Robbins, Mary	75	1685	EQC 9:484
Robbins, Thomas	55	1675	EQC 6:107
Robbins, Thomas	67	1684	EQC 9:344
Robbins, Thomas	67	1685	EQC 9:438
Robbins, Thomas	68	1685	EQC 9:482
Robbins, Thomas	68	1685/6	EQC WPA 46-24-6
Rober, Nathaniel	26	1680	EQC 7:380
Roberson, George	16	1677	MCC folio 77
Roberts, David	66	nd	SJC 18910
Roberts, John	24	1670	EQC 4:218
Roberts, John	27	1679	SCC 1099
Roberts, John	28	1674	EQC 5:286
Roberts, John	34	1680	EQC 8:67
Roberts, John	43	1671	SJC 1088
Roberts, Richard	52	1662	MCC folio 30
Roberts, Robert	40	1659	EQC 2:170
Roberts, Robert	40	1659	EQC 2:171
Roberts, Robert	40	1659	SJC 351
Roberts, Samuel	20	1668	SJC 924
Roberts, Timothy	38	1684	EQC 9:319
Robeson, Elizabeth	37	1686	MCC folio 125
Robeson, George	16	1677	MCC folio 76
Robeson, George	16	1677	MCC folio 77
Robeson, Martha	34	1680	EQC 7:410
Robey, Henry	50	1667	EQC 3:404
Robins, John	23	1672	EQC 5:66
Robins, Samuel	45	1686	MCC folio 120
Robins, Thomas	42	1680	EQC 7:385
Robins, Thomas	60	1678	EQC 7:108
Robins, Thomas	68	1686	EQC WPA 46-18-1
Robins, Thomas	68	nd	SJC 2770
Robinson, Andrew	19	1666	MCC folio 42
Robinson, Andrew	20	1672	MCC folio 60
Robinson, Andrew	28	1677/8	MCC folio 185
Robinson, Daniel	16	1683	EQC 9:87
Robinson, Daniel	17	1684	EQC 9:327
Robinson, Francis	52	1670	SD 6:217
Robinson, Francis	52	1670/1	SJC 1016
Robinson, Francis	53	1671/2	SD 7:275
Robinson, James	38	1657	EQC 2:29
Robinson, John	16	1677	MCC folio 76
Robinson, John	22	1662	EQC 2:388
Robinson, John	27	1694	SJC 3123e
Robinson, John	30	1683/4	SJC 2175
Robinson, Nathaniel	40	1664	SJC 746
Robinson, Nathaniel	50	1674	EQC 5:322
Robinson, Robert	40	1678	EQC 7:157
Robinson, Robert	45	1683	EQC 9:87
Robinson, Robert	56	1684	EQC 9:327
Robinson, Samuel	22	1658	EQC 2:128

Robinson, Samuel	23	1660	SJC 568
Robinson, Sarah	19	1676	MCC folio 74
Robinson, Thomas	18	1695	SJC 3123g
Robinson, Thomas	20	1686	EQC WPA 46-78-3
Robinson, Thomas	46	1666	SJC 813
Robinson, William	28	1662	MCC folio 30
Roby, Henry	50	1666/7	SJC 1277
Rock, Joseph	51	1670	SJC 1014
Rockett, John	59	1700	SJC 4845
Rodgers, Peter	64	1675	EQC 6:102
Roe, John	35	1677	SCC 804
Roffe, Abigail	16	1677	EQC 6:253
Roger, Ephraim	43	1691	MCC folio 142
Rogers, Ebenezer	23	1698/9	SJC 4714
Rogers, Ebenezer	24	1700	SJC 4714
Rogers, Ezekiel	26	1666	EQC 3:373
Rogers, Gamaliel	22	1679/80	SCC 1129
Rogers, Gamaliel	22	1679/80	SJC 1833
Rogers, Gamaliel	26	1684	SJC 2198
Rogers, John	24	1671	EQC 4:434
Rogers, John	28	1675	EQC 6:45
Rogers, John	34	1681	EQC 8:205
Rogers, John	35	1677	MCC folio 76
Rogers, John	45	nd	SJC 2817
Rogers, Joseph	75	nd	SJC 24815
Rogers, Margaret	16	1677	EQC 9:226
Rogers, Margaret	55	1665	EQC 3:234
Rogers, Margaret	55	1665	SJC 717
Rogers, Martha	16	1677	EQC 6:345
Rogers, Martha	49	1696	SJC 4714
Rogers, Martha	52	1698/9	SJC 4714
Rogers, Mary	21	1695	SJC 3110
Rogers, Nathaniel	24	1659	EQC 2:179
Rogers, Nathaniel	45	1698/9	MCC folio 209
Rogers, Susannah	60	1683	SJC 2198
Rogers, Thomas	26	1678	EQC 7:156
Rogers, Thomas	28	1678	MCC folio 82
Rogers, Thomas	30	1673	SJC 1341
Rogers, Thomas	38	1671	SJC 1041
Rogers, Timothy	20	1665	SJC 985
Rolfe, Benjamin	32	1669	EQC 4:137
Rolfe, Benjamin	37	1677	EQC 6:322
Rolfe, Benjamin	40	1678	EQC 7:157
Rolfe, Benjamin	40	1679	MCC folio 86
Rolfe, Benjamin	42	1681	EQC 8:171
Rolfe, Benjamin	44	1683	EQC 9:249
Rolfe, Edward	39	1672	SJC 1194
Rolfe, John	18	1678	EQC 7:156
Rolfe, John	21	1685	MCC folio 117
Rolfe, John	21	1685	MCC folio 128
Rolfe, John	21	1686	MCC folio 121
Rolfe, John	28	1663	EQC 3:67
Rolfe, Samuel	17	1685	MCC folio 117
Rolfe, Samuel	19	1685	MCC folio 114

Rolfe, Samuel	19	1686	MCC folio 121
Rolfe, Samuel	19	1686	MCC folio 128
Ronals, Alexius	25	1682	EQC 8:341
Roods, Samuel	40	1684	EQC 9:341
Roots, Josiah	60	1678	EQC 7:51
Roots, Josiah	65	1678	EQC 7:51
Roots, Katharine	62	1678	EQC 7:132
Roots, Sarah	24	1678	EQC 7:51
Roots, Susannah	53	1678	EQC 7:51
Roper, Ephraim	26	1677	EQC 6:251
Roper, Ephraim	33	1678	MCC folio 80
Roper, Ephraim	48	1690	MCC folio 136
Roper, John	16	1665	SJC 721
Roper, John	20	1670	EQC 4:337
Roper, Mathew	26	1664	MCC folio 38
Roper, Nathaniel	21	1674	EQC 5:307
Roper, Nathaniel	27	1680	EQC 8:41
Roper, Rachel	20	1660	MCC folio 25
Roper, Susannah	58	1669	EQC 4:154
Roper, Walter	45	1658	EQC 2:146
Roper, Walter	46	1659	EQC 2:179
Roper, Walter	48	1661	EQC 2:268
Roper, Walter	65	1676	EQC 6:159
Roper, Walter	67	1680	EQC 7:375
Roper, Walter	67	1680	SJC 1894
Ropes, Charity	50	1681	EQC 8:108
Ropes, John	18	1666	EQC 3:377
Ropes, Mary	50	1669	EQC 4:90
Ropes, Mary	60	1681	EQC 8:108
Ropes, Mary	70	1685	EQC 9:440
Ropes, Samuel	22	1678	EQC 7:246
Ropes, William	35	1685	EQC 9:440
Ros, Funall	50	1671	EQC 4:331
Ros, Susannah	18	1686	EQC 9:582
Rose, Abigail	34	1669	MCC folio 52
Rose, James	50	1685	SJC 2325
Rose, Roger	28	1667	MCC folio 44
Rose, Roger	37	1672/3	SJC 1194
Rose, Roger	38	1667	SJC 904
Ross, Hannah	19	1684	EQC 9:204
Ross, John	20	1661	EQC 2:308
Ross, John	25	1666	MCC folio 42
Ross, John	27	1667	MCC folio 24
Ross, Phenil	35	1684	EQC 9:204
Ross, Thomas	30	1662	MCC folio 32
Ross, Thomas	30	1663	MCC folio 35
Rotchford, Samuel	33	1680	SJC 1935
Roundall, Thomas	24	1684	EQC 9:396
Rouse, Roger	44	1680	EQC 8:58
Rouse, Suretrust	67	1667	SJC 814
Row, Anthony	40	1676	SCC 1111
Row, Anthony	40	1676	SJC 1526
Row, Anthony	40	1676	SJC 1828
Row, Hugh	49	1667	SJC 815

Row, John	27	1689	MCC folio 133
Row, John	35	1677	SJC 1635
Row, Sarah	20	1673	EQC 5:229
Rowden, John	50	1668	EQC 4:39
Rowden, John	72	1680	EQC 7:331
Rowden, Mary	48	1668	EQC 4:39
Rowden, Mary	60	1680	EQC 7:331
Rowe, Elias	31	1663	MCC folio 35
Rowe, Elias	40	1670	MCC folio 54
Rowe, Elias	50	1679	MCC folio 185
Rowe, Hugh	19	1666	EQC 3:328
Rowe, John	29	1692	MCC folio 154
Rowe, John	33	1695	MCC folio 180
Rowell, Thomas	23	1668	EQC 4:26
Rowland, John	15	1683	EQC 9:63
Rowland, John	17	1684	EQC 9:250
Rowland, John	26	nd	SJC 2769
Rowland, Mary	17	1667	EQC 3:417
Rowland, Mary	17	1667	EQC 3:418
Rowland, Mary	19	1669	EQC 4:146
Rowland, Mary	39	1666	EQC 3:367
Rowland, Mary	46	1673	EQC 5:180
Rowland, Mary	46	1673	EQC 5:180
Rowland, Mary	49	1674	EQC 5:421
Rowland, Mary	55	1683	EQC 9:5
Rowland, Mary	55	1683	EQC 9:64
Rowland, Richard	15	1674	EQC 5:421
Rowland, Richard	22	1680	EQC 8:65
Rowland, Richard	50	1672	EQC 5:41
Rowland, Richard	55	1673	EQC 5:180
Rowland, Richard	60	1671	EQC 4:378
Rowland, Samuel	20	1667	EQC 3:418
Rowland, Samuel	20	1667	EQC 3:419
Rowland, Samuel	26	1673	EQC 5:179
Rowland, Samuel	28	1675	EQC 6:19
Rowley, Aaron	28	1694	SJC 2989
Rucke, Elizabeth	58	1655	SJC 257
Rucke, Elizabeth	62	1660	SJC 387
Rucke, John	22	1679	EQC 7:326
Rucke, John	57	1684	EQC 9:184
Rucke, Thomas	24	1682	EQC 8:420
Rucke, Thomas	69	1660	SJC 387
Ruggles, Samuel	18	1695	SJC 3123a
Rule, John	25	1670	SJC 1046
Rule, John	42	1685	SJC 2346
Rumball, Daniel	62	1661	EQC 2:294
Rumball, Daniel	68	1668	EQC 4:75
Rumball, Daniel	70	1674	EQC 5:420
Rumball, Daniel	80	1681	EQC 8:205
Rumball, Sarah	70	1661	EQC 2:294
Rumsey, Simon	25	1682	EQC 8:348
Runnells, Cornelius	30	1676	EQC 6:328
Russ, John	19	1661	EQC 2:297
Russ, John	50	1661	EQC 2:309

Russ, Margaret	41	1661	EQC 2:307
Russ, Mary	16	1659	SJC 322
Russ, Nathaniel	28	1668	EQC 4:82
Russell, Benjamin	18	1690	MCC folio 137
Russell, Benjamin	30	1671	MCC folio 59
Russell, Benjamin	30	nd	SJC 1052
Russell, Elizabeth	8	1683	EQC 9:60
Russell, Henry	2	1683	EQC 9:60
Russell, Henry	24	1665	EQC 3:262
Russell, Henry	28	1668	EQC 4:313
Russell, Henry	40	1682	EQC 8:364
Russell, Henry	55	1665	EQC 3:287
Russell, Henry	55	1666	EQC 3:300
Russell, James	32	1672/3	SJC 1221
Russell, James	39	1679	MCC folio 185
Russell, James	39	1679	MCC folio 89
Russell, James	39	1679	SJC 1838
Russell, James	44	1684	MCC folio 111
Russell, Jason	27	1685	MCC folio 114
Russell, Jason	34	1691	MCC folio 146
Russell, Jason	34	1691	MCC folio 156
Russell, John	19	1682	MCC folio 100
Russell, John	23	1685	MCC folio 117
Russell, John	23	1686	MCC folio 123
Russell, John	26	1671	MCC folio 59
Russell, John	30	1675	EQC 6:67
Russell, John	38	1671/2	SJC 1148
Russell, Jonathan	21	1677	MCC folio 75
Russell, Joseph	15	1651	MCC folio 2
Russell, Joseph	22	1685	MCC folio 117
Russell, Joseph	55	1691	MCC folio 147
Russell, Joseph	55	1691	MCC folio 175
Russell, Mary	4	1683	EQC 9:60
Russell, Mary	45	1681	EQC 8:104
Russell, Mary	50	1685	EQC 9:537
Russell, Mathew	45	1660	MCC folio 22
Russell, Richard	23	1665	EQC 3:282
Russell, Roger	60	1665	EQC 3:282
Russell, Samuel	11	1683	EQC 9:60
Russell, Sarah	1	1683	EQC 9:60
Russell, Susanna	19	1667	EQC 3:455
Russell, Thomas	10	1683	EQC 9:60
Russell, Thomas	30	1672	MCC folio 59
Russell, Thomas	35	1685	EQC 9:537
Russell, William	30	1686	MCC folio 121
Russell, William	30	1686	MCC folio 128
Russell, William	36	1658	EQC 2:94
Rust, Nathaniel	19	1686	EQC WPA 47-15-5
Rust, Nathaniel	29	1670	EQC 4:222
Rust, Nathaniel	29	1670	EQC 4:258
Rust, Nathaniel	33	1673	EQC 5:144
Rust, Nathaniel	40	1680	EQC 7:375
Rust, Nathaniel	40	1680	SJC 1894
Rust, Nathaniel	44	1683	EQC 9:103

Rutherford, James	19	1685	MCC folio 118
Rutherford, James	19	1685	SJC 2389
Rutter, Jabez	20	1679	MCC folio 88
Rutter, John	27	1652	MCC folio 7
Rutter, John	37	1652	MCC folio 7
Rutter, John	50	1667	MCC folio 43
Ryall, Joseph	37	1692	MCC folio 154
Sabin, Benjamin	55	1699	SJC 4693
Saffal, John	30	1661	EQC 2:324
Saffin, Josiah	18	1685	SJC 2324
Safford, goodwife	35	1674	EQC 5:307
Salisbury, Nicholas	40	1682	MCC folio 99
Salisbury, Nicholas	48	1685	MCC folio 117
Salla, Bethia	16	1682	EQC 8:436
Sallos, John	40	1675	EQC 6:102
Salmon, Daniel	45	1657	EQC 7:128
Salmon, Daniel	50	1660	EQC 2:211
Salmon, Daniel	50	1661	EQC 2:331
Salmon, Daniel	50	1662	EQC 2:394
Salmon, Daniel	52	1662	EQC 3:11
Salmon, Daniel	61	1672	EQC 5:60
Salmon, Daniel	71	1681	EQC 8:198
Salmon, Daniel	74	1684	EQC 9:316
Salmon, Sarah	18	1659	EQC 2:194
Salter, Eneas	41	1671	EQC 5:66
Salter, Hannah	41	1682	MCC folio 99
Salter, Hannah	45	1683	MCC folio 104
Salter, Jabez	25	1671	SJC 1148
Salter, Jabez	32	1679	SJC 1800
Salter, Jabez	35	1681	SJC 2037
Salter, William	48	1655	EQC 1:399
Salter, William	58	1664	SJC 746
Saman, William	38	1674	EQC 5:402
Samms, Elizabeth	27	1684	SJC 2249
Samons, Ralph	80	1672	SJC 1281
Sampson, Edward	22	1676/7	SJC 1544
Sampson, John	50	1677	EQC 6:280
Sampson, John	50	1677	EQC 6:349
Sampson, John	52	1679	EQC 7:182
Sampson, John	53	1679	EQC 7:308
Samuel, Abraham	32	1694	SJC 3123d
Samuel, Abraham	32	1695	SJC 3101
Sanborn, John	48	1668	SJC 1372
Sanborn, John	48	1673	EQC 5:242
Sanborn, Josias	18	1666	SJC 1277
Sanborn, Lydia	27	1682	EQC 8:329
Sanders, James	19	1662	EQC 2:350
Sanders, James	22	1665	EQC 3:279
Sanders, James	36	1680	EQC 8:70
Sanders, Jonathan	40	1696	MCC folio 213
Sanders, Mary	26	1683	EQC 9:92
Sanders, Robert	24	1683	EQC 9:92
Sanders, Robert	36	1695	SJC 3127
Sanders, Sarah	30	1683	EQC 9:8

Sanders, William	23	1684	SJC 3349
Sanders, William	46	1681	MCC folio 97
Sanderson, Robert	30	1683	SJC 2145
Sanderson, Robert	45	1653	EQC 1:316
Sanderson, William	40	1681	MCC folio 92
Sanderson, William	48	1683	MCC folio 104
Sandford, Robert	45	1673	EQC 5:227
Sands, Sibbella	61	1678	SJC 1729
Sandy, Elizabeth	19	1680	EQC 8:89
Sandy, James	50	1654	MCC folio 10
Sandys, John	27	1672/3	SCC 206
Sandys, John	27	1672/3	SJC 1165
Sandys, John	29	1675	EQC 6:79
Sanford, John	39	1665	SJC 721
Sanford, Richard	77	1673	SJC 2120
Sanford, Robert	39	1667	SJC 962
Sanford, Robert	50	1678	EQC 7:12
Sanford, Thomas	30	1666/7	SJC 846
Sargent, Andrew	24	1680	EQC 7:419
Sargent, Elizabeth	19	1687	EQC WPA 47-52-3
Sargent, Rachel	45	1694	SJC 162329
Sargent, William	35	1662	EQC 2:386
Sargent, William	36	1663	EQC 3:42
Sargent, William	36	1663	EQC 3:43
Sargent, William	37	1664	EQC 3:185
Satterly, Nicholas	22	1686	EQC WPA 46-92-3
Saunders, James	20	1665	EQC 3:278
Savage, Ebenezer	23	1683	EQC 9:46
Savage, Ephraim	38	1683	EQC 9:46
Savage, Habiah	22	1660	EQC 7:27
Savage, Richard	28	1685	SJC 2324
Savage, Sarah	33	1686	MCC folio 121
Savage, Thomas	25	1665	EQC 3:261
Savage, Thomas	34	1674	SCC 455
Savage, Thomas	34	1674	SCC 495
Savage, Thomas	38	1678	MCC folio 79
Savage, Thomas	43	1683	EQC 9:46
Savage, Thomas	57	1664	EQC 3:210
Savage, Thomas	65	1673	SJC 1214
Savage, Thomas	67	1674	EQC 5:376
Savell, Patrick	25	1668	SJC 873
Savory, Mary	50	1682	EQC 8:300
Savory, Robert	48	1682	EQC 8:262
Savory, Robert	48	1682	EQC WPA 46-9-1
Sawdy, John	42	1662	SJC 467
Sawin, Munnings	21	1674	MCC folio 63
Sawin, Sarah	20	1685	MCC folio 115
Sawin, Sarah	20	1685	SJC 2348
Sawtell, Jonathan	40	1679	MCC folio 88
Sawyer, Caleb	30	1691	MCC folio 142
Sawyer, Edward	60	1668	EQC 4:52
Sawyer, Joshua	31	1686	MCC folio 123
Sawyer, Samuel	29	1679	EQC 8:37
Sawyer, Sarah	30	1682	MCC folio 101

Sawyer, Stephen	17	1680	EQC 7:361
Sawyer, Thomas	40	1691	MCC folio 142
Saxon, Thomas	28	1676	EQC 6:200
Saxton, John	35	1684	SJC 2217
Saxton, Mara	29	1684	SJC 2217
Saxton, Samuel	31	1684	SJC 2262
Sayer, John	28	1674	EQC 5:330
Sayer, Samuel	18	1665	EQC 3:238
Sayer, Samuel	29	1678	EQC 7:156
Sayer, William	65	1678	EQC 7:156
Saynes, Joyc	35	nd	SJC 25928
Sayward, Joseph	50	nd	SJC 28973
Sayward, Mary	48	1681	SJC 2057
Scadlock, Ann	27	1694	SJC 4114
Scadlock, Samuel	44	nd	SJC 2839
Scamp, Robert	40	1669	EQC 4:99
Scarlett, Benjamin	49	1674	EQC 5:324
Scarlett, Benjamin	49	1674	SJC 1503
Scarlett, Benjamin	54	1678	EQC 7:14
Scarlett, Tamasin	50	1680	SJC 1911
Sceals, Henry	19	1690	MCC folio 137
Scill, Elizabeth	16	1684/5	MCC folio 113
Scill, Joseph	42	1679	MCC folio 83
Scolly, John	26	1667	MCC folio 47
Scolly, John	31	1673	MCC folio 65
Scolly, John	37	1678	EQC 7:156
Scott, Benjamin	25	1675	EQC 6:15
Scott, Benjamin	40	1686	EQC WPA 47-18-1
Scott, Jean	20	1665/6	SJC 728
Scott, John	18	1662	SJC 874
Scott, John	50	1658	MCC folio 17
Scott, Joseph	20	1691	SJC 2600
Scott, Robert	62	1695	MCC folio 180
Scottow, Joshua	40	1657	MCC folio 16
Scottow, Joshua	43	1659	SJC 349
Scottow, Joshua	60	1677	SJC 1753
Scripture, Samuel	19	1668	MCC folio 51
Seager, Humphrey	24	1673	MCC folio 63
Seahon, Dennis	25	1671	SJC 1100
Seamon, George	25	1681	MCC folio 183
Searle, Andrew	56	1672	EQC 5:7
Searle, Grace	17	1680	EQC 7:373
Searle, Grace	17	1680	SJC 1894
Searle, Jean	35	1676	EQC 6:150
Searle, John	24	1681	EQC 8:194
Searle, Mary	20	1681	EQC 8:227
Searle, Thomas	42	1680	EQC 7:349
Searles, Philip	38	1672	EQC 5:65
Sears, Robert	39	nd	SJC 2851
Seaton, William	21	1671	SJC 1081
Seavare, John	35	1682	EQC 8:436
Seavey, Richard	35	1670	EQC 4:297
Secomb, Richard	35	1680	EQC 8:30
Secombe, Joanna	30	1680	EQC 8:30

Sedgwick, Robert	25	1676	MCC folio 74
Sedgwick, Sarah	21	1676	MCC folio 74
Seeley, John	31	1671/2	SJC 1148
Sehand, Anderos	25	1671	SJC 1100
Seldin, Joseph	40	1681	MCC folio 101
Sendall, Samuel	39	1659	SJC 349
Sendall, Samuel	50	1667	SD 5:340
Sendall, Samuel	57	1675	SJC 1562
Sendall, Samuel	60	1678	EQC 7:119
Sergent, Digory	35	1690	MCC folio 137
Sergent, Digory	35	1691	MCC folio 143
Sessions, Alexander	24	1669	EQC 4:117
Severance, Ephraim	27	1682	MCC folio 103
Severance, John	22	1670	EQC 4:231
Severance, Samuel	40	1678	MCC folio 81
Severe, Andrew	26	1682	EQC 8:348
Severns, Sarah	36	1680/1	SJC 1953
Severs, Shubal	25	1665	SJC 680
Sewall, Henry	60	1674	EQC 5:398
Sewall, Henry	60	1674	EQC 5:399
Sewall, Henry	60	1674	SJC 1352
Sewall, Henry	65	1677	EQC 6:333
Sewall, Henry	66	1678	EQC 7:156
Sewall, John	24	1678	EQC 7:156
Sewall, Robert	36	1679	EQC 7:297
Sewall, Stephen	24	1683	EQC 9:5
Sewall, Stephen	27	1684	EQC 9:198
Sewall, Steven	22	1679	EQC 7:327
Seymour, Thomas	36	1672	SJC 1135
Seymour, Thomas	36	1672	SJC 1153
Shaffel, Mary	46	1679	EQC 7:267
Shaffel, Mary	46	1679	EQC 7:268
Shannon, Nathaniel	38	1691	SJC 2621
Shapcott, Thomas	35	1670/1	SJC 1016
Sharpe, Nathaniel	33	1678	EQC 7:305
Sharpe, Nathaniel	35	1679	EQC 7:305
Sharpe, Nathaniel	35	1679	EQC 7:311
Shatford, John	21	1691	MCC folio 148
Shatford, John	21	1692	MCC folio 173
Shatswell, John	22	1673	EQC 5:233
Shatswell, Richard	50	1680	EQC 8:35
Shatswell, Theophilus	45	1659	EQC 2:365
Shattock, Samuel	58	1678	EQC 7:60
Shattuck, John	21	1666	MCC folio 40
Shattuck, John	24	1670	MCC folio 46
Shattuck, John	25	1671	MCC folio 59
Shattuck, John	26	1673	MCC folio 64
Shattuck, Philip	22	1670	MCC folio 46
Shattuck, Philip	25	1673	MCC folio 62
Shattuck, Philip	25	1674	MCC folio 63
Shattuck, Philip	25	1674	SJC 162133
Shattuck, Philip	30	1678	MCC folio 81
Shattuck, Philip	37	1686	MCC folio 121
Shattuck, Philip	37	1686	MCC folio 128

Shattuck, Rebecca	16	1671	MCC folio 59
Shattuck, William	30	1683	MCC folio 104
Shattuck, William	37	1692	MCC folio 172
Shattuck, William	38	1691	MCC folio 151
Shaw, Abraham	30	1664	EQC 3:155
Shaw, John	44	1676	MCC folio 71
Shaw, John	44	1676/7	SCC 761
Shaw, John	44	1676/7	SJC 1569
Shaw, John	68	1673	SD 8:171
Shaw, Thomas	37	1665	SJC 686
Shaw, William	40	1685	EQC WPA 46-38-1
Shaynes, John	27	1677	MCC folio 76
Sheafe, Jacob	36	1653	SJC 225
Sheafe, Sampson	21	1668	SJC 889
Sheafe, William	46	1693	MCC folio 176
Shed, Daniel	56	1677	MCC folio 77
Shed, Daniel	75	1677	MCC folio 78
Shed, Zachariah	20	1676	MCC folio 73
Sheffield, Daniel	27	1692	MCC folio 172
Sheffield, Daniel	27	1692	MCC folio 175
Sheffield, Joseph	21	1692	MCC folio 172
Sheffield, Joseph	21	1692	MCC folio 175
Sheffield, Thomas	24	1655	EQC 1:391
Sheldon, John	22	1683	MCC folio 102
Sheldon, Nicholas	28	nd	SJC 2785
Sheldon, William	58	1676	SJC 1526
Sheldon, William	60	1679	SJC 2011
Shelly, Thomas	35	1689/90	SJC 2540
Shelton, Robert	50	1683	SJC 2224
Shepard, Abraham	45	1684	MCC folio 109
Shepard, Abraham	54	1690	MCC folio 145
Shepard, Anna	52	1691	MCC folio 157
Shepard, Hannah	15	1680	MCC folio 183
Shepard, Jeremiah	33	1684	EQC 9:182
Shepard, John	20	1686	EQC WPA 46-149-2
Shepard, John	35	1668	MCC folio 50
Shepard, Juda	40	1691	MCC folio 145
Shepard, Persis	21	1689	MCC folio 135
Shepard, Ralph	60	1662	MCC folio 31
Shepard, Samuel	27	1677	EQC 6:291
Shepard, Sarah	16	1664	MCC folio 36
Shepard, Sarah	27	1678	MCC folio 78
Shepard, Thomas	17	1679	MCC folio 184
Shepard, Thomas	18	1680	MCC folio 183
Shepard, Thomas	19	1677	MCC folio 76
Shepard, Thomas	48	1683	EQC 9:124
Shepard, Walter	24	1667	MCC folio 43
Shepherd, Isaac	22	1665	EQC 3:291
Shepherd, John	15	1667	SJC 821
Shepherd, Thomas	26	1665	SJC 754
Sherburne, Henry	48	1662	SJC 470
Sherman, Abiah	19	1683	MCC folio 104
Sherman, John	17	1692	MCC folio 172
Sherman, John	46	1659	MCC folio 21

Sherman, John	61	1674	MCC folio 67
Sherwin, Richard	22	1685	SJC 2377
Shipley, John	79	1668	MCC folio 49
Shippie, Elizabeth	23	1671	MCC folio 57
Shippie, Grace	20	1679	MCC folio 85
Shippie, Thomas	20	1686	MCC folio 123
Shippie, Thomas	29	1693	MCC folio 177
Shippie, Thomas	40	1660	MCC folio 25
Ships, John	17	1686	MCC folio 121
Shore, Sampson	27	1695	SJC 3206
Shore, Sampson	62	1677	SJC 1753
Short, Henry	17	1669	EQC 4:180
Short, Henry	25	1677	EQC 6:357
Short, Henry	26	1678	EQC 7:156
Short, Sarah	50	1669	EQC 4:179
Shortrigs, William	28	1689	SJC 2540
Shrimpton, Epaphias	32	1685	SJC 2337
Shrimpton, Jonathan	32	1673	SD 8:173
Shrimpton, Samuel	39	1682/3	SJC 2120
Shubert, Ruth	22	1668	MCC folio 45
Shulet, Francis	35	1685	SJC 2346
Shunalloir, Daniel	28	1680	SJC 1941
Shute, Elizabeth	41	1671/2	SJC 1148
Shute, Richard	39	1672/3	SJC 1194
Shute, William	29	1672	SJC 1153
Sibley, John	33	1683	EQC 9:25
Sibley, Samuel	24	1683	EQC 9:47
Sibley, Samuel	24	1683	EQC 9:49
Siddall, Francis	23	1673	MCC folio 65
Sill, Elizabeth	17	1685	MCC folio 117
Sill, Joseph	33	1668	MCC folio 45
Silman, John	36	1677	SJC 1635
Silsbe, Samuel	23	1674	MCC folio 67
Silsby, Nathaniel	30	1680	EQC 7:400
Silsby, Nathaniel	34	1685	EQC 9:471
Silsby, Nathaniel	34	1685	SJC 2339
Silsby, Nathaniel	35	1686	EQC 9:580
Silsby, Samuel	38	1686	EQC WPA 46-145-2
Silver, Thomas	20	1678	EQC 7:156
Silver, Thomas	50	1674	EQC 5:330
Silver, Thomas	56	1678	EQC 7:157
Simentes, Joseph	34	1677	MCC folio 77
Simon, Jonathan	10	1688	EQC WPA 47-121-1
Simon, Nathan	14	1688	EQC WPA 47-121-1
Simonds, James	33	1691	MCC folio 146
Simonds, James	48	1682	EQC 8:346
Simonds, James	50	1685	EQC 9:472
Simonds, John	74	1669	EQC 4:109
Simons, Benjamin	16	1669	MCC folio 51
Simons, Benjamin	22	1676	MCC folio 71
Simons, Caleb	19	1668	MCC folio 48
Simons, Elizabeth	36	1685	EQC 9:471
Simons, James	50	1684	EQC 9:345
Simons, John	42	1680	EQC 8:16

Simons, Judah	40	1659	MCC folio 21
Simons, Judith	60	1676	MCC folio 71
Simons, Samuel	35	1675	EQC 6:55
Simons, Samuel	45	1685	EQC 9:471
Simons, Samuel	45	1685	SJC 2339
Simons, William	20	1680	EQC 8:21
Simons, William	21	1680	EQC 8:22
Simons, William	47	1656	MCC folio 16
Simons, William	47	1658	MCC folio 16
Simons, William	47	1659	MCC folio 21
Simons, William	50	1662	MCC folio 29
Simonson, Charles	26	1684	SJC 2251
Simpson, Andrew	40	1690	MCC folio 134
Simpson, John	39	1662	SJC 561
Simpson, John	53	1692	MCC folio 153
Simpson, Jonathan	45	1686	MCC folio 125
Simpson, Joshua	47	1686	MCC folio 125
Simson, Francis	55	1665	EQC 3:257
Simson, John	20	1677	EQC 6:354
Simson, John	40	1678	EQC 7:112
Simson, John	40	1680	EQC 7:400
Singletary, Jonathan	22	1662	EQC 2:381
Singletary, Jonathan	23	1662/3	SJC 543
Singletary, Jonathan	23	1662/3	SJC 549
Singletary, Jonathan	23	1664	EQC 2:121
Singletary, Richard	63	1662	EQC 3:7
Singletary, Richard	70	1663	EQC 3:27
Singletary, Richard	72	1664	EQC 3:214
Singletary, Susanna	46	1662	EQC 3:7
Sinkler, Edward	32	1692	MCC folio 146
Sinnott, Robert	50	1679	EQC 7:217
Skeath, Joseph	22	1691	MCC folio 141
Skerry, Frances	70	1678	EQC 7:108
Skerry, Frances	70	1680	EQC 7:390
Skerry, Frances	70	1680	EQC 7:391
Skerry, Francis	60	1669	EQC 4:145
Skerry, Francis	74	1680	EQC 7:390
Skerry, Henry	40	1678	EQC 7:108
Skerry, Henry	40	1678	EQC 7:111
Skerry, Henry	50	1663	EQC 3:104
Skerry, Henry	60	1668	EQC 4:50
Skerry, Henry	64	1668	EQC 4:54
Skerry, Henry	70	1674	EQC 5:335
Skerry, Henry	70	1674	EQC 5:414
Skerry, Henry	70	1675	EQC 6:67
Skerry, Henry	70	1675	EQC 6:88
Skerry, Henry	70	1677	EQC 6:288
Skerry, Henry	70	1678	EQC 7:108
Skerry, Henry	70	1678	EQC 7:25
Skerry, Henry	70	1680	EQC 7:331
Skerry, Henry	75	1677	EQC 6:356
Skerry, Henry	75	1678	EQC 7:30
Skerry, Henry	80	1684	EQC 9:199
Skerry, Henry	82	1684	EQC 9:345

Skerry, Henry	82	1684	SJC 2285
Skerry, Henry	83	1684	EQC 9:338
Skiffe, James	60	1700	SJC 4714
Skilling, Deborah	34	1657	EQC 2:37
Skilton, James	36	1681	EQC 8:102
Skinner, Mary	19	1685	SJC 2354
Skinner, Richard	16	1677	SCC 805
Skinner, Richard	16	1677	SJC 1635
Skinner, Richard	20	1683	EQC 9:68
Skinner, Thomas	79	1695	MCC folio 197
Skinner, Thomas	79	1695	SJC 3413
Skinner, Thomas	80	1695	MCC folio 178
Skinner, Thomas	80	1695	MCC folio 204
Skinner, Thomas	82	1696/7	MCC folio 204
Skinner, Thomas	84	1696/7	SJC 3413
Skinner, Walter	50	1680	EQC 7:400
Skolle, John	35	1677	MCC folio 75
Slade, Thomas	18	1671	MCC folio 56
Slater, Elizabeth	26	1663	EQC 3:103
Slaughter, John	26	1660/1	SJC 391
Slaughter, John	27	1663	EQC 3:102
Sleeper, Johannah	33	1656	SJC 256
Sleeper, Ruth	21	1671	SJC 1100
Sleud, John	25	1670	EQC 4:285
Slew, Barbary	35	1699	SJC 3967
Slye, Joshua	26	1691	MCC folio 141
Small, Ann	50	1666	EQC 3:380
Small, Benjamin	30	1676	EQC 6:190
Small, Benjamin	30	1677	EQC 6:281
Small, Benjamin	30	1679	EQC 7:308
Small, Edward	22	1676	SJC 1526
Small, John	68	1684/5	SJC 2285
Small, John	68	1685	EQC 9:439
Small, Mark	20	1681	MCC folio 94
Small, Stephen	20	1677	EQC 6:292
Small, Steven	22	1679	EQC 7:166
Smeade, Elizabeth	58	1698	SJC 3718
Smeadley, Benjamin	18	nd	SJC 2214
Smit, Mary	23	1690	MCC folio 138
Smith, Abraham	35	nd	SJC 2807
Smith, Andrew	52	1695	SJC 3299
Smith, Ann	19	1678	EQC 7:119
Smith, Asahel	40	1685	SJC 2370
Smith, Benjamin	30	1667	EQC 3:455
Smith, Benjamin	60	1673	EQC 5:226
Smith, Christopher	18	1677	EQC 6:280
Smith, Christopher	21	1680	EQC 7:401
Smith, Daniel	21	1664	MCC folio 36
Smith, Daniel	25	1669	MCC folio 52
Smith, Daniel	30	1671	MCC folio 56
Smith, Daniel	38	1682	MCC folio 99
Smith, Daniel	50	1696	SJC 3351
Smith, Elizabeth	20	1677	EQC 6:250
Smith, Elizabeth	29	1682	EQC 8:345

Smith, Elizabeth	41	1662	SJC 573
Smith, George	21	1685	EQC 9:472
Smith, George	21	1685	SJC 2339
Smith, Hannah	16	1656	MCC folio 15
Smith, Hannah	36	1680	EQC 7:372
Smith, Henry	49	1691	MCC folio 147
Smith, Henry	63	1667	EQC 3:415
Smith, James	14	1669	EQC 4:146
Smith, James	15	1669	EQC 4:151
Smith, James	33	1678	EQC 7:156
Smith, James	37	1683	EQC 9:11
Smith, James	43	1667	EQC 3:413
Smith, James	43	1667	EQC 3:417
Smith, James	45	1669	EQC 4:147
Smith, James	48	1672	EQC 5:41
Smith, James	48	1672	EQC 5:5
Smith, James	50	1674	EQC 5:283
Smith, James	50	1674	SJC 1323
Smith, James	56	1678	EQC 7:141
Smith, James	7	1674	MCC folio 67
Smith, Job	19	1682	EQC 8:298
Smith, John	21	1678	SJC 1734
Smith, John	24	1691	MCC folio 157
Smith, John	30	1653	MCC folio 6
Smith, John	30	1662	EQC 2:391
Smith, John	31	1678	EQC 7:157
Smith, John	37	1659	MCC folio 21
Smith, John	38	1694	SJC 3111
Smith, John	38	1694	SJC 4101
Smith, John	38	nd	SJC 2281
Smith, John	40	1674	EQC 5:308
Smith, John	42	1666	EQC 3:323
Smith, John	47	1695	SJC 162370
Smith, John	77	1668	SJC 1046
Smith, Jonathan	16	1675	MCC folio 70
Smith, Martha	26	1682	EQC 8:281
Smith, Martha	34	1673	MCC folio 62
Smith, Mary	19	1681	MCC folio 104
Smith, Mary	19	1681	MCC folio 97
Smith, Mary	23	1690	MCC folio 138
Smith, Mary	26	1681	EQC 8:95
Smith, Mary	26	1685	MCC folio 115
Smith, Mary	30	1680	EQC 7:411
Smith, Mary	48	1678	EQC 7:119
Smith, Mary	55	1683	EQC 9:64
Smith, Mathew	23	1691	MCC folio 146
Smith, Mathew	28	1691	MCC folio 156
Smith, Mathew	50	1676	MCC folio 72
Smith, Mathew	50	1676	MCC folio 74
Smith, Michael	45	1675	SJC 1390
Smith, Nathaniel	36	1679	SJC 1840
Smith, Nicholas	40	1671	SJC 1088
Smith, Rebecca	47	1686	EQC 9:606
Smith, Richard	19	1664	SJC 648

Smith, Richard	26	1653	SJC 225
Smith, Richard	36	1677	SJC 1621
Smith, Richard	39	1683	SJC 2224
Smith, Richard	40	1682	EQC 8:431
Smith, Richard	53	1693	SJC 3039
Smith, Richard	30	1664	EQC 3:212
Smith, Robert	23	1673	EQC 5:226
Smith, Robert	33	1658	EQC 2:141
Smith, Robert	33	1659	EQC 2:172
Smith, Robert	33	1662	EQC 2:364
Smith, Samuel	23	1672	EQC 5:35
Smith, Samuel	28	1679	EQC 7:270
Smith, Sarah	17	1678	EQC 7:119
Smith, Sarah	38	1682	EQC 8:284
Smith, Sarah	38	1682	MCC folio 99
Smith, Sarah	45	1694	MCC folio 161
Smith, Sarah	54	1675	MCC folio 69
Smith, Thomas	15	1662	EQC 2:350
Smith, Thomas	18	1674	EQC 5:444
Smith, Thomas	22	1670	EQC 4:241
Smith, Thomas	24	1672	EQC 5:34
Smith, Thomas	36	1684	EQC 9:251
Smith, Thomas	39	1682	MCC folio 103
Smith, Thomas	45	1681	EQC 8:101
Smith, Thomas	45	1681	EQC 8:102
Smith, William	16	1674	EQC 5:270
Smith, William	22	1662	SJC 467
Smith, William	26	1658	EQC 2:113
Smith, William	40	1674	EQC 5:422
Smith, William	46	1666	SJC 762
Smith, William	50	1676/7	SJC 1560
Smith, William	58	1684	EQC 9:246
Smith, William	58	1684	EQC 9:317
Smith, William	62	1681	EQC 8:108
Snelling, John	43	1671	EQC 4:420
Snelling, Joseph	25	1693	SJC 3125
Snow, Samuel	30	1679	SJC 1896
Snow, Samuel	32	1680/1	SJC 1956
Snowsill, Abraham	22	1672	EQC 5:109
Snowsill, Judith	35	1671	SCC 7
Snowsill, Judith	37	1671	SJC 1179
Snowsill, Thomas	32	1666	EQC 3:349
Snowsill, Thomas	32	1667	SJC 816
Snowsill, Thomas	32	1667	SJC 828
Sollas, Mary	17	1674	EQC 5:291
Somerby, Abel	27	1668	SJC 924
Somerby, Abiel	28	1669	EQC 4:153
Somerby, Anthony	52	1662	EQC 2:354
Somerby, Anthony	52	1662	EQC 2:355
Somerby, Anthony	54	1664	EQC 3:216
Somerby, Anthony	58	1668	EQC 4:12
Somerby, Anthony	60	1669	EQC 4:199
Somerby, Anthony	61	1671	EQC 4:335
Somerby, Anthony	66	1676	EQC 6:126

Somerby, Anthony	72	1681	EQC 8:172
Somerby, Anthony	68	1678	EQC 7:156
Somerby, Henry	16	1678	EQC 7:156
Somerby, Henry	33	1695	SJC 3150
Somers, Henry	28	1668	MCC folio 48
Somes, Morris	50	1654	EQC 1:329
Somes, Morris	58	1658	EQC 2:64
Soper, Joseph	33	1663	SJC 571
Soule, Abraham	45	1691	MCC folio 148
Soule, Benjamin	31	nd	SJC 3630
Souther, Joseph	25	1683/4	SJC 2183
Southerick, Daniel	48	1685/6	EQC WPA 46-22-3
Southwick, Daniel	48	nd	SJC 2770
Sowther, Nathaniel	62	1654	SD 2:85
Spafford, Mary	23	1683	EQC 9:113
Spalding, Edward	46	1682	MCC folio 99
Sparhawk, Arthur	26	1663	MCC folio 34
Sparke, John	27	1662	EQC 2:350
Sparke, Mary	36	1680	EQC 7:374
Sparke, Mary	36	1680	SJC 1894
Sparke, Thomas	22	1673	EQC 5:190
Spaulding, Andrew	17	1670	MCC folio 53
Spaulding, Joseph	22	1670	MCC folio 53
Speed, Samuel	30	1679	SJC 1800
Speere, Ebenezer	22	1676	SJC 1562
Spencer, Elizabeth	40	1691	SJC 2627
Spencer, Humphrey	43	1689	SJC 3006
Spencer, Roger	42	1661	SJC 507
Spicket, Nicholas	36	1683	EQC 9:28
Spierman, Francis	24	1671	SJC 1106
Spinney, James	35	1697	SJC 4705
Spinney, John	29	1697	SJC 4705
Spinney, John	30	1698/9	SJC 4705
Spinney, Samuel	38	nd	SJC 3608
Spinney, Thomas	67	nd	SJC 4705
Spofford, Hannah	21	1677	EQC 6:254
Spofford, John	50	1662	EQC 2:362
Spofford, Mary	20	1680	EQC 8:89
Spowell, William	76	1677	SJC 2016
Sprague, Elizabeth	26	1677	MCC folio 78
Sprague, John	38	1663	MCC folio 34
Sprague, Jonathan	23	1679	MCC folio 184
Sprague, Jonathan	28	1685	MCC folio 114
Sprague, Lydia	70	1698	MCC folio 167
Sprague, Lydia	70	1698	SJC 3936
Sprague, Mary	70	1667	SJC 814
Sprague, Mary	73	1669	MCC folio 52
Sprague, Phineas	27	1666	MCC folio 42
Sprague, Phineas	35	1673	MCC folio 65
Sprague, Phineas	40	1680	MCC folio 89
Sprague, Richard	40	1671	SJC 1081
Sprague, Richard	53	1679	MCC folio 183
Sprague, Samuel	28	1659	MCC folio 23
Sprague, Samuel	63	1695	MCC folio 179

Sprague, Samuel	63	1695	MCC folio 182
Sprague, Samuel	63	1695	MCC folio 197
Sprague, Samuel	63	1695	SJC 3413
Spring, John	40	1673	MCC folio 63
Spurr, Ann	61	1685	SD 13:408
Spurr, Robert	42	1663/4	SJC 606
Spurr, Robert	55	1672/3	SJC 1281
Squash, Edmund	30	1695	SJC 3123
Squire, Job	30	1654	MCC folio 9
Squire, John	32	1667	MCC folio 43
Squire, John	55	1691	MCC folio 147
Squire, John	55	1691	MCC folio 175
Squire, Philip	25	1681	EQC 8:95
Stableford, Thomas	33	1679	SJC 1809
Stackhouse, Esther	15	1666	SJC 762
Stackhouse, Richard	71	1684	EQC 9:343
Stackhouse, Samuel	16	1670	EQC 4:217
Stackhouse, Susanna	52	1666	SJC 762
Stackhouse, Susannah	60	1677	EQC 6:349
Stacy, Ellen	41	1674	EQC 5:348
Stacy, Henry	29	1681	EQC 8:103
Stacy, Henry	46	1667	EQC 3:419
Stacy, Henry	46	1667	EQC 3:443
Stacy, Henry	60	1674	EQC 5:348
Stacy, Henry	60	1680	EQC 8:5
Stacy, Henry	60	1680	SJC 2011
Stacy, Henry	60	1684	EQC 9:310
Stacy, Jane	30	1667	EQC 3:444
Stacy, John	23	1672	EQC 5:91
Stacy, John	26	1676	EQC 6:258
Stacy, John	35	1685	EQC 9:438
Stacy, John	43	1687	EQC WPA 47-67-3
Stacy, Mary	22	1666	EQC 3:420
Stacy, Samuel	25	1681	EQC 8:156
Stacy, Simon	41	1678	EQC 7:117
Stacy, Simon	42	1679	EQC 7:268
Stacy, Simon	44	1681	EQC 8:166
Stacy, Simon	46	1684	EQC 9:189
Stacy, Simon	48	1686	EQC 9:585
Stacy, Thomas	66	1687/8	EQC WPA 47-101-1
Staines, [Richard]	33	1655	EQC 1:399
Stalin, William	35	1672	EQC 5:105
Stamthorpe, Jonathan	40	1671	MCC folio 58
Stanbury, Thomas	40	1683/4	SJC 2173
Stanbury, Thomas	50	1693	MCC folio 176
Stanbury, Thomas	50	1694	SJC 4133
Stanford, John	38	1680	SJC 1894
Stanhope, Jonathan	53	1685	MCC folio 117
Staniford, John	30	1680	EQC 7:373
Stanley, George	44	1679	EQC 7:311
Stanley, John	27	1680	SJC 1909
Stanton, Robert	55	1670	SJC 993
Stanup, Jonathan	37	1668	MCC folio 50
Stanwood, Mary	20	1673	MCC folio 62

Stanyan, Anthony	59	1666/7	SJC 1277
Stanyan, Anthony	65	1672	EQC 5:100
Stanyan, John	18	1660	EQC 2:229
Stanyan, John	20	1669	EQC 4:134
Stanyan, John	23	1666	SJC 764
Stanyan, John	36	1678	EQC 7:6
Stanyan, John	36	1678	EQC 7:93
Starkweather, Anna	25	1680	EQC 7:372
Starkweather, Anna	25	1680	SJC 1894
Starkweather, John	40	1686	EQC WPA 46-68-3
Starlin, William	30	1667	EQC 3:387
Starlin, William	30	1667	EQC 3:388
Starr, Josaphat	21	1671	MCC folio 74
Starr, Robert	43	1670	EQC 4:299
Starr, Robert	47	1673	EQC 5:181
Starr, Robert	49	1675	EQC 6:35
Starr, Robert	49	1675	MCC folio 75
Starr, Thomas	19	1686	EQC WPA 46-100-5
Start, John	52	1685	SJC 2346
Stay, John	60	1654	EQC 1:332
Staynor, Elizabeth	27	1683	SJC 2144
Staynor, Roger	32	1680	SJC 2028
Staynor, Roger	32	nd	SJC 2374
Staynor, Roger	36	1683	SJC 2374
Steadman, George	19	1668	MCC folio 48
Stearns, Samuel	22	1660	MCC folio 25
Stearns, Samuel	24	1662	MCC folio 31
Stearns, Samuel	33	1672	MCC folio 33
Stearns, Samuel	35	1673	MCC folio 62
Stearns, Samuel	41	1679	MCC folio 84
Stebbins, Martine	68	1657/8	SJC 286
Stebbins, Rebecca	77	1699	SJC 3994
Stedman, Elizabeth	18	1659	MCC folio 23
Stedman, Isaac	59	1663/4	SJC 606
Stedman, Thomas	24	1665	SJC 680
Stedman, Thomas	25	1665	SJC 680
Steerman, Michael	28	1683	SJC 162218
Steevens, John	30	1678	EQC 7:157
Stenson, Jonathan	30	1672	MCC folio 64
Stephens, John	38	1677	EQC 6:325
Stephens, John	41	1675	EQC 6:43
Stephens, Thomas	20	1670	EQC 4:292
Sterling, John	21	nd	SJC 2788
Stevens, Benjamin	29	1686	EQC 9:607
Stevens, Charles	80	1695	SJC 3175
Stevens, Ciprian	22	1670	MCC folio 53
Stevens, Cyprian	28	1678	EQC 7:33
Stevens, Cyprian	40	1691	MCC folio 142
Stevens, Cyprian	45	1695	MCC folio 196
Stevens, Ebenezer	22	nd	SJC 2821
Stevens, Henry	60	1673	MCC folio 63
Stevens, James	48	1679	EQC 7:201
Stevens, John	28	1667	EQC 3:470
Stevens, John	30	1669	EQC 4:150

Stevens, John	32	1671	EQC 4:422
Stevens, John	56	1667	EQC 3:424
Stevens, John	60	1669	SJC 924
Stevens, Margaret	24	1677	MCC folio 183
Stevens, Margaret	38	1680/1	SJC 1959
Stevens, Moses	27	1686	EQC 9:582
Stevens, Nathan	27	1671	EQC 4:422
Stevens, Thomas	28	1679	EQC 7:318
Stevens, Thomas	29	1681	EQC 8:76
Stevens, Thomas	29	1681	EQC 8:78
Stevens, Thomas	33	1695	MCC folio 162
Stevens, Thomas	60	1680/1	SJC 1959
Stevens, William	21	1686	EQC WPA 46-137-2
Stevenson, Andrew	27	1677	MCC folio 78
Stevenson, Andrew	67	1677	MCC folio 78
Stevenson, Jonathan	30	1672	MCC folio 60
Steward, James	23	1685	SJC 2354
Steward, Thomas	27	1685	EQC 9:466
Stewart, William	24	1653	MCC folio 6
Stich, Henry	18	1653	EQC 2:97
Stich, Henry	18	1653/4	SJC 225
Stickeny, goodwife	37	1681	EQC 8:216
Stickney, Amos	18	1686	EQC WPA 46-6-1
Stickney, John	16	1682	EQC 8:262
Stickney, Sarah	35	1678	EQC WPA 46-11-1
Stickney, Sarah	35	1679	EQC 7:317
Stieff, William	36	1686	MCC folio 122
Stileman, Richard	51	1662	EQC 2:389
Stileman, Richard	55	1666	SJC 823
Stileman, Richard	64	nd	SJC 1632
Stillson, Grace	37	1676	EQC 6:149
Stilson, Vinson	32	1686	EQC WPA 46-87-3
Stimson, Alice	20	1676	EQC 6:238
Stimson, Andrew	34	1686	MCC folio 121
Stimson, George	27	1668	EQC 4:15
Stimson, George	31	1676	EQC 6:158
Stimson, George	32	1676	EQC 6:237
Stimson, Jonathan	52	1692	MCC folio 154
Stinner, Mary	45	1663	MCC folio 33
Stinson, Andrew	60	1672	MCC folio 61
Stinson, Jane	63	1677	MCC folio 78
Stinson, Jonathan	30	1672	MCC folio 59
Stitson, William	58	1658	MCC folio 16
Stitson, William	75	1676	MCC folio 72
Stitson, William	80	1680	MCC folio 89
Stitson, William	85	1686	MCC folio 122
Stocker, Ebenezer	35	1685	EQC 9:431
Stocker, Ebenezer	35	1685	EQC 9:465
Stocker, Joseph	18	1662	SJC 874
Stocker, Joseph	30	1677	EQC 6:329
Stocker, Thomas	55	1675	EQC 6:10
Stocker, Thomas	55	1675	EQC 6:78
Stockman, Dorothy	16	1695	SJC 4172
Stockman, John	29	1682	EQC 8:431

Stockman, Joseph	13	1685	EQC 9:533
Stoddard, Anthony	56	1662/3	SCC 67
Stodder, Daniel	62	1695	SJC 4202
Stodder, John	28	1697	SJC 4373
Stodder, Samuel	55	1695	SJC 3470
Stodder, Simeon	30	1682	EQC 8:328
Stone, Abigail	14	1679	EQC 7:182
Stone, Abigail	40	1679	EQC 7:182
Stone, Abigail	40	1683	EQC 9:152
Stone, Abigail	43	1678	EQC 7:53
Stone, Anne	69	1686	MCC folio 127
Stone, Daniel	50	1673	SJC 1216
Stone, Gregory	67	1658	EQC 2:112
Stone, Gregory	67	1658	EQC 2:130
Stone, John	46	1683	MCC folio 104
Stone, John	49	1667	MCC folio 43
Stone, John	55	1677	EQC 6:349
Stone, Josiah	27	1684	MCC folio 107
Stone, Nathaniel	34	1667	EQC 3:458
Stone, Nathaniel	48	1680	EQC 8:22
Stone, Nicholas	55	1671/2	SD 7:297
Stone, Richard	32	1678	MCC folio 82
Stone, Richard	76	1693	MCC folio 179
Stone, Robert	17	1679	EQC 7:248
Stone, Robert	35	1662	SJC 561
Stone, Samuel	26	1682	MCC folio 101
Stone, Simon	34	1665	MCC folio 38
Stone, Simon	42	1673	MCC folio 62
Stone, Simon	50	1681	MCC folio 97
Storer, Samuel	24	1679	EQC 7:318
Storer, Samuel	30	1680	SJC 1924
Story, Abigail	15	1669	EQC 4:124
Story, Hannah	17	1680	EQC 7:375
Story, Sarah	48	1668	EQC 4:80
Story, Seth	21	1669	EQC 4:104
Story, Seth	21	1669	EQC 4:125
Story, Seth	23	1670	EQC 4:218
Story, Seth	23	1670	EQC 4:259
Story, Seth	26	1674	EQC 5:413
Story, William	19	1669	EQC 4:104
Story, William	19	1669	EQC 4:125
Story, William	55	1668	EQC 4:67
Story, William	55	1668	EQC 4:69
Story, William	66	1676	EQC 6:155
Stow, Nathaniel	48	1670	EQC 4:288
Stower, Richard	60	1680	MCC folio 90
Stower, Richard	62	1682	MCC folio 100
Stower, Sarah	22	1678	MCC folio 78
Stowers, Richard	76	1693	MCC folio 204
Stowers, Richard	76	1693	SJC 162289
Stowers, Samuel	20	1685	SJC 2354
Stowers, Samuel	20	nd	SJC 26012
Stracher, Sarah	17	1677	MCC folio 183
Strague, Charles	22	1679	MCC folio 85

Strait, Thomas	47	1665	MCC folio 40
Strait, Thomas	60	1678	MCC folio 81
Stratton, Elizabeth	32	1673	MCC folio 63
Stratton, Elizabeth	37	1678	MCC folio 80
Stratton, Goodman	80	1672	MCC folio 61
Stratton, John	23	1681	MCC folio 97
Stratton, John	38	1672	MCC folio 60
Stratton, John	40	1673	MCC folio 63
Stratton, John	59	1672	MCC folio 61
Stratton, Samuel	23	1684	MCC folio 108
Stratton, Samuel	25	1684	MCC folio 107
Streeter, Sarah	26	1676	MCC folio 72
Strickland, Peter	24	1670	EQC 4:293
Strong, William	34	1684	SJC 2203
Strout, Christopher	33	1693	SJC 4114
Strout, Sarah	28	1694	SJC 4114
Stubbs, Elizabeth	17	1668	MCC folio 45
Stuckley, John	37	nd	SJC 512
Studman, Augustine	40	1678	EQC 7:157
Suddall, Francis	22	nd	SJC 162108
Suddall, Francis	23	1221	SJC 1673
Sumers, Susanna	35	1686	MCC folio 123
Summers, Humphrey	22	1668/9	SJC 924
Summerset, John	21	1679	MCC folio 85
Sumner, William	80	1685	SD 13:408
Sunderland, John	43	1661	EQC 2:286
Sunderlanᴅ, John	49	1667	SD 5:340
Sunderland, John	53	1671	SJC 1044
Suthicke, Daniel	42	1680	EQC 7:423
Sutton, Bartholomew	45	1673	SCC 309
Sutton, Bartholomew	45	1673	SJC 1209
Swaffer, Thomas	26	1684	SJC 2251
Swain, Eme	16	1658	MCC folio 17
Swain, Hannah	35	1691	MCC folio 157
Swain, Henry	32	1679	MCC folio 85
Swain, Isaac	46	1672	EQC 5:79
Swain, Jeremiah	25	1667	EQC 3:455
Swain, Jeremiah	28	1670	MCC folio 54
Swain, William	23	1673	SJC 1213
Swallow, Ambrose	27	1670	MCC folio 55
Swan, Ann	60	1675	EQC 6:15
Swan, Gershom	26	1681	MCC folio 93
Swan, Gershom	37	1691	MCC folio 148
Swan, John	13	1695	MCC folio 162
Swan, John	17	1685	MCC folio 117
Swan, John	18	1681	SJC 2031
Swan, John	45	1672	MCC folio 61
Swan, John	57	1682	MCC folio 101
Swan, John	68	1691/2	MCC folio 146
Swan, John	68	1691/2	MCC folio 175
Swan, John	74	1695	MCC folio 204
Swan, Mary	27	1689	MCC folio 135
Swan, Mary	28	1661	MCC folio 27
Swan, Richard	68	1675	EQC 6:13

Swan, Richard	70	1677	EQC 6:269
Swan, Robert	36	1662	EQC 2:381
Swan, Robert	54	1680	EQC 7:378
Swan, Robert	56	1682	EQC 8:300
Swan, Sarah	16	1695	MCC folio 162
Swan, Thomas	22	1666	EQC 3:302
Swasey, Stephen	22	1674	SJC 1360
Swasey, Stephen	40	1680	SJC 2055
Sweatland, William	34	1680	EQC 7:410
Sweet, John	66	1669	EQC 4:195
Swetland, Peter	29	1678	EQC 7:107
Swett, Henry	22	1679	EQC 7:170
Swett, Henry	22	1679	EQC 7:259
Swett, John	30	1678	EQC 7:157
Swett, Joseph	50	1673	SJC 1290
Swett, Stephen	26	1678	EQC 6:413
Swett, Stephen	58	1678	EQC 7:157
Swett, Steven	40	1664	EQC 3:188
Swinn, Owen	16	1658	EQC 2:112
Swinnerton, John	55	nd	SJC 2770
Sygus, John	28	1670	SJC 1046
Symmes, Timothy	23	1694/5	SJC 4118
Symmes, William	35	1660	MCC folio 25
Symmes, William	40	1668	MCC folio 48
Symmes, William	47	1675	MCC folio 70
Symon, Edward	40	1663	EQC 3:34
Symonds, Elizabeth	36	1685	SJC 2339
Symonds, Harlackenden	38	1666	EQC 3:373
Symonds, Harlackenden	40	1668	EQC 4:89
Symonds, Harlackenden	60	1695	SJC 162347
Symonds, James	50	1685	EQC 9:471
Symonds, James	50	1685	SJC 2339
Symonds, James	50	nd	SJC 2285
Symonds, John	18	1685	EQC 9:472
Symonds, John	18	1685	SJC 2339
Symonds, Mary	22	1685	EQC 9:439
Symonds, Mary	22	1685	SJC 2285
Symonds, Samuel	19	1662	EQC 2:437
Tabot, Jeremiah	39	1670	EQC 4:304
Taintor, Joseph	58	1672	MCC folio 59
Taintor, Joseph	60	1678	MCC folio 81
Taintor, Joseph	62	1676	MCC folio 74
Talbut, Mary	19	1674	EQC 5:315
Tally, Richard	30	1683	SJC 2198
Tanner, Arthur	29	1681	SJC 2010
Tapley, John	25	1664	EQC 3:211
Tapley, John	26	1664	EQC 3:210
Tapley, John	27	1666	EQC 3:333
Tapley, John	40	1678	EQC 7:306
Tapley, Tamsin	42	1673	EQC 5:216
Tappan, Abraham	20	1671	EQC 4:382
Tappan, Jane	48	1682	EQC 8:248
Tappan, John	20	1671	EQC 4:382
Tappan, John	27	1680	EQC 7:397

Tappan, John	43	1694/5	SJC 3148
Tappan, Peter	48	1682	EQC 8:248
Tappan, Samuel	25	1695	SJC 162373
Tappan, Susan	66	1674	SJC 1352
Tappan, Susannah	60	1671	EQC 4:379
Tappan, Susannah	74	1678	SJC 1791
Tarball, John	30	1683	EQC 9:55
Tarball, Susannah	56	1683	MCC folio 104
Tarbell, Mathew	18	1681	EQC 8:109
Tarbill, John	36	1686	EQC WPA 46-31-2
Tarbox, Samuel	22	1670	EQC 4:309
Tarbox, Samuel	29	1676	EQC 6:198
Tarbox, Samuel	34	1681	EQC 8:104
Tarbox, Samuel	35	1684	EQC 9:246
Tarbox, Samuel	35	1684	EQC 9:317
Tarbox, Samuel	37	1684	EQC 9:246
Tarbox, Samuel	37	1684	EQC 9:316
Tarlo, Jane	30	1696/7	SJC 3414
Tarlson, Margaret	60	1677	MCC folio 78
Tarvis, Andrew	42	1663	SJC 3138
Tarvis, Andrew	55	1675	EQC 6:102
Tay, Bathseba	32	1690	MCC folio 136
Tay, Isaiah	34	1684	SJC 162220
Tay, Isaiah	34	1684	SJC 2228
Tay, Jeremiah	35	1694	SJC 3033
Tay, Jeremiah	36	1694	SJC 3035
Tay, Nathaniel	36	1690	MCC folio 136
Taylor, Caleb	23	1669	SD 6:133
Taylor, Edmund	18	1694	SJC 4150
Taylor, Edward	26	1656	SJC 249
Taylor, Elizabeth	75	1681	SJC 2016
Taylor, George	18	1654	EQC 2:25
Taylor, George	60	1659	SJC 1046
Taylor, Henry	32	1664	SD 4:240
Taylor, James	64	1671	MCC folio 59
Taylor, John	27	1675	SJC 1422
Taylor, John	30	1678	SJC 1741
Taylor, Mary	40	1667	MCC folio 44
Taylor, Richard	60	1662	SJC 508
Taylor, Richard	68	1670	SJC 986
Taylor, Samuel	40	1658	EQC 2:140
Taylor, Thomas	36	1655/6	MCC folio 15
Taylor, Walter	55	1678	EQC 7:156
Taylor, William	46	1677	SJC 1613
Tearn, Hannah	22	1663	SJC 573
Teayn, John	40	1691	MCC folio 151
Teed, Joseph	28	1690	MCC folio 137
Teed, Samuel	22	1690	MCC folio 137
Tefts, Elizabeth	15	1669	MCC folio 52
Temple, Christopher	20	1677	EQC 6:288
Temple, Richard	21	1696	MCC folio 201
Tenney, Daniel	20	1681	EQC 8:216
Tenney, James	26	1678	EQC 7:97
Tenney, John	29	1670	EQC 4:283

Tenney, Susannah	34	1686	EQC 9:604
Tenney, Thomas	60	1674	EQC 5:277
Tenny, John	40	1676	SJC 1526
Tenny, John	40	1679/80	SJC 1828
Tenor, Thomas	40	1678	EQC 7:118
Teppett, Nicholas	38	1691	SJC 2602
Tewells, Richard	30	1668	SJC 910
Tewills, Richard	34	1668	MCC folio 48
Thatcher, Samuel	22	1671	MCC folio 56
Thatcher, Samuel	30	1681	MCC folio 97
Thatcher, Samuel	34	1685	MCC folio 117
Thatcher, Thomas	19	1663	SJC 602
Thaxter, John	28	1665	SJC 694
Thayer, Ann	48	1696	SJC 4342
Thayer, Benjamin	20	1700	SJC 4845
Thayer, Martha	25	1700	SJC 4845
Thayer, Nathaniel	22	1661	SJC 455
Thayer, Nathaniel	22	1662	SJC 828
Thayer, Richard	51	1680/1	SJC 1970
Thayer, Thomas	37	1659	SJC 347
Thing, Jonathan	46	1667	EQC 3:397
Thistle, Richard	22	1664	EQC 3:209
Thomas, Benjamin	24	1677	MCC folio 77
Thomas, George	40	1680	EQC 7:425
Thomas, George	48	1685	EQC 9:484
Thomas, James	30	1689/90	SJC 2540
Thomas, Richard	16	1685	EQC 9:442
Thomas, Roger	40	1695	SJC 3316
Thomas, Roger	50	1698/9	SJC 4705
Thomas, Roger	50	1699	SJC 4705
Thompson, John	22	1677	SJC 3349
Thompson, John	27	1684	SJC 2264
Thompson, Mathew	35	1680	SJC 1932
Thompson, Symon	60	1668	SJC 931
Thomson, Alexander	46	1674	EQC 5:414
Thomson, Alexander	48	1679	EQC 7:292
Thomson, George	20	1658	EQC 2:94
Thomson, James	69	1662	MCC folio 28
Thomson, John	30	1691	MCC folio 140
Thomson, Simon	50	1660	EQC 2:201
Thomson, William	27	1676	EQC 6:158
Thomson, William	29	1679	EQC 7:170
Thomson, William	30	1679	EQC 7:204
Thomson, William	30	1679	EQC 7:259
Thorla, Anna	50	1686	EQC WPA 46-118-3
Thorla, Anna	50	1686	EQC WPA 46-5-5
Thorla, Francis	50	1686	EQC WPA 46-5-5
Thorn, Sarah	37	1684	EQC 9:272
Thorndike, Elizabeth	20	1661	EQC 2:324
Thorndike, Mary	25	1674	EQC 5:290
Thorndike, Paul	42	1684	EQC 9:208
Thorndike, Paul	42	1684	EQC 9:208
Thorne, Bernard	24	1658	EQC 2:133
Thorne, Israel	43	1685	EQC 9:484

Thorne, Martha	36	1684	EQC 9:205
Thorne, Sarah	37	1684	EQC 9:273
Thorne, Sarah	38	1685	EQC 9:484
Thornton, Timothy	30	1680	SCC 1030
Thornton, Timothy	30	1680	SJC 1911
Thoyte, Jonathan	24	1689	SJC 2541
Thrumble, John	70	1677	SJC 162165
Thurla, Francis	45	1677	EQC 6:344
Thurla, Thomas	35	1670	EQC 4:261
Thurley, Anne	44	1678	EQC 7:138
Thurley, Francis	48	1678	EQC 7:156
Thurley, Francis	50	1684	EQC 9:238
Thurley, John	18	1678	EQC 7:99
Thurley, John	19	1678	EQC 7:157
Thurley, Jonathan	16	1678	EQC 7:99
Thurley, Jonathan	17	1678	EQC 7:157
Thurley, Jonathan	22	1684	EQC 9:327
Thurley, Richard	19	1684	EQC 9:238
Thurley, Thomas	47	1678	EQC 7:157
Thurriel, Johanna	26	1669	EQC 4:199
Thurston, Benjamin	33	1673	MCC folio 65
Thurston, Daniel	17	1678	EQC 7:157
Thurston, Daniel	40	1678	EQC 7:157
Thwing, Edward	42	1697	SJC 3897
Thwing, Jonathan	56	1673	SJC 1228
Tibbon, William	20	1666	EQC 3:333
Tidd, John	16	1671	MCC folio 58
Tidd, John	21	1676	MCC folio 71
Tidmarsh, Richard	25	1659	EQC 2:148
Tille, Thomas	50	1679	EQC 7:327
Tiller, Mary	50	1670	MCC folio 53
Tilly, Peter	18	1657	SJC 478
Tilstone, Thomas	76	1685	SD 13:408
Tilstone, Timothy	49	1685	SD 13:408
Tilton, Abraham	42	1686	EQC 9:584
Timberlake, William	26	1673	SCC 177
Timberlake, William	26	1673	SJC 1221
Timberlake, William	32	1678	SJC 1728
Tinkham, Isaac	30	nd	SJC 3630
Titcomb, Benajah	25	1678	EQC 7:156
Titcomb, Benajah	40	1695	SJC 3148
Titcomb, Mary	18	1662	EQC 2:410
Titcomb, Peniel	27	1678	EQC 7:157
Titcomb, Penuel	35	1686	EQC WPA 46-119-2
Titcomb, Thomas	17	1678	EQC 7:156
Titcomb, Thomas	18	1680	EQC 7:377
Titcomb, Tirza	17	1676	EQC 6:127
Titcomb, Tirza	17	1676	SJC 1481
Tite, George	22	1662	SJC 561
Tiver, Grace	22	1680	EQC 8:88
Tocker, John	18	1683	EQC 9:90
Todd, John	50	1672	EQC 5:35
Todd, John	54	1675	EQC 6:15
Todd, John	57	1678	EQC 7:84

Tolar, Sarah	18	1680	MCC folio 183
Tomlin, William	57	1682	SJC 2119
Tompson, Alexander	40	1667	EQC 3:430
Tompson, Benjamin	30	1674	MCC folio 67
Tompson, Benjamin	36	1679	MCC folio 86
Tompson, Francis	18	1689	MCC folio 134
Tompson, James	22	1670	MCC folio 53
Tompson, James	65	1658	MCC folio 16
Tompson, Sarah	40	1674	MCC folio 66
Tomson, Jonathan	55	1686	MCC folio 123
Tong, Steven	40	1680	EQC 7:376
Tong, Steven	40	1685	EQC 9:535
Toogood, Gartright	52	1695	SJC 3316
Tooky, Job	22	1672/3	SJC 1194
Tooky, Job	38	nd	SJC 2839
Tooley, John	20	nd	SJC 1257
Toope, Margere	17	1674	EQC 5:303
Toppan, Jacob	26	1673	EQC 5:155
Toppan, Jacob	31	1678	EQC 7:156
Toppan, Jane	40	1673	EQC 5:178
Toppan, John	28	1678	EQC 7:156
Toppan, Peter	44	1678	EQC 7:157
Toppan, Susannah	66	1674	EQC 5:399
Toppan, Susannah	74	1678	EQC 7:159
Torrey, Philip	59	1673/4	SD 8:392
Torry, William	58	1667	SJC 815
Tottingham, Henry	50	1658	MCC folio 16
Tottingham, Henry	50	1658	MCC folio 17
Tottingham, Henry	57	1664	MCC folio 36
Tover, Thoms	50	1680	EQC 8:2
Tovey, John	25	1683	EQC 9:110
Tower, Thomas	50	1681	EQC 8:198
Tower, Thomas	50	1682	MCC folio 101
Towers, Thomas	50	1680	SJC 1951
Towers, Thomas	50	1681	EQC 8:133
Towne, Deliverance	16	1680	EQC 7:410
Towne, Edmund	31	1660	EQC 2:205
Towne, Jacob	38	1669	EQC 4:110
Towne, Jacob	44	1675	EQC 6:4
Towne, Jacob	50	1680	EQC 8:74
Towne, Jacob	64	1685	EQC 9:440
Towne, Joanna	55	1677	MCC folio 78
Towne, Joanna	75	1670	EQC 4:249
Towne, Joseph	21	1660	EQC 2:205
Towne, Peter	33	1668	MCC folio 45
Towne, Peter	40	1679	MCC folio 85
Towne, William	60	1660	EQC 2:205
Townes, Mary	16	1672	EQC 5:22
Townes, Mary	33	1672	EQC 5:22
Townes, Sarah	15	1672	EQC 5:22
Townsend, Abigail	20	1691	MCC folio 141
Townsend, Abigail	20	1691	MCC folio 145
Townsend, Andrew	24	1678	EQC 7:29
Townsend, Joseph	20	1670	SJC 1005

Townsend, Martin	25	1667	MCC folio 44
Townsend, Martin	26	1674	MCC folio 63
Townsend, Martin	30	1673	MCC folio 64
Townsend, Martin	30	1677	MCC folio 76
Townsend, Martin	30	1677	MCC folio 77
Townsend, Martin	40	1684	MCC folio 107
Townsend, Martin	47	1691	MCC folio 141
Townsend, Martin	47	1691	MCC folio 145
Townsend, Martin	57	1691	MCC folio 141
Townsend, Penn	30	1681	SJC 2037
Townsend, Penn	38	1690	SJC 2570
Townsend, Peter	33	1677	SJC 1621
Townsend, Peter	41	1684	SJC 2198
Townsend, Thomas	60	1661	EQC 2:330
Toy, Nathaniel	30	1684/5	SJC 2327
Toy, Nathaniel	30	1685	MCC folio 116
Toysh, John	24	1653	EQC 2:94
Train, John	30	1664	MCC folio 36
Traine, Thomas	35	1692	MCC folio 172
Trask, Edward	19	1671	EQC 4:332
Trask, John	20	1662	EQC 3:20
Trask, John	21	1669	EQC 4:180
Trask, John	35	1678	EQC 7:108
Trask, John	35	1678	EQC 7:4
Trask, John	38	1680	EQC 7:388
Trask, John	38	1680	EQC 7:426
Trask, Osmond	38	1665	EQC 3:289
Trask, Osmund	35	1660	EQC 2:220
Trask, William	40	1680	EQC 7:385
Trask, William	69	1657	EQC 7:129
Trask, William	77	1664	EQC 3:207
Travis, Hannah	16	1677	EQC 6:281
Travis, Hannah	18	1677	EQC 6:348
Trayne, John	16	1667	MCC folio 44
Trayne, John	40	1691	MCC folio 145
Trayne, Mary	30	1685	MCC folio 115
Trayne, Mary	38	1692	MCC folio 172
Trayne, Thomas	30	1685	SJC 2348
Tre, Richard	39	1684	EQC 9:286
Treadwell, Nathaniel	48	1686	EQC WPA 46-67-1
Tredwell, Nathaniel	58	nd	SJC 25779
Tree, Joanna	41	1684	EQC 9:285
Tree, Richard	37	1683	EQC 9:19
Trerice, John	30	1667	SJC 909
Trerise, Rebecca	56	1662	MCC folio 29
Trescott, Dyer	19	1691	SJC 98514
Trescott, Elizabeth	16	1681	SJC 2024
Trescott, William	67	1681	SJC 2024
Tresteene, Robert	53	1677	SCC 830
Trevett, Anna	30	1691	SJC 162263
Trevett, Henry	50	1674	EQC 5:256
Trevett, Henry	50	1677	EQC 6:363
Trevett, Henry	60	1682	EQC 8:338
Trevett, Henry	60	1684	EQC 9:241

Trevett, John	22	1676	EQC 6:257
Trevett, Mary	19	1683	EQC 9:146
Trevett, Mary	45	1674	EQC 5:257
Trewolla, James	30	1681	SJC 2295
Triggs, Thomas	22	1658	MCC folio 17
Tringoe, John	24	1673	SJC 1245
Triplett, George	27	1663	SJC 612
Triplett, George	27	1663/4	SJC 612
Tristeen, Robert	53	1677	SJC 1627
Trowbridge, John	23	1671	MCC folio 58
Trowbridge, John	26	1675	MCC folio 71
Trowbridge, John	26	1677	MCC folio 72
Truant, Morris	61	1668	SJC 857
True, Henry	14	1662	EQC 2:411
True, John	17	1662	EQC 2:411
Truesdall, Richard	64	1670/1	SD 7:87
Truey, John	45	1672	EQC 5:110
Trull, John	40	1678	MCC folio 82
Trumball, John	36	1675	EQC 6:28
Trumball, John	70	1677	MCC folio 76
Trumball, Joseph	21	1679	SJC 2025
Trumball, Joseph	21	1680	MCC folio 88
Trumball, Joseph	24	1671	EQC 4:347
Trumball, Joseph	25	1683	EQC 9:45
Trumball, Joseph	25	1683	EQC 9:46
Trumball, Joseph	27	1675	EQC 6:14
Trumball, Joseph	27	1675	EQC 6:15
Trusdale, Richard	64	1670/1	SJC 1092
Tuck, Elizabeth	37	1680	MCC folio 183
Tuck, John	30	1679	EQC 7:182
Tuck, Thomas	55	1667	EQC 3:421
Tucker, Benoni	28	nd	SJC 2762
Tucker, Benoni	29	1691	SJC 162291b
Tucker, Henry	34	1653	SJC 225
Tucker, James	20	1690	SJC 2564
Tucker, John	24	1675	EQC 6:79
Tucker, John	24	1675	EQC 6:80
Tucker, John	28	1678	EQC 7:157
Tucker, John	39	1685	SJC 2377
Tucker, John	40	1694	SJC 3104
Tucker, Mary	20	1680	EQC 7:359
Tucker, Mary	35	1681	EQC 8:193
Tucker, Thomas	34	1683	EQC 9:90
Tuckerman, John	26	1684	SJC 2205
Tuckerman, John	27	1685/6	SJC 2388
Tuckerman, John	60	1684	SJC 2205
Tuckerman, Mary	28	1685/6	SJC 2388
Tudor, John	22	1671	SD 7:226
Tufts, Elizabeth	31	1681	MCC folio 94
Tufts, Mary	14	1669	MCC folio 52
Tufts, Mary	34	1662	MCC folio 31
Tufts, Peter	30	1679	MCC folio 83
Tufts, Peter	34	1683	EQC 9:124
Tuish, John	24	1655	EQC 2:93

Tully, Alice	66	1665	SJC 2233
Tully, Alice	66	1668	SJC 931
Tupe, Peter	26	1672	MCC folio 59
Turell, Daiel	70	1691/2	SJC 2650
Turell, Daniel	50	1672	SJC 1138
Turell, Daniel	50	1672	SJC 1163
Turell, Mary	50	1672	SJC 1148
Turland, Joshua	23	1658	EQC 2:108
Turley, Recerd	16	1682	EQC 8:284
Turner, Ephraim	27	1666/7	SJC 846
Turner, Ephraim	28	1667	SJC 846
Turner, Ephraim	31	1671	SJC 1092
Turner, Humphrey	26	1689	SJC 2539
Turner, Increase	38	1681	SJC 2034
Turner, Israel	21	1676	SJC 1449
Turner, James	34	1690	MCC folio 132
Turner, Japhet	25	1676	SJC 1449
Turner, Lawrence	32	1653	EQC 1:317
Turner, Penelope	41	nd	SJC 25969
Turrell, John	22	1670	MCC folio 56
Turrell, Joseph	20	1674	MCC folio 69
Turry, Francis	21	1661	MCC folio 26
Tushingham, George	27	1666	MCC folio 42
Tuttle, John	33	1659	EQC 2:143
Tuttle, John	33	1659	EQC 2:172
Tuttle, Sarah	19	1664	EQC 3:141
Tuttle, Sarah	30	1676	EQC 6:154
Tuttle, Simon	29	1664	EQC 3:142
Tuttle, Simon	46	1680	EQC 7:374
Tuttle, Symon	43	1674	EQC 5:292
Tuxbury, Henry	50	1676	EQC 6:163
Twelves, Robert	23	1654	MCC folio 13
Tyack, Thomas	25	1665	SJC 709
Tyler, Goodwife	40	1661	EQC 2:277
Tyler, Hannah	14	1662	EQC 2:367
Tyler, Job	40	1659	SJC 322
Tyler, Job	40	1661	EQC 2:277
Tyler, Job	40	1662	EQC 2:367
Tyler, Mary	15	1659	SJC 322
Tyler, Mary	18	1661	EQC 2:329
Tyler, Mary	18	1662	EQC 2:367
Tyler, Mary	18	1662	EQC 2:412
Tyler, Mary	40	1662	EQC 2:367
Tyler, Moses	19	1661	EQC 2:277
Tyler, Moses	19	1661	EQC 2:327
Tyler, Moses	19	1661	EQC 2:328
Tyler, Moses	20	1662	EQC 2:355
Tyler, Moses	20	1662	EQC 2:367
Tyler, Moses	24	1665/6	SJC 725
Tynge, Edward	46	1657	MCC folio 18
Tyson, Robert	34	1663	SJC 561
Underhill, Simon	33	nd	SJC 1024
Underry, Richard	21	1660/1	SJC 391
Underwood, James	50	1661	EQC 2:316

Underwood, Joseph	48	1668	MCC folio 45
Underwood, Martha	75	1676	MCC folio 73
Underwood, Mary	37	1666	MCC folio 40
Upham, John	17	1666	MCC folio 41
Upham, John	25	1672	MCC folio 60
Upham, John	25	1673	MCC folio 62
Upham, John	57	1657	MCC folio 20
Upham, John	60	1660	MCC folio 60
Upham, Katherine	60	1679	MCC folio 184
Upham, Phineas	36	1671	MCC folio 61
Upton, John	21	1676	EQC 6:193
Usher, Hezekiah	54	1670	SJC 986
Usher, Hezekiah	57	1672/3	SJC 1164
Usher, John	30	1678	SJC 2060
Vane, Henry	33	1672	SJC 1142
Vane, Henry	72	1657	EQC 7:127
Varney, Abigail	30	1673	EQC 5:195
Varney, Abigail	32	1676	EQC 6:159
Varney, Abigail	35	1676	SJC 1456
Varney, goodwife	40	1683	EQC 9:29
Varney, Thomas	20	1659	EQC 2:187
Varney, Thomas	32	1676	EQC 6:159
Varney, Thomas	35	1676	EQC 6:155
Varney, Thomas	35	1676	EQC 6:158
Varney, Thomas	35	1676	SJC 1456
Varney, Thomas	40	1679	EQC 7:218
Varney, Thomas	43	1682	EQC 8:408
Varney, widow	71	1675	EQC 6:116
Varnum, John	24	1696	MCC folio 201
Varnum, Joseph	21	1695	MCC folio 201
Varnum, Samuel	49	1668	EQC 4:3
Varnum, Samuel	64	1683	EQC 9:104
Varnum, Samuel	78	1696	MCC folio 201
Varnum, Thomas	25	1657	EQC 2:42
Varnum, Thomas	28	1695	MCC folio 201
Veazy, William	45	nd	SJC 2910
Veazy, William	50	1667	SJC 827
Veering, John	46	1681	EQC 8:192
Vening, William	32	1681	EQC 8:227
Vennez, Samuel	21	1654	MCC folio 10
Verin, Hillyard	23	1672	EQC 5:48
Verin, Hillyard	29	1678	EQC 7:35
Verin, Hillyard	37	1658	EQC 2:133
Verin, Hillyard	41	1662	SJC 561
Verin, Hillyard	52	1673	SJC 1226
Verin, Nathaniel	20	1675	EQC 6:45
Verin, Philip	20	1651	EQC 1:213
Verry, Thomas	30	1686	EQC WPA 46-23-3
Very, Frances	25	nd	SJC 2821
Very, Hannah	12	1664	EQC 3:137
Very, Isaac	17	1681	EQC 8:145
Very, Samuel	20	1674	MCC folio 63
Very, Samuel	64	1684	EQC 9:159
Very, Thomas	30	nd	SJC 2770

Very, Thomas	53	nd	SJC 2011
Vessell, Richard	49	1679	MCC folio 184
Vetter, Elizabeth	39	1659	MCC folio 21
Viall, John	42	1661	EQC 2:286
Viall, John	42	1661	EQC 2:325
Viccory, Roger	44	1686	EQC WPA 46-87-4
Vickers, Elizabeth	34	nd	SJC 2808
Vickers, John	31	1689	SJC 2552
Vickers, John	36	1692	SJC 4074
Vickers, Mary	50	1685	SJC 2346
Vin, Mary	21	1662	SJC 874
Vincent, Nicholas	67	1679	EQC 7:296
Vincent, Nicholas	67	1679	SJC 2011
Vincent, William	47	1658	EQC 2:68
Vine, Elizabeth	30	1681	MCC folio 97
Vine, William	28	1679	MCC folio 83
Vine, William	30	1684	MCC folio 111
Vine, William	40	1695	MCC folio 180
Vinson, Elizabeth	33	1670	EQC 4:216
Vinson, Elizabeth	33	1670	EQC 4:216
Vinson, Nicholas	46	1670	EQC 4:216
Vinson, Sarah	40	1660	EQC 2:238
Vinson, William	53	1663	EQC 3:42
Vinson, William	62	1675	EQC 6:116
Vinson, William	63	1675	EQC 6:116
Vinson, William	65	1674	EQC 5:358
Vinton, Blaze	21	1675	EQC 6:55
Vinton, John	26	1675	EQC 6:55
Voss, Edward	44	nd	SJC 1964
Voss, Henry	17	nd	SJC 1964
Voss, Robert	70	1671	SJC 1964
Vouden, Moses	30	1678	EQC 7:114
Vyall, John	34	1680	SCC 1029
Wade, Deborah	30	1677	MCC folio 76
Wade, Elizabeth	42	1662	SJC 874
Wade, Jonathan	40	1677	MCC folio 76
Wade, Jonathan	64	1678	EQC 7:87
Wade, Nathaniel	30	1682	MCC folio 99
Wade, Nathaniel	36	1684	EQC 9:210
Wade, Thomas	21	1672	EQC 5:11
Wade, Thomas	26	1676	EQC 6:159
Wade, Thomas	26	1676	SJC 1456
Wade, Thomas	28	1678	EQC 7:117
Wade, William	35	1668	MCC folio 50
Wadlin, Agnes	70	1682	MCC folio 99
Wadsworth, Timothy	25	1691	MCC folio 148
Waffe, Thomas	38	1684	SJC 2267
Waffe, Thomas	43	1689	SJC 2553
Waggot, Thomas	28	1672	SD 7:334
Wainwright, Francis	21	1685	MCC folio 113
Wainwright, John	31	1680	EQC 8:66
Wainwright, John	35	1684	EQC 9:241
Wainwright, John	44	nd	SJC 2820
Wainwright, Simon	20	1680	EQC 8:66

Wainwright, Simon	25	1686	EQC 9:604
Waite, Alexander	30	1667	EQC 3:455
Waite, Gamaliel	62	1663	SD 9:27
Waite, Gamaliel	82	1681	SJC 2016
Waite, Grace	61	1671	SJC 1092
Waite, John	19	nd	SJC 3614
Waite, John	25	1671	SJC 1092
Waite, John	30	1679	EQC 7:313
Waite, John	30	1679	SJC 1912
Waite, John	31	1693	MCC folio 176
Waite, John	42	1659	SJC 393
Waite, John	45	1663	SJC 789
Waite, John	46	1662	MCC folio 28
Waite, John	46	1663	MCC folio 34
Waite, John	50	1667	MCC folio 41
Waite, John	59	1676	MCC folio 71
Waite, John	60	1677	MCC folio 184
Waite, John	60	1677	MCC folio 82
Waite, John	60	1678	MCC folio 95
Waite, John	62	1680	MCC folio 89
Waite, John	62	1680	SJC 1914
Waite, John	74	1692/3	MCC folio 179
Waite, John	74	1692/3	MCC folio 204
Waite, Jonadab	18	1685	EQC 9:530
Waite, Jonadab	26	nd	SJC 3680
Waite, Joseph	38	1685	MCC folio 114
Waite, Mary	40	1681	EQC 8:112
Waite, Mary	40	1681	SJC 2008
Waite, Rebecca	50	1674	SD 8:406
Waite, Return	28	1668	MCC folio 49
Waite, Return	30	1670	SJC 985
Waite, Return	34	1676	EQC 6:167
Waite, Return	40	1681	MCC folio 93
Waite, Richard	50	1651	EQC 1:217
Waite, Richard	60	1660/1	SJC 2103
Waite, Richard	60	1678	EQC 7:27
Waite, Richard	60	1683	EQC 9:46
Waite, Richard	60	1684	EQC 9:254
Waite, Richard	60	1686	EQC WPA 46-102-1
Waite, Richard	61	1661	EQC 2:287
Waite, Richard	62	1662/3	SJC 664
Waite, Richard	66	1666	EQC 3:306
Waite, Richard	71	nd	SJC 1044
Waite, Richard	73	1672	SJC 1120
Waite, Richard	73	1672	SJC 1142
Waite, Richard	74	1674	EQC 5:394
Waite, Richard	75	1673	SJC 1432
Waite, Richard	79	1678	MCC folio 81
Waite, Samuel	24	1678	MCC folio 95
Waite, Sarah	29	1678	MCC folio 82
Waite, Thomas	16	1668	EQC 4:83
Waite, Thomas	20	1674	EQC 5:413
Waite, Thomas	21	1673	EQC 5:231
Waite, Thomas	27	1668	MCC folio 45

Waite, Thomas	28	1680	EQC 7:379
Wakefield, James	16	1680	EQC 7:401
Wakefield, John	21	1662	SJC 874
Wakefield, Samuel	29	1682	EQC 8:343
Wakefield, Samuel	30	1685	EQC 9:524
Wakefield, Samuel	43	1696	SJC 98546
Waker, John	35	1675	MCC folio 69
Walcott, Jonathan	39	1679	EQC 7:167
Walden, Richard	48	1663	EQC 3:171
Walden, Tamesin	16	1674	EQC 5:310
Waldern, John	42	1666	EQC 3:368
Waldern, Nathaniel	22	1683	EQC 9:13
Waldo, Daniel	34	1681	MCC folio 96
Waldo, Jonathan	14	1681	MCC folio 96
Waldren, John	18	1671	MCC folio 56
Waldren, John	22	1674	EQC 5:310
Waldron, Dorothy	30	1665	EQC 3:272
Waldron, John	40	1665	EQC 3:269
Waldron, John	40	1665	EQC 3:272
Waldron, John	46	1673	EQC 5:179
Waldron, John	47	1673	EQC 5:181
Waldron, John	48	1672	EQC 5:41
Waldron, Nathaniel	32	nd	SJC 2828
Waldron, Rebecca	16	1672	EQC 5:42
Waldron, Samuel	44	1661	MCC folio 27
Walen, Joseph	44	1690	MCC folio 136
Walker, Capt.	68	1681	EQC 8:123
Walker, Capt.	69	1682	EQC 8:397
Walker, Edward	23	1679	MCC folio 83
Walker, Edward	23	1680	MCC folio 183
Walker, Edward	35	1694	MCC folio 186
Walker, Isaac	28	1677	SCC 802
Walker, Isaac	28	1677	SJC 1584
Walker, Isabel	20	1668	MCC folio 48
Walker, Israel	20	1668	MCC folio 44
Walker, John	20	1684	EQC 9:205
Walker, John	23	1684	EQC 9:392
Walker, John	27	1692	MCC folio 172
Walker, John	51	1691	MCC folio 140
Walker, Jonathan	56	1694	SJC 3212
Walker, Joseph	40	1685	MCC folio 116
Walker, Joseph	40	1685	SJC 2327
Walker, Richard	27	1695/6	SJC 3680
Walker, Richard	41	1653	EQC 2:94
Walker, Richard	47	1684	EQC 9:209
Walker, Richard	49	1686	EQC 9:583
Walker, Richard	55	1665/6	SJC 726
Walker, Richard	63	1674	EQC 5:387
Walker, Richard	65	1677	EQC 6:300
Walker, Richard	65	1677	EQC 7:126
Walker, Richard	70	1684	EQC 9:339
Walker, Robert	72	1679	EQC 7:215
Walker, Samuel	6	1668	MCC folio 48
Walker, Samuel	23	1679	SJC 1908

Walker, Samuel	33	1676	MCC folio 71
Walker, Samuel	36	1679	MCC folio 87
Walker, Samuel	38	1654	MCC folio 9
Walker, Samuel	40	1684	MCC folio 109
Walker, Samuel	40	1684	SJC 2228
Walker, Samuel	45	1659	MCC folio 21
Walker, Samuel	46	1661	MCC folio 27
Walker, Samuel	50	1666	MCC folio 41
Walker, Samuel	52	1668	MCC folio 43
Walker, Sarah	31	1676	MCC folio 71
Walker, Shubael	36	1674	SJC 1389
Walker, Shubael	42	1680	EQC 8:80
Walker, Shubael	42	1681	EQC 8:215
Walker, Shubael	42	1681	EQC 8:92
Walker, Susannah	36	1681	SJC 26559
Walker, Susannah	36	nd	SJC 2017
Walker, Thomas	36	1678	EQC 7:30
Walkern, Margret	25	1691/2	MCC folio 157
Walkut, Jonathan	35	1675	EQC 6:8
Wall, John	24	1664	EQC 3:155
Wallatt, Samuel	39	1677	MCC folio 74
Waller, Christopher	41	1661	EQC 2:316
Waller, Christopher	42	1665	EQC 3:276
Waller, Christopher	44	1668	EQC 4:53
Waller, Christopher	54	1674	EQC 5:325
Waller, Christopher	54	1674	SJC 1503
Waller, Christopher	54	1675	SJC 1503
Waller, Christopher	56	1676	EQC 6:171
Waller, Christopher	57	1676	EQC 6:195
Waller, Thomas	14	nd	SJC 2021
Walley, John	35	1680	SCC 1145
Wallingford, Nicholas	26	1682	EQC 8:300
Wallington, Joseph	25	1669	MCC folio 52
Wallis, John	22	1678	EQC 7:74
Wallis, Nicholas	49	1683	EQC 9:2
Wallis, Nicholas	50	1684	EQC 9:189
Wally, John	35	1680	SJC 1910
Wally, John	38	1681	SJC 2037
Wally, John	39	1683	MCC folio 102
Wally, John	43	1673	SJC 1341
Walten, Elizabeth	34	1694	MCC folio 161
Walter, Elizabeth	52	1672	SJC 1148
Walton, Job	26	1667	SJC 909
Walton, John	26	1684	EQC 9:319
Walton, Josiah	20	1662	EQC 2:442
Walton, Mary	17	1662	EQC 2:442
Walton, Nathaniel	32	1670	EQC 4:268
Walton, Nathaniel	32	1670	EQC 4:286
Walton, Nathaniel	34	1671	EQC 4:400
Walton, Nathaniel	40	1678	EQC 7:119
Walton, Samuel	30	1670	EQC 4:267
Ward, Hannah	34	1682	EQC 8:370
Ward, Hopestill	15	1662	MCC folio 31
Ward, Increase	17	1662	MCC folio 31

Ward, Increase	23	1675	MCC folio 70
Ward, John	20	1660	EQC 2:219
Ward, John	20	1662	EQC 3:20
Ward, Mary	60	1661	SJC 874
Ward, Obadiah	30	1665	MCC folio 38
Ward, Obadiah	33	1667	MCC folio 44
Ward, Obadiah	37	1671/2	SJC 1097
Ward, Obadiah	53	1692	MCC folio 174
Ward, Obadiah	58	1692	MCC folio 174
Ward, Samuel	27	1665	EQC 3:262
Ward, Samuel	28	1666	EQC 3:343
Ward, Samuel	30	1671/2	SJC 1097
Ward, Samuel	40	1679	MCC folio 86
Ward, Samuel	40	1680	EQC 7:386
Ward, Samuel	60	nd	SJC 26521
Ward, William	61	1664	MCC folio 36
Wardall, Elihu	38	1681	EQC 8:112
Wardall, Elihu	38	1681	SJC 2008
Wardall, Uzal	42	1682	EQC 8:394
Wardner, An	20	1664	SJC 648
Wardwell, Elizabeth	26	1670	EQC 4:242
Warkman, Samuel	27	1668/9	SJC 911
Warner, Edward	18	1682/3	SJC 2123
Warner, Henry	50	1684	EQC 9:254
Warner, John	20	1679	SJC 1809
Warner, John	40	1690	MCC folio 148
Warner, John	45	1661	EQC 2:318
Warner, John	50	1697	SJC 3484
Warner, John	53	nd	SJC 25779
Warner, Nicholas	43	1679	SJC 1809
Warner, Nicholas	60	1690	MCC folio 145
Warner, Nicholas	60	1691	MCC folio 143
Warnsbe, Thomas	23	1663	SJC 571
Warr, Sarah	19	1667	EQC 3:395
Warren, Daniel	28	1674	MCC folio 66
Warren, Daniel	40	1668	MCC folio 44
Warren, Daniel	52	1679	MCC folio 84
Warren, Daniel	63	1690	MCC folio 135
Warren, John	49	1672	MCC folio 60
Warren, John	51	1673	MCC folio 62
Warren, John	57	1679	MCC folio 84
Warren, John	63	1686	MCC folio 125
Warren, John	70	1692	MCC folio 172
Warren, John	73	1695	MCC folio 179
Warren, John	75	1696	MCC folio 207
Warrent, Ann	70	1674	EQC 5:257
Warrin, Thomas	16	1670	SJC 1015
Warriner, James	52	1693	SJC 3301
Waters, Abigail	23	1677	SCC 804
Waters, Abigail	23	1677	SJC 1635
Waters, Jacob	27	1677	MCC folio 75
Waters, Jacob	40	1690	MCC folio 136
Waters, Jacob	41	1690	MCC folio 135
Waters, John	35	1677	EQC 6:292

Waters, Joseph	53	1681	MCC folio 94
Waters, Sampson	39	1680	SJC 1909
Waters, Samuel	20	1670/1	MCC folio 56
Waters, Samuel	21	1683	EQC 9:92
Waters, Samuel	25	1677	MCC folio 75
Waters, Stephen	36	1679	MCC folio 83
Waters, Stephen	43	1686	MCC folio 123
Waters, Steven	36	1679	MCC folio 185
Waters, William	33	1666	EQC 3:335
Waters, William	38	1672/3	SJC 1246
Waters, William	38	1673	EQC 5:168
Watkins, John	29	1690	SJC 2572
Watkins, John	30	1691	MCC folio 148
Watson, Abraham	23	1686	MCC folio 121
Watson, Abraham	23	1686	MCC folio 128
Watson, Isaac	16	1686	MCC folio 121
Watson, Isaac	16	1686	MCC folio 128
Watson, John	20	1664	SJC 825
Watson, John	20	1667	EQC 3:393
Watson, John	20	1682	EQC 8:248
Watson, John	24	1668	EQC 4:52
Watson, John	30	1674	EQC 5:276
Watson, John	33	1677	EQC 6:252
Watson, John	35	1679	EQC 7:269
Watson, John	41	1663	MCC folio 33
Watson, John	50	1682	MCC folio 101
Watson, John	66	1686/7	MCC folio 127
Watson, John	73	1692	MCC folio 172
Watts, Eleanor	50	1680	EQC 8:103
Watts, Eleanor	50	1681	EQC 8:219
Watts, Henry	67	1669	SJC 1046
Watts, James	35	1660	EQC 2:208
Waugh, Alexander	34	1672	SCC 138
Waugh, Alexander	34	1672	SJC 1194
Way, Richard	40	1664	SJC 625
Way, Richard	42	1666	EQC 3:322
Way, Richard	46	1670	SJC 982
Way, Richard	50	1675	SJC 1403
Way, Richard	50	1675	SJC 1503
Way, Richard	53	1676/7	SJC 1544
Way, Richard	59	1683	MCC folio 104
Way, Richard	60	1684	EQC 9:244
Way, Richard	60	1684	EQC 9:254
Way, Richard	60	1684	MCC folio 110
Way, Richard	60	1684/5	SJC 2391
Way, Richard	67	1691/2	SJC 2650
Waygood, Jonathan	20	1668	SJC 924
Wayman, John	70	1680	MCC folio 88
Weare, Nathaniel	66	1699	SJC 4028
Weare, Peter	29	1679/80	SCC 1129
Weare, Peter	29	1679/80	SJC 1833
Weare, Robert	46	1698	SJC 4700
Webb, Benjamin	49	1696	SJC 3413
Webb, Christopher	33	1663	MCC folio 34

Webb, Christopher	52	1682	SJC 162216
Webb, Christopher	52	nd	SJC 2126
Webb, Christopher	54	1684	EQC 9:139
Webb, Christopher	54	1685	SJC 2391
Webb, Christopher	55	1685	SJC 2391
Webb, Daniel	23	1674	SJC 1360
Webb, Daniel	30	1681	EQC 8:226
Webb, Elizabeth	30	1653	MCC folio 7
Webb, John	27	1682	SJC 162216
Webb, Jonathan	36	1653	MCC folio 7
Webb, Joseph	32	1673	SJC 2120
Webb, Joseph	34	1676	SJC 1465
Webb, Joseph	34	1677/8	SJC 1707
Webb, Joseph	37	1680	SJC 1914
Webb, Thomas	23	1675	MCC folio 71
Webb, Thomas	23	1675	MCC folio 72
Webb, Thomas	23	1675	SJC 1581
Webber, Benjamin	54	nd	SJC 26311
Webling, William	20	1680	SJC 2055
Webster, Abigail	30	1678	SJC 1705
Webster, Ann	40	1679	EQC 7:317
Webster, Ann	49	1686	EQC WPA 46-121-4
Webster, Benjamin	26	1679	MCC folio 87
Webster, Benjamin	26	1679	SJC 1829
Webster, Elizabeth	21	1663	EQC 3:97
Webster, Elizabeth	21	1663	EQC 3:98
Webster, Israel	18	1662	EQC 3:15
Webster, Israel	24	1668	EQC 4:13
Webster, Israel	25	1669	EQC 4:127
Webster, israel	35	1678	EQC 7:156
Webster, Israel	35	1680	EQC 7:377
Webster, Israel	38	1682	EQC 8:300
Webster, John	19	1675	EQC 6:25
Webster, John	22	1678	EQC 7:156
Webster, John	22	1679	MCC folio 86
Webster, John	35	1658	EQC 2:123
Webster, John	35	1668	EQC 4:12
Webster, John	38	1670	EQC 4:226
Webster, John	43	1675	EQC 6:26
Webster, John	45	1681	EQC 8:171
Webster, John	45	1682	EQC 8:283
Webster, John	46	1678	EQC 7:156
Webster, John	48	1681	EQC 8:172
Webster, John	48	1681	EQC 8:173
Webster, John	49	1682	EQC 8:265
Webster, John	49	1682	EQC 8:387
Webster, John	50	1683	EQC 9:11
Webster, John	50	1683	EQC 9:17
Webster, John	52	1684	EQC 9:256
Webster, John	55	1686	EQC WPA 46-126-1
Webster, John	63	1695	SJC 3223
Webster, Mary	32	1681	EQC 8:216
Webster, Mary	45	1685/6	SJC 2388
Webster, Nathan	16	1662	EQC 3:15

Webster, Nathan	35	1681	EQC 8:92
Webster, Steven	20	1657	EQC 2:56
Webster, Steven	31	1670	EQC 4:228
Wecom, Daniel	40	1683	EQC 9:58
Wedge, Thomas	40	1669	MCC folio 53
Wedge, Thomas	50	1677	MCC folio 76
Wedgwood, John	39	1679	EQC 7:217
Wedgwood, John	39	1680	EQC 8:11
Weed, John	36	1663	SJC 718
Weeden, Elizabeth	56	1677	EQC 6:293
Weeden, Joseph	39	1685	SJC 2375
Weeks, Christopher	47	1698	SJC 4490
Weeks, Joseph	33	1670	SJC 993
Weeks, William	44	1675	EQC 6:67
Welch, Philip	37	1680	EQC 8:5
Welch, Philip	37	1680	SJC 2011
Welch, Philip	40	1680	EQC 7:411
Welch, Philip	44	1686	EQC 9:581
Welch, Thomas	22	1679	MCC folio 87
Welch, Thomas	25	1679	MCC folio 184
Welch, Thomas	25	1681	MCC folio 102
Welch, Thomas	40	1667	MCC folio 41
Welch, Thomas	50	1678	MCC folio 84
Welch, Thomas	56	1682	MCC folio 100
Welch, Thomas	68	1692	MCC folio 153
Welcome, Richard	34	1675	EQC 6:48
Welcome, William	27	1670	SJC 989
Weld, Daniel	15	1658	MCC folio 16
Weller, John	30	1677	SJC 1586
Wellington, Benjamin	16	1663	SJC 566
Wellington, John	40	1681	MCC folio 92
Wellington, Oliver	24	1674	MCC folio 63
Wellington, Oliver	28	1681	MCC folio 97
Wellington, Roger	53	1663	SJC 566
Wellman, Abraham	24	1667	EQC 3:455
Wells, David	27	nd	SJC 2834
Wells, Hannah	25	1678	EQC 7:79
Wells, Ichabod	21	1682	EQC 8:328
Wells, John	34	1675	SJC 1402
Wells, John	36	1676	EQC 6:148
Wells, Jonathan	17	1682	EQC 8:328
Wells, Joseph	16	1672	EQC 5:12
Wells, Naomi	31	1668	EQC 4:78
Wells, Nathaniel	36	1674	EQC 5:287
Wells, Philip	35	1671	EQC 4:420
Wells, Richard	59	nd	SJC 206
Wells, Richard	64	1671	EQC 4:347
Wells, Richard	64	1671	SJC 1334
Wells, Thomas	27	1674	EQC 5:401
Wells, Thomas	42	1668	EQC 4:78
Welman, Abraham	49	nd	SJC 2712
Welman, Isaac	45	nd	SJC 2712
Welsh, Hannah	25	1680	EQC 7:336
Welsh, Hannah	30	1677	EQC 6:360

Welsh, Philip	36	1680	EQC 7:336
Welsh, Thomas	23	1683	MCC folio 185
Welsh, Thomas	30	1686	MCC folio 122
Welsh, Thomas	35	1690	MCC folio 132
Welsh, Thomas	50	1677	MCC folio 76
Welsh, Thomas	60	1690	MCC folio 132
Wessell, Gerrardus	25	1681	SJC 2010
Wesson, John	20	1681	MCC folio 96
Wesson, John	60	1681	MCC folio 96
Wesson, Mary	22	1681	MCC folio 96
West, Abner	51	nd	SJC 27405
West, Anna	29	1684	SJC 2242
West, Edward	29	1668	SJC 983
West, Edward	44	1682	MCC folio 106
West, Henry	49	1678	EQC 7:33
West, Henry	49	1678	EQC 7:56
West, Henry	52	1681	SJC 2021
West, Henry	55	1685	EQC 9:447
West, Henry	56	1685	EQC 9:473
West, Henry	56	1686	EQC WPA 46-80-2
West, John	20	1666	MCC folio 41
West, John	58	1673	EQC 5:195
West, Thomas	20	1662	EQC 2:440
West, Thomas	30	1665	EQC 3:276
West, Thomas	30	1669	EQC 4:118
West, Thomas	46	1680	EQC 8:69
West, William	30	1661	EQC 2:316
Westlebee, Bridget	31	1665/6	SJC 728
Weston, John	20	1681	MCC folio 96
Weston, John	50	1674	EQC 5:324
Weston, John	50	1674	SJC 1503
Weston, John	60	1681	EQC 8:118
Weston, John	65	1681	MCC folio 96
Weston, John	68	1681	SJC 2018
Wet, Susan	39	1662	SJC 874
Wharton, Richard	38	1675	SJC 1398
Wharton, William	52	1682	SJC 2119
Wheat, Thomsan	45	1660	MCC folio 22
Wheeler, Elizabeth	65	1667	MCC folio 43
Wheeler, Ephraim	19	1682	EQC 8:284
Wheeler, Ephraim	19	1682	EQC 8:387
Wheeler, Ephraim	20	1682	EQC 8:419
Wheeler, Ephraim	20	1683	EQC 9:11
Wheeler, George	65	1671	MCC folio 58
Wheeler, Henry	40	1673	MCC folio 65
Wheeler, Henry	43	1678	EQC 8:36
Wheeler, John	42	1684	MCC folio 107
Wheeler, Jonathan	20	1678	EQC 7:156
Wheeler, Joseph	16	1678	EQC 7:156
Wheeler, Joseph	57	1668	MCC folio 45
Wheeler, Mary	64	1687	MCC folio 148
Wheeler, Nathan	18	1678	EQC 7:156
Wheeler, Nathaniel	18	nd	SJC 2754
Wheeler, Thomas	21	1685	SJC 2377

Wheeler, Thomas	35	1670	MCC folio 53
Wheeler, Thomas	50	1658	EQC 2:91
Wheeler, Thomas	54	1682	SJC 2120
Wheeler, Thomas	57	1663	EQC 3:33
Wheeler, Thomas	76	1680	EQC 8:10
Wheeler, Thomas	76	1680	SJC 1973
Wheeler, Thomas	80	1684	EQC 9:316
Wheelock, Eleazer	45	1700	SJC 4696
Wheelock, Samuel	20	1691	MCC folio 174
Whefen, John	52	1679	EQC 7:306
Whetcombe, James	40	1673	SJC 1192
Whetcombe, James	44	1677	SJC 1630
Whetstone, Joseph	20	1663	SJC 721
Whetstone, Joseph	22	1665/6	SJC 721
Whicher, John	30	1677	EQC 6:254
Whicher, Nathaniel	37	1695	SJC 3782
Whicher, Thomas	53	nd	SJC 2772
Whipple, Jemima	17	1684	EQC 9:188
Whipple, John	36	1670	EQC 4:222
Whipple, John	38	1670	EQC 4:293
Whipple, John	60	1665	EQC 3:233
Whipple, Jon.	38	1666	EQC 3:373
Whipple, Mary	12	1680	EQC 7:362
Whipple, Mathew	20	1684	EQC 9:205
Whipple, Sarah	15	1672	EQC 5:97
Whit, Anthony	70	1678	MCC folio 81
Whit, James	39	1676	EQC 6:155
Whit, James	39	1676	EQC 6:157
Whit, James	40	1678	EQC 6:416
Whit, John	27	1678	MCC folio 81
Whit, John	40	1668	MCC folio 50
Whit, Philip	17	1678	EQC 7:23
Whit, Zachariah	23	1665	EQC 3:276
Whit, Zachariah	37	1682	EQC 8:413
Whitaker, Abraham	20	1677	EQC 6:262
Whitaker, Abraham	40	1666	EQC 3:370
Whitaker, Abraham	60	1664	EQC 3:221
Whitaker, Abraham	76	1674	EQC 5:348
Whitaker, Elizabeth	29	1664	EQC 3:167
Whitaker, Elizabeth	35	1677	MCC folio 76
Whitaker, John	14	1677	MCC folio 76
Whitaker, John	14	1677	MCC folio 77
Whitaker, John	25	1689	MCC folio 133
Whitaker, John	36	1677	MCC folio 76
Whitaker, John	37	1673	MCC folio 62
Whitaker, John	37	1673	MCC folio 63
Whitaker, Jonathan	23	1689	MCC folio 133
Whitaker, Mary	16	1677	MCC folio 77
Whitaker, Mary	30	1664	EQC 3:221
Whitaker, William	18	1677	EQC 6:262
Whitburne, William	20	1668	MCC folio 47
Whitcombe, James	28	1661	EQC 2:322
Whitcombe, Jonathan	20	1690	MCC folio 136
Whitcombe, Rebecca	22	1664	MCC folio 36

White, Abigail	72	1677	EQC 6:298
White, Abigail	74	1680	EQC 7:330
White, Abigail	74	1680	EQC 7:337
White, Abraham	80	1694	SJC 3104
White, Andrew	23	1689	MCC folio 133
White, Anthony	70	1678	MCC folio 81
White, Benjamin	16	1665	SJC 680
White, Benjamin	16	1679	MCC folio 184
White, Cornelius	30	1679/80	SCC 1128
White, Cornelius	30	1679/80	SJC 1833
White, Elias	45	1674	EQC 5:283
White, Elias	55	1679	EQC 7:297
White, Frances	80	1693	SJC 2738
White, James	23	1667	SD 5:182
White, James	25	1667	EQC 3:396
White, James	30	1673	EQC 5:132
White, James	38	1679	SJC 1908
White, James	39	1676	EQC 6:155
White, Joel	26	1662	MCC folio 29
White, John	22	1677	SJC 1682
White, John	27	1678	MCC folio 81
White, John	33	1664/5	SJC 721
White, John	34	1665	SJC 721
White, John	36	1695	SJC 3221
White, John	39	1680/9	SJC 1953
White, John	50	nd	SJC 2738
White, John	58	1668	SJC 905
White, John	62	1671	SJC 2997
White, John	62	nd	SJC 2997
White, Joseph	48	nd	SJC 2738
White, Nathaniel	36	nd	SJC 2728
White, Paul	84	1678	EQC 6:413
White, Philip	22	1683	EQC 9:110
White, Resolved	63	1678	EQC 7:112
White, Resolved	63	1679	EQC 7:239
White, Richard	44	1669	SJC 955
White, Robert	29	1676	EQC 6:181
White, Ruth	30	1667	EQC 3:457
White, Ruth	30	1667	EQC 3:458
White, Susannah	50	1700	SJC 4704
White, Susannah	69	1679	MCC folio 84
White, Thomas	12	1683	EQC 9:15
White, Thomas	17	1682	MCC folio 100
White, Thomas	17	1682	MCC folio 100
White, Thomas	32	1672	EQC 5:42
White, Thomas	39	1674	MCC folio 66
White, Thomas	44	1682	MCC folio 100
White, Thomas	46	1684	MCC folio 108
White, Thomas	55	1693	MCC folio 177
White, Thomas	73	nd	SJC 2772
White, William	18	1679	MCC folio 184
White, William	50	1663	EQC 3:37
White, William	50	1663	SJC 560
White, William	60	1670	EQC 4:258

White, William	60	1671	EQC 4:343
Whiteman, Hannah	50	1662	MCC folio 31
Whitenhall, Benjamin	34	1680	SJC 1935
Whiter, Mary	38	1687	EQC WPA 47-52-1
Whiteridge, William	65	1663	SJC 98508
Whites, Elizabeth	70	1676	EQC 6:195
Whitford, Walter	51	1679	EQC 7:253
Whiting, Jonathan	35	1672	MCC folio 60
Whiting, Joseph	18	1664	SJC 746
Whiting, Nathaniel	23	1667	SJC 830
Whiting, Nathaniel	63	1672	MCC folio 60
Whiting, Oliver	33	1698/9	MCC folio 209
Whiting, Samuel	65	1698/9	MCC folio 209
Whiting, William	35	1695	SJC 4697
Whitmarsh, Hannah	36	1677/8	SJC 1689
Whitmarsh, John	40	1665	SJC 815
Whitney, Benjamin	24	1685	MCC folio 115
Whitney, Benjamin	24	1685	SJC 2348
Whitney, Dorothy	25	1691	MCC folio 144
Whitney, Eleazer	30	1691	MCC folio 144
Whitney, John	9	nd	SJC 1050
Whitney, Jonathan	35	1672	MCC folio 59
Whitney, Jonathan	36	nd	SJC 1050
Whitney, Jonathan	40	1671	MCC folio 57
Whitney, Joseph	28	1681	MCC folio 97
Whitney, Moses	18	1675	MCC folio 70
Whitney, Nathaniel	19	1666	MCC folio 40
Whitney, Richard	53	1674	MCC folio 70
Whitney, Richard	72	1692	MCC folio 173
Whitney, Thomas	40	1697	MCC folio 205
Whitred, William	65	1663	EQC 3:87
Whitridge, John	25	1669	EQC 4:114
Whittemore, Abraham	17	1670	MCC folio 53
Whittemore, Benjamin	35	1675	MCC folio 70
Whittemore, Benjamin	37	1679	MCC folio 86
Whittemore, Daniel	37	1671	MCC folio 58
Whittemore, Elizabeth	26	1672	MCC folio 60
Whittemore, Francis	33	1659	MCC folio 23
Whittemore, Francis	35	1660	MCC folio 26
Whittemore, Francis	35	1660	SJC 386
Whittemore, Francis	47	1672	MCC folio 59
Whittemore, Francis	50	1676	MCC folio 71
Whittemore, Francis	56	1682	MCC folio 101
Whittemore, John	12	1673	MCC folio 62
Whittemore, John	31	1686	MCC folio 127
Whittemore, John	44	1681	MCC folio 184
Whittemore, John	46	1685/6	MCC folio 122
Whittemore, John	52	1690	MCC folio 132
Whittemore, Joseph	16	1681	MCC folio 94
Whittemore, Joseph	19	1685/6	MCC folio 122
Whittemore, Joseph	19	1686	MCC folio 121
Whittemore, Joseph	19	1686	MCC folio 121
Whittemore, Joseph	19	1686	MCC folio 128
Whittemore, Joseph	24	1691	MCC folio 148

Whittemore, Mary	39	1691	MCC folio 157
Whittemore, Nathaniel	28	1670	MCC folio 53
Whittemore, Samuel	19	1691	MCC folio 141
Whittemore, Samuel	37	1686	MCC folio 123
Whittier, John	30	1682	EQC 8:266
Whittier, Thomas	54	1674	EQC 5:330
Whittingham, Martha	14	nd	SJC 2245
Whittirin, Mary	15	1677	MCC folio 74
Whitwell, William	53	1672	SD 8:172
Whityear, Abraham	60	1669	EQC 4:156
Wiburne, John	15	1658	MCC folio 16
Wicke, Nicholas	70	1671	MCC folio 58
Wickham, Daniel	30	1671	EQC 4:347
Wickham, Daniel	40	1681	EQC 8:128
Wickham, Daniel	40	1681	EQC 8:214
Wickham, Daniel	40	1684	EQC 9:258
Wickham, Daniel	50	1686	EQC 9:584
Wicom, Daniel	40	1683	SJC 2227
Widger, Christopher	50	1661	SJC 909
Widger, Robert	33	1693	SJC 4105
Wier, Eleazer	23	1695	MCC folio 162
Wier, Robert	27	1691	MCC folio 148
Wiggin, John	27	1670	MCC folio 53
Wiggins, James	34	1668	SJC 955
Wiggins, John	17	1658	EQC 2:139
Wiggins, Thomas	26	1666	SJC 764
Wight, Elizabeth	16	1668	MCC folio 47
Wight, Ephraim	53	1699	SJC 4696
Wight, Ephraim	53	1699	SJC 4696
Wigley, Edmund	38	1669	MCC folio 51
Wigley, Edmund	38	1670	MCC folio 53
Wigley, Edmund	60	1692	MCC folio 173
Wiks, Abigail	18	1671	MCC folio 61
Wilcott, John	30	1664	EQC 3:196
Wilcott, John	30	1664	EQC 3:196
Wilcott, Thomas	35	1675/6	SCC 662
Wilcox, William	30	1668	SJC 873
Wild, John	50	1669	EQC 4:111
Wild, John	77	1695	SJC 3146
Wilder, John	25	1699	MCC folio 192
Wilder, Nathaniel	86	1690	MCC folio 136
Wilder, Thomas	35	1654	MCC folio 10
Wilder, Thomas	37	1681	MCC folio 95
Wilder, Thomas	40	1659	MCC folio 21
Wildes, John	40	1660	EQC 2:204
Wildes, Jonathan	21	1672	EQC 5:28
Wildes, Sarah	50	1679	EQC 7:299
Wiles, John	46	1665	EQC 3:259
Wiley, John	25	1679	MCC folio 88
Wilkes, Robert	24	1669	EQC 4:105
Wilkins, Bray	68	1680	EQC 7:392
Wilkins, Bray	68	1680	SJC 1884
Wilkins, Hannah	50	1695	SJC 3146
Wilkinson, John	34	1681	EQC 8:188

Wilkinson, John	36	1681	EQC 8:101
Wilkinson, Thomas	50	1676	MCC folio 73
Wilkison, John	37	1684	EQC 9:397
Willard, Daniel	20	1678	MCC folio 184
Willard, Daniel	20	1678	MCC folio 82
Willard, Dorcas	20	1690	MCC folio 145
Willard, Dorcas	20	1691	MCC folio 141
Willard, Henry	35	1690	MCC folio 136
Willard, Henry	35	1691	MCC folio 141
Willard, Mary	27	1679	MCC folio 84
Willard, Simon	29	1678	MCC folio 82
Willard, Simon	29	1679	EQC 7:220
Willard, Simon	35	1685	EQC 9:448
Willard, Simon	35	1685	EQC 9:470
Willard, Simon	35	1685	SJC 2339
Willcot, Thomas	30	1672	SJC 1194
Willett, Frances	50	1684	EQC 9:326
Willett, Francis	43	1678	EQC 7:156
Willett, Hezekiah	21	1673	SJC 1341
Willett, Jacob	54	1675	MCC folio 69
Willett, Thomas	65	1673	SJC 1341
Willey, Alexander	50	1666	EQC 3:333
Williams, Aaron	30	1643	SD 1:50
Williams, Alexander	42	1662	SJC 460
Williams, Anna	22	1658	MCC folio 17
Williams, Benjamin	17	1682	EQC 8:340
Williams, Ebenezer	22	1670	EQC 4:264
Williams, Ebenezer	32	1681	SJC 162204
Williams, Henry	43	1679	SJC 1828
Williams, Henry	43	1679/80	SCC 1110
Williams, Henry	44	1680	EQC 7:352
Williams, Isaac	20	1682	EQC 8:341
Williams, Isaac	25	1663/4	SJC 606
Williams, Isaac	33	1664	EQC 3:180
Williams, Isaac	34	1672	MCC folio 64
Williams, Isaac	36	166	EQC 3:348
Williams, Isaac	53	1683	EQC 9:525
Williams, Isaac	55	1685	EQC 9:524
Williams, John	22	1657	EQC 7:127
Williams, John	25	1670	SJC 1016
Williams, John	25	1671	SJC 1290
Williams, John	25	nd	SJC 1142
Williams, John	26	1672	SCC 137
Williams, John	26	1672	SJC 1194
Williams, John	27	1673	SJC 162121
Williams, John	33	1679/80	SCC 1124
Williams, John	33	1679/80	SJC 1827
Williams, John	40	1675	EQC 6:45
Williams, John	40	1678	EQC 7:107
Williams, John	40	1680	EQC 8:13
Williams, John	40	1681	EQC 8:73
Williams, John	40	1684	EQC 9:199
Williams, John	45	1681	EQC 8:156
Williams, John	77	1685	EQC 9:537

Williams, Josiah	26	1664	MCC folio 36
Williams, Margery	51	1685	EQC 9:524
Williams, Mary	16	1677	EQC 6:350
Williams, Mary	17	1691	MCC folio 151
Williams, Richard	30	1684	SJC 2228
Williams, Robert	37	1676	MCC folio 74
Williams, Ruth	35	1682	EQC 8:345
Williams, Samuel	30	1672	MCC folio 61
Williams, Samuel	50	1685	EQC 9:468
Williams, Thomas	21	1685	MCC folio 120
Williams, Thomas	27	1691	MCC folio 151
Williamson, Timothy	47	1668	SJC 857
Willington, John	62	1695	MCC folio 180
Willington, Joseph	16	1660	MCC folio 24
Willington, Palsgrave	22	1674	MCC folio 63
Willington, Roger	48	1658	MCC folio 17
Willington, Roger	64	1673	MCC folio 62
Willis, John	20	1691	MCC folio 156
Willis, John	23	1697	SJC 3530
Willis, John	56	1694/5	SJC 3185
Willis, Michael	26	1679	MCC folio 87
Willis, Nicholas	24	1672	EQC 5:91
Willis, Stephen	40	1684	EQC 9:211
Willison, Richard	30	1655/6	MCC folio 12
Williston, John	20	1668	EQC 4:57
Willmot, Mary	50	1676	MCC folio 74
Wills, Experience	50	1696	SJC 3470
Wills, John	34	1696	SJC 3377
Wills, Richard	19	1667/8	MCC folio 44
Wills, Robert	40	1675	SJC 1390
Wills, Stephen	37	1681	MCC folio 96
Willy, Timothy	29	1683	EQC 9:43
Wilson, Abigail	41	1682	EQC 8:270
Wilson, Deborah	18	1685	MCC folio 117
Wilson, Edward	28	1663	SJC 573
Wilson, Edward	49	1684	MCC folio 183
Wilson, Edward	49	1684	MCC folio 185
Wilson, George	13	1679	MCC folio 85
Wilson, Hannah	36	1662	MCC folio 30
Wilson, Hannah	36	1669	MCC folio 49
Wilson, Hannah	58	1689	MCC folio 134
Wilson, John	16	1675	MCC folio 74
Wilson, John	23	1679	MCC folio 87
Wilson, John	28	1679	MCC folio 87
Wilson, John	30	1684	MCC folio 107
Wilson, John	33	1685	MCC folio 120
Wilson, John	33	1685	SJC 2390
Wilson, John	34	1685	MCC folio 120
Wilson, John	40	1691	MCC folio 143
Wilson, John	40	nd	SJC 4696
Wilson, Joseph	26	1671	EQC 4:371
Wilson, Joseph	32	1677	MCC folio 74
Wilson, Mary	22	1673	EQC 5:143
Wilson, Mary	22	1673	EQC 5:190

Wilson, Mary	24	1663	SJC 573
Wilson, Mary	26	1678	MCC folio 78
Wilson, Mary	50	1699	SJC 3896
Wilson, Nathaniel	19	1681	EQC 8:124
Wilson, Nathaniel	40	1662	MCC Harvard #2009
Wilson, Paul	25	1659	MCC folio 24
Wilson, Paul	25	1660	MCC folio 25
Wilson, Paul	25	1660	MCC folio 26
Wilson, Paul	26	1662	MCC folio 31
Wilson, Paul	27	1663	MCC folio 34
Wilson, Paul	32	1669	MCC folio 52
Wilson, Paul	53	1690	MCC folio 132
Wilson, Paul	54	1691	MCC folio 145
Wilson, Samuel	17	1679	MCC folio 85
Wilson, Samuel	24	1674	EQC 5:340
Wilson, Sherborn	47	1683/4	SJC 2227
Wilson, Shoreborn	29	1666	EQC 3:373
Wilson, Shoreborn	47	1683	EQC 9:221
Wilson, Theophilus	75	1676	EQC 6:165
Wilson, Theophilus	79	1680	EQC 8:32
Wilson, Thomas	25	1656	MCC folio 12
Wilson, Thomas	45	1679	EQC 7:269
Wilson, William	30	1665	EQC 3:257
Wilson, William	30	1670	EQC 4:304
Wilson, William	32	1692	SJC 4085
Wilvatt, John	37	1696	EQC WPA 46-99-2
Winchcombe, Mary	41	1693	MCC folio 176
Winchester, John	60	1671	SJC 2997
Windsor, Widow	73	1675	MCC folio 70
Winfield, Sergan[t]	27	1671	SD 7:215
Wing, Robert	16	1690	MCC folio 139
Wings, John	37	1675/6	SJC 1471
Winn, Edward	25	1692	MCC folio 172
Winn, Edward	71	1670	MCC folio 53
Winn, Increase	43	1685	MCC folio 115
Winn, Joseph	46	1686	MCC folio 123
Winn, Sarah	69	1668	MCC folio 48
Winship, Edward	37	1691	MCC folio 146
Winship, Edward	46	1659	MCC folio 23
Winship, Joseph	29	1691	MCC folio 156
Winship, Joseph	30	1692	MCC folio 152
Winslade, John	48	1668	SJC 910
Winsley, Ephraim	19	1697	SJC 3780
Winsley, Isaac	23	1667	SJC 909
Winsley, John	75	1671	SJC 1090
Winslow, Edward	35	1668/9	SJC 911
Winslow, Jacob	15	1672	MCC folio 60
Winslow, John	60	1657	MCC folio 20
Winslow, John	75	1671/2	SCC 51
Winslow, Joseph	23	nd	SJC 570
Winslow, Richard	17	nd	SJC 2807
Winsor, Joshua	37	1685	SJC 2347
Winsor, Joshua	46	1694/5	SJC 4131
Winsor, Rebecca	59	1686	EQC WPA 46-100-4

Winsor, Samuel	29	1678	EQC 6:423
Winter, Abigail	20	1690	MCC folio 137
Winter, Deborah	31	1677	EQC 6:298
Winter, Deborah	38	1684	EQC 9:273
Winter, John	23	1690	MCC folio 137
Winter, John	25	1662	MCC folio 31
Winter, John	26	1660	MCC folio 25
Winter, William	73	1657	EQC 2:43
Wise, Joseph	22	1665	EQC 3:287
Wise, Joseph	22	1666	EQC 3:300
Wiser, James	39	1681	MCC folio 94
Wiswall, John	56	1658/9	SD 3:193
Wiswall, John	65	1667	MCC folio 43
Wiswall, Noah	20	1662	MCC folio 36
Wiswall, Noah	20	1663	SJC 28945
Wiswall, Noah	35	1673	MCC folio 63
Wiswall, Thomas	62	1663	SJC 606
Witherbee, John	24	1666	MCC folio 40
Witheridge, Silvester	23	1685/6	SJC 2385
Witt, Hester	18	1683	EQC 9:65
Witt, John	40	1657	EQC 7:128
Wodes, Mary	38	1683	EQC 9:148
Wolcott, John	32	1677	EQC 6:330
Wolcott, Jonathan	35	1674	EQC 5:324
Wolcott, Josiah	20	1677	MCC folio 77
Wolf, Henry	38	1681	EQC 8:165
Wolf, Peter	73	1674	EQC 5:290
Wollen, Edward	60	1684	EQC 9:349
Wood, Abraham	22	1679	MCC folio 87
Wood, Daniel	25	1675	EQC 6:55
Wood, Edward	21	1682	MCC folio 100
Wood, Elizabeth	25	1669	MCC folio 52
Wood, Esiah	41	1668	EQC 4:84
Wood, Isaac	38	1667	MCC folio 43
Wood, James	39	nd	SJC 2807
Wood, John	22	1673	EQC 5:157
Wood, John	24	1679	MCC folio 87
Wood, Jonathan	40	1676	MCC folio 72
Wood, Joseph	16	1680	EQC 7:373
Wood, Joseph	16	1680	SJC 1894
Wood, Josiah	23	1681	MCC folio 102
Wood, Josiah	23	1681	MCC folio 184
Wood, Josiah	23	1682	MCC folio 100
Wood, Josiah	24	1682	MCC folio 100
Wood, Josiah	27	1663	MCC folio 34
Wood, Josiah	32	1667	MCC folio 41
Wood, Josiah	44	1679	MCC folio 83
Wood, Josiah	44	1679	SJC 1798
Wood, Josiah	46	1679	MCC folio 87
Wood, Josiah	48	1682	MCC folio 100
Wood, Josiah	58	1691	MCC folio 150
Wood, Josias	33	1669	MCC folio 52
Wood, Mary	36	1680	EQC 7:391
Wood, Mary	37	1680	EQC 8:6

Wood, Nathaniel	38	1689	MCC folio 134
Wood, Nathaniel	38	1690	MCC folio 132
Wood, Obadiah	20	1673	EQC 5:157
Wood, Simon	38	1695	SJC 3223
Wood, Thomas	40	1675	EQC 6:14
Wood, Thomas	41	1674	EQC 5:303
Woodbery, Humphrey	70	1680	EQC 7:390
Woodbery, Mary	48	1678	EQC 7:51
Woodbridge, Joseph	21	1683	EQC 9:25
Woodbridge, Mary	25	1677	EQC 6:333
Woodbridge, Thomas	28	1676	EQC 6:201
Woodbridge, Thomas	28	1677	EQC 6:350
Woodbridge, Thomas	29	1678	EQC 7:156
Woodbridge, Thomas	29	1678	EQC 7:98
Woodbridge, Thomas	29	1678	SJC 1741
Woodbridge, Thomas	29	1679	SJC 1763
Woodbridge, Thomas	30	1679	MCC folio 86
Woodbridge, Thomas	31	1680	EQC 8:63
Woodbury, Ann	47	1673	EQC 5:215
Woodbury, Humphrey	61	1668	EQC 4:47
Woodbury, Humphrey	61	1668	SJC 879
Woodbury, Humphrey	70	1679	EQC 7:251
Woodbury, Mary	30	1670	EQC 4:216
Woodbury, Mary	46	1674	EQC 5:363
Woodbury, Mary	50	1680	EQC 7:411
Woodbury, Nicholas	40	1661	EQC 2:323
Woodbury, Peter	40	1682	EQC 8:323
Woodbury, Samuel	17	1668/9	SJC 924
Woodbury, Thomas	40	1679	EQC 7:308
Woodbury, Thomas	40	1679	EQC 7:310
Woodbury, Thomas	45	1684	EQC 9:209
Woodbury, William	18	1668	EQC 4:47
Woodcock, Israel	22	1673	SJC 1341
Woodcock, John	24	1673	SJC 1341
Woodcock, John	40	1691	MCC folio 148
Woodcock, Mary	19	1673	SJC 1341
Woodcock, Nathaniel	17	1673	SCC 353
Woodcock, Nathaniel	17	1673	SJC 1341
Woodcock, Thomas	22	1691	MCC folio 148
Woodcock, William	57	1677	SJC 1633
Woodcock, William	59	1677	SJC 1633
Woodey, Richard	21	1696/7	MCC folio 204
Woodhouse, Peter	25	1672/3	SJC 1194
Woodin, Hannah	17	1686	EQC 9:604
Woodis, Henry	32	1662	MCC folio 30
Woodise, Richard	73	1673	EQC 5:226
Woodman, Archelaus	60	1678	EQC 7:157
Woodman, Archelaus	80	1695	SJC 3217
Woodman, Dorothy	43	1679	EQC 7:267
Woodman, Edward	50	1678	EQC 7:156
Woodman, Ichabod	18	1694/5	SJC 3148
Woodman, Ichabod	18	1695	SJC 162356
Woodman, Joanna	60	1674	EQC 5:419
Woodman, John	19	1695	SJC 162352

Woodman, John	19	1695	SJC 3123
Woodman, John	19	1695	SJC 3123
Woodman, John	19	1695	SJC 3123d
Woodman, John	19	1695	SJC 3123f
Woodman, Jonathan	20	1695	SJC 162356
Woodman, Jonathan	28	1674	EQC 5:411
Woodman, Jonathan	30	1675	EQC 6:79
Woodman, Jonathan	30	1678	EQC 8:36
Woodman, Jonathan	32	1680	EQC 8:37
Woodman, Jonathan	35	1678	EQC 7:156
Woodman, Joshua	41	1678	EQC 7:156
Woodmansey, John	39	1664	MCC folio 38
Woodrow, Benjamin	48	1684	EQC 9:286
Woods, Henry	32	1662	MCC Harvard #1953
Woods, John	24	1666	MCC folio 40
Woods, Mary	20	1666	EQC 3:334
Woods, Mary	21	1669	EQC 4:108
Woods, Mary	26	1669	EQC 4:103
Woods, Samuel	30	1669	EQC 4:108
Woodward, Abigail	47	1671	MCC folio 59
Woodward, Amos	23	1668	MCC folio 45
Woodward, Anne	70	1671	MCC folio 57
Woodward, Arabella	20	1676	MCC folio 74
Woodward, Ezekiel	17	1682	EQC 8:436
Woodward, Ezekiel	58	1680	EQC 8:27
Woodward, Ezekiel	60	1686	EQC 9:579
Woodward, George	50	1669	MCC folio 52
Woodward, Henry	46	1679	MCC folio 88
Woodward, John	23	1685	MCC folio 115
Woodward, John	23	1685	SJC 2348
Woodward, Mary	16	1679	MCC folio 88
Woodward, Susannah	19	1671	MCC folio 59
Woodwell, Mathew	50	1680	EQC 7:331
Woody, Dorcas	36	1671/2	SJC 1148
Woody, Isaac	30	1659	SJC 349
Woody, John	24	1684	SJC 2242
Woody, Richard	61	1676	SJC 1465
Woodys, Henry	36	1666	MCC folio 40
Wooland, Edward	48	1674	EQC 5:266
Wooland, Edward	56	1680	EQC 7:349
Woolcott, Edward	59	1661	SJC 418
Woolcott, John	18	1678	EQC 7:156
Woolcott, John	19	1680	EQC 7:387
Woolcott, John	19	1680	EQC 7:388
Woolcott, John	21	1682	EQC 8:242
Woolcott, John	23	1683	EQC 9:11
Woolcott, John	23	1683	EQC 9:9
Woolcott, John	25	1684	EQC 9:237
Woolcott, John	45	1678	EQC 7:156
Woolcott, Jonathan	35	1675/6	SJC 1503
Woolcott, Jonathan	56	1694	SJC 3212
Woolcott, Joseph	18	1682	EQC 8:242
Woolcott, Joseph	19	1683	EQC 9:11
Woolcott, Joseph	19	1683	EQC 9:9

Woolen, Edward	34	1659	EQC 2:186
Woolworth, Richard	30	1678	EQC 7:156
Worcester, Elizabeth	44	1686	EQC 9:604
Worcester, Samuel	39	1672	SJC 1563
Worcester, Sarah	18	1685	EQC 9:534
Worham, William	26	1678	EQC 7:156
Wormall, Henry	50	1683	EQC 9:45
Wormall, Henry	50	1684	EQC 9:338
Worme, William	33	1684	EQC 9:326
Wormwood, Henry	23	1656	MCC folio 15
Wormwood, Henry	36	1670	MCC folio 53
Wormwood, Henry	46	1679	SJC 2025
Wormwood, Henry	48	1682	EQC 8:325
Wormwood, Henry	50	1684	EQC 9:341
Wormwood, Mary	37	1679	SJC 2025
Worro, Daniel	40	1655	MCC folio 112
Wreyford, John	55	nd	SJC 4105
Wright, Edward	34	1668	MCC folio 50
Wright, Henry	29	1678/9	SJC 1908
Wright, Henry	29	1680	SJC 1856
Wright, Henry	31	1681	SJC 2057
Wright, John	44	1678	MCC folio 82
Wright, John	57	1658	MCC folio 17
Wright, Mary	51	1675	SJC 1422
Wright, Robert	86	nd	SJC 3752
Wright, Thomas	24	1662	EQC 2:440
Wright, Walter	30	1672	EQC 5:20
Wright, Walter	46	1686	EQC WPA 47-20-2
Wright, William	61	1673	EQC 5:226
Wright, William	61	1673	EQC 5:226
Wright, William	63	1675	SCC 566
Wyatt, Richard	34	1663	SJC 512
Wyatt, William	44	1694	SJC 2989
Wyborne, Thomas	37	1672	SCC 127
Wyborne, Thomas	37	1672	SJC 1120
Wyborne, Thomas	39	1676	SJC 1575
Wyeth, John	17	1671	MCC folio 56
Wylie, John	25	1679	MCC folio 86
Wyman, Bathsheba	18	1676	MCC folio 71
Wyman, David	23	1677	MCC folio 77
Wyman, Francis	50	1676	MCC folio 71
Wyman, Francis	64	1684	MCC folio 115
Wyman, Isabel	28	1679	MCC folio 87
Wyman, Jacob	28	1693	MCC folio 180
Wyman, Jacob	28	1695	MCC folio 180
Wyman, John	39	1660	MCC folio 26
Wyman, John	47	1669	MCC folio 49
Wyman, Joseph	23	1686	MCC folio 123
Wyman, Nathaniel	21	1686	MCC folio 123
Wyman, Prudence	30	1691	MCC folio 142
Wyman, Sarah	37	1662	MCC folio 30
Wyman, Sarah	37	1662	MCC folio 34
Wyman, Timothy	23	1685	MCC folio 120
Wyman, William	30	1686	MCC folio 121

Yeard, Edward	25	1666	EQC 3:350
Yell, John	60	nd	SJC 2772
Yeomans, Edward	30	1662	EQC 3:6
Yeomans, Edward	30	1662	EQC 3:7
Yewen, John	30	1669	EQC 4:180
Young, Giles	49	1678	EQC 8:37
Young, John	33	1678	EQC 7:31
Younglove, James	27	1659	EQC 2:184
Younglove, Lydia	30	1673	EQC 5:190
Younglove, Margret	45	1668	SJC 931
Younglove, Samuel	20	1657	EQC 2:53
Younglove, Samuel	40	1678	EQC 7:157
Youngs, Richard	18	1681	EQC 8:194

www.ingramcontent.com/pod-product-compliance
Lightning Source LLC
Chambersburg PA
CBHW070408270326
41926CB00014B/2751